Advance Praise for Homegrown Hate

"*Homegrown Hate* explores the psychology of those who engage in violent behavior. Anne Speckhard has interviewed some of the most notorious extremists in America and beyond to produce a stunning insight into their thinking and beliefs. This is not just another book of composite cases; it is a book that takes the reader on a journey into the dark heart of America and the Western world. *Homegrown Hate* practically puts you in the interview sessions with these men and women of violence. These are stories of dispossession, hatred, exploitation, intense inequality, and cultural violence. Speckhard brings decades of professional expertise studying terrorism to the task of answering many complex questions about extremism. *Homegrown Hate* is no ordinary book. Speckhard's latest book challenges the accepted narratives about the issue and raises important and uncomfortable questions about the root causes of extremism in modern society."—**John Mooney**, The Sunday Times – Ireland

"Timely, incisive reading on the most controversial and fiery subset in the field of terrorism today: domestic extremism."—**Ambassador Alberto Fernandez,** Vice President of of the Middle East Media Research Institute, formerly President of Middle East Broadcasting Networks (MBN) and the Coordinator for Strategic Counterterrorism Communications (CSCC) at the U.S. Department of State – USA

"Anne Speckhard's new book affords deep insights into the minds and hearts of domestic extremists. Once again, her considerable interviewing skills lay bare the fundamental psychic processes, motivations and thought patterns that turn ordinary people into violent radicals. A must read to anyone who wishes to understand the working of the terrorist mind up close and personal."—**Dr. Arie Kruglanski** - Distinguished University Professor in Psychology at the University of Maryland – USA

"Anne Speckhard did it again! A must-read book. Anne keeps on focusing on subversive activities that seriously undermine democracy. The value of this book lies in the in-depth interviews. There are lessons to be learnt in order to develop and deepen activities to keep society resilient! All of us have a role."—**Stephen van den Bosch,** Superintendent Dutch National Police, CVE specialist – Netherlands

"Dr. Anne Speckhard's firsthand research on behalf of the International Center for the Study of Violent Extremism has taken her face to face with terrorists and extremists around the globe. We have much to learn from her research as we collectively tackle the challenge of extremism and radicalization on our home front. This book will serve as a critical primer to understanding the domestic problems of political and social division that we face as a nation. This book is a must read for anyone interested in truly understanding the scope and depth of extremism within the United States."—**Zack Baddorf**, Executive Director, Military Veterans in Journalism / Adjunct Professor, NYU – USA

"Thirty years in policing has given me a front-row seat to the intersection of policing and politics. I have witnessed the disturbing escalation in rhetoric and violence driven by political polarization. Every word of Homegrown Hate profoundly resonates with me. It is the most insightful and intimate look into the making of a domestic violent extremist I have read. It demystifies indoctrination, details the role of vulnerabilities in exploiting wounded people, and sheds light on how people become willing to do horrific violent acts. Dr. Speckhard's in-depth interviews reveal the disturbing truth of radicalization, like an iceberg, showing the reader the danger that lies unseen below the surface."—**Robert King**, retired commander of the Portland Police Bureau – USA

"Dr. Speckhard's work is illustrative of one's perceived rights as they conflate with public interests. In examining the freedom to express, coupled with the extent to which one is emboldened to act, violent extremism can be propagated. In this instance the following questions should be raised; "What is, in fact, violent extremist behavior, what are the factors that drive it and how can we prevent and remediate against violent extremism?" In pursuit of these revelations, *Homegrown Hate* provides essential perspective."—**Duane S.** – Award winning Criminal Investigator of Domestic Terrorism – USA

HOMEGROWN HATE

Inside the Minds of Domestic Violent Extremists

Anne Speckhard, Ph.D.

First published 2023
By Advances Press, LLC
McLean, VA

Editor – Susan K. Barnett, www.cause-comms.com
Cover Designer – JM InfoTech
Book Publicist – Susan K. Barnett, www.cause-comms.com
Cover Photo Design – Anne Speckhard

Every effort has been made to contact and acknowledge copyright owners,
but the author and publisher would be pleased to have any errors or omissions
brought to their attention so that corrections may be published at a later
printing.

Library of Congress Control Number: 2022951070
ISBN 978-1-935866-80-0 – Homegrown Hate – Hardcover
ISBN 978-1-935866-81-7– Homegrown Hate – E Pub

Dedication

For all the broken children whose futures have been harmed by family dysfunction, drug abuse, poverty, and bullying. May they find compassionate help from real healers rather than groups that teach them to blame and hate.

Table of Contents

Foreword by Daryl Davis

From 1789 to 2009 from George to George, in other words from Washington to Bush, only White males had held the highest job position in the United States. That 220-year monochrome continuum was short-circuited on January 20th, 2009, when Barack Obama was sworn into the office of President of the United States of America. It seemed surreal. White people who were predisposed of a racist and supremacist ideology couldn't believe it and Black people couldn't believe it either. These two groups at opposite ends of the ideological spectrum had one thing in common: neither believed they would ever see a Black man in the White House during their lifetime. Thus was born an earlier version of "woke-ism", not from the Black community but from the communities of White supremacy, White separatism, and White nationalism. The loudest chants became, "Wake Up White People!"

Racism, which had never gone away and remained lurking in a closet, under a rock, and behind the cover of darkness, was now in your face and unabashedly and loudly proclaiming its ugly and shameful beliefs front and center. Despite a private citizen's monumental and year-long effort leading up to the election to deny the Black candidate his American birthright, and despite elected officials immediately following the election with promises he will be a one-term President, Obama served the maximum two full terms. For eight years, while one group was celebrating another group was plotting.

As extremism was playing out on the other side of the world, it was also rapidly increasing and manifesting domestically as well. However, for the longest time in the U.S., the terms "terrorist" and "extremist," were mostly applied to people of Middle Eastern descent, especially in the wake of 9/11. Americans who were committing abominable crimes against humanity, such as Ku Klux Klansmen dragging a Black man to his death behind a pickup truck, or the proliferation of perpetrators of mass school shootings, were only being referred to as "troubled," "deranged," or "suffering from mental health issues." Finally, America was now starting to come to terms with the ugliness of its plague of racism, antisemitism, and "othering," also known as the "us versus them" mentality, exacerbated by rhetoric around immigration, both legal and illegal. High numbers of those not of the Anglo-Saxon persuasion prompted slogans "Take Our Country Back," and "Make America Great Again." When such slogans become rallying cries by those in positions of political power, they do not fall on deaf ears. Instead, they fall on the ears of extremists and serve as clarion calls, exponentially triggering them into action under the guise of patriotism.

It has been well calculated and predicted that around the year 2042, the United States will for the first time in its history see its white majority population drop to the level of 50/50 with non-whites, and shortly thereafter the white majority will become the minority. America was built on a two-tier society consisting of white supremacy at the top and slavery at the bottom. While there are plenty in the current white majority populace who are not concerned about this upcoming sea change, there are many who are convinced *their* country is being taken away from them. They believe their identity is being erased through "the browning of America," and "white genocide through miscegenation," and therefore a call-to-action is in order.

Such a call to action came on January 6, 2021, in the form of an insurrection at the U.S. Capitol Building, in which tens of thousands came to the nation's capital to protest the election of President Joe Biden and falsely claim it was stolen from the losing President Donald Trump. In an attempt to overturn the election, estimates are that over two thousand people, now referred to as insurrectionists, illegally entered the Capitol by breaking through windows and doors, destroying government property, and some threatening to hang Vice President Michael Pence for not overturning the election results. A man was seen carrying the

Confederate Battle Flag through the Capitol Rotunda while another man was seen in the halls of the Capitol wearing a Camp Auschwitz tee-shirt. It is not hard to connect the dots when you put both slogans together, "Take our country back and make America great again."

Author, Founder, and Executive Director of the International Center for the Study of Violent Extremism (ICSVE), Anne Speckhard, has connected the dots in her new book, *Homegrown Hate*. Dr. Speckhard has done the most extensive study to date on extremist behavior. This is not just another textbook consisting of composite cases of various people who have engaged in violent behavior. While most books on this subject provide bland psychologist's/interviewer's analyses, hypotheses, and reasons leading to extremist indoctrination and the subsequent carrying out of violence, *Homegrown Hate* practically puts you in the position of the fly on the wall during the interview sessions.

Dr. Speckhard's credentials and psychological background have enabled her to gain access to some of the most heinous and prolific current and former extremists in America. She puts the reader in her chair in the same room with her "clients" and gives them a rare and raw in-depth, firsthand look at them as they lie on the proverbial psychologist's couch and reveal all—from childhood to their present state of mind. You will hear the actual conversations and actual words of the interviewees. As they are talking, questions you want to ask them will pop into your head and within the next few paragraphs your questions will be answered. Being able to extract this type of information is an art form only experts at the top of their game in psychology and interviewing techniques and tactics can achieve to provide these invaluable results.

As Dr. Speckhard takes you on a tour of extremist mindsets, you, too, will learn the art of listening, analysis, and how to connect the dots. While each extremist interviewed is an individual, you will see many commonalities and similarities between our homegrown American terrorists and those involved in extremism on the other side of the world.

The COVID-19 pandemic has certainly dealt a deadly blow to the United States and fostered new genres of extremism in the form of anti-vaxxers, anti-maskers, and conspiracy theorists. The Coronavirus pandemic hit these shores in late 2019. But the longest lasting domestic pandemic is the one of racist extremism and supremacy which arrived on our shores in 1619 and is still affecting American citizens today with all its mutations of antisemitism, Islamophobia, homophobia, transphobia and a growing number of -isms and phobias. This book will provide you with a 360^0 scope of knowledge and help shape your perspectives while inspiring you to think about solutions to these ongoing extremist pandemics.

Introduction - No One is Born a Terrorist

I have crisscrossed the globe for the past 20 years studying the enemy outside. I've interviewed more than 800 militant jihadists, terrorists, and violent international extremists from ISIS, Al Qaeda, Al Shabaab and more—mostly men, but also women and even children who escaped and survived to tell their stories. Beginning a number of years back when presenting my research on international terrorists and counterterrorism, I was asked numerous times, "Why not turn my attention to domestic threats—white supremacists, skinheads, neo-Nazi, and nationalist violent extremists and create a similar program?" To be honest, my answer was I had my hands full.

It was never that I thought a domestic focus wasn't needed. I knew we had a significant domestic extremist problem among us. Domestic Violent Extremism, DVE, is in fact a bigger threat to the U.S. than external terrorism, something the FBI has been tracking and saying for years.

Then in late 2020 there was a sharp uptick in violent rhetoric and murmurings on social media among domestic white supremacists, fed by the Trump Presidency, and that's when I knew we had to try.[1] In fact, as more details come to light, we are learning that DVE groups, including the Proud Boys and Oath Keepers, whose leaders are being indicted, tried and convicted as of this writing, were among those who helped organize and carry out the January 6 attack on the Capitol Building and our democracy.

Make no mistake, homegrown extremists have been at the center of horrific carnage for decades—from Oklahoma City to January 6— inside daycares, dance clubs, grocery stores, houses of worship, and even a Fourth of July parade. Security experts expect more to come. Many homegrown extremists are now military-trained, and most are well-armed as they await RAHOWA, a racial holy war. Some think

January 6th was its harbinger and RAHOWA is closer than we think. Others believe in carrying out acts of racially and religiously motivated violence to accelerate the fall of society as we know it. The U.S. has a grave threat brewing from within and it is growing with violent vengeance, remarketing hate for the 21st century.

In *Homegrown Hate*, you will meet 15 domestic violent extremists and learn their stories. You'll meet Klayton, whose hate is literally (and now regrettably) tattooed from ear to ear, covering the lower half of his face; Kerry, who targeted the Oklahoma City Murrah Federal Building long before Timothy McVeigh; Benji and his failed attempt to emulate Dylann Roof, the young man who murdered nine Black church members during Bible study at the historic Mother Emanual Church in Charleston, South Carolina; and there's TM, a neo-Nazi "rockstar" at age 19, who went on to help spread the KKK into Germany and in the U.S. Thankfully, TM found his way out. He has worked with the International Center for the Study of Violent Extremism, ICSVE, which I founded, and is committed to helping extract others.

I have interviewed members of the Aryan Nations, Aryan Brotherhood, Christian Identity, Creativity Movement, English Defence League (EDL), Ku Klux Klan (KKK), National Socialist Movement (NSM), Oath Keepers, Proud Boys, various skinhead groups, Volksfront, and more. They were leaders and followers, propagandists and recruiters, security, chiefs of staff and more. They followed ideologies rooted in white Christian nationalism; some are anti-Christian; others adhere to white supremacism based in Norse paganism. Some ideologies and conspiracy theories are surprising, and some are truly bizarre. More recently, QAnon and its wild array of conspiracies are seeping in. Most, not all, are white, male, and American. Most, but not all, have denounced their former lives of hate.

Perhaps one of the most surprising and important findings in our work is the motivation to join these violent white supremacist groups. It is not hate. So how and why does this path into hate and violence evolve? Are these gangs or cults or something else? How do they recruit? Why are police and military prioritized? Where does religion, in particular Christianity, play a significant role and what does that look like? What roles do women play? What does DVE have in common with international terrorism? And perhaps most important, what can each of us do about it? This book will help answer questions many of us have about domestic violent extremists.

As you read their stories, you'll see I weave in theory and explanations, but part of what makes this book unique is I let each interviewee share in their own words what they saw as important on their paths into extremism, and what got them out. My approach to these research interviews gets personal. I get beyond the hate they've perpetrated to begin to answer the how and why they got there. I go deep into family and childhood histories, and early exposure to white supremacist groups and ideologies. Together, we track their trajectories into hate groups and their experiences becoming radicalized and violent. In the case of those who became disillusioned, we look at how they got away and what was needed to help them disengage, deradicalize, and rehumanize. In their stories, the reader will not find the stereotypical portrayal of men (and women) gone mad.

My roots are in psychology and international terrorism. The overlaps with DVE are many and my international experience has greatly informed my current DVE work. I've traveled into slums, refugee camps, and prisons; in the West Bank, Gaza, Morocco, northeast Syria, Baghdad and Sulemania in Iraq, Bishkek, Kyrgyzstan, throughout Europe, the Balkans, and the Maldives where I've met and interviewed more than 800 terrorists and violent extremists. They were soldiers, leaders, would-be suicide bombers, wives, and child soldiers who survived their ordeal and lived to tell their tale (and I've met with friends and families of those who did not.)

They came to believe they needed to join a violent group to bring just governance to the world, throw off the chains of occupation or repressive regimes, often with the aim to raise up an extremist Islamic State of one kind or another. These men, women, and children became convinced they would find dignity, purpose, significance, and belonging; and sometimes marriage, sex slaves, and material benefits, and even ethereal virgins and entry to Paradise, if they joined the battle. Some traveled across oceans and continents to join conflicts raging far from home. Some were manipulated into falsely believing their religion instructed them to strap on a suicide vest or drive a bomb-filled vehicle to detonate themselves and kill others as an act of "martyrdom." They were the enemy we all strove to understand.

I came to see patterns and conditions that make—and can unmake—a terrorist. I helped design and carry out the psychological and Islamic challenge portions of the *Detainee Rehabilitation Program* in Iraq in 2006-2007.[2] This program was applied to 23,000 detainees and 800 juveniles held by U.S. forces in Iraq, to take steps to prevent and stop terrorism "left of boom," as the military likes to say.

I also developed a creative prevention and intervention program called *Breaking the ISIS Brand Counter Narrative Project*. With the sponsorship of the U.S. State Department and later greatly expanded with funding from the State of Qatar, we videotaped my in-depth interviews with ISIS prisoners and returnees (with their permission.[3]) My team at ICSVE edits these interviews into short videos that intentionally look a lot like the powerful ISIS recruitment videos found online. Just like ISIS, our counter narratives are emotionally evocative and use music and imagery to appeal to potential recruits. Then the terrorist insider tells his or her true brutal story of life inside the violent group and denounces their group as un-Islamic, corrupt, and brutal. Their experiences are graphic and emotionally charged with the clear message that the terrorist group and its ideology did not meet expectations or needs, and their choice to join was a regretful one that had a terrible impact on their life and the lives of others.

To date we have released 250 *Breaking the ISIS Brand* counter narrative videos onto the internet.[4] We partner with Facebook which distributes them in over 150 campaigns on Facebook and Instagram, in 27 languages, where ISIS has been successful recruiting vulnerable people. The goal is to beat the terrorists at their own game.

Tracking the impact of these counter narrative videos on Facebook, YouTube, and Telegram and testing them face-to-face in focus groups, we've found they effectively engage vulnerable populations who watch, share, and comment on them, and often create heated discussions. By themselves these videos don't offer better ways to meet one's needs or perceived injustices, but they can derail someone about to tip into extremism. Viewers also follow the video links to our website, therealjihad.org, where they will find all our counter narrative videos as well as scholarly Islamic arguments countering militant jihadist claims.

Escape Hate is ICSVE's domestic-focused project built upon our existing expertise and success with *Breaking the ISIS Brand*. I have videotaped, with permission, 51 in-depth interviews so far with domestic violent white extremists. ICSVE has analyzed these research interviews across 375 variables. Then like the ISIS counter narrative videos, we edit these interviews into short anti-recruitment videos. Former domestic violent white supremacists share the high personal price they paid and condemn their former hate groups and actions; and they advise potential recruits to steer clear. We again partner with Facebook to distribute these short videos to fight homegrown extremists' recruiting techniques and we created a website (EscapeHate.org) where one can find all the videos, read blogs about the trap of violent extremism, and learn where to get help.

To be clear, my goal is to halt the growth of DVE. But we can't fix a problem we have not adequately acknowledged, and we can't bring good policy recommendations to bear that are not grounded in an understanding of the phenomena they are meant to address. Which means we cannot simply slap labels of bigoted, ignorant, uneducated, stupid, or just plain evil on this swath of humanity living across all 50 states and in most Western countries.

To some, I may come across as empathetic during these interviews, and I am. While people should be punished for the hate crimes they commit, it's crucial to remember, no one is born a violent extremist. They were made into haters by the forces in and around their lives. You will see patterns of vulnerabilities, often starting with dramatic childhood traumas which recruiters prey upon, offering a substitute family, belonging, a noble purpose, secret knowledge, and positive identity based upon "whiteness." For most, buy-in to the group's ideology, conspiracy theories, hate, and violence comes over time with isolation and the echo chamber of hate.

For these current and former members of hate groups, telling their stories is not easy. They are facing down deeply traumatic forces. It is my hope you will approach this book as I do with each interview— with a degree of openness to listening and learning from the stories of those who fell into hate and slowly found their way out and try not to judge them too harshly.

The 51 interviews took place during the course of a year and a half, October 2020-June 2022 (the study is ongoing.) All interviews were conducted via Zoom due to the COVID-19 pandemic. So the reader can meet the subjects more intimately as I do, dialogue is heavily quoted, edited for clarity, with names changed where requested.

Anne Speckhard
November 29, 2022
Washington, D.C.

Chapter 1 - The Threat From Within

I find myself looking into the eyes of one of the Proud Boys who stormed the U.S. Capitol Building just 13 days before. But our interview is not about the eight federal charges he will soon face. It's about his path into Domestic Violent Extremism, DVE. It wasn't easy to arrange this interview with Josh Pruitt. The police and FBI began making arrests in the days after the Capitol Hill invasion and suddenly no one wanted to talk. Even those who had previously bragged on social media and to news outlets were going radio silent.

Josh appears on Zoom dressed in a white sleeveless undershirt sporting a Nordic rune silver necklace, a large silver bracelet, and silver ring. He's a body builder, and his bare muscular arms and shoulders give evidence of that. His dark eyebrows, longish beard and mustache fully compensate for his completely bald head. His arms and wrists are tattooed but not with any symbols I recognize from hate groups. Despite the tough-looking exterior, Josh is scared.

January 6, 2021 is the day more than a dozen extremist groups including the Proud Boys, Oath Keepers, QAnon conspiracy supporters, militias, white supremacists, Christian nationalists, and newer hate groups, erected a gallows, marched with Confederate flags, attacked law enforcement, and desecrated our nation's capital.[5] Josh was among the hundreds of Proud Boys who entered the Capitol Building.

The FBI has warned for years that DVE poses the greatest threat to our nation's security.[6] FBI Director Christopher Wray testified at the Senate Judiciary Committee in March of 2021,

Proud Boys Symbol and Slogan

QAnon Symbol and Slogan

"Jan. 6 was not an isolated event. The problem of domestic terrorism has been metastasizing across the country for a long time now and it's not going away anytime soon."[7] Despite the alarm, few American researchers have been studying domestic extremists, instead focused on international terrorist groups like ISIS and al Qaeda.

A proliferation of domestic hate groups, white supremacists, armed militias, conspiracy theorists and political extremists have been violently acting out in our streets and seeping into our military, police, and politics. They have become candidates and elected officials in local and state governments and even our halls of Congress. They are influencing thinking and voting and exacerbating the divisions in our country. Yet most people had turned a blind eye to this growing danger, perhaps making the January 6 violence that unfolded in real time across our screens all the more shocking.

"Stop the Steal"—that pithy piece of MAGA propaganda—became a violent and vastly white and Christian nationalist extremist movement that led to the attack on our democracy and an attempt to stop the peaceful transfer of presidential power. Americans watched aghast as fellow Americans shouted through bullhorns, trashed and looted Senate offices, combed through private documents, hurled fire extinguishers, and clubbed law enforcement (114 officers were injured)[8] as they posed for selfies and videotaped their crimes.

We saw terrified Members of Congress and staff in hiding and calling loved ones to say a final goodbye, as a call to hang "the traitors," which included the powerful Speaker Democratic of the House, Nancy Pelosi, and Vice President Mike Pence, broke out in the historic hallways. The nation would later see Pelosi's husband, Paul, age 82, become victim of a brutal attack inside their San Francisco home in

October 2022. An assailant broke in during the dead of night and in a struggle, fractured Paul Pelosi's skull with a hammer. But the intended target was Nancy Pelosi, who had just returned to Washington DC. The assailant told police he was "fighting against tyranny without the option of surrender" and had intended to break the Speaker's kneecaps to send a message to other Democratic leaders.[9]

But it was the events of January 6, the violence, and deaths of five people including police officers in the days following the riot[10] (depending on the source, from two to five police officers died in stress-related causes from the Capitol riot[11]) that forced the American public to wake up to the reality that DVE is indeed a clear and present danger.

In the lead up, we saw President Trump fuel a MAGA movement, retweeting conspiracy posts, echoing QAnon slogans, and calling for violence. We saw President Trump's former national security advisor, Lieutenant General Michael Flynn and his family, apparently making a July 4th oath of loyalty to QAnon although they later denied doing so.[12] And President Trump made clear he might need the Proud Boys to defend him, telling them to "stand back and stand by," offering what the Proud Boys called an historic endorsement. Thus, when Josh Pruitt stormed the Capitol believing "I was being a patriot, following my commander-in-chief—when he said to go to the Capitol, I obeyed," it's not an inconceivable claim. He believed he was following Presidential orders.

I knew before our Zoom call Josh had been arrested by the Capitol police the evening after the insurrection and had not yet been charged. I take extra time to clearly warn him against self-incrimination during our interview, and to keep a careful watch on what he said to me so as not to be harmed by our research, particularly as I am video recording (with permission.) Yet with the incursion still very fresh in his mind, as soon as I go through our informed consent, Josh smiles and dives into how he fell into extremism.

He says he's a Trump supporter but "not in the far right, at first." Then three months before January 6, a friend called to say he had an expensive bottle of whiskey and invited Josh to come to the initial MAGA march in Washington D.C. in the fall of 2020 and share the bottle. A bartender, Josh knew his whiskey. "$130-a-shot whiskey, so sure I'll come for that! Have a shot, have a beer. We walked Pennsylvania Avenue to the Capitol."

That's when trouble began. "I'm a little amped up as it is. I see Antifa. I walk up to a fence. I want to hear what they are saying."

Antifa, a loosely organized movement of antifascists, are the bogeyman of white supremacists. Sometimes it seems anyone protesting DVE is labeled Antifa. However, Antifa is real, and its adherents will show up at rallies to provoke and clash with far-right protesters. Barricades and the police often stand between the two sides as was the case here. Josh says, "One of the guys started coming at me to rile me up, with a bull horn yelling at me. He said that he was going to fuck me in the ass and taunted me, 'Come over the fence.'"

Antifa followers antagonize, and they justify violence against those they see as fascists as a means of restraining the spread of fascism. Many endorse the slogans, "Punch a Nazi in the Face" and "Punch a MAGA in the Face" and deny property destruction is violence. The hardcore Antifa counter protestors will show up as a "black block" dressed in all black, faces covered in black scarves, and with gas masks and black umbrellas to ward off tear gas. Indeed, reciprocal radicalization[13], a process that has been going on all over this country, finds Antifa and others on the far-left clashing with the far-right and white supremacists, antagonizing each other until both sides are spoiling for a fight. (Antifa do not like to speak to reporters or researchers; however, I recently gained rare access and have so far conducted five interviews with a range of self-identified Antifa activists, included in Chapter 9.)

Josh is a trained Mixed Martial Arts (MMA) fighter, and he was riled up. After the MAGA march, he let off steam by drinking with friends. As he was leaving a bar, he says he was followed by 10 people he identified as Antifa. "Me being the knucklehead, [I think] 10 of you, one of me. I'll get five of you before they hit me." But then some guys appeared behind him, he later learned were Proud Boys. "They kept me from getting jumped."

The Proud Boys, established in 2016 by VICE Media co-founder Gavin McInnes, is an all-male organization describing themselves as "western chauvinists" who purport to be dedicated to "anti-political correctness" and "anti-white guilt." Many experts and lay people, myself included, at first found it hard to decipher what the Proud Boys actually stood for as their leadership denied connections to the racist alt-right. Overtime it became clear in public statements by leaders and members, the Proud Boys support white nationalism, are antisemitic, and misogynistic.[14] The Southern Poverty Law Center has documented their violent activities and the FBI designated them an extremist group with white nationalist ties as early as November 2018. Canadian authorities took that a step further designating the Proud Boys as a terrorist entity in 2021.[15] Their leaders have been indicted for seditious conspiracy for their role in the January 6 attacks.

"I didn't even know who Proud Boys were," Josh continues. That night at the bar, he says there were multiple scuffles, and he is clearly proud of his fighting ability, telling me someone swung a knife at him but no one could touch him. He says no one got hurt but, "apparently the person I was right besides—I pulled someone off him—it was Enrique Tarrio, the leader of the Proud Boys." In classic gang mentality, he fell in with his protectors, despite not knowing much about them. By the end of the night, he was asked to join and inducted by Tarrio. The video of it went viral on social media. "Seventeen million views of me being inducted into the Proud Boys, right outside the JW Marriott," Josh boasts.

But the repercussions for Josh across social media were immediate. "Bald, white, and big with a beard, so I fit the narrative [of a racist]. So, I know why they attacked me. I was in the majority of videos, partly because I was with Enrique." He got doxxed and pulled off the schedule at a bar where he worked. "Doxxing" is a tool used by Antifa to publicly reveal the identities, addresses, and personal details of white supremacists and former members with the intent to shame, ostracize, and prevent them from being able to hold jobs, relationships, etc. (The far-right also employs this tool.)

Later I go looking on social media and see photos of Josh in Washington, D.C., posing with Enrique Tarrio, then leader of the Proud Boys. Tarrio and four other Proud Boys have since been charged with seditious conspiracy for their alleged planning of and participation in the January 6 attack on the Capitol.

When I ask how he felt about being accused of being racist and called out on social media for joining the Proud Boys, he answers, "Last thing you think is that you are joining a racist organization when the leader is

Josh Pruitt and Enrique Tarrio

Puerto Rican and Black. I wasn't mad. More scared than mad, worried about people noticing me." Growing up in diverse Washington, D.C., Josh says he has had friends and romantic relationships of many races and ethnicities.

Though he denies being racist, I do notice Josh is wearing a Thor hammer necklace, an early Norse symbol that's been appropriated by neo-Nazis and other white supremacists. We talk about it. He tells me his ex-girlfriend from Poland got him into Norse mythology. "She has spears and hatchets and swords on the wall. It has nothing to do with [white supremacy] and I didn't know it was a thing," he tells me. "The Thor hammer is racist? I didn't have a fucking clue. It wasn't when it was originated."

Perhaps the same might be true when Josh would again claim his innocence a year after our interview, this time to CNN, after he posted a video on his Parler social media account flashing a white power hand gesture (albeit upside down) alongside two Proud Boys. He said he had no idea it was considered a white supremacist symbol; it was just a "what's up" statement among Proud Boys.[16]

Josh Pruitt Flashing Okay Sign

However, Josh's disavowals of racism seem somewhat disingenuous months later when he again posts videos, this time on Tik Tok in the Spring of 2021, showing off a "wife beater" t-shirt with the words "Stand Back, Stand By" framing the Proud Boy emblem, as he flashes his Thor necklace. At that point he has got to be well aware others consider these to be racist symbols.

We continue discussing his social media notoriety. "My best friend [told me], 'There's no bad media. Infamous is still famous. No one is going to touch you. No one is going to do anything.'" That did not turn out true, but Josh still had that lesson to learn. "I went to the next rally."

Josh says he had laid low and hadn't stayed in contact with the Proud Boys, but they remembered him when they saw him at the large

November 2020 MAGA rally, the second one in D.C. "I apparently made a name for myself," he tells me. "They said I held my own, stayed in the front line." There were a few more scuffles and "after that night, I heard I had a price on my head, from Antifa and BLM." Josh's sense of importance and belonging to the group was growing. He went from joining a MAGA march to enjoy some expensive whiskey with a friend, to feeling a sense of belonging, significance, and purpose, like many who join white supremacist, violent extremist, and terrorist groups.

The vitriol on social media increased. He was particularly angry when a woman he never dated accused him of beating his ex-girlfriends. "'You look like someone who hits your girlfriend.' What does that mean?" Josh rants about the post. Josh is adamant he's never been violent with women and demanded she take down the post, which she did.

Later I learn Josh has a criminal history. At least two exes have obtained restraining orders against him. He was convicted of theft at age 18 and has multiple DUIs. After I learned about the first restraining order, I asked him about it and he claimed it was for texting his ex nonstop after their breakup, because he was still in love and wanted to get back together. She responded by filing for a restraining order. Josh repeated the same explanation about the restraining order to CNN.[17]

Josh has a temper and strong streak for justice which can lend itself to vigilantism. When he heard Antifa and others were spraying "bottles of piss at the cops, I was infuriated." As a bartender, he says he knows a lot of cops and he told his law enforcement friends, "I can do what you are not allowed to do." They didn't take him up on it. "I wanted to protect the cops." Despite his "Back the Blue" sentiments, Josh ended up on the other side of events when January 6 rolled around.

Before interviewing Josh, I revisited social psychology literature on mob mentality. Some authors argue individuals lose their sense of self in crowds, de-individuate, and take on groupthink and temporarily suspend their judgment to take on the norms of the group. Likewise, there is good evidence that individuals in mobs, particularly those who hide their identities under balaclavas or masks, tend to be more violent than they would be on their own. Yet other researchers argue that mobs tend to bring together like-minded individuals who often share a grievance and a continuum of views, and some in the mob instigate violence where others may not be interested in violence at all. Clearly there were instigators present on January 6. Weapons were brought into Washington. A gallows was erected. As I listen to Josh, it seems that once falling in with those who endorse violence, he is the type to be swept up in a mob mentality. His needs for belonging and validation are strong.

Indeed, Enrique Tarrio was arrested on January 4, 2021, for allegedly stealing and burning a Black Lives Matter banner from a D.C. church, and for bringing a high-capacity magazine into D.C. Josh put up a threatening rant the next day on his Parler account, "Bring it, motherfuckers. Y'all motherfuckers just started a war. You wanna arrest Enrique? OK, we got you. You're gonna have to arrest fuckin' all of us."[18]

(A condition of Tarrio's release on January 5th was that he leave Washington. So, he was not physically present in the January 6th insurrection though he was later arrested and charged with seditious conspiracy for his alleged role in its planning.)

Josh describes January 6th. "We started at the other end where Trump was speaking," the events still fresh in his mind. "[It was a] clusterfuck. I didn't hear a single word that he said. You couldn't get that close." He says he marched to the Capitol Building with the Proud Boys, 15 at a time, and got separated from them once at the building. "Then we see the fuckery happening. It was getting really weird. The last thing you think is anyone would go into the Capitol. See them rushing up, I waited a few minutes. I walked up and I walked through the front door, an open door, cops waving us in. I think it's okay if they are waving us in. Now it seems like a set-up. Why not let everyone in and charge everyone?" While it's unclear if Josh is being honest, there are reports that once the mob started surging, the police did wave people in through the doors. He is pictured on Twitter jumping over a four-foot metal barrier before entering.[19]

Obviously, some intruders had prepared for crimes. Josh agrees there were very nefarious actors inside the Capitol but denies sharing that mindset. "I'm not going to hurt a congressman. That was not even in the back of my mind" and reiterates he "had no ill intentions."

Inside the Capitol, he says he was completely shocked by what he saw. "I don't believe in that, stealing shit, and taking pictures of people's office, fucking disgusting, I saw that and it pissed me off." He describes trying to pull people back and hitting one person who took a swing at a cop. "How do you say, 'Back the Blue' and then attack the blue?" He says two cops asked him for help, telling him, "'You are obviously the voice of reason,' because I was backing people up and saying, 'We need to leave.' I could see there was no purpose, and it was disgusting."

Josh's cognitive dissonance was overwhelming him, and he didn't know how to make sense of it. "There was a picture of me throwing a sign in aggravation. We had just gotten gassed. You're mad. You hit a wall instead of hitting someone else. I threw a sign."

Later I will see the video of Josh throwing "a sign". The sign was actually a large stand which he picked up and held over his head, then hurled toward police.

"I have to get the fuck out of here," he recalls thinking. "I don't want any part of this." He says he was in the building for 30-40 minutes and out by 3:30. He was arrested that night for breaking curfew when he offered to escort a young woman to her hotel. In custody, he says he was surprised by how badly he was treated by police and says he doesn't remember being read his rights. He was shown photos of himself at the Capitol and was told he'd be charged with felony rioting. He didn't deny he was there and says he was very cooperative.

The facts shown in security video footage and in his federal indictment tell the story this way: Proud Boys used a shield taken from Capitol police to smash through a window to illegally enter the building, after which the marauders kicked open the door through which Josh entered.[20] According to the court offense statement against Josh, as Senate Leader Charles Schumer was evacuated from the Senate Chamber, his security detail attempted to reach a motorcade to move the senator to a secure location. As they waited by the elevators, "a member of Senator Schumer's security detail saw Pruitt and one other man approaching. The security detail and Senator Schumer reversed course and ran away from the elevator, back down the ramp, and away from Pruitt.[21]"

Whether or not Josh meant to menace Senator Schumer, he was seconds away from him and Members of Congress were in fear for their lives, especially leadership. "Kill Mike Pence" was being chanted in the hallways and President Trump did not intervene, showing callous disregard for his Vice President's life, according to subsequent testimony in the House Select Committee to Investigate the January 6 Attack.[22]

Josh says he was following what he thought President Trump asked he and the others gathered to do. And clearly, he was preparing to do something. He posted a body building photo of himself on January 4th, on Parler, with the caption: "Getting ready for those clowns on Wednesday. Wrong patriot to fk with." According to court records, Josh also posted a photo of

Josh with Automatic Standing on BLM Banner

himself on the morning of the riot, posing with an assault rifle while standing on a Black Lives Matter flag. The black tank top he wore to the riot bore the logo of the comic book vigilante "Punisher"[23] and Josh also wore what the government described as "a tactical glove with knuckle pads" on one hand.[24]

Josh will be charged with eight separate counts and will wind up in prison, but at the time I interview him, he was not yet charged and was hoping it would all go away. He was scared and asked me several times if I could help "find the video of the cop asking me to help them, backing the people up and thanking me?" He told me he can't afford a lawyer and was afraid he could be charged in the murder of the police officer who died. "I'm 'Back the Blue'," he repeated several times. "That person who hit the cop with the fire extinguisher should go to prison, not cool."

In the aftermath of January 6th, Josh once again found himself tried in the court of public opinion. "They make me out to be a monster…I get my character assassinated now." He's gotten death threats. "People can be really nasty just for having another opinion [from] them." (The irony was lost on him.) It's impossible not to feel pity for him as he looks terrified at the potential criminal charges and says, "It's not so goddamn black and white." He again insists there are "videos of me actually helping. They are not going to say that. They want to nail me on the one charge. I was cooperative with the arresting cops. Most [rioters] said 'Fuck off.' They thanked me," he reiterates.

He then launches into a far-right conspiracy I will later hear from others at the Capitol Building—that Antifa was at the Capitol disguised as Trump supporters. "The guy with the horns on his head is Antifa, and he was the first one in the building. He goes to everything. I saw him earlier in the day talking on a bullhorn. We walked by him laughing as he was acting a fool." I decide not to engage on this but as Josh continues to text me after our interview, sharing his anxiety about his court date and fears of ending up in prison, he continues this line of thought and sends me QAnon videos as confirmation. I try to point out he needs to vet his news sources and become a better critical thinker, but he's pretty convinced the riot was a set-up and he's a pawn in a bigger game.

Within months after the Capitol Building was overrun, the Biden Administration conducted a sweeping assessment of domestic terrorism and repeated earlier FBI warnings, labeling white supremacists and militia groups as the top domestic security threat.[25] Twelve U.S. Army National Guard members were removed from President-Elect Biden's security detail for having ties to right-wing militia groups or posting extremist views; and there are allegations that Trump's Secret Service team had advance knowledge of threats against House Speaker Nancy Pelosi, Vice President Mike Pence, and President-Elect Biden on January 6, yet did not report those threats.[26]

Analysis of the Capitol Hill rioters revealed a significant and disconcerting portion, and the most violent among them, involved former and current military. Twelve percent of the January 6th Capitol Hill rioters charged with federal crimes are veterans or active-duty military. Of that subgroup, 25 percent are commissioned officers and 44 percent had been deployed at least once, so they were trained in active warfare.[27] U.S. Secretary of Defense Lloyd J. Austin III vowed to take steps to eradicate extremism from our armed forces. He has called for Extremism Stand Down Days to conduct trainings. The U.S. Department of Defense has asked ICSVE to help them better understand how extremism occurs in the military, and how to prevent and mitigate it. We have also started doing police trainings funded by the U.S. Department of Homeland Security and research funded by the U.S. Department of Justice.

Our institutions have been infiltrated and DVE is metastasizing across the U.S. at a staggering pace. The number of violent white supremacists and other hate-motivated domestic extremists has almost tripled in recent years, egged on by a cocktail of conspiracy theories.[28]

They are deadly. When the Anti-Defamation League, ADL, analyzed extremist-related murders in 2019, they found an overwhelming 90 percent were linked to right-wing extremists.[29]

It's a scary time for global democracy as well. New Zealand and Norway have suffered horrific mass murders carried out by domestic white supremacists,[30] and most European countries are seeing an uptick in hate-motivated, violent attacks against minority populations. The domestic terror threat appears to be growing alongside far-right populism. Italy elected Georgia Meloni as Prime Minister, whose party, Brothers of Italy (Fratelli d'Italia), traces its roots to dictator Benito Mussolini. Viktor Orban leads Hungary; France's perennial politician, Marine Le Pen, maintains a growing popularity; Sweden's recent elections showed a surge in their far-right party, right wing extremists are infiltrating German police and security agencies[31], and in Croatia, men marched with fascist symbols in support of Donald Trump.[32]

What we do to counter the rise of DVE depends upon our understanding of it. I want to share an example here, as a case in point that directly links to January 6th:

For weeks after the January 6th attack, conversations over encrypted social media platforms like Signal and Telegram claimed gallows had been erected around Washington D.C. QAnon posts and YouTube videos purported to show areas where a secret liberal elite who kidnap, sexually abuse, and traffic children were to be hung. QAnon claims Hillary Clinton, George Soros, and other prominent Democrats lead this secret cabal. Their hanging would be Trump's ultimate "reckoning" against pedophiles, liberals, non-whites, and Jews who sought to steal America. Rather than Biden being sworn in, Trump would be reinstated as the legitimately elected president and swiftly enact justice.

Allegations of those gallows invoked a longstanding special meaning for white supremacists who were well-represented among the rioters on January 6. In fact, it was a day they have anxiously awaited for decades called "The Day of the Rope."

"The Day of the Rope" comes from a 1978 dystopian novel by a white supremacist, William Luther Pierce, who wrote under the pseudonym Andrew Macdonald. Called *The Turner Diaries,* the FBI refers to this book as "the bible of the racist right."[33] The Anti-Defamation League says this book has achieved a kind of cult status and is "probably the most widely-read book among far-right extremists; many have cited it as the inspiration behind their terrorist organizing and activities."[34] It has explicitly influenced violent extremists, from January 6th to the Oklahoma City bomber, Timothy McVeigh.[35]

The Turner Diaries Book Cover

The novel depicts the U.S. federal government, referred to as "the system" run by Jews, violently overthrown by a fictional white guerilla group called "The Organization." Whites, who have been dispossessed of their firearms, are subjected to surveillance measures and unable to defend themselves until they band together to carry out low-level resistance activities that include assassinations, economic sabotage, and bombings. The Organization mounts attacks against law enforcement, politicians, and others using tactics described in the novel in such detail they can be read as a how-to manual. When The Organization takes control of a territory, they carry out "The Day of the Rope," a mass hanging of non-whites, Jews, liberals, "race traitors," and politicians. The author's protagonist, Earl Turner, is part of the underground revolution against "the system" and eventually engages in a global race war in which all the groups opposing his group are ultimately exterminated.

Tragically, the fictitious Earl Turner and his diaries have inspired dozens of real terrorist events. Chief among them are the operational similarities between the 1995 Oklahoma City bombing and the fictional bombing of the FBI building in Washington, D.C., described in detail in the *Diaries*.[36] Likewise The Order (aka Brüder Schweigen/The Silent Brotherhood) is a real group that embarked upon a

The Order Logo and Slogan

series of bank robberies and was responsible for at least three murders, including the assassination of Jewish radio host Alan Berg in 1984. The Order was founded by white supremacist Robert J. Mathews who named the group after The Organization in *The Turner Diaries*. The novel also promotes suicide terrorism, a technique more often employed by militant jihadists who claim religious "martyrdom," but is increasingly referenced in white supremacist chat rooms, to escalate their lethality and influence.

The Turner Diaries glorifies what many white supremacist "patriots" believe is a very real and deadly racial holy war they await and try to incite, to destroy corrupt democratic institutions and replace them with white domination. From fears of losing Second Amendment rights to becoming a minority by 2040, from factories moving offshore to ingrained racism and more, fears and feelings of inadequacy are being channeled into a desire to secure what essentially has been a racist caste system in the U.S. and beyond where whites dominate other races and profit from it.[37] "The Day of the Rope," is the ominous phrase they frequently employ, referring to a coming RAHOWA, racial holy war, which will include public lynchings. In this race war, whites who fear "white genocide" and "the great replacement" will be restored to power by driving out or executing Jews and minorities and hanging collaborators and liberal politicians. To that end, domestic hate groups have stockpiled weapons and carried out attacks with the hope of inciting this war.

It's a threat we are also exporting. Consider this familiar scenario: A plan to storm the capitol, arrest lawmakers and kill the leader, urged on by QAnon conspiracy theories of a shadowy deep state that needs taken down. This time it's December 2022 in Germany where QAnon has fed the conspiracy group, the Reichsbürger, or Citizens of the Reich, a loose network of some 20,000, who believe Germany is run by a corporation set up by the Allies after World War II.[38] Police officers and Special Forces raided 150 homes across Germany and arrested 25 suspects that included a former special forces officer, an active-duty soldier, a police officer, and two army reservists. Hajo Funke, a political scientist, told the *New York Times*, "We are seeing now the mistake in the downplaying this danger."[39]

Which brings us back to January 6th.

Experts believe the gallows outside the U.S. Capitol was not a coincidence but inspired by "The Day of the Rope." As counterterrorism expert, Bruce Hoffman, so aptly noted in an op-ed one year after the attack, "The 2021 true-life version [of *The Turner Diaries*] revealed the dangerous, continued resonance of the so-called accelerationist strategy the novel advocates."[40] Indeed, a number of former extremists I have interviewed for *Escape Hate* warn we are closer to realization of the fictitious *The Turner Diaries* than ever.

That is the political climate we face, seen inside the halls of power and seen in far too frequent deadly breaking news. Perhaps it's hard for our country to admit we have this growing cadre of flag-waving haters fed by outlandish conspiracies and debunked propaganda, willing to become violent at a moment's notice, and helped along by elected leaders and even a president who panders to extremists. But that is the threat, and it comes from within.

I ask Josh to turn back to what he was thinking as he joined the events of January 6. "We had control and cared about a real election not being cheated," he responds. Control. It's a big word and one that extremist groups promise their members, that they can assert themselves and take control, making things that worry them right.

Then Josh returns to his confusion about the legal trouble he's now embroiled in, ruminating over his innocence about entering with the other rioters. "I went in there as a goddamn patriot, not as a rioter, not to fight cops, to take pix on people's desk, steal podiums. Put 300 people together, 30 will be dumbasses," he concludes.

Seeing the tension on his face, I ask how he's coping with the distress and confusion. He says drinking is his "go to" though he'd rather be working out. But he's scared to go to the gym or leave his house. "I'm getting noticed everywhere I walk to. I'm scared to go to the grocery store. I can't catch a fucking charge now. If someone talks shit and swings at me, I'll be the bad guy, because I'm all over the news. If someone hits me in the face and I hit him back, guess who is going to jail? It's me."

At this point, the social media attacks, real-life threats, and the charges hanging over his head are wearing him down. "I am scared for my goddamn life," he says, and then this big burly man bursts into tears. "I want to leave so bad. I'm scared. There is nothing like everyone hating you. People who don't even know you, people who don't know you, hate you. That's the worst."

In many ways, Josh seems naïve and childlike in his strong need to belong. Like most violent extremists, a rough childhood is part of the package. He saw his mother overdose on heroin when he was around six years old, and his father contracted AIDs from needles. He says he was the outcast of a large family because he reminded them of his deceased mother. The family gave up his younger and older sisters for adoption, doing them "a favor," but his father kept Josh and would pass him back and forth with an aunt. He only found out six years ago his "cousin" is actually his older sister. He finally left home at age 16 and got his GED. "I'm not dumb," and tells me, "I went to college for digital media and animation" and says he worked his way up in sales at various places, becoming top in the stores where he worked.

Given all that has passed, I ask Josh if he still considers himself a Proud Boy. "I would say yes. It's a good question. I don't really know these guys. Am I affiliated? Yes. What they stand for is not what they are being told they stand for," Josh tries to explain. Then Josh lays out his own code of loyalty and honor. Though he didn't know who the Proud Boys were when they came to his rescue against Antifa, they "helped me from not getting jumped. Fuck it, I'll hang out with them…I'm going to have their backs. That was my thought process. I don't regret."

Despite its designation as an extremist group by the FBI, Josh says he hasn't heard "one guy say one racist thing when I am hanging out with them" and says they definitely don't stand for white supremacism or even lean that far to the right. They support Trump and many are ex-military who "just don't want our country taken over; don't believe in a stolen election which is what we think."

Josh then launches into a rant. "No one gives a fuck if Trump is President again. I'm not even going to vote again. For what? They just pick who they want anyway," he asserts. "Me and my sister are not voting again. No point," and I think, this is how we can lose our democracy, when voters no longer believe in it. "Seems there was fraud, don't know if it was enough to steal the election, but fraud yes. I don't think it was 20 million votes. Georgia, idea of Pennsylvania, he's winning by seven million, and then only 500 in the morning. Doesn't make sense to me. That's me thinking I'm being logical." When I ask where Josh gets his information, he admits to watching far-right videos and names Ben Shapiro, Officer Tatum, Conservative Twins. "I probably watch way too much shit from certain people," he admits. The "Big Lie" has had far reaching consequences and it's going to be people like Josh who pay a big price.

Josh agrees to participate in our *Escape Hate* counter narrative video project, which offers more insight into his mindset. "You need to think about what you're doing before you do it. That spur of the moment thing is not a thing. That's when you make bad decisions…your intent to be good, then it can turn into something completely different. No one knows what you are actually thinking, what is seen from the outside is for them the truth."

"Definitely another piece of advice," he continues. "For kids or anybody, don't become a part of anything you don't know the whole background or story on…The idea that anyone is really going to have your back at the end of the day is a joke, not if it compromises them."

I ask Josh if we should refer to him as a former Proud Boy in his counter narrative video, still thinking he may want to distance himself, but he again says no, he is with them. Then to make the point that he thinks the Proud Boys are being vilified and Antifa is ignored by the mainstream media, he points out to me that Antifa has attacked a U.S. Immigration and Customs Enforcement (ICE) building in Portland, and no one is doing much about it. He says Black Lives Matter and Antifa can get away with things for which he's going to be crucified.

Josh ultimately pled guilty and faced a statutory maximum of 20 years in prison and a fine of up to $250,000.[41] He was repentant when he talked to me and similarly at his detention hearing in January 2022, telling the court, "I regret going inside. I was disgusted with what I saw."[42]

Yet he publicly flip-flopped on his regret six months after I interviewed him and six months before his detention hearing. With a steady diet of QAnon propaganda and YouTube videos that claim January 6 was a false flag operation run by Antifa, designed to entrap people like him, Josh puts up a video in June 2021 on a new Tik Tok account (his earlier one was taken down.) His video consists of rotating images of the January 6 rioters, Donald Trump, the U.S. border, and an American flag with a Christian cross, captioned, "Do I regret Jan 6th? Not even a little!!! Patriots rise!"[43] His new account had 8000 followers in June 2021 so he's still attracting attention. Indeed, the attention seems to feed a deep need for significance, and it appears he likes taking the victim stance while dodging responsibility for his own bad choices.

And there are more bad choices still being made. For the first year after the insurrection, Josh was under the federal government's High-Intensity Supervision Program (HISP) requiring him to stay home nights. But in January 2022, a judge ordered him to jail to await sentencing for repeatedly violating the order. His GPS tracker showed him out nights in the vicinity of nightclubs and bars.[44]

Josh is an underdeveloped man with an alcohol problem (he later admitted to me over text,) who consistently fails to think through the consequences of his actions. He is lonely, has an unsteady temper, a deep need for belonging and significance, and mixes with online conspiracy theories. Perhaps that combination partly explains why Josh remained connected to the Proud Boys despite his conviction and the heavy prison sentence he faced. He has even remained loyal to former leader Enrique Tarrio who was outed as working with the FBI. Understanding he may serve significant prison time, perhaps he's setting himself up to be a "martyr" for the cause. Josh is a walking cocktail ready to be pulled into violent extremism.

You can watch Josh tell his story at www.EscapeHate.org

Chapter 2 - The Day of the Rope:
A Fictional Novel becomes a Calling

With the words, "I will see you in Valhalla," Brenton Harrison Tarrant's heinous act traveled the globe and the world recoiled with revulsion.

The 28-year-old white supremacist mass murderer posted those words on Facebook right before his killing rampage in Christchurch, New Zealand, on March 15, 2019. He gunned down 51 mosque goers and injured dozens more, and to the world's horror, he live-streamed the bloody crime as those aligned with his hatred of Muslims and nonwhites helped him globally magnify the terror by repeatedly reposting it.[45]

Tarrant's massacre was accompanied by a 74-page manifesto that referred to the "great replacement" and "white genocide" conspiracy theories.[46] Minutes before the attacks he dispatched his diatribe, emailing it to more than 30 recipients, including the Prime Minister's office and several media outlets, with links shared on Twitter and 8chan (an online chat site linked to right-wing extremism and now mass shootings.)[47]

What could possibly drive a young man to commit such a horrifying crime and make sure the world witnessed it in real time?

One answer lies with Ed Schofield. It's January 2021. I'm interviewing the 48-year-old former skinhead and former adherent of the Creativity Movement. Despite its innocent-sounding name, the Creativity Movement is hardcore. This white supremacist group dates back to the 1970s and is notable for its attempt to assume the guise of a religion as a way to promote its extreme racist and antisemitic views that define only white people as human. Originally known as the Church of the Creator, then the World Church of the Creator, it was later renamed the Creativity Movement or simply Creativity. The Anti-Defamation League, ADL, defines it as a "white supremacist pseudo-religion."[48] For

Ed, this racist "religion" that extols white supremacy is now an ideology he has committed himself to debunking.

"A lot of people never heard of it, how far spread it was," Ed tells me. I admit, he can count me among them. "They are dangerous. I wish I had done it [worked to debunk them] sooner. Maybe people would have recognized it in New Zealand. Maybe that massacre in the mosque would not have happened."

I think back to the moments after the attack, and I remember it very well. Ardian Shajkovci, my Muslim research colleague who traveled with me to interview ISIS prisoners in Syria, had forced himself to watch the video of the massacre as it reverberated across the internet, taking in the carnage of men, women, and children slaughtered in real time. I can't forget his feelings of confusion and horror watching innocents murdered during prayer.

Ed's face takes on a somber look. "As horrible as that was, it inspired me to let people know how far spread they are: Australia, South Africa, New Zealand. They are dangerous," he reiterates.

Indeed. While most white supremacists will never carry out acts like Tarrant, it is crucial to realize the influence these groups and their racist ideologies have in propelling people into extremist violence and copycat crimes such as the El Paso shooter in August 2019 who killed 22 and injured many more in a Texas Walmart. His online manifesto echoed that of Tarrant as did the 18-year-old Buffalo shooter who killed ten and injured three in a grocery store.[49] Nowadays we are seeing school shooters and violent extremists carefully studying those who went before them, echoing and quoting from their manifestos as well as advising those who follow to conduct careful surveillance, test their weapons beforehand, figure out how to livestream their attacks and cause as much carnage as possible—each one learning and improving in lethality and striking terror as far as possible from those who went before.

After my interview with Ed, I look into the writings of the Creativity Movement. They are militant and extreme:

We gird for total war against the Jews and the rest of the goddamned mud races of the world—politically, militantly, financially, morally and religiously. In fact, we regard it as the heart of our religious creed, and as the most sacred credo of all. We regard it as a holy war to the finish—a racial holy war. RAHOWA! is INEVITABLE. (1987)

We are in harmony with the Leadership Principle as expounded by Adolf Hitler and consider the former Nazi Party and governmental organization as a model structure for our own future development. We consider Hitler's Nazi Germany between 1933-39 as the finest and most efficient society the White Race has ever produced." (1987)

We believe that in the battle for individual survival and the survival of our race, Nature tells us that any means is morally justified…In the matter of survival of our race, we take the firm position that any means justifies this end, and no price is too high. (1981)

When persuasion and reason fail, the only recourse is violence, legal or illegal. (1981)[50]

The 'W' of our Emblem stands, of course, for the WHITE RACE, which we regard as the most precious treasure on the face of the earth. The Crown signifies our Aristocratic position in Nature's scheme of things, indicating that we are the ELITE. The Halo indicates that we regard our race as being UNIQUE and SACRED above all other values. (2005)[51]

Ed, balding with a short dark beard appears on the screen framed by what almost looks like a little shrine behind him, white twinkle lights arranged in a frame on the wall with a shelf of what look like tiny icons arranged behind him. I begin our interview as I often do, by asking Ed about his upbringing. His family was intact, but deeply troubled. "Both my parents were addicted," he tells me. "My father was a Vietnam vet and later became a plumber. He was an alcoholic. He drank a lot and was fairly abusive. Neither were racist," he points out, assuming I'm looking into his childhood for the origins of his entry into white supremacism. "My mother, I don't speak to any longer. She's still alive. She chose heroin over her children. My father passed away in 1996."

Ed had four siblings. They family was poor, but his father was able to buy a house in southern New Jersey. "My mother went to prison for the first time for a drug charge after we bought the house. Dad went to the VA. I went to foster care at 11-years-old."

He went back to live with his dad but was very rebellious. Always looking for a fight, "that ended me in military school, Hargrave Military Academy. Welcome to your new home. I was 14."

"It definitely put me on a better path for quite a while, straightened me out. I quit fighting everyone. They just laugh at you and give you something harder to do." His grandmother also intervened. "My grandmother tried to give me advice, slapped me upside the head more than once. She was an old Italian woman. I think she was one of the people who really helped me to get myself figured out in the military school. She told me, 'Don't miss this opportunity. Make something of yourself.' That's when I got into martial arts and focused."

He was smart, did well in school, and skipped a couple of grades." Being smart landed Ed an early graduation at age 16, but he was hardly ready for life as an adult, which he was soon to prove.

With a black belt in Aikido and Brazilian jujitsu, Ed tried to become a Mixed Martial Arts (MMA) professional. At age 19, he won a fight in Atlantic City. But things turned very bad at the after-party along the crowded boardwalk. "I saw this guy beating up his girlfriend, just wailing on her, no one doing anything. I took it upon myself to intervene. I pushed him off her." Things got out of control. "He pulled a knife, 'Get off my face! I'm going to kill you!' I answered, 'I will stab you if you come at me.' He came at me, and I bent his hand back, and it cut his neck."

Ed had had plenty of run-ins with the police as a troubled kid and he had a strong distrust of cops. Even though he'd pretty much acted in self-defense, the cops would blame him. His immediate instinct was to run. He was caught three days later. He got 30 years for first-degree involuntary homicide. It was later overturned, but he served 12 years attempted robbery of a car when he was on the run." Ed's young life was shattered.

It was in the county jail, before heading to prison, where he met up with a couple guys he'd grown up with. "They were neo-Nazi skinheads. It was my first introduction to that. I had heard about them, but since everyone in my family was very military oriented, if I saw skinheads or swastikas, I'd say, 'Oh, you are a Commie' and blew them off. But they told me, 'No, we are not Commies. We are against communism. We are for National Socialism.'"

"What attracted you to them?" I ask.

"I was so angry at how things had turned out, it gave me an outlet, gave me a reason to fight. This system screwed me. Everyone else screwed me, so I'm going to join this group. And that was 20 years of being in the movement," Ed tells me. "We formed the State Prison Skinheads with the okay of the older members of Aryan Nations on the west coast. We were the only sanctioned white supremacist prison gang on the east coast." Ed seems to boast, although I'll soon learn about his deep sense of shame over his years of involvement in white supremacism.

He remained an active member of the State Prison Skinheads and long before quitting in 2012, he found church. Though it was not the kind of church most would think of.

"I was an atheist before I went to prison," Ed says. "I had wanted to be a preacher and I became ordained at 18. But later I learned that nothing I had learned proved there was a God, and much disproved Christianity. So, I decided to leave religion behind."

"Then I came across the Creativity Church. They said, 'We're atheists, too. Our race is our religion.'" He read their literature and "it was something I could agree with at the time, so I became a practicing member of the Creativity religion and followed it to my release in March 2004."

The Creativity Church, according to Ed, is the same white supremacy group the New Zealand mass murderer followed, although Tarrant seems to have followed many groups on the internet.

"Creativity teaches that every ethnicity is a different species. The only humans on the planet are the white race. I thought Black people are another species. Blacks are inherently more violent." There is no co-existence. "What species reproduces outside its species or lives together? You don't see lions and tigers living together, a cow mating outside its species."

Ed was young when he went to prison and his new mentors easily captured his attention. "They are older than me and talking to me about science. I was more into sports. My focus was martial arts. I didn't think about science and sociology. They were throwing terms out and they suckered me in."

Now Ed realizes it was all pseudoscience, outdated theories, and just plain garbage. "They are showing me papers that are so old and out-of-date, from the 1800s, for brain mass and measuring skulls." But he had little with which to challenge them. "When I told them, 'I never heard that,' their answer was, 'Of course. They don't want you to learn that. Jews don't want you to have that knowledge.'" Ed became a true believer, and a hater.

"One of the biggest things they try to tell you, 'It's not hate to love your own race,'" he explains. I will hear this refrain many times during my interviews with white extremists. "That's one of the things I used to use when I was recruiting in the '90s. That gets people thinking, 'Yeah I'm not hating anyone to love myself.' You tell them, 'Love your family first, but your family is white. Love your race above others. Those races are jealous of everything the white man has. We worked for it, and they want it.'"

These recruiting tactics, of course, totally gloss over the fact that white people subjugated and oppressed other races. The tactics are effective. "They would ask for books and pamphlets. They would read it and it was stuff they had never seen before that goes contrary to the mainstream. Then you tell them of course, because the Jews want to hide the truth. That gets them thinking, maybe he's right." The goal was to move recruits from the free literature he handed out to buying more expensive texts, then funneling the money back into the church to bring in more recruits.

"I can honestly say in my six years following the Creativity religion, I indoctrinated at least 15-20 people and that's just the ones I can remember," Ed says of his prison recruitment. Given Ed's martial arts expertise, and success in recruiting, I wanted to know if he had weapons training as part of this group.

"I didn't because I was in prison, but some take weapons training. The state imperator [commander] for New Jersey, Henry Barret, was the highest-ranking member in prison for the church at that time. He asked me, 'With your background in martial arts, would you mind training other Creatives who are in prison with us?' We had a system. I would purposely get in a fight, stab someone who was with the Black Hebrews or Nation of Islam—get in a fight, stab them—to be put in administrative segregation, to get communication with other Creators in there, to keep communication going. That's how extreme I was. I would give up my time in general population to transfer information and training to those locked up in the hole."

As an MMA champion, Ed was a deadly weapon.

"Yes, I taught them everything I could: Aikido, Taekwondo, Jujitsu, hand-to-hand combat from my dad and military school. Whatever I could train them. I showed them prison weapons—if you find yourself on the street, take your socks off and load them up with a bunch of rocks to hit and defend with. I taught a lot of guys how to make a shank real quick, and how to use it; how to fold a single piece of paper to puncture skin."

"What did you believe at that time? What were you preparing for?"

"We are building our strength. Someday we'll take our country back from everyone that stole it from us."

"Were you waiting for a race war?"

"Oh yeah!" his eyes lighting up, remembering what that used to mean to him. "Yes, everything that's happening right now, January 6th, this is the scenario that I always thought was just a pipe dream. We used to talk about this exact thing happening. How we were going to kick off a second civil war and get rid of all the nonwhites and take this country back. It's called RAHOWA, racial holy war," Ed says, spelling it out for me. RAHOWA has been a rallying call for the white supremacist cause for years, and it originated in the Creativity Movement.[52]

"How would you know when this race war starts?" I ask, and add, "Would you have killed for them?" Horror creeps up my spine as I wonder just how brutal Ed used to be.

"If someone higher up in the church declared this is RAHOWA, every Creative that got that message would have geared up to go to war. They say they don't promote violence and extremism, but it is well known that if you hear the order for RAHOWA, it's time to get violent, time to go to war," Ed explains. "We came very close on January 6th," he adds. "The Feds don't know how close it came to being more than a riot and stampede into the Capitol Building."

Ed says he even alerted the FBI, telling them the January 6 plan was far broader than the Capitol Building, and would involve destroying emergency response capabilities. "They will start with the 911 cell towers and police stations, and then ER rooms in high traffic—they are going to hit those—attack fire departments and EMT centers and their main goal and first goal is disrupting cell towers and 911 centers." Ed says Creativity and members of other groups would talk and "had planned that they will talk back on older technology, using ham radios and bouncing messages. [I told the FBI] 'Listen for ham radio signals. That's where they are going to make their actual plans.'" Indeed, that is now emerging as evidence in the sedition trials of Oath Keepers and Proud Boys involved in the Jan 6 insurrection.

Since he thinks the Capitol Hill mob almost triggered RAHOWA, I ask Ed a bit more about his view of the rioters. I think about Josh Pruitt and how heavily the Proud Boys were represented. "I don't view Proud Boys as white supremacists," he responds. Indeed, the Proud Boys vehemently deny they are part of the alt-right, although the Southern Poverty Law Center, SPLC, which does excellent work tracking hate groups, reports them regularly spreading white nationalist memes and associating themselves with known extremists.[53] "They are fascist far right, but they don't understand the groups they are working with. In reality, we would see groups like them as cannon fodder. We'd put them on the front line. Let them take the beating. They are not white. They are expendable."

"And QAnon?" I ask, as many of the rioters were also QAnon conspiracy theory followers and I have learned in my years of research that nearly all terrorists and violent extremist groups have elements of conspiracy theories in their ideologies. "There are conspiracies galore there," he says. "They have these conspiracies that people believe wholeheartedly with no evidence. That's what makes them so dangerous. They don't need evidence. They will do it for the cause. You just tell them, and they do it. That makes them more dangerous than other groups."

I've spent decades talking to ISIS, Al Qaeda, and other foreign extremists. Even so, Ed's warning about QAnon gives me pause.

I wonder how actively engaged Ed had been in these kinds of long-term plans for RAHOWA.

"I had talked about that with Henry Baird [one of the Creativity leaders], who had a direct line to Matthew Hale. Hale was the Pontifex Maximus [the leader of Creativity]. Hale hadn't been arrested yet. We would also talk to Stormfront, Volksfront, the Klan. We would say we don't agree with you, but we are all fighting for the same cause, and this is what needs to happen."

"Then what?" I ask, trying to imagine this doomsday scenario for nonwhites and Jews, once emergency services are shut down and "regular citizens are in a panic."

"Once you have defeated the military, once you have someone from the white race take over, as long as you are all fighting together, and you know the U.S. military has surrendered and this country is under martial law. Then the highest-ranking white member, you go around for 'The Day of the Rope.'"

My heart catches with the unexpected casualness with which Ed refers to mass lynching.

"You send troops to pick up anyone deemed to be a nonwhite. After you take care of nonwhites then you get the race traitors, those who helped, those who are in interracial relationships, who have nonwhite children."

"The Day of the Rope?" I repeat.

"The name says it all," Ed says, shrugging. "Rope is cheaper than bullets.

"Who are you killing exactly?"

"Hispanics, Blacks, Jews, Latinos, Native Americans, Muslims, whoever."

"How do you define white?" I keep running into white supremacists who at some point learn they have Jewish ancestry or are partly Native American or Hispanic.

Ed laughs at my question about defining whiteness and tells me a genetic test revealed he is 14.9 percent west Asian. One more for the "not-so-white" white supremacy group, I think to myself. The whole time I've been listening to him, I've been noticing his dark complexion and hair. He's already said his grandmother was Italian. Not so many years ago, Greeks and southern Italians were considered Black by many in the U.S.[54] If there ever is to be a so-called "Day of the Rope", perhaps many white supremacists would be surprised to find they would not, in the end, be only perpetrators.

The ADL confirms Ed's view that Creatives are violent, citing the case of Matthew Hale, who rebuilt the group after the 1993 suicide of its leader, Ben Klassen, perhaps yet another version of a white supremacist taking in all the hate he spewed onto others, and turning it on himself, back to where hate had likely originated. This self-hatred is another theme I've found woven into white supremacy. The feeling of personal deficiency, and a need to find a home in a group that breeds hatred turned outward. If you remain busy hating others, you never need to attend to your own deficiencies, it seems.

The Creativity Church was started in 1973 by Klassen, in Florida. "He was a politician, maybe a state Senator," Ed tells me. "He founded the religion of Creativity. The prison aspects didn't come till later on." Creativity has a logo consisting of a crown on top of a large letter W.[55] Ed explains, "W is for the white race, the crown for royal and the holy cloud—race is their religion.

Creator Logo

After Klassen's suicide, Hale branded the group the World Church of the Creator. When in the early 2000s, Hale and his group lost the right to the name in a trademark lawsuit, Hale sought vengeance against the federal judge who oversaw the case. Hale was subsequently caught and convicted to 40 years in prison for soliciting murder. With the death of its founder and imprisonment of their subsequent leader, the group then became known as the Creativity Movement or simply Creativity, but lost its organizing capabilities, dwindling from 88 chapters in 2002 to just five by the following year.[56]

Since then, the Creativity Movement has splintered and proliferated in the U.S. and abroad. In 2009, the U.S. had 14 groups, eight of them based in Montana, with an estimated 40 to 50 members and at least one of them lethal. At age 18, member Allen Goff was indicted, but not successfully convicted, for what he claimed as an accidental shooting that wounded a Latino teen. Prosecutors alleged the motivation was racial.[57]

Out of the Creativity Movement, (which for a short period was also called the White Crusaders of the RAHOWA (WCOTR), grew the Creativity Alliance founded by former members of the World Church of the Creator. In 2015, the Creativity Alliance had groups in Georgia, Pennsylvania, South Carolina, Utah and Vermont.[58] Coming full circle, the current Pontifex Maximus of Creativity Alliance is Joseph Esposito (Church of Creativity Oregon), a former supporter of the church's originator, Ben Klassen.

Today, adherents band together in small Creativity factions across several continents, and individuals claim personal adherence, the New Zealand mass murderer among them according to Ed.

Ed continues to tell me about the violence bred by Creativity followers. "I can't remember the gentleman's name off the top of my head, but in North Carolina in 2018, there was someone arrested for manufacturing ricin." (Ricin is an extremely potent and deadly toxin made of easily procured castor beans, but that's difficult to manufacture.) The Church of Creativity denied he was a member. "Of course, they are going to do that. If they admit it, the Feds will investigate them. This person had all their holy books, claimed to be a member of the church. He was creating ricin for this belief."

Later, I look it up and find Ed's recall is not exact but still very concerning. The actual story is of William Christopher Gibbs, from Georgia, who was arrested in 2017 after admitting to emergency medical workers he thought he had exposed himself to ricin in his possession, leading to questions about its intended use. Gibbs identified himself on one of his social media accounts as "belonging to the Georgia Church of Creativity" where he is seen posing in front of the Creativity logo. On another profile, he posted Creativity graphics.

On the website of the Creativity Alliance, the group that has tried to take up the Creativity Movement's mantle, he is featured and has posted photos of himself wearing a Creativity jacket.[59] It seems hard to disavow him as belonging to their group, yet officials from both the Creativity Movement and Creativity Alliance made official statements to that effect.[60]

When I ask Ed how many members he thinks Creativity has now, he tells me growth tamped down after the New Zealand massacre. "I knew they grew exponentially in the last few years in the U.S. and UK, Australia and New Zealand, but not as much after the mosque shooting. They have been laying low. The Pontifex for the Creativity Movement in UK and Europe has brought in hundreds, if not thousands of members, in the past years. They have the Creativity Alliance in the U.S. It's supposedly a different group, but same beliefs, same doctrines, both are aligned with one another." Ed adds that despite their promotion of racist violence, the Creativity leaders are careful. "They don't want to be classified as an international terrorist movement."

They certainly look like one. Now that he's turned against them, Creativity doesn't admit Ed was ever an insider. Ed insists he was a dues-paying member and a true believer for 20 years, from 1992 to 2012. "Otherwise, the prison imperator wouldn't have asked me to train [the other Creatives] in hand-to-hand combat." And he tells me something else about this movement.

"Creativity is definitely a cult," he says. "When I joined the church, under no circumstances am I to have contact [with my family] because they are race traitors, my mother being a heroin addict. They are also anti-religion. Christianity is a Jewish-created religion to bring about the downfall of the white race. If you are dealing with someone out of the church, they have to be white. You only do business with white businesses, no Hispanic or Black, especially Jewish business. There is a Jewish occupational government. It may seem like we elect our government, but they are placed there by the Jewish cabal.

We are under the guise of a free country but are really just slaves for Israel."

It's no accident "Jews will not replace us" was chanted by torch-bearing neo-Nazis in Charlottesville in 2017. Whether secular or quasi-religious, at the heart of white supremacism is a deep-seated, millennia-long scapegoating of Jews who are now blamed for orchestrating "white genocide" and "the Great Replacement." This modern-day theory that Jews are orchestrating demographic changes and a takeover of white Christian dominance was created by white supremacist ideologues, American David Lane, and French writer Renaud Camus in the 2000s.

The Jewish publication, *The Forward,* created a database of some 1,500 monuments, statues, and plaques honoring Nazi-collaborators and perpetrators of the Holocaust, currently found on streets and inside schools in 29 countries, including in the U.S. far-right and white supremacist groups rally around these monuments. As *The Forward's* Nazi Monument Project states, "The monuments and the figures they honor stand at a crossroads of fascism and neo-fascism, the losers of WWII and today's white supremacists who believe they're on the brink of a global race war."[61]

As a kind of cult, I wonder if Ed has identifying tattoos, the answer is surprising.

"Creativity doesn't believe in blemishing your body." In fact, Creatives promote healthy living alongside hatred. "Creative has a very strict regimen for diet and workouts. They don't smoke tobacco, drink, no processed foods, you eat raw fruits and veggies, nuts and grains, no meats."

Without identifying tattoos and their so-called healthy lifestyle, I'm curious about how they recruit and how one becomes a member.

"Does this group recruit on the internet?" I ask.

He smiles, "In 1991, there was no internet back then. Those people didn't have cell phones. My daughter showed me Myspace when I got out of prison!"

Creativity recruits the old-fashion way. "It's still out in the streets, flyers handed out, posters on trash cans and poles. There [recently] was a leaflet drive in the UK. The Creativity Movement left thousands of leaflets in people's mailboxes, all over the place. I know they get members that way."

Distributing leaflets and flyers is an obligation for members who are, according to its website, "expected to distribute a minimum of 600 church flyers of their choice or perform other duties equal in priority to flyering." New members must fill out an application and fulfill a mandatory minimum of six months as prospective church members prior to being granted full membership. The website further describes conditions of commitment: "You may have to work alone for long periods, or you may have to assume responsibility and form your own Church Primary Group. You also may have to accept directions from more experienced Creators. Whatever your situation,

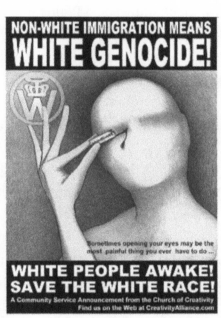

Creativity Church Flyer

remember that the Church of Creativity does not carry passengers. Anyone that does not pull their weight will be dismissed from the Church." Annual dues of $100 are mandatory.

The group's propaganda is still available when I later go poking around the web. I see since the January 6 Capitol Hill riots, Twitter and Facebook have cracked down on them, but there is a new Twitter account in their name and their website is still encouraging "militant" activism. Disturbing pop-ups appear upon entering their site. "Non-white immigration means white genocide!" "White people awake!" Save the white race!" An unsettling graphic depicts a white person using a razor blade to cut open his eyes with the caption, "Sometimes opening your eyes may be the most painful thing you ever have to do…"

The Creativity Alliance website states: "Our Mission is to educate and awaken White Europeans and people of European descent everywhere, to the possibilities currently being kept from them by the tripartite oppression of the alien Judeo-Christian religion, Multiculturalism and Political Correctness. Our Vision is to build a Whiter and Brighter World."[62]

Ed says members must also memorize their 16 commandments. When I ask him to recite them, he doesn't recall. "I will give you something from the church that everyone remembers," he offers. "The highest virtue of the church: 'What is good for the white race is the highest virtue; what is bad for the white race is the ultimate sin.' That's their mantra. Everything you are doing for the church is good for the white race and if you step out of the church that's bad for the white race. You are committing a sin."

"What happens if you commit a sin?"

"There were more drugs than you found on the streets, in prison," Ed offers as an example. "If they had a weak moment and they were in Creativity, they would be sanctioned if caught. Had to work prison ministries, extra workouts, pay a fine, cough up x amount of money so we can send three of the *White Man's Bible*."

Yes, the Creativity Church has a Bible. As Ed explains, the *White Man's Bible* is a "holy book of Creativity" divided into three books. *Nature's Eternal Religion* is pseudo-science explaining why white people should not have children with other ethnicities whom founder Ben Klassen claims are other species. *Salubrious Living* contains diet and workouts to be a healthy white person; and part three, called the *White Man's Bible,* explains the how to's of this white religion—from dealing with nonwhites, to exclusively doing business with only whites, to buying property in predominantly white areas.

Speaking about "sin," I am always curious about the role of women in extremist and terrorist organizations. Women can take on many roles, from sex slaves held captive by some ISIS groups to female "freedom fighters." Most white supremacist groups in the U.S. are misogynist.

"They view it as honorable for women to also know how to fight and be warrior women, but at the same time they are supposed to have the next generation and hold the house down. You can't be a strong white man without a strong white woman. Also, we have to protect them. They do have women's groups promoting the religion, to raise money."

I now turn to how and why Ed left Creativity. The reasons for leaving a white supremacist group are as important as those for joining.

"Right before I got out of prison, I got a book on biology and genetics. I dove into these books, and I couldn't debunk that science," Ed answers. "That was the beginning of my road out of the movement."

"First group I left was Creativity. So many reasons: they claimed not to advocate for violence, but member after member was committing violent acts. People were saying they are a hero, but they are as bad as the people we claim to be against. Then I read biology and genetics and found out that everything I had learned from Creativity was pretty much a lie. My family always told me be honest. Above all be honest. After I realized they had lied to me, I was done. I didn't want anything more to do with them, none of it. I informed the church. 'I want nothing more to do with your organization. Don't contact me.'" He told the State Prison Skins he was "retiring" a couple years later, in 2012. Ed says he held onto some of his skinhead beliefs for those couple extra years, but "some would say I left in 2010. That's when I started having dialogue with an old Army buddy of my father, a Black man."

This friend of Ed's father took Ed under his wing and trained him as a machinist. They worked together in a machine shop. He'd become one of the pivotal people to pull Ed all the way out of white supremacism.

Now Ed's voice takes on a new softness. Perhaps, I think, reflecting the unconditional acceptance now being extended to him. "When we started working together, it was regular everyday talk…Wow, he's being like my dad. How is he any different than my dad? He served two terms in Vietnam, volunteered, served this country, never been arrested, never arrested in a bar, and they want me to believe Blacks are more violent?" Ed started asking questions. "I started talking to him about it, that Blacks are more violent. He said, 'That's a myth. You need to understand statistics.' 'Why do Blacks get more help from the government?' I asked him and he answered, 'I wish! I don't get nothing. I work for my dollar.' 'Jews, do you think they run Hollywood?' 'I don't think so. Who works here [referring to the machine shop]? We are the only ones not related [to the shop owners], so if Jews run a production studio wouldn't they hire people close to them, too?' I'd present all these things without letting him know I used to believe them, until he asked me why."

Then Ed revealed his truth. "I told him in prison I became a skinhead, and he was like, 'Why??' I couldn't give him an honest answer. I honestly don't know. That's when I knew I can't do this anymore. I'm not being honest to myself. This is pointless."

Perhaps Ed was also finding a new kind of family. "He would sit there and tell me dad advice. He knew my dad was gone. He'd say, 'I'm not trying to take the old man's place, but cut back on the drinking, stay away from drugs. Don't do that stuff.'"

"Talking with him, our dialogue back and forth every day, was the catalyst. That was the biggest one, and the education, reading about biology and genetics and knowing ethnicity-wise humans are 99.9 percent the same DNA. There is no superior species. Black people don't have lower IQs simply because they're Black. There is no Jewish conspiracy. We are different ethnicities due to evolution, but that's it."

The man's wife was another curiosity and opportunity for Ed to grow. "I asked her, 'What's it like being a white woman married to a

Black man?' She was flabbergasted. 'Why would you ask me that? He's a man, I'm a woman. We've got kids. We do the best we can.' 'How do other people treat you?' 'It depends. If they are racist and act like an idiot, I ignore them. Normal people don't have an issue and are fine.' I realized she wouldn't view me as a normal person, something wrong with me. That made me think about it, made me tell her husband I had become a skinhead. When she found out, she was not happy. She came to my apartment and laid into me, pretty heavily. We had a nice long talk about it. I told her I did believe that for a long time, but I knew now that it wasn't true."

They became close friends. Both of us have kids that are addicts." Ed tells me as he breaks into tears.

"Two of them together are an inspiration for me today. They have been the biggest support to leave the movement. They helped me leave New Jersey. I started getting death threats when I started speaking out against white supremacy."

Many white supremacist groups will allow members to exit, often with the warning they will be reviled and rejected if they leave. On that note, they are probably right, which needs to be taken into consideration when helping white supremacists exit hate groups. It isn't easy to exit from hate and the repercussions can be long lasting. Tattoos that forever identify them, alongside practices of doxxing, have resulted in many losing their jobs or finding themselves unemployable. As I would learn later in interviews with Antifa, it isn't only the left that practices doxxing on white supremacists; the far right also doxx's, stalks, and harasses its enemies.[63]

Those are the standard difficulties, but when an individual publicly speaks out, the group's hate and violence may be re-directed at those who dare denounce their former group. Ed started receiving threats when he began to publicly speak against Creativity.

"I've had unmarked envelopes in my mailbox that said, 'We know what you are doing. We know you talked to STG [security threat group] officers. If we catch you, we are going to take you out,'" Ed tells me. "I had someone right after I left Church of Creativity shoot a bullet into the side of my house in New Jersey. That was two weeks after my daughter moved out. They shot at my house and the bullet went through the bedroom that would have been my daughter's. I decided I have to get out of New Jersey. I moved to upstate Pennsylvania."

The threats followed. A box was left on Ed's doorstep with a sticker of the emblem of the Church of Creativity. "It was them letting me know, 'We know where you live.' When I saw it sitting there, I thought, 'Oh boy, what's this? I didn't want to touch it. I did call the police. They came and said it was empty and asked, 'Why would they do that?' I said, 'I used to be a follower and was speaking out.'"

I'm trying to better understand that important personal mix of needs, vulnerabilities, and motivations that always play into a person joining and remaining in a violent extremist or terrorist group. No one joins without the group meeting some need. "When you look back, what do you think you got from them? What was the reward for you, being in their group?"

"People ask me if you join for protection," Ed muses. "That does happen, but not as often you think. Most often when people join these groups, they are already angry at something, angry and they join this group because it's an angry mindset. It gives an excuse, saying this is the right way to be a white man."

Sometimes joining is an outlet for rage as Ed notes. Other times it's about belonging, sometimes it's for political reasons, sometimes for love. I've identified at least 50 variables that can play into joining a violent extremist or terrorist group. I've constructed a model of what I call the Lethal Cocktail of Terrorism made up of four essential ingredients: a group, its ideology, the social support, and the interaction between these elements and those individual needs, vulnerabilities and motivations. For each person it's going to be their own combination of variables.[64]

For Ed who remained very violent in prison "fights, stabbing charges, fighting with guards, just whoever. I used the excuse that I was a political prisoner. I was an oppressed white man. That was the only reason I was in prison. If you're going to punish me, then it's my excuse to lash out. That's what it was for me, an excuse. I spread that lie that I'm doing this for my race. I'm fighting for the white man, but in reality, I was just fighting because I was mad, really just fighting against myself."

"You think it went back to your troubled childhood?" I ask. With a heroin addicted mom and alcoholic dad, Ed had been an angry child shuffled between homes and foster care and military school.

"Not necessarily. I had let that go. My life was on a good path," he reflects and offers this answer. "I was getting ready to be a professional fighter and in an instant, trying to defend myself, it went away. I felt like I was a victim. At the time, New Jersey didn't have a self-defense law. When I got convicted, if I had a knife like his it would have been called equal force and I would not have got convicted. But that I was able to turn his knife on him, it was excessive force. [The court ruled] I should have been able to disarm him."

He then returns to his early years, "I got kicked out of every school I went to, public and three Catholic schools. I was a hellraiser and I had a reputation with the police. Part of that was being bounced around from home to home. When I was put in youth shelters, I knew I didn't do anything wrong. My parents were screw-ups, and I was being punished. Why?"

Ed has learned to forgive. "I don't have any contact with my mother because she refuses to change. She's 67 and is serving 30 years for selling a large amount of drugs to an undercover agent. With my father, I started understanding PTSD, things he suffered, and why he was the way he was, that he was not purposely abusing me. He was trying to lead me down the right pathway, just didn't know how."

Still, I wonder what kept him in the extremist groups for so long. People join to meet their needs, but often stay for additional reasons and then finally leave when they get disillusioned or are pulled out by an active intervention.

"[Creativity] was my identity then. They were my support group…Most of my family is very military oriented. Going to prison for homicide and armed robbery, they didn't know how to respond to that. A lot of them didn't write me. They wouldn't pick up the phone if I tried to call. They didn't know what to say, so they kind of pushed me to the side. That kept me in the movement a lot longer. The people in the movement had become my family."

This is a frequent theme with white supremacists, trying to forge a sense of family among broken, angry, and hurt people who cling to each other and bond over shared hatred and injustice, when what they are really looking for is love, nurture, and protection. This is the common psychological phenomena of enmeshment—when two or more damaged people deeply bond as they try to create within their broken union a wholeness that each of them individually lack. Of course, they seldom find it among the people with whom they bond over a shared hatred of others.

"I tell my family now, 'Don't let this happen to anyone else. If someone else goes to prison, call me. Don't leave them there.'" Ed broadens to general advice, "Have dialogue, speak to your family. If you don't know how, there are plenty of groups, plenty of formers who can answer about 'What do I say?'" Ed is one of those formers now and works hard to both debunk the Creativity Movement and pull others out from white supremacist and hate groups.

"What in your opinion is the best intervention?" I ask.

"You have to have empathy. You don't have to agree with their ideas, but they are people, and there is a reason why they have these ideas. Ask them and listen to what they are trying to tell, and then give the best honest answer you can." He thinks back to his own situation. "If my father or my grandmother or aunts or uncles that I respect so very much, if they would have even come to the county jail and came and sat down with me and found out how angry and on edge I was, they would have talked and given me advice, and let me know in the end this was going to be okay. If they had let me know they were supporting me..." Ed's voice breaks and his face crumples. It's clear he remembers how alone and abandoned he felt.

"I saw it so many times, guys would come to prison, and they wouldn't even have that much time, three or five years at the most... It was easy for me to draw them into the movement because they didn't have anyone else. They were so alone. Families need to understand that just because they made a mistake you don't have to cut them off. They are your family. Support them. Go and talk to them."

This is kind advice, but as I listen, I think about how many families are broken and incapable of offering this type of support to a fallen family member. Violent extremists in gangs, prisons, and even on social media actively seek out and prey upon lonely and hurt people.

"What do you think of Facebook, Twitter and YouTube taking down the white supremacists these days? Do you think de-platforming is a good idea?" I ask, as the giant social media companies have been pressured to ban white supremacists, causing many to migrate over to Parler, and then to the encrypted chat site, Telegram, when Amazon refused to host Parler any longer.

"De-platforming is a double edge sword," Ed tells me. "I understand people don't want these horrible ideas spread out over social media, but it makes it harder for someone like myself to debate these ideas and make people stop listening to them. Now I don't know where to counter them. They're in private discussion groups. I can't get in there and counter it while people are hearing and are being drawn in. A couple of people I was having dialogue with got thrown off Twitter. One wrote me an e-mail: 'I'm done talking to you! See how they are suppressing us. Why should I believe anything you have to say?'"

I explained our *Escape Hate* counter narrative project and Ed has given us permission to make a short video from this interview. "Best advice I can say to anyone contemplating joining in is slow down, think critically—for real think critically—and ask yourself, are you looking at both sides of this issue honestly? And speak to people like me even if you think the far right is absolutely right. And if I can debunk any of your ideas you have to question all of them." He adds, "If someone is preaching division or telling you that you need to pick a side, they are on the wrong side. People who say it's not hate to love your own race, but they want you to hate those who are not exactly like you, are wrong. We are not meant to be robots."

He also speaks to personal pain. "In a lot of cases just because you don't feel anyone loves you doesn't make you worthless," and advises, "You are not being thrown away. The world is bigger than you and just because you don't feel others love you, if you take it on yourself to say, 'I care about you for the fact you are a human being', a lot of good people will reciprocate that, and love you for being human and being kind."

You can watch Ed tell his story at www.EscapeHate.org.

Chapter 3 - Seed of the Serpent

When parents dropped their young children off at daycare on April 19th, 1995, never could they have imagined how that day would forever change their lives, and our nation. That's the day Timothy McVeigh drove a rental truck containing a mixture of over 4,800 pounds (2,200 kg) of ammonium nitrate fertilizer, nitro methane, and diesel fuel into the Alfred P. Murrah Federal Building in Oklahoma City. The bomb blast destroyed one third of the building, the onsite daycare, killing 168 people including 19 children, and injuring more than 680 others. The bombing remains the deadliest act of domestic terrorism in U.S. history.

While McVeigh and the Oklahoma City bombing are infamous across America, what is not known is the Murrah Federal Building was a target of white supremacists well before McVeigh carried out his deadly attack. Kerry Noble was involved in one of those early plots.

As we begin to talk, a wry smile crosses his face. Kerry is now 68 years old with snowy white hair that makes him look like he wouldn't be a threat to anyone. He was born in 1952 in Abilene, Texas, and says "I had a happy childhood for the most part." His mom worked for the state school for mentally challenged young people. His parents divorced when he was three and his mother remarried when he was 10. His biological father "pretty much disappeared."

They weren't poor and he and his younger sister were raised with a strong female presence in his mother and his grandmother. But he suffered respiratory problems growing up which he says led to a lot of school bullying. "Anytime when we went to a new school, I had a target on my back. I couldn't do sports. In second grade I had to be in girls' PE. Whenever it was cold, I couldn't play outside." That bullying would make far more of an impact than Kerry likely understood.

"In 1977, my wife and I were both going to Bible college," Kerry tells me, as we start to explore how he found his way into violent extremism. Newly married with one child and a second on the way, the young couple sought out natural home birth options after a complicated first birth.

"We had friends in a group up in Arkansas. Everything fell in place to have the baby up there. They had plenty of midwives, so we went up there to visit and to have the baby, and then planned to return to Dallas. But we ended up loving it and stayed. There were eight young families at the time, some with children and others that didn't. We were a group of Christians that wanted to live and work together; just church, no guns, no para-militia."

"It was just a church," he repeats of this community compound called The Farm. "I'd been a minister since I was 19. It was a place to fellowship and minister. The leader of the group, his name was Jim, he said, 'Why don't you move back up here and be my Bible teacher?' I wanted to finish school, but then we decided I could learn by doing."

What Kerry may not have understood in those early days was who Jim Ellison really was, what he envisioned, and what he would become.

"I loved it. The Christian community thing was just great. Because I'd been sick and bullied a lot, I didn't fit in. I never had that real male bonding thing growing up. It was the first time I experienced male camaraderie. The men cut cedar. It was the first time I got to work hard. That was new and good for me. That whole thing, one purpose, all doing the same thing."

"How long did that last?" I ask. I can't keep the cynicism from my voice. I've interviewed hundreds of ISIS members, many who traveled to Syria from around the world expecting to find an Islamic utopia. I know promises of an ideal made by any religious group rarely materialize, and communities, especially those led by charismatic leaders with their own strong ego needs, often disappoint and disintegrate into unhealthy patterns.

"It lasted a year," Kerry answers, a sad and perturbed look crossing his face.

Kerry says the group was apocalyptic, "founded on typical church eschatology of Jesus coming back at any point. Jim didn't believe in the rapture," the Christian belief that in End Times believers will be taken up in a cloud while unbelievers will be left to suffer under years of what is referred to as the tribulation. The group started talking about the need to protect itself against the bad forces to come. Thinking that "makes sense" Kerry went along with the need to protect their community.

"Jim spent $52,000 on guns, military equipment, and we started training. We became a paramilitary survivalist group and we practiced with a mock town. Word started spreading and more joined us. We had to form squads. If you wanted to join you had to live with us and commit 100 percent to us, no outside job. We grew to 150 men, women, and children, 32 families."

Still, Kerry describes it as peaceful for the next year. "We had church services four nights a week and Bible study and military night, and then a night off." Anyone lonely or looking for belonging would have found it here, I think to myself, but at a price.

Things turned when Jim, working as a welder on military silos in Missouri in 1979. It was the 'red scare' and he met a man whose church taught Christian Identity. "That was the first we heard of it. We had met Christian-Patriots Defense League."

This Christian doomsday paramilitary group is part of the Christian Identity movement, a deeply racist and antisemitic theology based on a 19th century pseudo-doctrine called

British Israelism. This doctrine identifies Anglo-Saxons with the Lost Tribes of Israel, and England and its colonies as the Israel of Biblical promise. This line of thought made its way to America in the 20th century where it became popularized by Christians who believed the U.S. has a special God-ordained destiny. In America, the theology rebranded as Christian Identity where it became intensely antisemitic, claiming Jews are descended from Satan. Asserting white Europeans, not Jews, are the real Israelites, Christian Identity has become influential in white supremacist groups in the U.S. since the 1980s and gave birth to what is called the "two seed theory."

According to the Southern Poverty Law Center, the Kingdom Identity Ministries promulgated teachings in the U.S. of the Christian Identity movement since the early 1980s. Mike Hallimore, the group's founder and leader, calls his operation a "politically incorrect Christian Identity outreach ministry to God's chosen race, true Israel, the White, European peoples" and he supports the death penalty for idolatry, homosexuality, blasphemy and abortion as well as slaying race mixers. The Kingdom Identity Ministries logo states, "Conquer we Must, For our Cause is Just."[65]

Kingdom Identity Ministries Logo

"At first we rejected hate materials, but this guy introduced it as patriotic," Kerry recalls. "They sang 'America the Beautiful' and preached Jews are not God's chosen people. That was totally new and foreign to us. But we began to believe about the lost tribes of Israel, that Americans were the chosen people. I bought a bunch of books, and we incorporated their teachings into our group."

"In Christian Identity," Kerry continues. "Jews were the literal seed of the devil."

I ask him if the "two seed" theory was something he had believed in during his previous church life.

"I was Southern Baptist and my church didn't address race, but the Christian Identity guys said, 'We want to talk about race from a Biblical point of view.'" Kerry then launches into the Christian Identity retelling of the Garden of Eden story: "Dan Gayman, who introduced this to our leader, said that in the Hebrew text Eve was seduced by an individual by the name of Nachash. That's the Hebrew name for snake. But it was a person in human form, and we know seduce commonly means sex. That's why it says in the Bible there will be enmity between your seed and the seed of the serpent, meaning Adam's and Nachash's descendants. Everything in history is centered around sex and perversions of sex, so okay," Kerry says, trying to explain how they bought into this extremist retelling.

Dan Gayman is widely regarded as one of the contemporary theological leaders of the Christian Identity movement who helped popularized this "two seed" theory, now widely accepted by Christian Identity believers. The "two seed" theory, also known as the dual-seed or two-seedline theory, was originally developed by Wesley Smith, a former Methodist *minister* from Southern California, known for his racist and white supremacist views. His theory says Jews descended from a sexual union between Eve and Satan that produced Cain, the father of the Jewish people. Only white Christians are descended from Adam and Eve, who produced Abel. In the Old Testament, Cain famously slew Abel, but according to this theory, Abel already had children—the lost tribes of Israel—from whom white Europeans are descended.

Kerry continues building the biblical case that only whites are descended from Adam and God's chosen people. Describing how Adam blushes before God after their sin was discovered, "Only the white race can blush." Referring to Isaac's son and Abraham's grandson, Esau, "Only whites have red hair. They are all white." When Jacob cheats his brother Esau out of his birthright, the Christian Identity interpretation is the antisemitic trope of the wily cheating Jew.

"So now we are a racist, survivalist, paramilitary. We grew. In December 1980, I prophesized to the group that our name would be spread across the land. Jim said we need a name that the public can remember, so we renamed to Covenant Sword and the Arm of the Lord (CSA)."

The group made an insignia and shoulder patches for their uniforms. They started to publicize the group and grow; Jim maintained strong control, as Kerry further explains.

"We believed we got purged of worldly desires and personality conflicts. But even though we were all white, we had conflicts. Jim was very strong and would not let conflicts brew. He made them talk it out and hug. Unity is the main thing, common vision, not letting petty things divide us. We had so many

Covenant Sword and the Arm of the Lord Logo

church services, everyone prayed with you; confession—we had the chair. You would openly confess what was bothering you. So it was not encouraged to hold grudges and conflicts."

"So, you were a healthy group of people?" I ask, wondering where the rub will come.

"Yes, I think so," Kerry answers. "We never really did anything until 1983. In 1982, we had our first national convocation with all the groups: Aryan Nations, Klan, Posse Comitatus, etc. It was a weeklong survival course." The 1982 recruitment flyer for the group states only "white, patriotic and serious Christians" need apply and advertised classes including weapons and wilderness training and addressing topics of racial truths, the Jews and the betrayal of America among others.

"We wanted people to find out about us and form a coalition together, a national organization of white supremacists who would be under the leadership of Jim. Everyone else wanted it to be under their leadership. But it was a good convocation."

And there it is. The ego coming out in their leader who up until then had kept the group unified and conflicts abated, even as he led the group from peace-loving Christians banding together in anticipation of the End Times, to an armed and dangerous militia, and a polygamist one at that.

CSA National Convocation Flyer

"Right after that we found out that one of the elders had adultery in the group," Kerry continues. "He was leaving his wife. Jim thought God told him to take this woman as his second wife. In 1978 we had decided against polygamy, unless it was the End Times, so this caused a major split in our group."

And finally, the group gained law enforcement attention when a man killed two federal marshals in North Dakota and fled to Arkansas where he had a shootout with the FBI and the local police. A sheriff was killed. As a result, law enforcement attention shifted to CSA. It was 1983 and CSA decided it needed to get even. "We didn't want to lose face, so we decided we had to do something. We made plans for retribution. We planned to bomb the Murrah Building in Oklahoma City with a multi-rocket launcher. But the man who was building it had an accident with one of the rockets."

"Sometimes it seems there is a God," I couldn't help but think to myself. It's reminiscent of the ISIS and al Qaeda bombmakers and instructors who delivered themselves straight to Paradise by accidently blowing up themselves and their compatriots.

"He burned his hands badly, so we said, 'God didn't want that.' Then we decided to handle the federal judge and prosecutor in the case. But we had a car collision with another couple and that stopped that.

When those two events fell through, we decided not to carry on with them. We also had tried to blow up a pipeline. It didn't work. We tried to burn a gay place and a synagogue but only scorched the doors with no effect. We thought these were signs from God that he didn't want us to go down that track. We had an assassination attempt that didn't go through, so we decided to abandon it." Whether God, incompetence, or dumb luck, I can't help but stifle a chuckle.

"Then Jim and I started arguing. In March '83, I had a revelation that we were going in the wrong direction. Jim didn't see it that way. I gave up arguing with him. In '84 I said, 'Give me a silencer weapon and briefcase bomb and I'll make it happen.'" And the mishaps continued.

"We had heard about a gay park where gays openly picked each other up on Saturday nights. Our plan was to assassinate anyone we saw at the park. We got there and drove around several times but never saw a single person. We had the bomb, so we went to the adult bookstore. I went in with the briefcase. 'Welcome, but you can't take a briefcase in here,' the attendant said. That left me in a quandary, so I went back out to the car," and I admit I again suppress laughter at this ridiculous caper. Except it's not the least bit funny, of course. It could well have been deadly.

"We spent the night and asked God what to do. So, we went to my friend's church. It was now a gay church." Thinking this must be their God-given target, Kerry says the two men carried their briefcase bomb into the church. "I told my friend, 'Once we go in, we can't just set the timer and walk out. We should set the timer and stay a half-hour or so.'"

"We had never been around homosexuals before. We thought it would be a sexual orgy going on. The pastor came out and talked about his sexual relations with the music director. It seemed what we should do, as it was the epitome of what we were against."

But once again something stepped in to stop them. This time it seemed to be their conscience.

"We knew we should not put a face on the enemy, but here we were doing it, whether we wanted to or not. I was looking around. 'They don't look any different than me. What have they ever done to me? They haven't hurt me. They haven't hurt my family.' I started to not hate them so much. The music started, traditional church music, a bit peppier. They started praying and raising their hands up. It was almost like our church services. I started to realize these people are only trying to find their place in God as I am. For the first time I didn't see them as homosexuals, but as Christians."

So, they left. I asked Kerry about his escape plan, how they planned to evade the law had they blown up scores of people.

"Just go back to the community," Kerry answers nonchalantly. "It was a briefcase full of C-4. I didn't think there would be any evidence left over. If they did discover it was us, our fingerprints weren't on any registry. We'd have a shootout at CSA."

No one had known of the plan ahead of time except Jim, not even Kerry's wife. Others were told after they left. They found their friends watching the news when they returned. When Kerry explained what had happened, "Jim said, 'You're just a coward.' That hurt. Then I was on the outs with him."

"So did you think of leaving at this point?" I ask.

"I was just tired of it all and just wanted to leave," Kerry says nodding, knowing had he blown up 60-70 people in the church, it would have been the biggest domestic terror act in the U.S. to date. "When I was in the church I was wondering, 'What will happen? Will this start the second American Revolution, or will I just be discovered and arrested and spend it on death row, or shoot it out with the cops?' None of this appealed to me. I wanted to leave. It was no longer what I had wanted to join. It had become a nightmare for me."

But Kerry's God wasn't finished with him yet.

"I felt the Lord said, 'You cannot leave.' It was not the answer I was looking for...I prayed repeatedly about this, but same answer. If I cannot leave, I need to restore it to how it was when I had moved there, but no one remembered it. Only Jim and I were original."

The groups split. Some joined the Aryan Nations, became The Order [a prominent violent white supremacist group, which killed Jewish radio host, Alan Berg.] They "robbed armored cars, were counterfeiting money, funding right-wing groups, and got busted. When some former CSA members turned state's evidence, I knew raids were coming. I went to a man who had befriended me in the Arkansas police. I said, 'If you get a warrant for Jim, please talk to me first, so you don't get a bloodbath that you can't imagine.'"

When the arrest warrant was issued, April 18, 1985, Kerry told Jim "but he refused to surrender. We started a four-day siege with FBI and locals [police], 300 of them. I became the negotiator for a peaceful resolution." Knowing they'd be overwhelmed Jim finally agreed to surrender.

With former members turning state's evidence, charges mounted up: unregistered weapons, silencers, machine guns, rockets, harboring members of The Order, RICO (federal organized crime statute.) The leaders were arrested. Kerry found out Jim was working out a plea agreement even as he threatened the others, "'If any of you betray me, I'll put a bullet in your back.'" Jim told Kerry to say he was blackmailing him and making all the decisions." Jim's reasoning: "'I need you to take the blame so I can go back to CSA, so I can start over again.'"

Kerry then knew he had to take a plea bargain. "I had already an offer to testify against him and be free but had refused it. So, I knew I had a way out. I tried not to cry. I knew I was facing 210 years, so I agreed to plea bargain and plead guilty and move back to Texas. I told the others, 'You all do what you want. I'm tired and want to go back to my family. They all pled out later."

The Bureau of Alcohol, Tobacco, and Firearms (ATF) later determined that the CSA had obtained 155 Krugerrands, one live light antitank rocket, 94 long guns, 30 handguns, 35 sawed-off shotguns, and machine guns, one heavy machine gun, and a quantity of C-4 explosives and the group members had been involved in all sorts of criminal activities.[66]

Jim was sentenced to 20 years. Kerry got a five-year sentence and served 26 months for crimes committed while in CSA.

He also faced another trial of sedition. Under pressure and to avoid being convicted, he now agreed to testify against Jim.

"I was 32," he concludes, noting the year his life ground to a halt.

CSA unraveled, but its links to violent extremism continued on.

"What did you think of Timothy McVeigh blowing up the Murrah Building?" I ask.

"When I saw it on TV, I said to my wife, 'They've done it, the right-wing movement has finally done it.' I knew it was not foreign terrorists. April 1995. It was 10 years since our event, two years after the Branch Davidian fires. He'd been at the siege watching it. I had known about *The Turner Diaries*. All the pieces fit together. He did everything *The Turner Diaries* said to do: the explosives, the truck, only significant difference was the Murrah Building, not the FBI in D.C. It bothered me that it was an inconspicuous federal building. Why? It was nowhere."

Kerry believes he knows why McVeigh chose the Murrah Building on April 19, 1995 at 9:02 AM. "On April 19, '95 [Robert Wayne] Snell was going to be executed. He was a quasi-member of our group. He never lived with us. He had been arrested in '83 for killing a Black state trooper and later a pawn shop owner he thought was Jewish. He got the death penalty. He also was talking to groups similar to ours, in Elohim City," referring to a right-wing commune in northeast Oklahoma known as Elohim City, founded by Robert G. Millar, a group to which McVeigh was also linked. "So, it was tied into us. Wayne Snell was tied to us. He wanted us to target that building...He was a provocateur in many groups." When Snell was pulled over by the state trooper he subsequently killed, one of the weapons found in his van was traced back to CSA's Jim Ellison, Kerry tells me.

"I never liked Wayne Snell, I never considered him spiritual. He seemed like bad news to me. It was too much of a coincidence for [McVeigh] to pick that building." Kerry concluded that McVeigh "had to be in contact with Wayne Snell who would have said, 'CSA tried, but do it again.' McVeigh blew up the building as a going away present for Wayne Snell. [Snell] knew it was coming. But the FBI could never tie anyone to McVeigh but his two associates." McVeigh, who incidentally was a Gulf war veteran, was executed in 2001, the controversial first federal execution since 1963. Kerry has written a book about his experiences called *Tabernacle of Hate: Why they Bombed Oklahoma City.*[67]

As CSA morphed into hatred and arming members under Ellison's spiritual direction, Kerry who doesn't seem truly evil went along helping to build a white supremacist militia. Why would he do so rather than resisting? Kerry describes Jim Ellison as "very charismatic, and very merciful, and calm in the early days. He was like a calm in the storm." Jim was not only a charismatic character but also hyper-masculine and conveyed upon Kerry a special purpose, an elevated position and a group of men to belong to as he manipulated Kerry's religious beliefs to support violence. In combination this was too strong a draw for Kerry who couldn't break ranks with him, even going against his better inner guidance (and many failed terrorists attempts). Kerry told me me, "The only reason I went to bomb the church was to appease Jim because we were on bad terms. I wanted to earn my right in the Kingdom. I was under the delusion to earn my place in the Kingdom of God I had to earn Jim's good graces."

Kerry turns to an early story about Ellison: "That first summer when I had moved up there and we had decided to stay one or two months, we were out in the woods working. The couple we were visiting, [his] wife came crying and bawled to Jim, 'I'm sorry! I'm sorry!' She could barely talk. She said, 'I accidentally ran over Joseph [their 3-year-old son] with the truck, three times!' In her mind she'd killed him. Jim didn't blink an eye and said, 'Don't worry. Everything is fine.'"

"We ran to see Joseph. There was gravel in his face, tire marks on his body. He was limp in her arms. He's still breathing. Jim's wife said, 'The devil tried to take him. I wouldn't let him.' Jim said, 'Let's take him to the hospital. You all just pray.' We lived 45 minutes from town. In 2.5 hours, Jim comes back. Joseph is smiling, happy, energetic. Doctors hardly believed it. They did x-rays for us. It was a miracle, and Jim remained calm. He was just a rock in those days."

His stalwart leadership continued as CSA morphed into a paramilitary outfit. "He was looked at as the general of the Army. Jim had that James Dean haircut, nice thick, longish hair. There was a point after the paramilitary started, he told Ollie he wanted a military style haircut. She cut his hair and said as she did that, she saw the look in his eye just changed. He ceased to be as merciful and compassionate as he had been, became more demanding—'my way or the highway'."

In this regard, Kerry is like many extremists who went into it incrementally not noticing how violence endorsing he had become. As his group was using Christianity to justify their violence, once he realized how wrong it was, Kerry had to backtrack slowly taking his theology of hate apart as well.

We turn to his struggles to leave extremism behind. Kerry tells me for 10 years, he struggled "to get Christian Identity out of my head, to be able to read the scriptures without reading them from the point of view of Christian Identity."

"Why was that hard for you to do?" I ask, somewhat surprised he couldn't more easily reject the clearly bogus claims. But I also remember Ibn Omar, the ISIS teen I interviewed who was all set up to drive a suicide vehicle. He was luckily pulled out of ISIS by his parents just before his turn came up. Ibn Omar told me he'd been eager to become a "martyr" for the group and it took him a full year to get the ISIS ideological indoctrination out of his head.

"I'm the Bible teacher. I'm the propaganda guy. Everything came through me," Kerry answers. "Nobody understood Christian Identity to the degree that I understood. They didn't get it most of the time. They just went along, but it was so engrained in me to read [the Bible] from a different point of view. How could I look at what Adam and Eve did apart from sex? In Christian Identity it's the Jews who wanted to kill Jesus. So, it's still an anti-Jewish point of view. Paul is hunted by the Jews. Paul was killing Christians as [Jewish] Saul before he converted. Even though I was raised anti-racism and anti-violence, I had to go a full revolution around and I had to un-explain Christian Identity scriptures to myself."

ICSVE's TM Garret, a former KKK Grand Dragon who translated some of the first Christian Identity literature in Germany and taught this doctrine to the members of his European KKK group, agrees, "You can still find my old teachings on the internet, and reading them makes me shiver. If you are looking for something and are already getting radicalized, it sounds completely logical. And later it's always harder for the teacher to unlearn this than for the regular follower. It can mess with your mind for a long time and haunts you for a lifetime."

"I had to go back to the scriptures and sort. It was like sorting through the trash to find something of value," Kerry tells me.

"Are you still Christian?"

"I don't go to church anymore. I just don't fit in," though Kerry says he's still a Christian.

"Do you feel a sense of cynicism or fear being part of a church nowadays?" I ask, exploring how he "just doesn't fit in."

"I guess you could call it cynicism, fear of being told what to do. I went through that at The Farm, CSA," Kerry answers. "Also, part of it is doctrinal. I don't believe in hell or damnation. I'm not going to be part of that. Most Christian preachers believe 97 percent would go to hell. That's sad. I can't sit for that. We went to Unity church for a while, tried that, no judgments, no talk of hell, but not enough Jesus. We went to a gay/lesbian church for six months. We were one of two heterosexual couples there. We went to Messianic church [so-called "Jews for Jesus"] for several months, but they still believed in hell. I never get it. Jews as a whole don't believe in hell."

Looking back to what he got from being in the group, Kerry reflects, "For the first time in my life, when I first moved up there, I fit in. Guys didn't care about my background; how weak I was. The first day I went to the woods to work, Jim told them, 'Just tell him how to do it. Don't help him.'" By the end of the day, Kerry was learning how to load heavy logs onto a truck. "I was so proud of myself. It was the first day I had worked hard in my life. The guys didn't judge or condemn me, and I was so proud—I couldn't even walk. First time in my life I just fit in. Once you know you fit in, you are almost ready to do anything to stay in."

This statement is such an important one. To those of us who have strong families and social supports, fitting in can seem like the oxygen in the air we breathe, not noticeable until it's not there. For those without oxygen, belonging can mean everything, and many will sacrifice a great part of themselves for that oxygen. Some will even fuse their identity to their group, lose themselves in it and its mission, because belonging, as well as the positive sense of identity they receive, becomes their world.

"If you put a frog in cold water and heat it up it would boil to death," Kerry continues, referring to the false but common claim in which a frog that is gradually heated to boiling will die before realizing the danger. "If I had moved to CSA I would never have stayed. But in the beginning, it was everything I was looking for. Then when it became CSA, I almost died for it."

Kerry, who has since helped others exit hate groups, sees that for the most part people don't get into extremism because they hate Blacks or Jews, unless it's generational. "I've had good conversations with people who are in the movement and find that if I talk to them with respect, it doesn't take too awful long for why they are in it: 'I want to be part of something bigger than me. I wasn't happy with my life and here people made me fit in and I stayed to be part of something.' Then they are afraid to go back to when they weren't a part of something."

This is so important to underline. Humans are a social species. Embedded in our genes and deeply sensed by all of us is a need to belong to some group, to have others who are looking out for us, on our team. No one is immune to this need to belong.

I ask how he approaches helping someone leave a group and he shares his imagined dialogue:

"First thing, I would just ask, 'Have you ever been around Blacks that you know? Have you ever sat and talked with them and hung? If no, why don't you? What is it you fear of being around them?' 'They are lazy, on welfare, whatever.' If he's willing to be around some Blacks, great."

'Tell me about your life before you joined the Klan? Unhappy about something?' That's the hot button. 'Can we fix that?' 'I'm not making enough money because the Jews are making all the money.'

'What do you have against Blacks and Jews?' The typical answer is going to be rhetoric they've heard. Find those points they are the strongest on: 'Jews are the seed of the devil.' 'What makes you think of that?' 'The Bible says.' 'Where?' They can't tell me where. They just believe what they are taught. 'Why can't you tell me the exact scripture? You got into this because you weren't happy with your life, and you believe Jews are the seed of the devil, but you can't prove that, and you've never been around Blacks. Does that make sense to you?'

"'Let's talk about your life before you joined.' 'I was unemployed,' whatever the case was. 'Could you have not straightened that out?' 'I couldn't do anything. I couldn't work. The Mexicans have all the jobs.' 'Did you try? Try to get training?' 'No. No. No.' 'So, you are saying you had a problem you couldn't fix or weren't willing to fix and needed someone to blame?' 'I guess so.' 'You are not happy with your life and want someone to blame.'"

As Kerry points out, approaching those in violent groups and movements by seeing them as humans with real needs that the hate group has met, a group they both need and fear, is crucial to creating a rapport and drawing someone out.

This intervention technique Kerry has been reciting is also the one he used to recruit new members. "I'm going to find what's unhappy with your life and who to blame." Terrorist and hate groups and their ideologies always have some conspiracy element that puts the blame for a grievance onto someone else. Personal grievances are exploited to teach the recruit to see oneself as a victim, and direct blame and violence toward an enemy "other," an outgroup. The person gets sucked further into the hateful ingroup, often losing his individual sense of identity in the process, as well as any sense of personal responsibility for failures in his own life.

Kerry concludes with something I've been saying for years about extremism: "You don't get into anything unless you are unhappy about something," he says. "If you are not unhappy you won't go in." I agree. Very few join a terrorist or violent extremist group, at least in the beginning, unless it somehow meets his or her needs. Of course, over time groups of this sort overtake the individual and no longer meet their needs, and instead use them for the group's purposes.

Kerry admits it took him awhile, but he has walked away from racist hatred. "I called the director of the ADL [Anti-Defamation League] and apologized for what I did and what my group did," he tells me. "It's not scriptural to hate others. Jesus at the well helped the Samaritan woman and treated her with respect, as should we."

When he was released from prison, he called his kids together: "They were 12 down to three but I told them all, I made it very plain, 'Now that I'm home here's the rules. I don't care what color your friends are. They are welcome to the house. No judgments.' [Now] I have a son-in-law that's Black and a grandson that's Black and a daughter-in-law that's Black and another grandson that's Black and a Native American daughter-in-law and grandchild."

You can watch Kerry tell his story at www.EscapeHate.org

Chapter 4 - Warrior for My Race

Sean Gillespie smiles matter-of-factly and rubs his forehead as he explains, "Eight and a half years in solitary confinement, I did a lot of introspection. I read cognitive behavioral therapy books and thought about where the hate came from." Less than a year ago, 37-year-old Sean received early release from a 30-year prison sentence for bombing a synagogue.

Sean is white, well built, bald, and looks intently as he tells me his story of how he became a member of the Aryan Nations, perhaps the most notorious of the neo-Nazi, white supremacist terrorist organizations.

"He was Asian..." Sean tells me, then hesitates for a moment. Then he decides to open up and tell me his full story.

"I was repeatedly molested from ages seven to 10, raped. He was an Asian male named ML. He was Korean and babysat me. He molested kids in the community. He had us do stuff to each other and to him."

"I'm so sorry," I say softly. "How did you deal with that?"

Sean explains he dealt with it through hate. Hate groups reject minorities and homosexuals, and given his molester's identity, that felt right to him. They also linked the hate back to Jews. "Hate groups said Jews pervert culture," Sean tells me. "It's not his fault. It's theirs. And that exacerbated my anger."

Sean eventually tried to report the crime. "At age 10, I revealed it to a counselor. The police were called. No follow up. He was allowed to continue."

"He's still out there?" I ask, stifling a horrified gasp.

"He is. I drove by his house. I found the guy in 15 minutes. How could law enforcement not find him?" he asks incredulously. "I made a police report, but if it's over 25 years ago, there's a statute of limitations and it's my word against his."

Though I'm conducting a research interview and not a therapy session, I've been in this exact point in the therapy room many times over my 20 years of clinical work with adults grappling with how to handle childhood sexual abuse. In some states the clock on the statute of limitations for the sexual abuse of children may only start at the point the adult recalls or is able to psychologically deal with reporting the abuse. Sean confirms that is his situation and explains his desire to stop the man who derailed his life and says he's identified one of the other victims. This is too important for him, so I decide to sidetrack, and we have a short discussion on the implications of remembering and reporting childhood sexual abuse as an adult.

"Do you want me to treat this as confidential, Sean?" I ask about this portion of the interview. Sean has agreed to be in one of our counter narrative videos, but this is a very sensitive story.

He shakes his head and laughs cynically, "There was a time I was ashamed. That's what he wanted. I'll be damned." He wants his story told, all of it, if it will help others. I believe it will.

Sean is speaking to me from his home in Washington state. He's a well-built and well-spoken white man who could quite easily personify the idealized image of "white power" and if he still had his facial tattoos would be totally intimidating.

"What would my life have been like if this hadn't happened?" Sean ponders as we move back into memories of his childhood in Spokane, Washington.

Sean's parents split when he was two. His mother got custody, but traded it, Sean says, "for about 300 and some odd dollars, so she could go down to Reno and continue to live her party lifestyle." Sadness laces his words. "She's been married four times. She had an extensive history of drug abuse and alcohol. She did meth. She still smokes weed, uses cocaine, pills." He says his father, a disc jockey, also used drugs when his parents were together. And both his grandparents died at that time. "I witnessed my grandfather have a heart attack in explicit detail."

Sean says his childhood wasn't all traumatic. He remembers "really good family life." He says his father had cleaned up by the time he was four or five. Still, he saw the struggles of his father, a single dad, working three jobs. (Although he started out rough, Sean's father later went on to get his master's degree and work for a congressman.) Sean says his father was not abusive, but he was a disciplinarian who spanked not to excess. "He was very strict, and I had behavioral issues."

Sean who was acting out from having been sexually abused was institutionalized young. He went from the children's wing of a psychiatric facility to a group home at age 10. "I was receiving counseling as part of the group home. I broke down and told them." Pain furrows his brow. The psychologist stopped the interview, called his father, and the police. Despite Sean's report, his molester was not stopped.

Like many traumatized children who develop conduct disorders, Sean learned that asking for help accomplishes nothing and it was better to bottle up his painful secret. That only worked for so long, as it kept exploding outward, making him appear to be a "bad kid." He kept getting in fights and expelled. He threatened to kill himself. "I was an antisocial kid. I was very, very difficult to deal with. Now I joke with my dad—he's had four or five heart attacks—that I'm at fault. He said, 'Just the first two.'"

He kept running away from group homes; from ages nine to 12, he was in 10 different group homes. At age 12, he threw a rock over an overpass which got him into juvenile detention. As he narrates, I inwardly wince, recalling the stupid things my friends and I did as adolescents, antics for which we never paid such a heavy price. He was on a tragic and inexorable downward spiral of a kid deep in trouble, acting out pain he can't put into words, or when he does, no one responds correctly. He ended up assaulting a guard in juvenile and from there, "I was in and out of juvenile. If you just shove a kid, they have to press charges. I had 4th degree assault charges, but they were all just for shoving. I got two years in juvenile."

As social beings, and we all need group support, particularly in our youth, to help us manage our emotions and to help us make sense of the world around us. Sean was no different. "I hung with punk kids, called myself a Satanist, but I didn't even know what it was," Sean scoffs. "I listened to Marilyn Manson, had a mohawk, but I was just looking to belong."

Then chance, as it often does, provided the necessary exposure to a hate group that matched his inner pain and gave outlet to his rage. "In juvenile detention I didn't feel comfortable with the punk kids, too leftist. I was raised in a Republican home." Then he saw a news story about "a group that shot up a daycare—Aryan Nations." Still a kid, he looked into the group and concluded, "I'm white. I like the military. These people are a militia—I don't know what that means. I was released and immediately ran away to where the news said they were, on Rimrock Road [in Idaho]. I stole a bike and rode 45 miles on a BMX bike."

Looking back at how little adults did to protect him on his teenage journey into a hate group, Sean says he's "disappointed. I'm a kid stopping people asking, 'Where is the Aryan Nations compound?' and no one did anything to stop me. They just pointed down the road."

"Did you already hold racist views?" I ask, curious as to why he would specifically seek out white supremacists.

Sean shakes his head, no. "My family is very diverse. I may be part Native American. I have an aunt that's Japanese, a cousin that's gay. I was never raised racist, but these people didn't ask any questions. They took me in right away. My family was like, 'If you're a runaway and antisocial you can't live with us.' They [Aryan Nations] were like, 'You're a runaway and antisocial? Come on in.' It was a surrogate family. I was 15."

Arriving at the Idaho compound, "I knocked on this trailer house where I met Shaun Winkler, at the time their national youth leader. Shaun just took me in. He said, 'You need a haircut. Let's shave your head' because he was a skinhead. 'You're white,' he said, and they gave me a little bit of literature. That's when my indoctrination started."

They were Christian Identity which Sean says provided the basis for their racist views. "They were teaching me antisemitism with the Bible." Similar to Kerry Noble's Christian Identity militia group, they believe Jews are the spawn of Satan and the root of all evil; and whites are supreme and should not mix with other races. Here's how Sean tells it: "The way Christian Identity believes, basically nonwhite races existed before Adam, and he was the first white man created. Adam means to show blood in the face. That's why [we know] he's white. The other races were here first, and the white man was given dominion over them."

"And Cain came from the serpent?" I ask.

"Cain was according to two different theories," Sean explains. "In the one seed [theory] Cain was cursed. That's where Jews came from. We were two seed. Eve slept with the serpent. Cain was not Adam's child, but the serpent's child." Sean rattles out Bible verses Leviticus 20:13, Romans 1:26-27 and John 8:44. I notice he still has them memorized. Later when I look them up, I see the first two condemn sodomy. Sean explains in the third, a verse from the Gospel of John, "Jesus is speaking to the Jews and says, 'You are of your father the devil, and your will is to do your father's desires.' That proves that the Jews were Cain's children [fathered by the serpent]."

I'm wondering if he was raised with religion and this Biblical interpretation resonated somehow but Sean said he never had a religious upbringing. "I just wanted something to believe in. I just needed someone to direct my hate. I was an angry kid." Getting to the heart of the matter, "If I had come from a liberal background, I could have been a Weatherman," referring to an anti-government extremist group active in the 1960s. "I was ready for any type of radicalization."

As he says it, I think of Oliver, an Austrian foster kid who fell in with extremist Muslims in Vienna. They convinced him first to convert and then travel to Syria to join the ISIS Caliphate. Looking back at how vulnerable he was, Oliver told me he could just as soon have joined white supremacists—it didn't matter who the group was, just that he could belong.

Sean left the Aryan Nations for the first time after three months because he was asked to leave for shoplifting. The Aryan Nations was embroiled in a serious lawsuit at the time, as Sean puts it, "losing the compound due to the Southern Poverty Law Center. They said, 'We can't have you doing that right now.' I said, 'I'm stealing from the Jews. It's a Jewish corporation. The Order [another prominent violent white supremacist group] stole from people. Why can't I steal?'"

Sean left and turned himself in as a runaway. he returned to Spokane, but the indoctrination had won him over. "I did a month in juvie. Before, I never had problems with Black inmates. Now I was n-word this, n-word that. People were shocked. 'What happened in the last months?'"

"Where was your father in all of this?" I ask.

"I'm sure he worried about me," Sean says. "He remarried. I came back and ended up being a street kid. My parents didn't want to take me...I was a juvenile thug." As he tried on identities, Sean gravitated to those that were "badass" and violent. "I tried to join the Hell's Angels even though I don't ride a motorcycle. I was just a little asshole."

After several months on the streets, he says his aunt and uncle told him, "If you give up that Aryan Nations shit, we'll take you in." It was too late. Sean had tasted acceptance and with his anger over family failures and his sexual abuse firmly redirected at minorities and Jews, he wasn't about to give that up. "I had no intention, but said, 'Oh yeah, cool.' They took me in, and it was some of the most stable time I ever had, with a church group, youth group, with activities." He was maintaining a 3.6 GPA, played football, and loved wrestling. "The wrestling team was like a family, the team bond." But Sean couldn't fit in. "These kids had on the surface perfect families. Everyone seemed to be happy. Here I was, a kid from the streets having done drugs, lived more than they ever have. After three months, I got tired of my aunt and uncle's rules and in trouble for having skinhead literature and white laces in my boots," a sign of white supremacy among skinheads. "They gave me an ultimatum, and I said, 'Fuck you' and went back to the homeless shelter."

Sean ran away for another three months and this time his father tried to save him when he returned. "He actually moved out from his wife and got an apartment to offer me an opportunity. I was 16 and did really well for a while, but I wasn't willing to give up Aryan Nations."

White supremacism had put meaning in his life and though family members and even his school all were trying to save him, no one was treating the trauma burning inside. Without finding a way to work through the sexual abuse, Sean continued to dive deeper into hate.

He ran away again, and this time lived with Richard Butler who founded the Aryan Nations in the 1970s. "I was living with Pastor Butler in his house," Sean clarifies. During the 80s and early 90s, neo-Nazis, racist skinheads, Klansmen and other white nationalists convened regularly at the Aryan Nation's Idaho compound for its annual world congresses but by then the Aryan Nations had lost their property in a million-dollar civil lawsuit.[68] Yet the group struggled along. According to Sean, "Some Silicon Valley millionaires, Vincent Bertollini and Carl Story, bought him [Butler] a house. Vincent later went to federal prison. [Butler] ran Aryan Nations out of his house." Sean's good organizational skills won him favor with the Butlers and his youth made it easy for him to go to the local high school and hand out propaganda materials,

Aryan Nations Logo

including CDs filled with violent skinhead music. He helped Pastor Butler's wife run their "prison ministry" where she showed him how to correspond with prisoners and send white power literature.

Then at age 17, with his father's permission, Sean joined the Army National Guard. Even now he wishes he could rejoin the military, but his felony charges prevent him from doing so. "I loved the military, the structure," and I hear a wistfulness entering his voice. "I'm a hyperactive hard charger. If something needs to be done, I'll do it. It was the happiest time of my life, other than wrestling."

I ask him why pursuing his dream of the military wasn't enough. "What was the Aryan Nations giving you that you weren't getting anywhere else?"

"I felt like I was part of a cause," Sean explains. "Here I am a soldier for my race, always race, race. I don't have anything else that gives me a self-esteem boost. They were telling me, 'At all times you are superior to everyone else, because you are an Aryan man.'"

Hate was also covering over that well of deep-burning anger and shame over having been molested. "Hate is like a drug. It's a rush. If you walk into a room with a swastika shirt, people are afraid of you. I'm only 130 pounds. They aren't scared of you, but your message. You have something—a purpose—when you are a disenfranchised kid with nothing to belong to." Sean then refers to one of the central slogans of the American white supremacist movement, the "14 Words" authored by David Lane of The Order: "We must secure the existence of our people and a future for White children."

"Those 14 words," Sean explains, "refer to our future children. It's not just for yourself,

The Fourteen Words

but your family, your heritage. They teach you that if you don't believe this, you are letting down all your ancestors."

If his National Guard recruiters had known about his racist activities, he would not have been allowed to enlist. So, for the most part, he hid his membership in the Aryan Nations. "But there were people that knew. I joined prior to 9/11 but after 9/11 they didn't care. 'We need bodies!' They needed meat for the grinder."

The military did not work out for Sean. He says he wound up eventually getting kicked out "for being racist, but it took a lot." He'd protested a Martin Luther King parade wearing a swastika and got arrested. Sean says he should have been kicked out immediately with a dishonorable discharge. Instead, he was charged with two counts of malicious harassment due to a racial slur, given a month of probation because he was under 18, and sent to basic training. "The Army should have kicked me out," Sean reiterates. "My company commander was not too happy. I got a stern, stern lecture with a bunch of four-letter words."

A military unit's cohesiveness is threatened by extremism, and it cannot be tolerated. However, this punitive approach by the military, regarding white supremacism as an attitudinal and behavioral problem to be reprimanded, doesn't address what underlies it. Alcoholism, drug addiction, posttraumatic stress disorder or suicidality are treated by military medicine with some level of compassion, while requiring compliance to remain in the military. Discharging those who have been weaponized, without treating them, is unfair to the rest of society as these are angry and dangerous individuals. The need to claim superiority, resulting in white supremacist extremism, may also have a strong mental health component. When extremism is found in the military ranks, it might best be considered a mental health condition that also needs addressed.

Since the January 6 Capitol Hill riots in which scores of active-duty, reservists and military veterans took part, the U.S. Department of Defense has begun admitting they have an extremism problem among their ranks that must be routed out. It's not new. During the U.S.-led war in Iraq, the DOD found white supremacist infiltration in the ranks in graffiti it found in Baghdad, and it found a special forces veteran officer encouraging skinheads to join the military to get training.

I ask all our interviewees about recruiting and engaging military and police and a recent ICSVE study identified scores of examples across the U.S. and other Western countries of both military and police affiliated with, members of, or acting on behalf of, white supremacist groups.[69] Similarly, a leaked membership list of Oath Keepers set the media on fire in September 2022. The ADL's Center on Extremism analyzed the list of 38,000 alleged members and estimated:

- *Law enforcement:* 373 Oath Keepers are currently serving in law enforcement; 10 are chiefs of police and 11 sheriffs; more than 1,000 are former law enforcement.
- *Military:* 117 Oath Keepers are currently in the U.S. military; 11 in the reserves; 31 hold civilian positions or are military contractors
- *Emergency responders*: 86 are active fire fighters including several fire chiefs; 19 active paramedics; 31 emergency technicians
- *Elected officials*: 81 Oath Keepers hold or are running for public office in 2022
- *Other:* The ADL also identified significant professions held by Oath Keepers, including: religious figures, teachers, civil engineers, government employees and some individuals who report having top secret clearance or jobs with access to critical infrastructure such as nuclear facilities.[70]

Keep in mind, this list is just a read-out of Oath Keeper members. Dozens more DVE groups no doubt have members participating in these many professions that touch our daily lives.

In the end, Sean was put on military probation a second time, this time for a full year, for being a vocal skinhead. During probation, he says he remained "very active with the Aryan Nations, recruiting, passing out literature, at the same time I was joining the Army again." And he also got married. His wife was a skinhead. I know there are female skinheads, though they are outnumbered by the men. "There are a lot," Sean tells me. "They are treated like property sometimes. They are hypocritical. They say women are our future, but they pass them around. This is how you treat your Aryan goddess?"

The couple was married by Pastor Butler. They'd known each other for five days. Sean went back into the National Guard, and she went back to an old boyfriend. And his Aryan recruiting activities gained notice. "The Army said, "'You need to renounce this.' I was like, 'Screw you! White Power!'"

Sean was 20 years old. He was separated from his wife and working at Taco Bell.

"I felt like my life was over. I lost the career I loved. I didn't have high school wrestling anymore. I didn't care and thought, 'I'm going to do something like The Order,' inspired by *The Turner Diaries*."

At this point it sounds like Sean was going out of his way to find trouble. He starts to list for me the giant mess that became his life and eventually got him sent to prison. There was vandalism, fist fights, and violence. "I put a guy's mouth on the curb and stomped on his head." He tells me he decided "to go around the country doing hate crimes. So that's what I did!" Then he describes for me his brief white supremacist terrorist career.

Sean's voice is thoughtful but detached from emotion as he recounts horrific crimes he committed, almost like he's describing another person.

"I drove to Vegas. I looked at a synagogue. I was going to firebomb it with a Molotov cocktail, but there was a heavy police presence."

"Where did you learn to make a Molotov cocktail?"

"It's not a complicated device, but it will get you 30 years. I found out the hard way," he foreshadows, and chagrin turns his cheery demeanor to a frown.

"I beat up some Black guy with a baseball bat in Vegas," he continues, then he moved on to Oklahoma City. "My plan was to find some random stranger with a Jewish sounding name and firebomb their house. I had gasoline in a can, so I wasn't stopping for gas. I picked up a beer bottle wearing gloves," to ensure no evidence could trace the bomb back to him. However, his plan went askew.

"I found Temple B'nai. I filmed myself like any criminal mastermind would, totally incriminating myself. I ended up throwing the Molotov at the temple. I caused 250 dollars of damage to the building, scorched a brick wall, and nicked a window," downplaying the seriousness of his hate crime. Still, he wasn't caught, at least not yet. He went onto Arkansas to meet the number three leader of the Ayran Nations, a man named Rick Spring.

"I didn't know he was an FBI informant."

"I showed him the film. He said, 'Don't break the law.'" Rick Spring was likely required by the FBI to give this advice in the course of extracting information from Sean. "I got a job at Burger King. He got me a place, but I didn't know that he's setting me up to get busted. I lent him my camera with the footage. I trusted him. I thought, he's my brother. He's not going to tell on me. Then I met some skinheads in Little Rock. A couple of days before I was arrested, I did seven hate crimes. I ran over some Black guy with my truck, busted in the NAACP headquarters in Little Rock," Sean starts cataloguing his crimes.

"It's a dry county, but there is one bar," Sean recalls the night before his arrest. "I had 12 shots. I was late for work and Rick Spring shows up. There was no reason to come to my trailer." Rick drove him to work and on the way, told him he needed Sean to pawn his camera to pay Rick back for money he'd lent him, "but the truth was that he wanted it in my possession." The Pope County Sheriff arrested Sean as he left work.

"I got 39 years," and I hear regret filling his voice. "I was sent to federal prison at age 21."

He succumbed to the rules of his new environment with a string of violence. "I went to USP Florence in Colorado, a high max prison... At the time there were no consequences. You stab someone you're in the hole for a couple of days, or we confiscate your phone. They didn't give a shit. I stabbed four people in prison, one guy for being a coyote, the one who brings the immigrants in... We had a race riot in Florence. It was bad. I beat people with padlocks. We stomped people. It was an incredibly violent environment. I spent two years there, then got a disciplinary transfer to USP Coleman where there was only one active [white supremacist]. I stabbed a child molester 29 times. It's the only thing I don't regret. He's a child molester. I don't feel guilty about that. He molested a kid. I stabbed the molester with an army duffle bag clip that can be made into a shank."

Sean also thought he was superior because he was now a skinhead and not in a prison gang. "Prior to prison, I was prospecting for the Hammerskins [skinheads]," referring to the process of being accepted into a white supremacist group. "We are not a prison gang. They wrote in and gave me permission to become one because of my [hate] crime."

Sean was transferred to a prison where he says, "all the terrorists are." There he spent 8 1/2 years in solitary confinement. "It's good that you have a cell to yourself, not that stress, a lot of time to introspect." Though even there he was violent, "I stabbed a guy for being a SHARP, one of the Black skinheads, Skinheads Against Racial Prejudice."

Sean may have been in a phase of introspection and growth, but he was also in dire straits enduring solitary confinement. "I was physically tortured by guards at some time. I was one of nine plaintiffs.

We successfully sued, but the lawyer got the money." He also started cutting. "I cut my entire arm. I lost 3 pints of blood."

"What was the cutting about for you?" knowing some do it to trigger an endorphin high, mimicking opioid use.

"I just wanted to feel something. I used to think [about other cutters], 'You're a cutter. You are mentally weak.' Then I tried it. Spurting blood felt good. I was doing a lot of self-harm at the time." He would go to desperate lengths to express his anger just to interact with other human beings. "If you smash up your cell, they have to extract you. They shoot you with bean bags, gas you, and beat you up. You aren't going to win. I did that, but I got tired of it." Sean was getting some treatment, but even that provided a path to more self-harm. "I took an overdose of lithium. I had no hope. I'm serving 40 years for something I don't even believe anymore. I didn't think I'd ever get out of prison."

After years of prison time, violent white supremacism was clearly turning out to be less fulfilling than the initial promise of a positive identity, purpose and a strong sense of belonging.

"I knew I couldn't be racist anymore. I was tired of the hypocrisy. Skinheads don't do drugs. These guys were all addicts. I served time with David Lane, the one who did the 14 Words. I was looking at these people thinking, 'These people are ridiculous!' I wrote Morris Dees of the Southern Poverty Law Center, and he wrote back." (Years earlier, when Dees had come to his town, Sean had had a very different exchange with him, holding a protest sign, "Mr. Dees don't you know God hates fags?")

Getting out of hate wasn't easy. He says he was labeled a "race traitor, nigger lover" and was moved to another area of the prison for his own safety. "I was put in gang dropout. If I was on mainline, I'd be beaten and maybe killed."

Still, Sean persisted and continued to try to heal his broken mind. He spent three years in Dialectical Behavior Therapy. He says his weekly therapy sessions helped eventually heal him from cutting and taught him other ways to cope. Therapy also "showed me to find the middle ground. I'm still against abortion, but in the past, I'd be, 'Let's bomb the clinic!' I can still be conservative, but that doesn't mean I have to be radical. A lot of [white supremacists] became radical anti-racist, one thing I've noticed with former white supremacists. I'm glad they changed, but they went all the way from the right to the complete opposite—Antifa, liberal."

The Supreme Court would rule on a case that signaled Sean's 39-year-conviction might be overturned. Sean understood he needed to lie low, be patient, and stay out of trouble. Now in USP Tucson where he claims 80 percent of the inmates were child molesters, Sean really struggled to control his anger. "There was a guy there that had killed two people. He studied Nietzsche. He kept me from being stupid." After another six months, a court overturned Sean's sentence, saying he should have been given nine years maximum. He had already served 16.

"I am very happy to get a second chance," he tells me, a smile lighting up his face. "I got out last June. I went to work the second day I was out. I reached out the first week I was out—my ex-wife had left the movement. I asked if she had my stuff. We rekindled our love. I just bought her a huge ring so she's happy," Sean says, laughing.

Noting how clean cut and "boy next door" Sean appears, I ask him about tattoos because these markings of hate, difficult to remove, can create fear and alienation, and spoil employment and relationship opportunities. And Sean has plenty of tattoos. He tells me he has two swastikas on his arms and an iron cross, an SS on the back of his neck, and unfortunately: "I got boots on my face, a triple seven, 777 over my mouth, SS bolts on my hands." He has had the most obvious tattoos removed. "I got laser. It's not fun. It's bad. They burn your face off. I was trying to get my hands covered to join the Army. Laser on the fingers is so bad." At work, Sean explains, "I wear gloves so they can't see my tattoos."

I'm finding the desire for tattoo removal is an important point of intervention. Many white supremacists who want to leave their movements will reach out for help from groups offering free tattoo removal, which is otherwise costly. A local tattoo artist offered to help Sean, telling him after hearing his story, "'I was a junkie in prison. No one gave a shit about me. I'm going to do it for free.'" Sean goes once a month, "I'm glad to get this hate off my body."

Sean has gotten into mixed martial arts, MMA, where he's found acceptance. "I thought with swastikas and stuff, a lot of African Americans and Cubans would react. But I have not had one person of any race say one thing negative to me about my tattoos. I've gotten sideways looks. 'Does he really have that tattooed on him?' Everyone has been cool and supportive. I do MMA and I'm their mascot," Sean explains about the gym. "I get beat up by these world champions. They know about my past, but they don't care."

As we wrap up our interview, I tell Sean that while a news story made him aware of the Aryan Nations, nowadays a lot of recruitment is over the internet, and he agrees to be a part of our *Escape Hate Counter Narrative Project*.

We first discuss how white supremacist skinheads recruit. "Skinheads recruit by providing a family just like any gang," he explains. "'Hey kid, hang out with us. Here's a beer. You like music. We have some really cool music that you'll like.'"

I ask him what advice he'd give to that young kid he used to be.

Sean pauses and thinks for a moment before he answers. "Get treatment. Therapy is the best way to deal with traumas. Being abused sucks. You can continue to be a victim and blame other people. Getting help and being honest about being raped as a kid helped me exponentially." Sean offers additional personal perspective, "My family is very conservative. I thought I was molested so that means I'm a fag. I was afraid of telling them. If you have experienced any of this, there are hotlines, therapy. Cutting, suicide, none of that is worth it. There is help."

Sean says a lot of people tried to help him. His family; his wresting coach "always talking about racism is wrong. 'Be a better man. If you quit in this room, you are going to quit on your kids.'" As much as these people meant to Sean, without providing him with a way out of his shame and confusion over his sexual abuse, and an outlet for his rage while also building him up with a positive new identity, they were poor competition for the Aryan Nations.

Sean also shared advice for vulnerable youth looking to join white supremacism: "These people will use you. It's not about a cause or a movement. It's about using kids that have no other option or no self-esteem. The minute I got arrested, all your supposed friends will leave. They don't care. They won't write you. You'll see how hypocritical they are. I spent 16 years in prison for the cause. I regret every minute of it."

Still, it was hard to walk away. "When I was in prison, I watched 3700 movies. Film and literature had a big impact on opening up my mind. I read Gandhi's autobiography, Martin Luther King's biography, Sidney Poitier's *A Patch of Blue*."

I think of Sean's young mind, blocked by abuse, finally taking a long draught of wisdom from all these sources. Sean appears not only disengaged from white supremacism but also significantly "deradicalized." He no longer holds racist views or hatred toward other races, religions, and the LGBTQ community, and appears to feel genuine remorse for his previous actions.

However, he still endorses violence in one regard. "I have a 'Shoot your local pedophile sticker' for my truck," he says with a sarcastic smile. "The only reason I would go back to prison is if someone molests my nieces and nephews."

I later show Sean's counter narrative video to Jeff Schoep, the former charismatic head of the National Socialist Movement, NSM, at one time among the biggest and most active neo-Nazi groups in the U.S. (You will hear much more from Jeff later in this book.) Jeff had known Sean from the violent extremist movement and said the hyper masculine environment of white supremacy doesn't make room for people to talk about things like sexual abuse. "Sean opening up like that is pretty incredible. I can't even imagine how hard that was for him to share that." Jeff had not been aware of Sean's childhood trauma. "I watched Sean's video right before going to bed, that wasn't the best idea, but had no idea his sad story would hit me as hard as it did." He hopes others will be moved by Sean's story and see they "can re-think their lives before it's too late and they end up like what happened to Sean, or locked away longer, or dead."

Sean later texts to tell me he won his first MMA fight. I text him back, sharing with him that when I spoke at the Secretary of Defense's mandated military extremism Stand Down Days, I showed Sean's counter narrative video as an example of how discharge might solve the military's problem, but it foists the now military-trained hater back out onto society when left untreated. Hundreds of service persons from high level generals and colonels down the ranks saw his story and were very moved. "They may not let you back into the military, but your message is being heard and making a difference," I write back.

You can watch Sean tell his story at www.EscapeHate.org

Chapter 5 - The Few, the Proud

Law enforcement officials across the country have been pulling the alarm about growing threats against their forces, elected leaders, and government buildings. On October 8, 2020, the FBI announced the arrests of 13 men suspected of orchestrating an astounding domestic terror plot to overthrow the Michigan state capital, kidnap its Democratic governor, Gretchen Whitmer, and charge her with treason. Half the men were part of a paramilitary group who called themselves the Wolverine Watchmen and they were well trained by none other than the mightiest military in the world.

The group's alleged leader, Joseph M. Morrison, had served in the U.S. Marine Corps Reserve since 2015. Another member, Daniel Harris, served in the U.S. Marine Corps as a rifleman for five years, June 2014 - June 2019.[71] Paul Bellar, according to his father, had trained for a year with the U.S. Army at Fort Jackson, South Carolina, before being discharged in 2019 with a diagnosis of posttraumatic stress disorder, PTSD. The militia amassed significant weaponry and equipment and also included night vision googles, a boat, a dashcam, and a rifle with a silencer. Morrison allegedly used his home as a training camp with human silhouettes for target practice,[72] and Bellar was allegedly responsible for designing the tactical training exercises which included firearms and medical treatment.[73]

That some of the Wolverine Watchmen were former military members who had been professionally weapons-trained and knew how to organize attacks is chilling and brings up the alarming prevalence of active duty and veteran military members being targeted for recruitment and joining hate groups.

Those charged with storming of the U.S. Capitol on January 6th included 81 current and former members of the military (including one active-duty Marine and four active members of the Reserves or National

Guard),[74] and at least two current or former members of law enforcement. [75] Had there been even more of them or better planning among them, who knows how much worse the end result could have been.

As former KKK leader TM Garret has told me, "We always believed that at some point we would need strategically placed persons in the military and police so that when the time came, we would be able to overthrow the current government and put in place our system of governing."

Recruiting members of the military and police has many advantages for white supremacists. They can pass along weapons training and may even be a source of weaponry and inside information. Ties to the police can help avoid arrest. From the vantage point of white supremacy leadership, military members usually have developed a sense of discipline that make them valuable cadres; and for military members, joining extremist groups with a rank structure is often appealing, as is finding a sense of belonging to a group purportedly fighting a noble cause. These groups also like to recruit former and active-duty military members because they convey a sense of legitimacy and an air of patriotism and are often very good at recruiting others to the white supremacy cause.

Jeff Schoep built up and ran the largest neo-Nazi organization in the U.S. for 22 years, the National Socialist Movement, NSM. Jeff was among the first former white extremists I interviewed for *Escape Hate*. When I asked Jeff how many of his members were in the police or military, as active-duty members or as vets, he told me it was a priority for the group to recruit these types. Keith Schneider, who led NSM's security, claims over half his "storm troopers"—NSM's security force—were from police and military backgrounds and had specifically been recruited for that reason. "They liked that we had ranks and they followed orders and were disciplined so they were good for us to recruit," Jeff confirms. Later, I find these sentiments to be true across many other white supremacist groups.

In a post-NSM speech in 2019 to New America, a public policy think tank, Jeff told the audience NSM members also intentionally seek out military training, predicting a civil war or a race war. [76] "That's why we were sending people into the military all the time. By the time I left, about 50 percent of the membership had military experience." Ten years earlier, in 2009, when the Southern Poverty Law Center, SPLC, had identified over 40 active-duty military personnel on a social networking site run by the NSM, Jeff told the military newspaper, *Stars and Stripes,* that roughly half the group's members had served in the military. That same year, Charles Wilson, an NSM spokesman told *Salon,* "We do encourage them to sign up for the military. We can use the training to secure the resistance to our government."[77]

Both white supremacists, and groups like ISIS and al Qaeda, try to infiltrate militaries. In the case of militant jihadists, it's often to mount insider attacks, while in the case of white supremacists, it is to gain training, and possibly weapons as patriots who have served in the military.

Thirty-five-year-old Ryan Lo'Ree, from Flint, Michigan, is one of these cases. He was recruited into white supremacism after his discharge from the U.S. military, which included a particularly grueling stint in Iraq.

Ryan who lives in the Flint, Michigan area is a good looking, heavier set, young man with a reddish mustache and short beard, full head of wavy hair and a genuine smile.

Ryan grew up around the military. His father was in Special Forces, and they lived at Fort Bragg when he was very young. But a military environment did not ensure stability. Ryan is the eldest and has three siblings from different fathers. He saw a lot of abuse growing up, including his stepfather who was an abusive alcoholic. "My mom was trying to put food on the table. He was abusive, but not to us. He threw my mom down a flight of stairs in our apartment. He threw a bottle at her head. He tried to hide his abuse, like he'd pinch her." She divorced both the stepfather and Ryan's father due to abuse. "The reason why my mom left [his father] is also that he was very abusive. He shoved a key in her ear one time."

In spite of the spousal abuse, Ryan says his mother was the positive light in his childhood. "My mom is an awesome drummer for a blues band," he boasts. "She manages a group home, works in home healthcare special needs, and volunteering in schools. She is very loving. They are all a bunch of hippies on her side. My grandfather fought in Vietnam, but my grandmother was a soul sister. They were all Baptist. They were very loving, accepted everyone, and people loved them."

Ryan was smart and excelled in his studies, but he says he distanced from others and acted out. His dad lived in the suburbs and his mom lived in Flint's tough city center. He describes being "two different personalities, hanging with preppie sports guys, and at my mom's house it was, 'Let's smoke weed, drink beer.'" In some ways, Ryan was set up to fall into trouble. His mom worked the third shift, so she wasn't home nights and "dad didn't care about us."

Ryan says his first big challenge was when he thought he got a girl pregnant. "Being a stupid teenager, I stole my stepmother's car to take her to get a pregnancy test, but I crashed it on another car. I didn't know what to do—I took off to my mom's house. My mom made me go back to the crash." He wound up on probation. It turns out the girl was not pregnant, but Ryan began skipping school and "started to hang out with more people on the streets."

Ryan was sent to Glen Mills for two years, the oldest reform school in the U.S. (shut down in 2019 after a child abuse and cover-up scandal.) Glen Mills' attempt at "reform" didn't work. He started hanging out with gangs, doing drugs and stealing, and getting caught. He does, however, credit the school as a good influence, although punitive. "There were staff members who put their hands on kids more than they should have. Not sexual, but physical abuse. But overall, when it came to leadership, self-discipline, academics, and sports, if I hadn't gone, I don't know if I would have had my high school diploma."

As Ryan opens up, I learn about a driving force underscoring his life, a story I've sadly heard too many times before. He was molested when he was three years old. "My uncle molested me and my cousin. He used to babysit." Ryan's mother found out and put a stop to it, but serious damage had been done. "I don't remember all of what happened. My cousin remembers. He's been diagnosed schizophrenic. He said a lot of different stuff happened to him." While Ryan's mental health didn't suffer like his cousin's, Ryan thinks the experience contributed to him being overly sexually active as a teen and says even now he doesn't like to go to male doctors.

Ryan enlisted in the Army right after high school and was assigned to Fort Dix in New Jersey. He deployed to Iraq for 18 months. "It was probably one of the worst deployments for the units. It was 2004 when I joined. I came back from the Army and didn't reenlist."

He served in Mosul, an area rife with insurgents and al Qaeda operatives. "We called it the Swiss cheese roads, so many IEDS." It was a dangerous time, before the U.S. military began to install detectors for improvised explosive devises called IEDs, on all its vehicles. Until then, safety depended much more on visual identification of IEDs. "If we saw something that looked wrong…" and his voice trails off with painful memories.

Ryan recalls the impact of combat trauma among his returning military mates: "guys killing themselves, killing their families." Returning to Flint, his unit faced troubled personal lives and harsh economic times. General Motors has left, and jobs were scarce. Ryan had been married when he deployed, had a daughter while I was Iraq, and the relationship was rocky. "We were having a very rough relationship. Ugly words, but no abuse," he adds.

Ryan faced his demons alone and he didn't want to be around his mother who didn't understand what had happened to him and asked too many questions. Unfortunately, the abusive uncle showed up right at the most vulnerable and particularly triggering time in Ryan's life, when he was angry about everything. His uncle had just been released from prison, for a second time. He'd gone to prison for stealing credit cards, then again for assault. Like many abuse survivors, Ryan had an approach/avoid relationship with his abuser and easily fell back into the sphere of his manipulative uncle's influence.

Ryan was unemployed, his wife was pregnant, and he was having a tough time putting food on the table. It was an ordinary incident that became his turning point into the white nationalist movement. "Two Black guys came over, friends of mine. They asked me if they could have a slice of the pizza. I thought my pregnant wife needed it. But when I left, the pizza was gone. My uncle heard about it." And he swooped in.

Though Ryan says his uncle had never been racist, he came back from prison the second time with swastikas and Aryan Brotherhood tattoos. He wanted to take Ryan to meet and tell them "how these Black guys stole this pizza from me." Ryan was intimidated at the thought of meeting these ex-cons and for good reason. The Aryan Brotherhood is not only the nation's oldest, largest, and deadliest white supremacist prison gang, it is also a national crime syndicate, according to the SLPC.

Ryan describes the scene: "There were hate flags—confederate, white nationalist—a swastika burnt into the grass. One kid had a pistol by his side." He was to meet the group's leader, Ron Chadwell, who was under investigation for ordering the killing of a Jewish infiltrator. "They stabbed him and drowned him. The murderers were found, and they were very, very proud of what they did. They are still in prison to this day."

Yet the meeting was not at all what Ryan expected.

"I had a fight or flight response, but Ron was a very charismatic, little guy, not a lot of tattoos. He was missing some of his fingers, lost from his job, and he talked low and mysterious. He was charismatic, knowledgeable on history, hate knowledge. He played on my anger at the time—my father, my childhood, the army that had abandoned me and did nothing for me. He was a cult leader."

Ryan says Ron took a liking to him and invited him to hang out more. Though the Aryan Brotherhood purports to not believe in harming their bodies with drugs and alcohol, Ryan says there was plenty of beer, marijuana, and cocaine to keep people around. "I found a place I could party. There were some girls there. He used women to his advantage— the party life that he kept going."

Ron saw the positives of recruiting someone like Ryan, a proven warrior from the U.S. military, trained to be disciplined, respectful of rank, and hard working. Ryan embodied that air of legitimacy and helped portray the group as patriotic, and he says Ron loved that. As Ryan got into the hate rhetoric, Ron realized Ryan had leadership potential. Ron wanted to rebrand and make use of new technology. "At that time Myspace was becoming a thing. They were starting to veer away from the shaved head, swastika look, and I was a techie and I spoke well." And Ron shied from the media, "he used other people to do those things."

Ryan easily rose to leadership in this group of angry misfits. "We rebranded ourselves to become the Rollingwood Skins. Ron was not a skinhead, he was Aryan Brotherhood," Ryan explains, "but we knew the skinhead part attracted the younger guys who were into punk music. We'd have bands come and play. They'd be attracted to that—and the drinking." Ryan became a purveyor of local violence and hate against immigrants and Blacks, using racial tensions for recruiting.

Thinking back to how Ron drew him in, Ryan explains, "I was angry. He started to say they have never been your friends if they are willing to steal from you when you had nothing. Black people are not your friends. Look at how white European communities have flourished. I started to believe it, that we were smarter than Black people."

This illustrates the essence of how hate groups operate and the process they use to inculcate hate—a process ICSVE calls Directed Hate.[78] First recruiters figure out what you need, or you figure it out yourself and go to the group looking to fill that need for dignity, belonging, purpose, significance, protection, shifting blame from your own failures, finding an outlet for enacting violence, a group to party with, girls to meet, etc. Once hooked into believing your needs will be met by the group, then its leaders begin to ideologically indoctrinate you. First, they make it clear you are only in the group because you are white, inculcating a sense of specialness about whiteness. Then you are brought into hidden secrets about the inferiority of people of color and the destructive plotting by Jews. Then the group insists you must join in the hate to belong, so the mutual hate becomes the bond that glues the group together alongside conspiracy theories of white genetic superiority, being spiritually chosen by God in some cases, and threats of Jews orchestrating white genocide and white replacement.

Ron knew how to work Ryan. He appealed to his ego and his intellect, telling him he could be a leader, and fusing him to the group and what it could deliver to him.

Ron asked Ryan to become vice president and his uncle was made president. Ryan says Ron didn't want to be in the leadership position, at least not formally. Ryan got a tattoo that everyone in leadership roles has, two points at the top of a swastika. "I felt like people were looking up to me. Now that I know how power works, I realize it was an adrenaline rush. It feeds your ego." Ryan says Ron's motivations for running this hate group "was his ego, having this huge group of people. I didn't realize he was a cult leader until later on. He had a group that he kept drunk and high that fed his personal ego. He was having threesomes. The money [from criminal activities] was coming back to his house. Whatever drink they wanted he'd have around, and he used it to manipulate sex for himself."

"What were the girls' motivations for joining this group?" I ask him.

"The girls were just like us. They were poor and were looking for the same thing we were—acceptance. He also knew that the girls helped him to keep the young guys around." Ryan says the women were treated as beneath men and never given leadership roles.

Ryans says the men had ambitions and understood mainstreaming their movement would help it spread. They didn't dress like typical skin heads, instead chose dress shirts, suits and ties. Ryan was researching groups operating on a more national level and found the NSM. "We met with them to put our group on the map more." Ryan was invited to a barbeque in Cadillac, Michigan "to meet some influential people. I had never seen anything like this in my life," he recalls. "Pavilions right off the water, Nazi and swastika flags all around the pavilion, families all around.

Michigan has a history of militias and at this point in our interview, Ryan harkens back to the history of Michigan and Henry Ford. Indeed, the history of Henry Ford is important to understanding the context and current strength of white supremacy. The famed industrialist who brought the Model T to the American middle class also heavily promoted antisemitism.

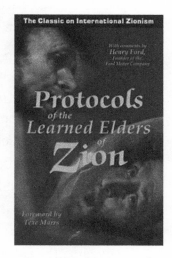

In the 1920s, Henry Ford's newspaper, The Dearborn *Independent,* published a controversial front-page series every week entitled *The International Jew: The World's Problem.* This series promoted a conspiracy theory based on *The Protocols of the Elders of Zion*, fabricated propaganda originating in Russia in the early 20th century.[79] *The Protocols* purported to be a series of secret documents describing a global conspiracy of

Protocols of the Learned Elders of Zion Book Cover

Jews trying to unseat whites from their dominant position in Western societies, whose ultimate goal is to take over the world. Many of the old antisemitic tropes contained in the long-debunked *Protocols* are still incorporated into current day white supremacist literature.

"The guys we met in Cadillac, they were into eugenics," Ryan recalls. "We had very dangerous conversations; that the white population is smarter, and Blacks are inferior and should be wiped off the face of the earth. They had money to try to make these things happen. They had a lot of money." They decided to have a rally targeting the NAACP building in Flint. "There were shootings there all the time and we wanted to cause a ruckus. It was a perfect opportunity to get into the news. [We] made the *Flint Journal.* I was quoted saying Hitler was not a bad person and misunderstood." In the article, Ryan was described as busy passing out red fliers asking white people to join to reclaim their "White Heritage" and unafraid "to parade down neighborhood streets in a brown shirt with his swastika flag aloft."[80]

"As much as I was spitting this stuff out, deep down I felt like it was just wrong," Ryan admits. "I was being used. I was being ignorant." I've heard from others that joining hate groups to meet unmet needs created a sense of unease. Ryan was well aware of what he was promoting and knew what he was doing was wrong. He was also supporting himself in the movement by crime. "When you made that chapter your whole life, that's the way money was brought in."

The crime/terror nexus is well known in extremism studies and many flagrant compromises of alleged principles result. Al Qaeda has funded some of its activities by members running liquor stores or sharing proceeds from drug lords and gang activities. Hezbollah, to this day, deals in the amphetamine, Captagon.[81] Ryan recalls the same sort of thing. "Funny thing is, this extremely racist group collaborated with Mexicans, doing crimes with them."

Eventually, it all caught up with them. They were stealing boat motors, using the proceeds for beer, drugs, and their pockets. "We got greedy, and the police started to investigate. They put a tracking device on one of the motors." His house was raided, and Ryan was arrested. "They came with AR-15s and pistols. They had my whole street blocked off. It was the craziest thing in my life," Ryan recalls. "They knew who we were. There was already the gang task force keeping their eyes on us, our conversations, and they were looking back on these murders." Ryan is referring to the killing of a Jewish infiltrator and Ron's suspected involvement.

Looking back, "It was also the best thing at the time because I was so scared. They had me shook. I didn't know my rights, so I admitted to doing everything. After they arrested me, it was my first time in jail. I was scared. You are getting searched down. I have this huge swastika on my arm. I tried to proudly fly this flag thinking maybe it will save me. It didn't save me."

Ryan quickly learned prison is a place to find safety and protection in numbers, and people gather in groups often bonded by race, ethnicity, and hate. "I started seeing Black guys. Next thing I know I get jumped. I'm getting hit from everywhere, I got one guy in a submission hold and I remember looking over at the guys in the hate groups. They didn't come to help. But one guy who did was my cellmate. He was Black. He was swinging on them. He went down in the hole. I went to medical."

For some, hitting bottom is a time of soul searching and reorganization. Ryan says he and his cellmate started to build a relationship. "He called himself a radical Christian. He was all about the Bible. He was leftist. He said, 'You don't seem like the guy that would be part of a hate group.' He talked to me about certain Bible verses. He had a strict workout routine we did. He taught me how to live in jail, wash my socks and hang them under the lights. He talked to me about kids, and he gave me a reading list. He read books all the time." Ryan's indifference was wearing thin. "I started to realize it doesn't matter what color skin you have. We all make mistakes. We are all human." That appreciation helped him remember who he'd once been, and it helped him avoid going back to the hate group upon his release.

His uncle was furious. He and others in the hate group accused Ryan of being a snitch. Ryan went back to his old friends, "even my Black friends, who still loved me. To them, I was Ryan. The two guys that had stolen the pizza from me, I made up with them."

Ryan says from there he "self-educated like crazy, I filled myself with books." He started paying attention to the messages of Cornel West, Angela Davis, Malcolm X, John F. Kennedy, Martin Luther King, and Robert Kennedy. He began to realize the importance of forgiveness and empathy both for himself and others—as he puts it—the importance of "looking at someone as a human being. I realized that what I was holding onto at that time was my own fears and anger."

Community members began to reach out to Ryan and a mentor told him, "'We don't condemn people for the mistakes that they made in their life. If we do, we just chase them back to those corners of their life.'"

Ryan realized he really wanted to help troubled kids in Flint. "I started to ask myself, why did I hang out with gangs when I was younger, or go into this hate group?" He was looking for what he didn't have growing up. "We didn't have mentorship programs, outlets for kids to go into. I researched the school-to-prison pipeline, the judges and lawyers getting kickbacks for sending kids to out-of-state schools; and I started looking to programs that kids were really drawn into."

Mixed Martial Arts, MMA, rose to the top. As many of my colleagues in Europe have also recognized, young men and boys drawn into white supremacism, or militant jihadism like ISIS, are often first attracted to MMA. Perhaps out of a need to consolidate their sense of toughness, these groups can be a force for bad, or good, depending upon the group one joins. Cynthia Miller-Idriss, a researcher at American University who studies white supremacism both in the U.S. and abroad, found MMA groups in Germany are indeed purveyors of hate, drawing in vulnerable young men and filling them with a sense of purpose and mission as white warriors for their race.[82]

Youth who are into martial arts closely follow the champions, and these sports icons can be great spokespeople against violent extremism and its recruiters. ICSVE worked with a group in Austria to platform such role models and we produced a video profiling a bullied immigrant Muslim kid who almost gave in to hate and joined ISIS. Instead, he got into an MMA group and became a countrywide champion in Austria. As a role model, he encouraged kids to rise above hate and find their own paths to success, even when facing significant barriers and hate from others.

In Flint, boxing was popular. Unfortunately, Ryan says that's due to the violence in Flint. He approached some social workers and MMA experts and asked if they'd be willing to volunteer if he got a program together to help kids get off the streets. Joined by some friends, they went bigger. They started tutoring, tackling addiction. A church let them use a gym and with small grants they got an MMA-style cage which attracted more kids. The project grew from 10 kids to over 100 kids. Some were on probation and Ryan says, "I saw these kids make changes I've never seen. I took a liking to this kid who had been in hate groups himself. I focused on him to get him away from that mentality." Ryan says probation officers expressed interest in the program.

Unfortunately, they hit a wall, figuratively and literally. The church pastor built a wall without a permit and the fire department shut things down. Ryan said it put him in a downward spiral. "It almost sent me into an anti-government spin."

As Ryan was trying to get his youth program funded, he began to learn more about systemic and institutional racism and the roots of some police forces organized to recapture slaves. He began to ask himself how this early U.S. history was currently affecting the city of Flint, with a population that is 50 percent Black. He started to follow the money. "A lot of our county commissioners were underfunding Flint. There was corruption. We found it and went public."

And that began an unexpected political career for this former white supremacist.

"Some politicians were leery that I was a prior member of a hate group but then I learned how to tell my story." Ryan didn't share it publicly, at first. "I didn't want people to know the stupid thing I had done." But "I learned your story can change so many people's lives. You could open so many people's eyes. You just need to learn how to tell your story. It worked."

Then came the infamous Flint water crisis. In 2014, state officials looking to save money switched Flint's drinking water supply from the Detroit city system to the Flint River, exposing thousands of children to lead poisoning that can cause irreversible damage to the brain and nervous system, leading to lifelong learning and behavioral problems. Citizens of Flint were also exposed to legionella, a bacterium that causes a potentially fatal form of pneumonia.[83]

They engaged in peaceful protests to raise awareness, which brought needed media coverage. Ryan says he also started to see how government failures can push extremism and become power levers and recruiting tools for violent extremists. Unfortunately, domestic hate groups as well as international terrorist groups capitalize on these situations. Terrorist groups identify grievances in a community, pointing to where governments are failing their citizens, then attract new adherents by offering services the government is failing to offer. In Lebanon, for example, Hezbollah has offered schools and training camps for kids, and services such as medical care to poor families. In return, Hezbollah has gotten a steady stream of young boys to join its ranks, along with increased community support. ISIS has distributed graphic videos of harm happening to Muslims in conflict zones, to convince Muslims in Europe and the U.S. that Muslims are under attack and hated by the West, then they've found recruits to help build a utopian Caliphate they claimed would dominate in world power.

As Ryan correctly notes, "Even in Syria with al Qaeda and ISIS, it started with a terrible drought. 'Look, the government is not giving you water, we will give you water.'" He saw that play out in Flint as the county militia, a racist hate group, showed up during the Flint water crisis. "On several occasions, they came and passed out water. They had military fatigues and AR-14s and they started to use the water crisis like a recruitment tool. They used environmental impacts to say, 'Hey, we're the good guys. The government doesn't help you.'"

As Ryan continued to learn more about Michigan's militias, he says, "I started to realize there were a lot more hate groups than I ever thought." Ryan started letting haters know there is a way out and he was ready to help anyone who wanted to exit. He opened his phone 24/7 and found some success with this method, but says, "There are not many people doing this. I felt alone." People were outing white supremacists by identifying and doxxing them, but Ryan had another vision: to heal them of hate...I saw guys who went from extreme right who then went to the extreme left. How? They never went through that healing." The move from white supremacism to leftist ideologies may sound odd, but it is not all that dramatic because an enemy is still identified and needs to be fought.

Reciprocal radicalization also plays a role when the actions of one group end up radicalizing another and that plays out in Michigan, too. Michigan has one of the largest populations of Muslims in the U.S., and there is plenty of Islamophobia to go around. "In Michigan, it's because they've been fed this fear that every Muslim you meet must be a terrorist," and as Ryan explains, militant jihadi terrorists fuel Islamophobia which in turn can fuel white supremacism.

Ryan was finding his way toward deradicalization. His breakthrough involved meeting with Holocaust survivors. "I still had my tattoo," he reminds me of his swastika and pain briefly passes across his face as he tells me, "I bawled my eyes out when I sat down with Holocaust survivors. It was a deep transformation for me."

I ask Ryan what his advice is for others who might get sucked into white supremacism as he did. "One of the things I wish I would have done, even as a Christian," he tells me, "and I'll say to a child now, is to be open-minded, and don't believe everything you hear the first time you hear it. A lot of these [recruiters] have learned how to make you feel psychologically comfortable and you think they're your friends, but they are not your friend. They are after their own egos. If someone tells you something, go research it. It's just propaganda."

Ryan knows researching this propaganda isn't so straightforward these days and further advises, "Don't believe anything you see on the internet without checking correct sources. It's too easy to put lies out on the internet now." In response to the current atmosphere of political polarization, Ryan says, "You don't have to be into it. Peace and love in your heart is going to make you feel so much better than to hold on to hate. Hate eats you up. It tears you up."

"What is the real power of hate?" I ask.

"It's fear," he replies without missing a beat. "Ron could dissect you and find your fears and play off of those with me. 'You don't have a father. I'd never beat you. I love you. I'll be that father figure.' He'd pretend he loved me. It's the fears. Even to this day I struggle. My dad never told me that I would amount to anything."

As we conclude our interview, Ryan says, "We are born with love in our hearts, but hate is taught, and it can be untaught." Ryan smiles warmly his face lighting up with optimism. "There's so much more in this world to offer, not just your white world. Diversity is so rich. Have an open mind," he restates. "Fears hold you back from your purpose. Everybody is a disaster and also a miracle. We all have our personal issues. We are all a miracle."

That his life took a turn for the better may just be a miracle. It has certainly turned out far better than others from his white supremacy days. One of those is his group's leader, Ron Chadwell. He was killed in 2018 at age 48. Police were not able to identify a suspect but said it looked like a homicide.[84] And Ryan's predatory uncle—"He's a meth head and heroin addict...We have no contact now."

Two of the Wolverine Watchmen didn't fare so well, either. An Army veteran who joined the paramilitary group became alarmed at talk about killing police and became an FBI informant. Two of the perpetrators went to court facing the possibility of life in prison for conspiracy in the plot to kidnap Governor Whitmer, and conspiracy to use a weapon of mass destruction to blow up a bridge and stop police from getting to the scene of their crime.[85]

Governor Whitmer said, "Plots against public officials and threats to the FBI are a disturbing extension of radicalized domestic terrorism that festers in our nation, threatening the very foundation of our republic."[86]

The Assistant U.S. Attorney said, "They wanted to set off a second American civil war, a second American Revolution, something that they call the boogaloo. And they wanted to do it for a long time before they settled on Gov. Whitmer."[87]

You can watch Ryan tell his story at www.EscapeHate.org

Chapter 6 - Defending the Constitution

Jason Van Tatenhove is clearly defensive as we start our interview, wanting to dissociate himself from his role as propagandist for one of the largest far-right anti-government militias the United States has ever seen. But as he will come to explain, anyone who surrounds himself with lies and conspiracy theories will get drawn in. And overtime, Jason slid down that rabbit hole, working as the main propagandist for the Oath Keepers, alleged to be among the key perpetrators of the January 6 attack on the Capitol Building. Eleven Oath Keepers, so far, have been charged in U.S. federal court for their actions before, during, and after the U.S. capitol attack.[88]

As of this writing, these men are being prosecuted by the U.S. Attorney's Office for the District of Columbia and the Department of Justice National Security Division's Counterterrorism Section.[89] They face up to 20 years in prison for seditious conspiracy and up to 20 years for obstruction of an official proceeding, along with potential financial penalties."[90]

Jason is not among them. But their leader is. Oath Keeper founder and leader, Stewart Rhodes, is a former U.S. Army paratrooper, and a key distinguishing feature of the Oath Keepers is their explicit focus on successfully recruiting current and former military, law enforcement, and first responders (although anyone can join.)

Among Rhodes' co-conspirators is 45-year-old William Todd Wilson of North Carolina. Wilson was the first Oath Keeper to breach the Capitol Building on January 6. He helped literally bust open the doors of the Capitol's rotunda so others could invade the building. Wilson was well-prepared. According to the U.S. Department of Justice, on January 5th he drove to Washington, D.C. and brought with him an AR-15-style rifle, a 9-millimeter pistol, approximately 200 rounds of ammunition, body armor, a camouflaged combat uniform, pepper spray, a large walking stick intended for use as a weapon, and a pocketknife. Wilson stored his firearms, ammunition, and combat gear in his hotel room and was prepared to retrieve the weapons if called upon to do so. The person who would call upon him would be Stewart Rhodes. Wilson has pled guilty.[91]

A question looms. How were former U.S. military personnel, who have all sworn an oath to defend the U.S. Constitution, convinced to arm themselves, organize what many are calling an attempted coup, and move in military stack formation up the steps of our U.S. Capitol to try to stop the peaceful transfer of power, in contravention of a lawful election process, not to mention the U.S. Constitution itself?

The answer may lie in my interview with Jason Van Tatenhove, the Oath Keepers' former propagandist. I spoke with him one month before he testified, on July 15, 2022, before the U.S. House Select Committee on the January 6 Attack.

Jason begins our interview by telling me he was never a member of the Oath Keepers. He was an aspiring journalist who saw an opportunity to embed with a powerfully influential group rising on the political horizon. Only after embedding with them was he offered the job of national media person, which he took out of a growing excitement at the large audiences the Oath Keepers and groups like them were able to draw in.

He also tells me, "Stewart was not racist at all. He told many stories that his mother was an immigrant from Mexico, and how he travelled the Southwest with her in the agricultural industry." Yet Rhodes catered to the alt-right. Jason explains, "There was a dynamic shift in the two years I was exposed to the Oath Keepers, to when I said, 'I gotta go. I cannot abide this anymore.'"

Officially launched in April 2009 as a Nevada-based nonprofit following the election of Barack Obama, the country's first Black president, the Oath Keepers present themselves to the public as defenders of the U.S. Constitution, that is, the constitution as they interpret it.[92] By 2014, Rhodes, a Yale Law School graduate in addition to being former U.S. Army, claimed the group had 35,000 dues paying members said to be mainly active and former military, law enforcement, and first responders with state, county, and local chapters scattered across the country.

Oath Keepers often show up in armed standoffs against the government. Likewise, the group has a history of vigilantism, providing voluntary armed security (not affiliated with any law enforcement entity) at various protests and venues; again purportedly in defense of the U.S. Constitution. Armed Oath Keepers patrolled Ferguson,

"Guardians of the Republic"

Oath Keepers Logo and Slogan

Missouri, after riots broke out in the wake of the 2014 police killing of Michael Brown, an unarmed Black man. Armed Oath Keepers patrolled the site of the deadly 2017 "Unite the Right" rally in Charlottesville, Virginia, and they have sent patrols to the U.S. southern border. They've provided security for staff of the conspiracy website, Infowars, and to those promoting Donald Trump's "Stop the Steal" campaign, and even to controversial Trump presidential advisor, Roger Stone. They've also offered security to business owners who defied COVID-19 public health mandates.[93]

"I don't really hold extremist views," Jason tells me, obviously ashamed of his previous activities. He describes himself as a libertarian-leaning anarchist before serving the Oath Keepers. "I was never an extremist. I was an employee of the Oath Keepers. It was a writing gig." That gig helped spread the Oath Keeper's core message, which essentially says the federal government is a danger to its own citizens, engages in attacks against citizens and is working to strip our civil liberties. They advocate for U.S. citizens to arm themselves and prepare for inevitable federal showdowns by stockpiling goods and supplies, engaging in paramilitary training, and organizing small self-reliant community networks, including militias to protect against the feds.

The group's name reflects its core principle, that members vow to uphold the oath they swore as law enforcement and military personnel, which in the case of the military members is to "support and defend the constitution against all enemies, foreign and domestic." In reality, its defiant propaganda and actions are alarming.

Rhodes offered this chilling rant in 2012 against any restrictions on military-style weapons:

> And you can bet that if you let them take away your military semi-autos, next on their list will be bolt action rifles, which they will call 'sniper rifles' (and By God, that is certainly what they are good for.)[94]

His group has published a list of "Ten Orders We will Not Obey" detailing what they see as impending threats coming from the U.S. government. In this list they refuse the government's potential to impose martial law, confiscate citizens' guns, and force Americans into concentration camps.[95] Then when Donald Trump claimed a stolen election by Joe Biden, Rhodes published an open letter to President Trump in December 2020, on the Oath Keepers website, calling for martial law to avoid a militia-led civil war over what he and Trump's right-wing were claiming was a coup attempt in the form of a stolen election by the Democrats. Rhodes urged:

> You must act NOW as a wartime President, pursuant to your oath to defend the Constitution, which is very similar to the oath all of us veterans swore. We are already in a fight. It's better to wage it with you as Commander-in-Chief than to have you comply with a fraudulent election, leave office, and leave the White House in

the hands of illegitimate usurpers and Chinese puppets. Please don't do it. Do NOT concede, and do NOT wait until January 20, 2021. Strike now![96]

In this letter he urged Trump to invoke the Insurrection Act against "domestic traitors" and command "trusted military units" to "seize all databases of the CIA, FBI, NSA, DNI, etc. and the records held by all state electoral systems and administrators."[97]

On January 4, 2021, Rhodes sent a callout to his followers to gather in Washington, D.C. "We need prior military, LEO [law enforcement officers], security professionals, skilled martial artists, emergency medical, communications, and intelligence personnel."[98] Rhodes wrote online:

> It is CRITICAL that all patriots who can be in D.C. get to D.C. to stand tall in support of President Trump's fight to defeat the enemies foreign and domestic who are attempting a coup, through the massive voter fraud and related attacks on our Republic. We Oath Keepers are both honor-bound and eager to be there in strength to do our part. [99]

Many answered his call and Oath Keepers and others violently attacked the buildings, institutions, and democratic processes Rhodes claimed to be defending.

Given the radical propaganda of the Oath Keepers, Jason's family background comes as a surprise. His mother had attended the original Woodstock concert in 1969 ("on the coffee table of my mother there is a hardcover book of the original Woodstock, she was there"); his grandfather was an abstract expressionist ("I may have met Andy Warhol, I didn't know any different"); and the family has "Martin Luther King's handwritten letters to my grandmother during the civil rights movement." He describes his family as "very leftist."

Then his parents split and like many kids growing up in a divorced family, Jason's life shifted when his mother remarried. He was 10 when they relocated from New Jersey to tech-heavy Fort Collins, Colorado. But Jason followed his grandfather's artistic bent. He dropped out of university, went to several art schools, had his first museum show at age 24. He then found his way into alternative media journalism and became a writer. He's also owned "a few tattoo shops, I'm a tattoo artist." Not surprisingly, Jason has tattoos all over his body.

Jason is now 48 years old, has been married for 27 years and has three daughters. He hints at a marriage that is "a very nontraditional relationship throughout." And in breaking tradition with his upbringing, he decided to try his hand in politics in the aughts, "Joining the Republican party was rebelling for my family," he jokes. "I got elected to the Larimer County Republican committee. I became the PR director of the party for a while. We got people appointed to several positions in the county. Then they started catching on" to him, referring to his unusual lifestyle, appearance, and bent for anarchy.

I was personally curious about his interest in anarchy. I lived in Greece when anarchists wanted to destroy the government and kill many of the social elite and top journalists. My husband, the U.S. Ambassador to Greece at the time, was on a hit list.

I briefly describe this experience and ask Jason if this is what he means by anarchist—if he means those who want to violently tear down everything in hopes of rebuilding something better. He backtracks a bit, "I don't think the human race is ready for anarchy, but [I endorse] the 'Live and Let Live' philosophy."

Yet that live and let live idea was leaving him "feeling fairly lost" and wanting to reconnect with his biological father. He moved his family to Butte, Montana, where he worked alongside his dad building cabins and lodges. His dad listened to Rush Limbaugh, "who I couldn't stand, and Alex Jones. I started listening to Alex Jones. You get a minor in conspiracy theory in talk radio," Jason jokes about the popular and angry conspiracy theorist and founder of the website, Infowars. Yet this is when he started falling down the radical rabbit hole.

"I knew about Waco, with the Branch Davidians," Jason recalls. Anti-government conspiracy groups frequently rally around the "never another Waco" sentiment. Waco was the disastrous 1993 51-day standoff in Waco, Texas, between the federal government and a religious sect believed to be stockpiling illegal weapons. Tragically, a fire erupted during the siege, engulfing part of the compound and resulting in the deaths of 76 Branch Davidians, including 25 children, two pregnant women, and their leader, David Koresh.[100]

Then came Bundy Ranch. This 2014 armed standoff with the federal government was preceded by a two decade long dispute in which cattle rancher, Clive Bundy, refused court orders to pay more than one million dollars in back fees for grazing his cattle on public lands. He claimed the federal government did not have the authority to manage public lands. His claims were consistently rejected by scholars, federal courts, even the U.S. Supreme Court. A violent standoff ensued which garnered national attention. With rumors of law enforcement sniper teams, some thought the Bundy Ranch standoff could turn into another Waco. Rhodes came to Montana and issued a callout, bringing in people, supplies, and ammunition.

Jason says this growing standoff was a bit of a dream for him. He'd hoped to emulate the journalist, Hunter Thompson, who had embedded with the Hell's Angels biker gang for about a year in the '60s and later wrote a book about his experience.

"I started connecting with the right wingers and I got the okay to embed with Stewart Rhodes at Bundy Ranch." Rhodes was just getting his alt-right enterprise going and saw opportunism. Jason says, "Stewart found he could make money by these callings. [In the Bundy Ranch standoff] he would make 40K in a week, but he only gave 12K to the Bundy family. That flipped a switch."

"I was never a member of the Oath Keepers," Jason repeats at this point in our interview. "When I came to work for them, my thought was it's a historic event, like writing my own version of *Hell's Angels*. But I got lost."

Over time Jason says he came to understand that Rhodes had stumbled upon a money-making machine he exploited to raise himself into the national and international spotlight. In his quest for money and power, Rhodes "began finding events that he could plug into" and he kept inviting Jason back and granting access to events. Jason says they developed a rapport.

At White Hope Mine (a dispute between the U.S. Forest Service and a small, dilapidated Montana mine) the Oath Keepers assigned a public information officer and Rhodes asked Jason to look over the press release. Jason similarly helped at Sugar Pine Mine (another standoff at a small mine in Oregon.) This time, unbeknownst to him, his name was added to one of these press releases. His employer at the time, the state of Montana, was not happy. He ended up resigning. Rhodes offered him the job of national media director and associate website editor. "My job was to be the liaison with the press, be a gatekeeper for who would treat Stewart the friendliest, what news stories were hot at the moment, and how to spin it to plug in some belief of the Oath Keepers. They are really good at social media and internet messaging and Alex Jones dwarfed all mainstream media. I knew I was getting unprecedented access."

Rhodes and Jones fed each other. Rhodes was a frequent guest on Jones' Infowars show, playing into Jones' penchant for claiming the federal government couldn't be trusted.

"I was never a member. I told Stewart I'll work for you," Jason repeats, again distancing himself from the group he served.

But they got under your skin after a while?" I ask.

"I didn't have any other options," Jason protests. "I'm six foot, have a Mohawk more than I don't, I'm tattooed up. It's not easy for someone like me to find a job. My wife's health has been challenged since we got married. She is medically disabled. We lived below the poverty line most of our life. [Oath Keepers] was a steady gig." And then he adds the real hook that drew him in and fed his ego. "I put out an article and 70 to 100,000 people read it overnight. Their reach was massive." And Jason descended into the conspiracy world.

Jason moved to Eureka, Montana, to live among the "who's who of radical extremism." Money was suddenly not an issue. Jason was paid well, and they lived on the property of "some very big supporters of the Oath Keepers."

I ask how Rhodes is funded.

Jason said Rhodes raised money doing callouts. "Stewart was playing to the right side, the alt-right rise." His formula was to find emotional hot button issues that get people worked up. "Emotional intensity will drive people to spend money. His callouts resulted in only a dozen who actually showed up, but a lot of time those who didn't come would donate. Stewart would say, 'We need boots on the ground,' these skills, and 'if you can't make it yourself you can support the effort through your donations.' It was a show put on to drive this show, to feed his ego, to become this paramilitary rebel leader."

Oath Keepers Patch

Jason saw the power of triggering strong emotions. "People will spend money and let go of their core beliefs," and adds, "Extremists are very good at doing that, like Alex Jones, and it's compounded when we have these echo chambers on social media today."

Jason used the propaganda echo chamber and saw its real and tangible effect on critical thinking. "I can tell you there are underground lizards controlling the government and when it's echoed everywhere, you begin to think, 'Shit maybe there are?' We can't discount the power of conspiracy and social media very quickly ratcheting up this hype. We are stuck in this brain chemical."

I agree. Emotions are powerful forces with extremist and terrorist groups. It's the emotional component of internet and face-to-face messaging evoking fear, pride, anger, and feelings of belonging to a like-minded group, that confers a sense of purpose and significance—even if one has to change beliefs and conform to fit in.

Rhodes also raised money by providing security for high profile situations that were getting national and international attention. For example, Jason says Rhodes offered security during funerals for school shooting victims. He offered protection to the Kentucky county clerk who made national news when she refused to sign marriage certificates for gay couples. This situation, it turns out, was walking a troubling line for Jason. Jason recalls flying out to Kentucky to cover the story for the Oath Keepers. "I wrote it from the perspective of the queer person."

"I am an openly queer person," Jason reveals. "The message [Stewart] puts out in the public realm and what he accepts in private are two different things. There was a queer couple who did all the merchant services tech IT and me [on the national staff]. But he knew it would not play well with the base. He was hanging with Chuck Baldwin," Jason adds, a homophobic right-wing politician, radio host, and pastor of Liberty Fellowship in Kalispell, Montana.

So, when it came to the Kentucky county clerk who refused to issue marriage licenses to LGBTQ couples, Rhodes rejected Jason's article and rewrote it. "That was a red flag, but I didn't pay attention." Jason was on the rise, enamored by the influence and audience he had at his fingertips, and perhaps a bit enamored of Rhodes as well.

When I ask how the group functions and what its actual ideology is, Jason answers, "Stewart Rhodes is the Oath Keepers."

"Their ideology? Let's just say, what we need to do to make money. Selling the revolution. Some groups are true believers," he says. "The Idaho Three Percenters, Bundy and his groups." (The

Three Percenters are another militia, far right and extremely anti-government. Their leaders appear to have been involved with Rhodes and the Oath Keepers in the January 6 insurrection.[101] To which Jason adds, "They are at a higher threat level. Although I underestimated the Oath Keepers stack formation on Capitol Hill, the insurrection, the coup attempt.")

Three Percenter Flag

Three Percenter Meme

Returning to the essential contradiction of the Oath Keepers, I ask about their attraction to active and former military and police officers, who claim patriotism and defense of the constitution. They even put themselves in positions where they will face-off and come into violent contact with police and military forces.

Jason says the former military who are attracted to the Oath Keepers are those who, as he puts it, "worked in the kitchen, who didn't see actual combat." Rhodes attracts those who feel alienated, may want to bolster their sense of masculinity and offers them the opportunity to "be part of the solutions. They find disenfranchised people and give them something to live for." Not all Oath Keepers are lost military vets, however. Special Forces would do trainings, "but those people realized quickly what Stewart was really like and they didn't want to be associated, didn't like the optics."

Many anti-government extremists believe the government is out to get them. Jason references Jade Helm 15, an Army Special Operations training exercise that conspiracy theorists turned into a plot to sweep through the Southwestern U.S., shred the constitution, and place Texas under martial law. Decommissioned Walmart's would be turned into concentration camps to contain the far right. Rumors gained fuel when Texas Governor Greg Abbott ordered the Texas State Guard to monitor it, prompting Texas Senator Ted Cruz to inquire at the Pentagon about its true purposes. Alex Jones, of course, was right in the middle giving the conspiracy theory legs.[102]

Jason experienced the allure. "I was training because I loved training. And if there is ever going to be some collapse, better to have these skills. I was never training to take down the government and I didn't think there was an imminent collapse, but it was fun and interesting skill sets to have. Society can be interesting with civic upheaval, natural disasters. Right now, a lot don't have drinking water in Montana. I was learning to hunt and fish, rappelling, it was a damn fun thing to do for me. I always wanted to live an adventurous life while young."

I think of all the ISIS guys I've interviewed, most who said they loved training with guns and heavy equipment, even if they were shocked that ISIS was drafting them to become actual warriors and disillusioned with the battles they ultimately fought. From militant jihadists to white supremacists, young men especially, seem to experience a deep excitement and sense of fulfillment playing warrior roles.

"It was fun training with the guys, although I'm not a big gun guy," Jason admits. "Stewart wanted me to have an assault rifle in my car at all times, 'All should be armed at all times!' But I had kids!"

A more personal look at the Oath Keeper leader is enlightening. Jason said Rhodes is dysfunctional in many ways. "He lived in my basement for eight months [after his divorce.] He'd take all our plates and leave them dirty in his car. He'd work out of his house in his underwear." I hear conflicting admiration on Jason's part, too. "He's an amazing sculptor. He'd make these beautiful sculptures for stage shows out of Styrofoam." Jason seems to have had a love/hate relationship with Rhodes.

Jason notes Rhodes was never a combat vet. "He was Army Airborne, injured in a parachute accident. He was discharged honorably. His missing eye—he shot out himself with a Derringer." And though he lost his law license, Jason says he would assure followers if there was trouble, "'We'll fund a defense. I'm a Yale educated attorney. I'll mount a defense for you'. But when [members] got arrested, those who participated in these callouts, he never did anything."

Rhodes also had plenty of fallouts with other extremists. He was "kicked out of Bundy Ranch." Jason says he returned to the ranch two to three weeks after the iconic showdown. There were false rumors that a drone strike may have been authorized. Rhodes swooped in and "pulled everyone back from the ranch, but the other militias saw that as turning tail and running, so they kicked him out. I think that had an effect on Stewart."

Jason says Rhodes would travel a lot to "get in front of cameras all the time." This kind of showboating caused rifts, including with the Proud Boys and Patriot Prayer (another anti-government extremist group that often includes the Proud Boys in its rallies.)[103] "Stewart was always showing up for pictures of himself with the riot shields, Kevlar, gloves, all looking like he was going down to brawl and engage with Antifa, but in truth, he was always behind the police line. But the Proud Boys were fighters. They didn't like that he was saying one thing and doing something else."

These various groups, including the Oath Keepers, fallout, crossover, merge and converge around key events and reinforce the violent racist and ethno-phobic messages of one another. Jason says these groups "are incompetent in some ways, but they are pulling this off. A small force has an effect, creating perception in the broader community and it inspires further action in people more squared away." He also thinks self-policing is on a decline. "More and more groups that would have kicked out the far-right are now embracing them." Indeed, white supremacist movements have learned over the years to tone down their rhetoric, lose their Nazi emblems and uniforms, and mainstream into society to gain more power and support for their ideas and ultimate goals.

While fringe ideas are being pushed toward the more mainstream, Jason warns the fringe may also serve to absorb society's most troubled elements. In a horrifying example, Jason tells me about an unwell couple who were kicked out of the Oath Keepers and proceeded to execute sheriff's deputies in Las Vegas, "and draped their bodies with a swastika and Don't Tread on Me Flag."

Jason finally hit his wall and decided he needed to get out. His turning point was in the local supermarket, the town's "gathering place." He finally blew up when he overheard three Oath Keepers openly denying the Holocaust. He has Jewish cousins and was raised in a very inclusive environment. "So, I said, 'You are just full of shit. If you really believe that something is wrong.'" Jason talked it over with his wife, worried they weren't going to be able to make ends meet, then he called Rhodes and said, "Look I'm done. I can't do it. I'm moving on. We are going to have to part ways."

Except it wasn't over. Rhode's wife kicked him out and he showed up at Jason's front door. "He had no other friends. I guess I considered him a friend, at least we had a rapport. You do create connections. He is a human being when not in front of a camera." As for his wife, "She was just done. She tried to get a restraining order. From her side he was very controlling and threatening physicality." Jason now indicates Rhodes may have some potentially serious mental health issues. "He would get very aggressive, threatening with the firearm he always had on him, threatening to kill himself, the family dog." Jason sensed Rhodes may also be bipolar.

Rhodes lived in Jason's basement for eight months while Jason was recovering from an injury. Rhodes said he would help with rent and medication for his wife. "So, I put up with him, but none of it worked out. So finally, I told him, 'Look dude, you've got to go.'"

Jason said Rhodes then couch surfed in Texas at about the time the alt-right and Roger Stone were connecting to the militias. Jason says Rhodes again saw opportunity. He wanted to be a rebel leader and here is Trump saying, "Stand back and stand by." Trump validated a lot of his members' beliefs and Jason believes "his administration [was] reaching out to the militias, I assume to make connections for something like January 6. At that point, Stewart really began to radicalize." The Oath Keepers began "courting the alt-right, [Robert] Spencer—the actual Nazis, Proud Boys. I just couldn't do it," Jason says. "I couldn't stay in."

Jason believes "they gave a blueprint" for government takeover. "Stewart mapped out how to create decentralized cells; how to network on social media; how to recruit" and "propaganda has normalized things. Seeing people in full fatigues, assault rifles, side arms and all their magazines. A person may think it's cos play [in-costume role playing] but it shifts into more of a real thing. If you keep going to protests and standoffs dressed for war, eventually war is going to break out."

He thinks we've just been very lucky so far. "So little bloodshed has actually happened. There has been potential for mass bloodshed," referring to the January 6 insurrection, which he believes was an attempted coup. "Unfortunately, luck runs out. Just being lucky is not a survival strategy."

In Jason's eyes, Rhodes was a smart and disorganized egomaniac who did not make a good leader, and he fears a better militia leader may pick up where Rhodes left off. "My worry is less Stewart. He's going to do time or reconsider things, but what's going to happen when a true believer, more dedicated comes along, and there's not just a dozen storming the capitol, but 200?"

Alex Jones is sinking under multimillion dollar defamation lawsuits for despicable claims that the Sandy Hook Elementary School shooting was a hoax, with the part of grieving parents played by "crisis actors." Rhodes and his leadership face prison. But "there will be another Alex Jones, and another Stewart," Jason warns.

Jason says he "feels bad about it all" and admits he got "swept up" in the movement. "I never brought a gun, but I did bring a keyboard, camera, and microphone and that, in the end, was a much more effective tool than a gun ever would be, because it hijacks critical thinking functions, changes perceptions. That's why I have been working against it now."

Jason testified before the House January 6 committee one month after this interview and he trained to become an EMT and fire fighter "to do some repentance after I left. I wanted to give back to the communities that had been intimidated by the militias that had been inspired by my writing." Clearly shamed, he has found that crossing back out of the echo chamber in which he had sequestered himself is breaking down walls he erected. When training as a first responder, "a guy came up to me saying, 'Hey Jason, I'm Forest Service law enforcement. I've been watching you before you moved into the county.' I said, 'Let's get a beer,' and to his credit he did. He became my best friend in Montana." Jason had a similar experience with a trans woman who also became a family friend. "I realized, 'Oh shit, I had no idea what I was talking about.' If my friend wants to spend time with my daughters, I know this person is a good human being. A lot of it is ignorance...We have to work on making real human connections."

"There is this twisted thing in the subconscious," Jason warns. "We as a species are hard-wired for storytelling, every night sitting around the fire. Stories become our myths, our religions. It has real tangible cultural effects...We need to really figure things out with the best storytellers we have." As for solutions, "Best thing I've been able to come up with is we have to re-weaponize for the good side...We have to look at our most successful storytellers in mass media. I'm a big *Star Treks* fan and sci-fi, *Strange New Worlds*. They hit topics so relevant to what we are doing now and really tackling issues and planting these seeds. It sprouts into new ways of thinking. Shootings breed more shootings."

I couldn't agree more. Stories are the most powerful form of how we learn. Some stories, repeated enough, are dangerous; and some are redemptive. And to leave a hate group, it's crucial for extremists to have some way of seeing themselves in a redemptive story, with value, hope, and the possibility of connection to and rehabilitation in the eyes of others. Otherwise, the journey out can be psychologically way too hard to accomplish. Jason notes, "The unintended effects of cancel culture are believing once you are blacklisted it's over, but that's not true. You can still change. For those who have plugged in to these groups, we need to have an exit ramp."

Jason found his exit ramp. With the help of "a good-hearted journalist and an expert on right wing extremism," who "saw my personal moral challenges with this stuff" and confronted him. "He encouraged me to do that critical thinking and that influence was critical for me to forge my own path." Having someone see his potential helped Jason reimagine himself, not as the failed journalist turned right-wing propagandist, but as someone who could use his intellect and creativity to rebuild and do something good. In sociology, this is called the "looking glass self" phenomena, the way we see ourselves in the eyes of others.[104]

Jason returned to writing. "Now, the stories I write weave in social issues that may spur conversations. Absolutely I'm sorry and I'm working to counteract the influence I had." Jason moved back to Colorado and runs the *The Colorado Switchblade*, a counterculture magazine covering Colorado culture, arts and music, and featuring editorials and news coverage. And he is writing a book about his time in the Oath Keepers—perhaps the unexpected insider story he had always hoped to write.

You can watch Jason tell his story at www.EscapeHate.org

Chapter 7 - The Human Behind the Hate

At the heart of every one of these Domestic Violent Extremist groups is the individual. Throughout my DVE interviews thus far, I've sought to go deeper and learn what lies behind why people join hate groups; their grievances, their indoctrination into hate, how they come to believe violence is heroic, and why they choose to engage in hate crimes. (Also important is the need to better understand why and how extremists leave their hate group and ideologies, discussed later in this book.)

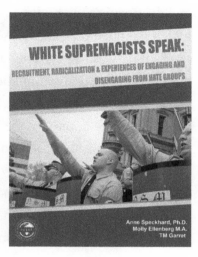

ICSVE's Report

Who is the human behind the hate? From personal vulnerabilities and motivations for joining, to influences and recruitment strategies, our *Escape Hate* study, focused on data from my first 50 DVE interviews, offers important patterns and we examine some of them here.[105] And of course I think it is important to hear directly from many of the former violent extremists.

Vulnerabilities

Vulnerabilities include life-course variables such as experiences with different types of abuse, histories of criminality and drug use, economic hardship, experiences with unemployment and poverty. The subjects of our study had many vulnerabilities for joining. Family traumas loomed large—from broken homes and substance abuse to familial violence and abuse, as well as traumas experienced outside the family.

Traumatic Childhood & Family Violence

Our sample had a much higher level of adverse childhood experiences than is expected in the general population. Family conflict and dysfunction in childhood was self-reported by 26 interviewees, which included physical abuse reported by 19 interviewees. As a result, our sample was more vulnerable to groups that provided the expectation of belonging or familial relations.

Former Volksfront leader, Brad Galloway recalls, "I felt like I was kind of the outcast in the family. They painted it on me, so I am going to act like, 'why should I care, if they don't?' I guess the street and the people I knew became my second family." Chris Knack, formerly of the far-right National Democratic Party of Germany, also expressed a feeling of rejection by his family. At age 13, he got into trouble at school for drawing a swastika, a crime in Germany for which he could have been charged had he been 14 years old instead of 13. His mother kicked him out of the house and sent to him to live with the father he hadn't seen in 10 years. Chris recalls feeling glad to be reunited with his father, but it didn't last long. His father hadn't paid child support for other children, was arrested and sent to prison just two months after Chris went to live with him.

Volksfront Logo

Essentially abandoned, he lived with his father's girlfriend.

Substance Abuse

Twenty-three interviewees said someone in their household during their upbringing struggled with substance abuse, a vulnerability which is one of the empirically derived Adverse Childhood Experiences [ACEs] which predicts a slew of mental and physical health outcomes.[106] Twenty-eight interviewees struggled with their own substance abuse. Drugs of choice included marijuana (13), methamphetamine (7), cocaine

(7), unspecified (7), unspecified pills (5), heroin (1), mushrooms (1), and 20 reported abusing alcohol. Many of those who abused substances seemed to be trying to self-medicate deep psychological pain and posttraumatic stressors.

Jonathan Strayn (Aryan Brotherhood) used heroin. He said, "It did everything that nothing else could do. It took everything away. It took all my feelings that I ever had and put them by the wayside and let me experience a sort of calm in the midst of a storm." The opposite is true for those abusing methamphetamine who reported often being extremely violent during days awake and hyped up. Those drinking in groups often ended up seeking out street fights or attacking members of minority groups.

Trauma

Twenty-five interviewees named specific traumatic events they believed contributed to their later membership in a hate group. Trauma comes in many forms. Timothy Zaal (Hammerskins and White Aryan Resistance) says his dysfunctional family dynamic was exacerbated when his older brother was shot by a Black man—triggering an outpouring of racism at home. "I don't like to blame, but looking longitudinally, no wonder. I would have gotten involved with something else if not this [violent extremism]. By his late teens, the drinking and drug use were becoming life-threatening. "By 21, I had hepatitis. I was drinking like a fish. I already had several DWIs. I was imploding."

Hammerskins Logo

Janet Louise (a pseudonym), who describes herself as a non-active current member of the National Socialist Movement, NSM, shared her trauma story. A straight-A student in high school, when she was 16, "a trusted friend of mine gave me some alcohol and took

me home and took advantage of me
and raped me. And from there, my
grades and life and depression and
anger plummeted, and I became full
of rage and anger and anxiety." The
trauma also created a pathway toward
hate. Her rapist was Hispanic. "I just

National Socialist Movement Logo

despised all Hispanic men…and believed that's all that they stood
for was rape and cheating and beating." Joining NSM, "I wanted
protection and acceptance and loyalty and respect, and I received all
of that."

Romey Austin Mons (Arkansas-based prison gang White
Aryan Resistance) faced a very different kind of traumatic experience,
a diagnosis of leukemia at age 13. "I just watched my grandma die of
cancer. When I got diagnosed, I told my mom, 'I want to die on my
couch. I don't want to go through what my grandma did.'" The disease
also stole his identity and purpose. He'd always dreamed of being an
Air Force pilot. "I would write the governor all the time with my report
cards, I wanted to go to the Air Force Academy. I lost all hope with [the]
leukemia diagnosis. They wouldn't take me. I felt like a ghost."

Motivations for Joining

Motivations range from the tangible (e.g., employment) to the
emotional/psychological (e.g., desire to fight for a noble cause.) Two
reasons for joining a hate group stood out among our 50 interviewees
and notably, hate was not among them. Evenly tied was the desire to
belong and the sense of dignity and positive identity that conveys (32
interviewees), and a sense of significance (32 interviewees).

Belonging

Scott Shepherd (KKK and NSM) recalls, "I went to one of their
rallies in Mississippi. They put that [arm] around me, 'We'll take you in

and take care of you. You had a bad life. We'll
take care of you.' And they did." Red (a
pseudonym, NSM) concurs, "Growing up
in [a] shit household, I needed a place to
belong, that family aspect, to be better than
what I was." Recall Chris Knack (German
National Democratic Party), who dealt with
a deep sense of rejection by his mother. His
far-right hate group gave him "a lot of
friendship and family; you could talk with
them about everything, and they were

German National Democratic
Party Logo

going to help you." Jonathan Strayn (Aryan Brotherhood) also says the
feeling of family "was the driving force, belonging when I didn't feel
like I belonged in a family." Skinhead Jason Downard, "It was just a
comfort thing; somewhere to belong. I was always trying to try to figure
out where I belong. I was always alone growing up." And Lukas Bals
(Die Rechte, a far-right German group) articulates it this way, "The
reason why I stayed so long—they gave me a reason, an identity…My
comrades are my friends, we have the same enemy…I like it, being told
I have worth: 'Lukas, you are worthy, you are worthy by birth.' I didn't
have to do something first. I'm just German."

Recruiters understand this power of belonging. Before they offer
up hateful ideology, they first offer care and acceptance and community.

Fred Cook (NSM) was assaulted at age 15 by "11 to 13 Black
guys." Traumatized, he approached a man who had been trying to recruit
him into his skinhead gang. As Fred recalls, the 19-year-old recruiter
told him, "Don't worry, we'll walk you to and from school, you just
have to be there for us when we need you." Fred says, "You didn't feel
like they wanted anything in return, just looking out for white people,
nothing else." Later, when he moved to North Carolina and didn't know
anyone, he found NSM online. "I messaged the leader, and he said come
to a barbeque in Georgia. Everyone was hugging me, 'What's up? Who

are you?' It was one of those connections. I didn't have any identity, so I made my identity the white nationalists."

Romey Austin Muns (White Aryan Resistance) was in prison for armed robbery while using methamphetamines. He was approached by a recruiter for the prison gang, Aryan Brotherhood. As he tells it, "White guy came up to me, 'I'm so and so, I see you are new here and you have heart. I'm an Aryan. We've been watching you. Do you want to prospect?' I said, 'No, I'm good, I don't want to join a gang.' He said, 'We're not a gang. We're a family. We fight together, we eat together. It's for the kids, the white race.'"

Jared Mickelberg joined the Aryan Brotherhood in prison and after he got out, the local branch "brought me into the little group, helped me out with a place to live," but with a criminal twist. In exchange for drugs, "any time I needed help, any time I found a place to rob, they were all in. Later, I basically became a hired hand. If there was a job to do they called me—kicking in doors, putting people on the ground, running up to a house, anything with guns, jewelry, and medicine cabinets. We could run through a house in four minutes and clean it out."

Significance

Equally as impactful as the desire to belong was the desire for significance, to feel important and to matter. As former KKK member, Benji McDowell, clearly states, "To me, it was a sense of royalty, being a white man and proud."

Each of these former NSM members share similar feelings. Acacia Dietz says running NSM's social media propaganda gave her "a sense of purpose, doing something good, using the skill sets that I had...Nobody could do it, and I'd say, 'look what I can do.'" Similarly, Janet Louise, whose academic trajectory was derailed by a high school rape, was proud to become an NSM radio host: "The radio show, and being a coordinator, planner, organizer, and everything, and almost a sergeant at this point, I felt pretty good. Pretty responsible, and like I could be entrusted with all these kinds of responsibilities, so I kind of left my past behind and started looking into the future at this point."

Greg Howell (skinhead) was primed as a child to believe violent action granted significance and his father reinforced it. He remembers playing football in the backyard and one of his father's friends got too rough. "I got angry. I was a little skinny kid. I went after him with a rake. My dad turned to him, 'I told you, he's not afraid of anybody, don't mess with him.'" Greg (KKK, not his real name) similarly describes his initial attraction as a bullied middle schooler. "Hoods on and fires—for kids, it comes off, like, powerful...I wasn't a hateful person. Coming from a kid who is insecure and very afraid, and gangster rap was popular. White kids were acting like that. Klan was a counterbalance to that. I was [looking for] anything powerful."

Noble Cause

The third most commonly reported motivation relates to that feeling of significance, but significance of the movement rather than of the individual. Joining "a noble cause" was cited by 17 interviewees. Of course, a great deal of overlap exists between individual and group purpose. Individuals join groups to serve a higher power be it their country, their heritage, even their God.

Red (NSM) says he liked the personal "feeling of power that I never had, confidence, holy shit. You felt you were part of something bigger than yourself, part of a revolution." In his journey up the ranks of the White Aryan Resistance, JJ Chivers says, "They don't attract extremists, but normal people who become extremists without even realizing it. I don't think I was an extremist going in when I first got with the skinheads. I'm not defending myself and my friends, it's my race, because this is a bigger problem. While I was in, I didn't think of it as extremism. To me, it was a noble cause."

Though skinheads are usually pagan, Raine (a pseudonym) combined the sense of power created by belonging to the National Alliance, a violent skinhead gang, even as she adhered to Christian Identity. "It was like we were put here, we are God's people" and that noble purpose, the white race, needed protection against dark forces, which the skinheads could provide.

Influences for Joining

Different from personal motivations are outside influences that encourage engagement with hate ideas, settings, and groups. Influences can be in-person such as parents, extended family, friends, speakers, recruiters; online such as chatrooms, encrypted communications, direct contact with recruiters, passive video viewing and other content on various social media platforms; and influences can be cultural such as books, clothing, history—and especially music. Eleven interviewees said their beliefs were influenced by listening to White Power music. Young men, who may not be attracted to older neo-Nazi and KKK groups, were drawn to the counterculture surrounding skinheads. Though skinhead music is not exclusively about the white power movement, it does draw young men into a wider culture that includes white supremacy.

Sean Gillespie used the white power music scene to help recruit for the Aryan Nations. "I burned CDs and handed them out at high schools. It was violent skinhead music—Skrewdriver, Midtown Boot Boys, very violent message like, 'destroy everyone that is not white.' They have songs like "Six Million More", "Coon Hunt." TM Garret, who wrote and performed music filled with violent hate lyrics, still finds his songs distributed over the internet to this day.

Brad Galloway (Canadian Volksfront) recalls bumping into a guy with a shaved head and bomber jacket, someone he'd hung out with back when he was a teen. They had a beer and "he started telling me about his new way of life and definitely trying to recruit me… telling me the woes of the world, Jews running the media, multiculturalism ruining

Toronto." Always searching for someplace to belong, he attended some meetings and "a couple of white power concerts. I was wearing [Doc Martens], adopted the skinhead subculture. The music was what I was really attracted to, violent metal."

Interviewees' descriptions of prevailing influences reflect distinct cultural settings over time and shed light on longstanding ingrained biases. While these factors may not have singularly pushed individuals into their hate groups, they made ideologies easier to swallow. Tony McAleer (Canadian skinhead) recalls meeting counterculture skinheads while living in England. "My coping was—befriend the bully, become the bully, because I was not big. They had the one thing I didn't have, that people feared them. They were tough...That false sense of power, the notoriety, and fear that created was intoxicating."

Whereas Tony and Brad were attracted to a counterculture movement, 13 of the study's subjects were moved to join their hate groups by what they say was history, sparked by white supremacist literature. The literature "offered access to esoteric knowledge" says Søren (NSM). "You feel like you are learning new truths that others don't know. Gave me something to believe in, gave me purpose and meaning. If you believe you are in a revolutionary struggle, it gives you something to fight for, to live for—lots of reading and books—especially when you are lonely and isolated. I learned a lot of terrible things, and things that are probably not true, but also learned new words, new points of view, so it was an intellectual adventure in a way. It was a chance for me to have something to be good at, to excel at."

Similarly, Keith Schneider, at age 56, had been reading and studying Nazism for decades and says he joined NSM "not so much out of hate" but a sense of self-made expertise. "I may know more than some historians and book writers on Nazism," he told me. That self-education was also a boon to his NSM status, and he eventually became the personal bodyguard to its leader, Jeff Schoep. Keith describes his feeling at the top of NSM: "Euphoria. I was on a very silent and very reserved power trip. I had full control of something becoming very vital. When the movement proclaimed me as a potential presidential candidate, I'm on top of the world looking down on creation."

In contrast, some of the interviewees, especially from the American South, felt joining a white supremacist group was simply not out of the ordinary but part of their culture. Jvonne shared this disturbing, early influence. She was just six years old when her father "had my mom sew a little Klan robe for me" and remembers being told she could no longer play with a friend who was Black. She remembers being exposed to extremist violence throughout her childhood. She saw her father "shooting someone's car up like a drive-by shooting. Another time [he] threw a Molotov cocktail through a white woman's window who had a Black baby. I saw curtains go up in flames. I was seven."

Veronica (pseudonym) became a skinhead when she was 14 years old. "My parents were Southern. It was heritage. Rebel flags. My dad was racist, so it was easy for me to transition into this." Scott Shepherd (Grand Dragon, Tennessee KKK) was blunt, "I was in the state of Mississippi in 1959, born in 1959, grew up in the '60s and '70s. I was surrounded by the Klan."

William Trull (NSM) expressed a distinction between what he perceived as real racism and what he experienced growing up in North Carolina. "I never considered myself a racist. I never hated anyone for the color of their skin. I had that instilled into me as a kid. My mom told me not to mix races—whites were better than them—but never to hate." His grandfather was in the Klan. "Most people were in the Klan. I played football in high school. Football deterred the hate away because the Blacks and Hispanics had my back on the field and off the field. I wore confederate flags to school but never hated anyone."

This type of influence is of course not exclusive to the southern U.S. Shaun Grimsley is a former member of the British West Midlands Infidels. "My dad was racist. He called Indians 'wogs' and 'crackies'."

Shaun recalls an incident in which his dad was pushed around at his mother's gravesite by some young Muslim men, "calling him white trash. I shouldn't have made the association with the color of their skin. [They] were just bad kids." In fact, Shaun later converted to Islam, but back then, "We regarded them as bacteria, cockroaches, something that wasn't human."

Recruitment

Just 10 years ago, most international terrorism experts would have said only face-to-face recruitment could compel a person to travel to Syria to join ISIS. Yet in ICSVE's sample of 273 ISIS men and women, we found 20 percent were recruited into the group solely through internet contacts.[107]

Older DVE interviewees who joined hate groups in decades past, engaged in message boards and telephone banks which have since been replaced by social media, websites, and encrypted apps. Though leafletting remains a surprisingly common devise to recruit (and terrorize), everyone agrees internet recruiting is today's primary vehicle and it's highly effective. YouTube, Snapchat, Tik Tok, Instagram, Facebook use algorithms to generate posts and videos that engage, confirm, echo, and reinforce messaging, including hateful propaganda. Encrypted sites add to the security of personalized attention and offer more platforms now that mainstream social media is attempting to bar some extremism.

Whether militant jihadists, ISIS, QAnon conspiracists, or white supremacists in-the-making, we consistently find the internet plays a huge role in both recruitment and incitement to violence. As the ways we connect online increase, so does the intimacy and the ability of extremists to find impressionable people who will respond to sophisticated propaganda across states, countries, and continents. The lethal cocktail of international terrorism I've frequently written about pulls together a group, an ideology, and social support with the vulnerabilities of an individual, to create a potentially violent actor. This cocktail applies to homegrown domestic extremists as well.

TM Garret describes internet recruitment like this: "Kid falls into the rabbit hole and parents react with, 'I'm right, you're wrong.' On Telegram, they will take you by your hand and warn you that your teachers, parents, and friends will be against you: 'They are your enemies. They will tell you that you're wrong, we're right.' Then this is exactly what happens with all these authority figures freaking out saying, 'Why are you doing this? Don't you know this is wrong?' And this confirms that the recruiter is right." ISIS does the same thing although they couch their warnings about parents and teachers in religious terms, warning the "true believer" to not be dissuaded by family members but to stay true on the path of Islam—*takfir* Islam that is—the distorted ISIS version that allows for killing other Muslims and a plethora of other crimes.

Of course, in-person efforts remain highly effective. Sixteen DVE interviewees were drawn into their hate groups through face-to-face recruiting and 14 recruited new members face-to-face. William Trull (NSM) remains proud of his accomplishments. "I got a recruitment award. I recruited 15 that year, more than anyone else." William recalls most of those he recruited were not dedicated racists at the time of recruitment.

While Jeff Schoep says he changed NSM rules and refused members under age 18, many groups actively prey upon minors. Many interviewees talk about targeted youth recruitment, with older members reaching out to and offering substitute "father" relationships as a means to bring youth from troubled homes into the movement. Not surprisingly, those recruited as youths can recall how powerful that sense of family and belonging was in their decision to join these extremist groups.

While leafleting may seem old-fashioned in the age of the internet, many explained provocative leaflets left in primarily Jewish neighborhoods often got press attention, even nationally televised press, with a group's insignia and contact details shown on camera, resulting in new recruits reaching out. Likewise, putting leaflets in mixed-race areas with racial tension appealed to whites living in these areas, and generated responses. Søren (NSM) recalls, "They'd throw flyers in people's driveways to recruit and to make a news story."

Roles in the Group

In a hate group, as in any organization, everyone has a role. Our interviewees were event planners, recruiters, propaganda specialists, security details, fighters, internet and media specialists, ideologues, public speakers, and leaders. While 20 interviewees specified that they held rank-and-file roles, it is notable that our sample included a disproportionately large number of group leaders (22) of which nine were speakers and ideologues.

Propaganda also plays an important role and 15 interviewees reported acting as propagandists in a variety of roles. Alt-right leader Brian (a pseudonym) recalls an event he organized around themes of discrimination against white people and white history being torn apart by slavery "which all people throughout history did. You wouldn't tear down the Mayan pyramids because of human sacrifice and slavery."

Though Acacia Dietz (NSM) says she didn't buy into the whole ideology and "never intended to be in the propaganda role" she took over their social media, graphic design, and video after their media director quit. For her it was about "compartmentalization." She bought into some of the propaganda, even as she was spreading all of it. Then as Facebook and other mainstream social media platforms' takedown policies started to be implemented, one of her responsibilities was to find ways to disguise and downplay anything that would result in removal, to keep the group's recruiting and propaganda presence.

TM Garret translated hate literature into German and started his own KKK group in Germany. Another German, Lukas Bals (Die Rechte) generated free propaganda through large events that would garner news coverage and attract new members. He says he organized concerts and demonstrations and would speak publicly, otherwise, "the people become bored. You have to do these things, provocation, have something to offer to the people in the far-right, so that they can do something on the weekend."

When it comes to the human behind the hate, the blanket presumption of hate as prime motivator clearly oversimplifies and undercuts efforts to counter these groups and rehabilitate former members. ICSVE offers readers the opportunity to hear directly from former violent extremists via the counter narrative videos we create. These videos can be found on our ICSVE YouTube Escape Hate playlist and at www.EscapeHate.org.

Chapter 8 - Hate Etched on My Face

Perhaps no domestic extremist I've interviewed for this study embodies the human tragedy behind the hate more than Klayton Bindon. I've heard a lot of terrible childhood stories during the hundreds of interviews I've conducted with violent extremists, both foreign and domestic. But his story is truly one tragedy after another. The painful world of Klayton Bindon is hard to miss—it's literally etched into his face.

The name of his former prison hate group, Aryan Nation Skins, is tattooed in big black letters from ear to ear, completely covering his cheeks and chin. Large swastikas are tattooed onto either temple, another even larger swastika covers his throat. This 26-year-old would otherwise be good-looking, with sandy blonde hair, green eyes, and a nice smile. Instead, he looks bizarre and permanently disfigured by hate.

As we begin our Zoom interview, Klayton is sitting on the edge of a double bed. He appears anxious as he talks, his mannerisms nervous, and he fidgets around. I'm momentarily caught off guard when his girlfriend suddenly pushes back the covers and sits up beside him, pushing her long hair to the side and rubbing the sleep from her face to see what's going on, before laying back down and throwing the covers back over herself. Maybe it's the time change? Klayton is in New Zealand. I want to laugh but this subject is serious.

Klayton has been told that sometime between his first six months and a year "someone found me at my birth mother's house covered in shit in the corner." He was informally fostered by a woman Klayton describes as a gangster. When this woman whom he refers to as his "gangster mother" was arrested, she was unable to get out of her sentence "as she had expected. She was dealing drugs and was in 12 years, so she passed me off to her friends." Her friends were addicts and criminals.

I am amazed to hear a little child could be passed among a myriad of offenders for years on end without the juvenile protection system noticing, but here is living proof. Somehow, Klayton remained unknown to child protective services throughout his entire childhood. It's no surprise he would wind up in prison and in a notorious prison hate gang by age 20.

"Did your 'gangster mother' care about you?" I ask, still easing into the interview and careful to use Klayton's words when asking about the people in his early life. We are definitely in painful territory.

"She cared in her own way. Breeding animals was her addiction. She bred them and had 150 pets. She sold drugs [to pay for their expenses]."

"Would you say any of your homes were happy?" I ask, as I try to make sense of what can only be described as a disastrous childhood from day one. Even though I sense the answer is likely no, perhaps the 'gangster mom' with all her animals was loving. Instead, his story gets worse.

"I was sexually abused quite a lot with my foster parents, by both males and females," Klayton answers matter-of-factly. Most people don't admit to sexual abuse so readily, but Klayton seems to have open boundaries or perhaps, no boundaries, and a somewhat childlike manner, which would make sense with an upbringing like his.

"So, it was confusing growing up?" I ask gently.

"Yes," he answers, and then goes on to tell me he had girlfriends and worked small jobs as a teenager. "I was in one foster home for seven years. They were good."

"This was an unofficially arranged foster home?" I confirm.

"Yes," again with little emotion.

I'm wondering if he even attended school with this kind of upheaval. "How did you do in school?" I ask him.

"I was the class clown" and that I can see clearly, despite the tattoos and nervousness. He's got a goofy presence and the pictures sent

my way before our interview, by my colleague TM Garret who arranged
it, included one of Klayton clowning in a hat and showing off his tattoos
in a making-fun-of-himself sort of way.

"I did okay, not too bad," he continues. "I didn't have to try
in school," indicating he was a smart kid and adds, "I took drugs as a
child and teen." Despite the odds, he finished high school. "At one point
everyone went off to do university, but I carried on partying. Then my
friends were carrying on with schooling and I wished I had."

Klayton's birth parents promoted white supremacism in New
Zealand before he was born. "My old man tried to start white power."
Apparently, they were prominent. "I finally met my birth mother when I
was 15."

"Why did you look up your birth mother at age 15?"

"I had run away from my foster home to my gangster mother and
we were in the car. There was a woman there and she asked me, 'Do you
want to meet your mother?' She was there standing in front of the car.
She was crying and shaking. I got her phone number, and it went from
there."

The reunion was definitely fraught, as it led to Klayton's arrest
just one year later, and his descent into the white supremacy imprinted
on his face. Klayton explains, on the way to get pizza with friends, he
realized his mom lived down a nearby side street, so they decided to stop
by to say hello. "Her partner told me to leave. He had a baseball bat and
attacked me, but I turned it around on him. I went to prison. He lost his
leg after bone grafts."

Klayton sounds innocent in the telling, but he'd have to have
been either drugged or a brutal fighter to have pulped someone's leg so
badly it needed to be amputated.

He was sent to prison and became a member of the Aryan Nation
Skins. "That's where I got these tattoos on my face."

The Aryan Nation Skins is a violent skinhead prison gang local
to New Zealand although there are similar prison gangs bearing similar

names and ideologies in the U.S. Trying to decide which aspect of his compelling story to explore first, I ask him how he wound up joining this ruthless prison gang. Klayton says he was a drug addict and weighed about 99 pounds. "The prison was full of gangsters. I saw that as soon as I got to the gate. Convicted murderers, full face and body tats of all the gangs. They [the Aryan Nations Skins] said they were going to take all my food off me, beat me, unless I joined them. I asked the prison authorities for segregation but was denied. I got tired of getting beat up, so I joined," Klayton concludes, still emotionless.

"How do you get tattoos in prison?" I ask, naively not realizing that for years, inmates have been devising jailhouse techniques for demarcating one another as members of various gangs and to convey coded messages about origin and criminal acts. Most prisons prohibit tattooing but that doesn't stop prisoners from applying their own creative and risky methods.

"Getting a tattoo in prison?" Klayton laughs at my lack of knowledge. "You break down a stereo, get some soot…"

Improvised tattoo tools are made from mechanical pencils, magnets, radio transistors, staples, paper clips, and guitar strings. Ink can be derived from pens, melted plastic, soot mixed with shampoo, and melted Styrofoam. A *Vice* report describes inmates who created an improvised tattooing machine using the motor of an electric toothbrush and the coiled spring from inside a pen.[108] Prison tattooing is not without serious risks, of course, given the contaminated needles and inks, and lack of proper equipment and sterile environments. Severe infections can result, as can the spread of diseases like Hepatitis C and HIV.

"They did my throat and face in one sitting. It took nine hours and was pretty intense. They did the chest the day before."

White supremacist tattoos are endless in variety, beyond the ever-present swastika. Words like "Skinhead" "Aryan" "White Power" are commonly tattooed, as are group-affiliated tattoos with abbreviations and logos. Symbols include SS lightning bolts which are sometimes an indication of having carried out an assigned assault on other races; there are SS skull heads, three interlocking triangles called Valknuts or Odin's symbol, a white fist for white power, the letters SWP for Supreme White Power, and 100% indicating racial purity. The number 14 refers to the "14 Words", the popular white supremacy creed, "We must secure the existence of our people and a future for white children." 1488 is the 14 Words plus the eighth letter of the alphabet repeated, HH for "Heil Hitler". 1483 is the 14 Words with 83 altered by Christian Identity members to signify "Hail Christ".

Some prison groups, like the one Klayton joined, pushed him into being marked as a member. Often illicit prison tattoos are done in exchange for food, stamps, cigarettes, phone time, canteen items, or other favors. "Did you want to join them at that point, when you tattooed yourself?" I ask, wondering if he was going along for protection or had begun to take on their ideology of hate.

"I was looking for a family," he answers honestly, admitting to his deep sense of vulnerability. "I felt like no matter what, they will be there for me if my mom died."

"Were they?" I ask gently.

"Sometimes yes," Klayton answers as he shakes his head no. "There was one man, Ryan, who really made me want to join. He said, 'I'm your mate. I'll look after you.' I felt love for him, and I wanted to give it back."

Remembering Klayton had been sexually abused by both men and women, making him more vulnerable to sexual exploitation, I ask if they were sexual partners in prison.

"There were, but not me," Klayton answers, unperturbed by the question. "I loved him like a brother." Later Klayton will further clarify that Ryan was in for life on murder charges and they were not lovers.

Knowing other white supremacists who went to prison were made even more vulnerable to prison radicalization when their families turned their backs on them, or were never there to begin with, I ask if his family stayed in touch with him while in prison.

"I spoke to my gangster mom every day. She gave me money," which I will learn his Aryan Nation brothers would extort.

Klayton served two years and seven months and during that time he started to buy into what was "going to be the ultimate statement, being loud and proud." Aryan Nation Skins required members to adhere to white supremacist views and follow the Odinist religion, a pagan tradition named after Odin, the chief god of Norse mythology.

Klayton Face Tattoos

Odinism, in its various interpretations, refers to the pre-Christian Norse gods and portrays the god Odin as the founder of the Germanic race. White supremacists the world over reconstruct pre-Christian European polytheism and mythology alongside Germanic, Norse, and Anglo-Saxon paganism, which they reclaim as the true religious roots of the white race. They reject Christianity as something that came later and was imposed from the outside. White supremacists who follow Odinism, for example, might denigrate the crucified Jesus as a "Jew hanging on a stick" and instead prefer gods and heroes that promote valor over humility.

Odinism also appeals to white supremacists because it credits white tribes, or *folk,* with building civilization and holding a strong ethic of individual responsibility, emphasizing a pure and genetic closeness, and mythologizes the virtues of early northern European whites seen as "deeply involved in a mystical relationship with nature, struggling heroically against the elements."[109] Courage, truth, honor, and self-reliance are highly valued in Odinist traditions.

Odinism was naturally also favored by the Nazi Third Reich, influencing even SS initiation rites. Decades later, Odinism influenced George Lincoln Rockwell's American Nazi Party, and an Australian Nazi sympathizer named Alexander Rud Mills is credited with having deeply influenced a key American Odinist, Else Christensen, who published *The Odinist* newsletter in the early 1970s.[110]

Asatrú (Icelandic for belief in the gods) is Odinism's closely related Icelandic interpretation and particularly interesting because it has been officially recognized as a religion in Iceland since 1972. While not all Asatrú followers are white supremacists, and their leaders have tried to step away from political links to their religion, Asatrú and Odinism both appeal to racists as they bind them together by recreating a sense of heroic white legend and myth.

In 1998, Asatrú leaders opened prison ministries in at least five states in the U.S., according to the Southern Poverty Law Center. These ministries, alongside other informally constituted groups following the Nordic religion, attracted hundreds of white supremacist prisoners to their ranks. Among them was violent white supremacist, ideologue, and author of the 14 Words, David Lane, a member of The Order. These Odinist groups adopted and proselytized a series of related beliefs. "The old gods and the old religion are ours and thus relate to our race-soul," David Lane wrote in praise of Odinism. "Through our myths and legends, we find a link to our past, and a rudder for our floundering race vessel."[111]

Klayton says they were drilled and quizzed every day about the teachings of Odin, Odinic Rite, and Valhalla ruled by Odin, the mythic place where some heroes who die in combat go in the afterlife. They also trained in Odinism's religious aspects of self-reliance and being in good physical shape. The gang routinely fought with and beat up minorities in prison. I assume Klayton took part, but it's my practice not to ask interviewees to incriminate themselves.

Looking back now, he says, "I was young and dumb." He says he was indoctrinated into the Aryan ethos. "Before, I was not a racist," he explains. "I've got Samoan family members. To me the word 'nigger' is an attitude. Anyone can be like that."

I ask him his opinion of the 2019 mosque shooting in Christchurch, New Zealand, in which white supremacist Brenton Tarrant live-streamed his massacre of 51 Muslims during prayer. [112] "I was in jail and thought it was absolutely disgusting. There's no reason to take innocent lives. It was unjustified. In prison some were happy and chanty, but not me."

Though he's now out of prison and out of the Aryan Nation Skins, Klayton says he still believes in some of the Aryan teachings: "'May your word be a bond of steel.' Some of it was racial, but a lot was just being honest, a genuine human being. 'Take no quarrels with your family.'"

"What was racist?" I ask.

"'Advance your folk.' 'Only believe in your God.' 'Alien Gods will destroy you.'"

Klayton deeply regrets the hate tattooed across his face. "I feel like an idiot to be honest. I can't walk down the street. People keep their kids away from me." He's in the process of getting them removed which is painful, time-consuming, and expensive. "People would attack me on the street, thinking I'd breed terror. Muslims…" and his eyes grow wide with fear. "People refuse to serve me in restaurants, dairies, supermarkets." He tells me he's scared all the time. "I hate looking over my shoulder. I just got ran off the road because of my facial tattoos."

It will take years to remove these visible marks of hate. Klayton is collecting donations to pay for treatments which has been a problem due to the tattoos he's trying to erase. "They see my swastikas; TikTok, they kicked me off. I had 5000 followers in a week." Klayton says strong shutdown policies and cancel culture impact people like him. "I just tried to start a GoFundMe page. Three thousand people said they'd help me but as soon as they see a swastika, I get kicked off TikTok."

I ask to see his tattoos more closely and he turns his face so I can read "Aryan Nation Skins" starting from his ear, crossing his entire cheek and chin, and connecting over the other cheek to his other ear. He has 12 swastikas on his body and he shows me the ones on his neck and temples. Later he sends me a picture of his body covered in tattoos.

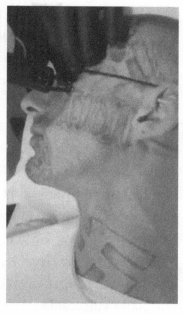

Klayton Tattoo Removal

Tattoo removal is vital for people like Klayton who literally cannot reenter society while wearing the permanent markings of their former white supremacist loyalties. From personal to professional, people immediately fear, judge, and hate them. As Shane Johnson, whose story you'll read, said to me, "Who would want this behind their counter, dealing with customers?"

Klayton was a roofer before going to prison and can't get employed now, so at age 23, he is on public benefits. He also still uses drugs "but less often. I use them for coping, to shut my brain from going all the time." With no hesitation or sense of shame, and clearly seeing his drug habit as necessary for survival, he tells me he will "self-medicate mostly once or twice a week." I'm neither surprised no one wants to hire him, nor that he has turned to drugs given his upbringing.

Apparently Klayton has sought help from a psychologist, "I suffer with posttraumatic disorder from mental abuse and sexual abuse. In the foster homes they would say I was worthless. 'Your mom and dad are no good. I'll make sure you never see them again.'"

"What are your symptoms of PTSD?"

"I'm profusely sweating just talking with you," Klayton answers, shaking his arms around as if to cool off. It's likely the hyperarousal of the childhood and prison memories is activating his sweat glands.

"How do you cope, apart from using?" I ask.

"I just have to deal with it. It's life. I'm angered easily. I struggle with my anger," another possible symptom of the hypervigilance often present with PTSD or anger modulation issues he grew up with. He says his partner helps a lot.

When I suggest meditation as a possible route, he tells me in prison they had a mindfulness session once a week—and he used it to grab a safe hour of sleep. His Aryan Nation "brothers" would routinely beat him up and warn him to stay awake and vigilant against other gang attacks so a safe place to snooze was precious. "I'd say, 'It's going to happen either way.' I had more worry about being punched over by the Skins than anyone else," Klayton admits. Maybe Klayton's low body weight when he first entered prison, likely from drug use, made him look especially vulnerable to the others. "They'd embarrass me in trainings and beat the shit out me. If they had gotten me on with love instead of intimidation, I'd still be there for them," Klayton also admits, pointing out the limits of loyalty that can be enforced with violence alone.

"Do they still contact you from prison?" I'm curious to know if the Aryan Nation Skins has the long reach beyond the prison walls that many terrorist and violent extremist groups do, especially if they have phones smuggled into the prisons.

"Yes," and adds, "They don't intimidate me anymore. Even when I was 45 kilos, I stood up at the end of it. Words hurt me more than punches."

Klayton gave up on white supremacism. With his face an unrelenting reminder of his past, I ask Klayton if white supremacists get doxxed in his part of the world by Antifa. Klayton says it doesn't happen in New Zealand and then begins to freak out entertaining that possibility. "If people put me or my partner in jeopardy, I'd be in jail for murder," reverting to his violent edge. "It frustrates me. They hate, you know what I mean? They are saying that's what we are doing, but it's a problem, too, but they don't see it." In his own way, he' making pretty clear that he's got a serious anger modulation issue himself and trying to explain the reciprocal radicalization that occurs between white supremacists and those who try to stop them using violence and other illegal or harmful methods. Indeed, when we analyzed our interviewees' experiences with doxxing, counter protests, and violence, we found little positive effect; and in many cases it helped bolster the white supremacist's narrative of being under attack and justifying their violence.

"Every life matters not just Black lives matter," Klayton says, repeating a put down to those who think black lives should be protected. Though I don't sense he means it that way.

Klayton's girlfriend is starting to stir, and he indicates he doesn't have much more time for our interview. So, I move onto asking if he'd be willing to appear in a counter narrative video and, if so, what advice he would give to those thinking about joining or already in a white supremacist group.

"One, don't do it," he says, jumping right in. "To start with, the brotherhood, what they try to sell you is not true. There are always other motives behind it. Money. They got me to extort my mother, and they beat me up." They promised to look after him upon his release, and instead, he says his gang disbanded and reorganized as the Skinhead Soldiers. "We had to take an oath for blood in or blood out. The only way of leaving is by death, but they all left me. They didn't follow their own rules." Klayton had expected he'd be a life member of a protective "family" gang, but now "I'm the only member with this on my face and I'm the small one! I got beaten every day. I felt like, what was all that for? I was devastated."

"You joined for survival, but they left the group right after you got the group's name tattooed on your face?" I ask, just to be sure I understood correctly.

"Yes, same guys," Klayton affirms. "Eat or be eaten."

When I ask if he has other guidance for those thinking about joining a gang, he advises to "reach out to anyone. Your family, your friends, look online for a helpline—people who will listen." He says, "The only place a gang is going to leave you is jail and death."

Then perking up momentarily from the sadness, he says he has a supportive partner and now that he's an adult, he's moved away from his gangster mother, "I'd end up back in prison otherwise." He has reached out to his biological father. "He hasn't replied. He's never been there for me." Then in a really unexpected twist, Klayton tells me his biological mother, who used to be a skinhead, is now an extremist Muslim on the national watch list. She married an ISIS fighter. She had also been in the mosque at the time of the Christchurch shooting. As Klayton unravels this part of his story, I try to keep up. "She's got a partner in New Zealand and is married to two other partners in Syria," he tells me. "She's a con artist. She's an attractive white woman in another country. They like her and send her money." So, nothing has really changed. His mother still finds any way that works to supply her lifestyle.

Klayton is aware of my years of work interviewing ISIS members and notes how he admires their fearlessness. "One thing I like about ISIS, this dude picks up a rocket launcher, no fear in him. But gang

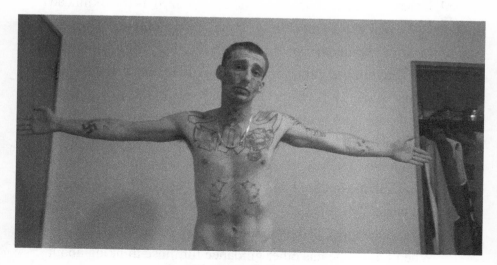

Klayton Body Tattoos

swastikas just cause more severe anxiety and more PTSD. And once I have this label it is so hard to take it off. I'm labeled with this for the rest of my life, from one bad decision." Though ISIS members don't tattoo themselves, they actually feel the same—their bad decisions label them for life and limit their futures, no matter how reformed they may be.

Again, referring to the Aryan Nation Skins' broken promises, Klayton says, "It's honestly terrible. I put everything into them. I put my whole life on the line for them and they just leave me. At the end of the day, I have nothing. I changed my whole life for them? What do I have from them? It is what it is." And Klayton breaks into tears.

I see his dog, probably sensing he is upset, come and nudge Klayton who reaches out to hug him. "Dogs are so comforting," I say.

"When I was homeless," Klayton tells me, "I had my own dog for four and a half years. He died while I was in prison," and he starts to cry again. "I suffer such bad anxiety. It's hard to leave the house. People try to pull me out of cars. It's ruined my whole life. Sometimes I feel like committing suicide."

As I begin to realize just how fragile Klayton is, I ask him if maybe it's not worth participating in our counter narrative project, that I don't want any harm to come to him from putting himself and his name out in one of our videos. Klayton protests as he insists, he wants to take part. "If one kid can see the pain, sweet, if I can change one person's life and stop them going down this road to bullshit."

We make Klayton's video, and I send it to him to be sure he's satisfied with it. He is, although he asks us to remove one detail about his birth mother and gangster mother, which we do because as he says, he can't afford to harm his relationship with either woman.

You can watch Klayton tell his story at www.EscapeHate.org

Chapter 9 - The ICSVE *Escape Hate* Study

Looking beyond these individual stories and motivations, our research also set out to examine the psychosocial profiles of current and former members of DVE groups, taking a lifespan, human development, and systems approach to understanding participation in hate groups. In this chapter we share our main findings.

The sample for this study is by necessity a convenience sample. Our sample includes current and former members of any white supremacist group who would speak to us in a video-recorded, in-depth, semi-structured psychological interview. Not only is it by its nature difficult to gain access to this population, even more so to obtain informed consent for an in-depth interview. Thus, random sampling was not possible.

We did attempt to obtain a representative sample in terms of men and women and a diverse sample of white supremacist groups and nationalities. Participants were recruited through a snowball system, and we are very grateful in particular to two former, high-ranking extremists, Jeff Schoep, former head of the National Socialists Movement, NSM, now with *Beyond Barriers*, and TM Garret, former KKK leader and now with ICSVE, for helping us find the majority of the interviewees. In the case of German interviewees who did not speak English well, TM, who was born in Germany, also skillfully and compassionately translated, often helpfully adding social and political context as well.

The interviews were coded for 375 variables and the study's results were analyzed and written up when we reached a sample of 50 interviews.[113] However, our research is ongoing and expanding the sample is a goal.

The 50 individuals in our study were at various stages of disengagement and deradicalization. Four were still relatively active in their hate groups at the time of our interview. Some had exited but remained committed at some level to their groups and ideologies, with a significant part of this sub-sample continuing to adhere to all, or parts, of their ideologies. For instance, Janet Louise (a pseudonym) claimed to have disengaged from NSM yet she proudly showed me her Third Reich Nazi flag and her copy of Hitler's *Mein Kampf.* Others had renounced their groups but acknowledged their difficulties in finding new beliefs and purpose in life. Many others had completely deradicalized and felt deep remorse for their hateful and violent actions and were trying to make amends where possible.

Study Process

I took all interviewees through a video-recorded informed consent process, in accordance with the American Psychological Association [APA] guidelines and United States legal standards. A strict human subjects' protocol was followed (approved by ICSVE's Internal Review Board) in which I introduced both myself and the project, including the risks and benefits of participation. Participants were warned to not incriminate themselves and to refrain from speaking about any crimes they had not already confessed to the authorities, and those still within the statute of limitations or otherwise prosecutable. Participants were informed they could opt out at any time, refuse to answer any and all questions, and could determine whatever level of confidentiality they wished in terms of the video recording and write up of their interview.

With one exception, each interviewee was also invited to take part in ICSVE's *Escape Hate Counter Narrative Project* by giving permission for their videotaped interview to be edited into a short counter narrative video message against joining extremist groups. Because denouncing their hate group posed a risk of harm from current group members, those who judged it a significant risk either asked for their faces to be blurred, their location withheld, or a pseudonym to be used (or they chose to not participate.) Nearly everyone agreed to appear in the *Escape Hate Counter Narrative Project.* In one case, the interviewee was not asked to participate because he could not credibly denounce his group. In another, a woman admitted to still being ideologically indoctrinated though currently disengaged from the group and spoke about the downsides of being in it rather than a full denunciation.

Interviews have a shared structure, and each lasted between one and a half to two hours. Each interview began with a brief history of the interviewee, focused on family, early childhood and upbringing, and covered life experiences prior to becoming interested in their hate group or far-right ideology more broadly. Demographic details were gleaned, as were vulnerabilities that may have impacted the individual's choice to join, including familial conflict, violence, physical and sexual abuse, divorce, health problems, school problems, bullying, substance abuse, etc.

Questions then turned to how the individual was introduced to the hate ideology and hate group and how they were influenced to join. I explored the various motivations for joining and obtained a detailed recruitment history that included how the individual interacted with their group prior to joining; whether recruitment took place in person or over the internet, or both; and intake and initiation procedures for the group. Many questions focused on what the individual's needs were at the time and what he or she expected to gain and actually gained by joining. The interview then turned to the interviewee's experiences in the group such as roles held, whether they attended events such as protests or rallies, and whether they ever witnessed, participated in, or were victims of violence (again with the warning to not self-incriminate.)

Finally, interviewees were asked about changes in orientation toward the group, including any sources of disillusionment with the group, its violence, or its ideology. At the very end of the interview, those willing to appear in a counter narrative video were invited to say anything they wished to denounce their former groups and give advice or warnings to anyone thinking about joining an extremist group. Many became very enthused at this moment and spoke from the heart about how harmful being in a hate group had been for them and how they now suffered guilt and trauma over their involvement; adding they feared the consequences of being doxxed, or otherwise discovered for their past violence.

While some interviewees avoided certain questions, I believe most were forthright and honest, including speaking about often painful circumstances growing up, and participating in violence. Because I have been conducting in-depth psychological interviews for decades, and specialize in violent extremism, I am comfortable dealing with traumatic material and find I am able to quickly build rapport in the interview setting. I often find subjects want to talk about their traumas but are terrified to do so, and if I am gently supportive, they gain a lot from carefully going through the traumatic circumstances of their life trajectories and seeing connections. The subjects shared a great deal of personal information, sometimes openly weeping, other times temporarily shutting down then returning later to address a particularly painful subject. I slowed down and digressed as needed when emotionally fraught topics became temporarily overwhelming.

While I cannot say I was entirely shocked, it was surprising to learn just how many of these individuals had traumatic childhoods. In fact, that the interviews often touched on highly traumatic material and probed deeply into painful events made it clear to me I needed to be present as a trauma expert and offer support for them to be able to continue speaking about these painful issues, which I always gently did.

Although I always made clear it was not a therapeutic intervention and the interview was for research purposes, many of the interviewees said they found the interview experience therapeutic, some even writing about subsequent and even profound growth from the insights they had gained during our time. For example, Greg (name changed), whose story is told in Chapter 15, wrote to tell me he was renouncing his membership in the KKK for what he said was his final time.

Everyone seemed very appreciative of having the time to review their lives in a nonjudgmental environment; to think through what had gotten them in and then out of extremism; and what they still need to escape the hate they had come to embrace. I offered to be available after the interview for anyone who wanted to continue the discussion. They thanked me and likewise, I am grateful for their time and the candidness with which they approached our time together for ICSVE's *Escape Hate* ongoing study.

ICSVE's research projects are a team effort. While I am the interviewer for ICSVE's extremist and terrorist interviews, TM Garret helped to identify and invite many of the sample participants, and he, with my help and Zack Baddorf, produced the counter narrative videos. Molly Ellenberg launched our counter narrative video campaign on Facebook as we continue to study and modify it for impact. Molly coded every interview on the 375 variables identified ahead of time by our team and carried out all statistical analysis. The analysis represents her work as well as my own, and together we have produced many academic articles presenting this research in greater detail. [114]

Demographics

Our sample of domestic extremists analyzed here includes 40 men, eight women, one trans woman, and one person who identified as non-binary. Thirty-six of the interviewees are American, five are Canadian, five are German, three are British, and one is from New Zealand. Current ages range from 24 to 70; they joined their groups at very different ages and years—between ages 5 to 56, and between 1978-2020.

Table 1. Demographic Details

Variable	Minimum	Maximum	Mean	Standard Deviation
Age when joined	5	56	21.80	10.001
Age when left	18	62	31.21	8.862
Age at interview	24	70	40.02	10.191
Yrs. of Education	7	16	13.28	1.556
Social and Economic Status in Childhood	20.0% working class; 74.0% middle class; 4.0% upper class			
Marital Status Prior to Joining	74.0% single, never married; 12.0% married; 12.0% divorced			
Current Marital Status	34.0% single, never married; 36.0% married; 26.0% divorced; 2.0% separated			
Sexual orientation	92.0% heterosexual; 8.0% LGBTQ			

Many reported being raised by a single parent working in blue-collar jobs or underemployed. After joining their hate group, 16 people got married once and six got married twice; 13 got divorced once and one got divorced twice.

Women comprised 18 percent of the sample, likely representative of women's far lower level of involvement in hate groups. Likewise, most of the respondents noted their groups were led by and made up primarily of men.

Ideologies

The ICSVE study includes interviews with white extremists who were members of a wide spectrum of groups and movements, including: Aryan Nations, Aryan Brotherhood, Christian Identity, Creativity Movement, English Defense League, National Socialist Movement (NSM), Oath Keepers, Proud Boys, Ku Klux Klan (KKK), various skinhead groups, Volksfront, and an organizer of the Unite the Right rally in Charlottesville.

Though diverse, today's white supremacist groups can be said to fit into three broad ideological categories: political, religious, and youth subculture.[115]

Political Ideologies

The political groups are authoritarian and militaristic, with strict hierarchies and strong, charismatic leaders at their helms. These groups laud what they might call "traditional values" and narrow definitions of national identity with ideologies largely fascist and neo-Nazi. Racial-ethnic nationalism is a means to define in and out groups, and the latter are demonized and scapegoated in order to strengthen the in-group's sense of unity and pursuit of power.

Political white extremist groups often stay inside the law and are especially dangerous for how they can legitimize and mainstream their virulent ideology by running for elected office and holding legally sanctioned events which serve to threaten their defined out-groups. They also use the media, for instance, by holding rallies to garner press for the hate they engender and to help recruitment. Some political white extremist groups include the NSM, Unite the Right, Proud Boys and Volksfront. Paramilitaries also fit into this group such as Oath Keepers and III Percenters (aka 3 Percenters) and Kerry Noble's paramilitary group, the Covenant Sword and the Arm of the Lord (CSA).

The "Great Replacement Theory" has been cited in some of the worst DVE attacks. May 2022 in Buffalo, New York a shooter massacred 10 people in a grocery store in a primarily Black neighborhood. The 18-year-old gunman's 180-page screed fixated on the false claims that America's whites are being "replaced" as part of an elaborate Jewish conspiracy.[116] Likewise, the perpetrator of the August 2019 massacre at a Walmart in El Paso, Texas, that killed 23 and wounded another 23, the deadliest attack against Latinos in modern U.S. history, cited the Great Replacement Theory,[117] as did the New Zealand terrorists who murdered 51 people and injured 40 in the Christchurch mosque.[118]

Religious Ideologies

Like militant jihadists, white supremacy based on religious ideology can chillingly lead members to believe their violent actions against others are divinely sanctioned. Christian Identity, followed by many KKK groups, for example, holds white Aryan Christians as God's chosen people; defines Jews as the spawn of the devil and the primary enemy of white people and humanity itself; while minorities are subhuman over which whites have dominion. Jews, likened to the Garden of Eden's serpent itself, constantly use trickery to replace whites with people of color, the "white genocide" feared by white extremists. This ideology expands to the "Great Replacement Theory."

The Creativity Movement and its offshoots are another religious strain of white extremism; however, it considers Christianity to be a religion polluted by Judaism. The Creativity Movement's sacred texts put whites first, stating "spirituality is expressed through nature as the collective will of the white race," and "what is good for the white race is the highest virtue; what is bad for the white race is the ultimate sin."

Youth Subculture

Finally, there is a strong youth subculture among white extremists tied to the white power music scene, a subsection of the skinhead scene, which developed in the 1960s among British working-class youth as an apolitical subculture. These groups hold a general white supremacist ideology similar more to the political hate groups than the religious (though not always.) These groups are tied together through music, hard partying with plenty of alcohol and drugs, shared dress and symbols, and often engage in street fighting. All of which creates a sense of belonging, bonding, and brotherhood.

Skinhead attire often includes Doc Martens boots in which racists use white laces to signify "white power" or red laces to distinguish themselves from other wearers of the trendy footwear. For insiders, red bootlaces indicate the wearer has shed blood for the racist skinhead movement. Racist skinheads will often randomly attack non-whites to "earn" their red laces.

Some hate groups look down upon the skinheads as akin to Hitler's Brownshirts (Stormtroopers), riff raff which can be liquidated in the end.

Gender

DVE, like most terrorism around the world, is male-dominated and at times a highly misogynistic phenomenon which includes women in a range of subservient and support roles, often venerated as "breeders" of white offspring. Women are often told their job for the movement is to stay home, support their men, and have more white children. In some cases, primarily in street and prison gang-like groups, women were reported to be badly treated and passed around between men for sexual exploitation.

Few female leaders are permitted, except where women lead ladies' auxiliaries as in the KKK. A Klan woman is sometimes referred to as a Lady of the Invisible Empire (LOTIE). One former KKK member told me, in his group women "made the Klan robes. They had different titles than in the Klan. They set up food, organized rallies." NSM is a notable exception in terms of allowing women to assume leadership roles.

Yet women do carry out violence, although in this study, women who had been violent on behalf of their groups declined to talk about it due to self-incrimination. Our subjects did tell us about women who fought alongside the men, wearing brass knuckles and being every bit as tough in street fights.

A notable finding in our study involved the LGBTQ community. Many participants either knew active members who were part of the

LGBTQ community, or they were themselves. LGBTQ members appear to join groups with internalized homophobia, accomplishing this through splitting and projection, a process we call Projected Hate.[119] They reject their closeted identity out of shame, fears of rejection from others, etc., then pour out their self-loathing for their closeted self onto others. I see this with both ISIS and white supremacists. Being gay is so reviled in their group cultures that gay men often identify with strong traditional male images and outwardly project their hatred over their own sexuality, seeking to destroy it. It's why both groups tend to attack and kill LGBTQ people.

Psychologists call this splitting because it's like trying to split off and destroy a part of oneself, the part that got them in trouble, wasn't able to protect them, or their own vulnerable self they were unable to protect. Consider, 29-year-old Omar Mateen who attacked the gay nightclub in Orlando, killing 49 and wounding 53 in a mass shooting on behalf of ISIS and al Qaeda, before killing himself. He was known to have frequented this club and its patrons claimed he had partners there. Coming from a conservative Muslim Afghan background, being gay was likely an anathema to him and rather than accept himself, he lashed out and destroyed those who represented his "sinful" self.[120]

I also see a lot of splitting and projected hate in white supremacists who reject their own weaknesses as they strongly identify with the violent persons who hurt them—violent parents, school bullies, and others. They revile and want to destroy the weak and vulnerable parts they see in others which are the parts that strongly remind them of their own weakness and vulnerability.

Hate is not the Prime Motivation

Despite all we've written so far, one of our most surprising and important findings has been that the majority of individuals we studied were not motivated to join white violent extremist groups out of hate.

Other researchers have described white extremism as an ideologically driven process. Participants undergo an "awakening" to a radical ideology,[121] after which the radicalization process occurs, according to Schafer and colleagues' theory. They base their theory on 115 open-source, online individual accounts of radicalization. This awakening plants "the seeds of discontent" which can happen in ordinary environments or due to specific triggers, such as negative personal interactions with members of minority groups, a fear of assault, bullying, etc. Then after being radicalized, they join a hate group. Schafer, Mullins, and Box note individuals with these "seeds of discontent" then utilized networks, such as family and friends, to play a role in radically awakening others by introducing individuals to their ideology.[122] The internet, of course, has greatly accelerated this process by facilitating sharing white extremist ideology between total strangers.

Our research differs. While we found some cases to support this theory, we did not find radicalization in our sample as the primary element at all, rather we found the opposite—ideological indoctrination followed joining a group out of a desire to meet specific emotional and psychological needs. Moreover, few in our sample reported negative personal interactions with minority groups that served as a grievance or "seeds of discontent" that propelled them into white supremacism.

That said, a significant portion of our sample, 42 percent, admitted to prejudice against certain people at the time of joining. Specifically, six individuals said they were motivated by racism against Black people before joining; five named anti-Semitism; eight were anti-immigrant or against people of immigrant descent (namely Hispanic and Turkish); seven named Islamophobia prior to joining their group. Only a few reported having had serious negative interactions with minorities, for example, one woman had been raped by a Hispanic man, and some were bullied by minorities.

However, the main motivators for joining a hate group were not ideological but a desire for belonging (64 percent) tied with a need for personal significance (64 percent). Once they became members in an extremist group, then ideological indoctrination followed, leading those who were already bigoted to solidify their beliefs, and those who were not bigoted to adopt those beliefs. Indeed, some never fully took on the group's ideology and remained silent about it to retain their sense of belonging. Most however, described gradually taking on the ideology and hatred, with some moved to lethal acts of violence as they became convinced, they were purpose-filled "warriors for their race" on a heroic mission.

Directed Hate

Here we delve deeper into this ICSVE concept, Directed Hate.[123] How groups take individuals not looking to join a hate movement, and over time inculcate hate into their members, even convincing them to engage in acts of violence, is important to understand. In sum, a sense of specialness is conveyed in order to meet the strong need for belonging and significance. Specialness comes in the form of membership in an elite, superior, and exclusively white club. Members are told this significance is threatened by those who seek to upend the world order and depose white people from their position of dominance. Members come to believe if they do not staunchly adhere to the white extremist ideology, they will lose their newfound sense of superiority. Hate is directed toward the threats.

Directed Hate has three distinct and sequential steps:

1. Joining the Noble Cause: New members find by virtue of their "whiteness" they are able to join a "whites only" group, and not only belong, but play a significant role in the fight for the noble cause. This feeling of having joined a noble cause was reported by 32 percent of our interviewees.
2. Superiority and the Fight for Power: As the white extremist groups begin to indoctrinate new members, they convey the

message by virtue of their whiteness, members are special and superior. They feel part of an elite group of likeminded people, and they have this right to white privilege and advantage. Importantly, their failures are not their own fault but caused by outside forces, most often Jews, who are portrayed as plotting to elevate minorities for white genocide and white replacement. This ideology is reinforced through informal conversations with group radicalizers, recruiters, and leaders; through White Power music and novels like *Hunter, Siege* and *The Turner Diaries*; pseudo-religious texts like *Nature's Eternal Religion*, older texts like the *Protocols of the Elders of Zion* and *Mein Kampf*, and biblical lectures and sermons explaining Christian Identity ideology and other far-right biblical interpretations. Importantly, these texts and conversations make clear the newfound sense of significance is not secure. Pride and status as white men and women are under dire threat.

3. Group Compliance to Belong: The third and final step on the Directed Hate continuum are demands by the group that the individual adheres to its ideology and norms; works toward enabling its noble cause; and even supports violence on its behalf. Demands must be satisfied in exchange for maintaining one's belonging to the elite group and to bolster the significance and purpose it conveys. Members comply out of fear of rejection or ostracism as well as the relief that comes from belonging and shifting blame for one's own failures onto others. Belonging and significance are secured through various actions, such as taking part in rallies, concerts, street fights; taking on leadership roles; propagandizing and recruiting; carrying out acts of violence against alleged enemies; and by avoiding "race mixing.". [124]

Dehumanization and the Ultimate Villain

Learning to dehumanize is an important factor in radicalization. Dehumanizing Muslims and immigrants was reported by about a quarter to half of our sample (13 and 20 respectively). Dehumanization of Black people was more pervasive, reported by 33 interviewees. Statements from among our interviewees are telling: Lukas Bals (Die Rechte, Germany) admitted to easily falling into his group's ideological indoctrination because "I hundred percent believed white people are more worthy than Black people. I didn't even think about it." Ken Parker (KKK and NSM) also admitted how little rumination went into his acceptance of white supremacist ideology: "I thought Blacks were a subspecies of humans. Founding Fathers say they stink, need to be educated. I thought just like that." Tony McAleer, (Canadian skinhead leader): "[We] referred to them as mud people." But as Tony further explains, "It was less about Blacks and Hispanics—it was Jews."

While our study found very few of our participants had started out hating Jews—they didn't even know Jewish people—all of them were ultimately directed into virulent antisemitism. Jews as the ultimate enemy is an ideology that cuts across all white supremacist hate groups. They were taught the definitive enemy is the Jewish people who control the banks, the media, and run the so-called Zionist-Occupied Government [ZOG] with its evil plan to dethrone and displace whites with "mud races." Tony told me, "Jews were the ones who were engineering the downfall of the white race—all these other races were a threat to that. UN endangered species, it's us." As such, their belief was, "if you take care of the Jewish question, everything will be OK."

TM Garret affirmed this sentiment. "It started with unintentional jokes against minorities. Then as an early skinhead, I thought the enemy were Turkish street gangs, but as I got deeper indoctrinated and became a nationalist, it was the communists who wanted to swap out the Germans and replace them with immigrants. But at the end, it became a world-wide problem where the white race was under attack and I was presented with the ultimate villain, like the 'final boss' in a videogame: The Jews who want to take over the world. And we could be the heroes. Noble warriors fighting against evil, saving everybody."

Those who adhered to Christian Identity ideology were indoctrinated with biblical justifications for their hatred, which also resulted in directing their anger and hatred toward Jews above all others. Again, this ideological shift occurred despite the fact very few had been prejudiced against Jews prior to joining their groups and hardly any had actual interactions with Jews.

The Echo Chamber and Bond of Hate

Like cults, extremist groups demand ideological and behavioral loyalty and begin to isolate members from dissenting opinions, including friends and family, as well as people from hated minority groups to make it hard for them to have any positive exposures and change in perspective. Twenty-four of our interviewees reported being isolated from the outside world during their time inside hate groups. As isolation and the echo chambers of hate increase, fusion with the ideology and buy-in to conspiracy theories set in. That's why when it comes to disengagement and deradicalization, measures designed to create positive interactions and dialogue across racial, ethnic, and religious divides are invaluable.

Bonds are further created by rituals and ceremonies; and fights are often construed as self-defense against counter protesters or rivals. This is one reason we've found Antifa's violence in counter protests seems to backfire, and creates deeper bonds forged among white supremacists during violent interactions.[125] Strengthening bonds helps to fuse identity with the group's ideology in a rigid and cohesive in-group and a well-defined and reviled, out-group. This fused individual identity with the group's ideology also happens in militant jihadist groups and has been found to be challenging to break once it occurs.[126]

Adherence to the group is reinforced through outward expressions of loyal adherence by our interviewees, including shaving one's head (16), tattoos (21), using hand symbols, and wearing clothing portraying shared hateful symbols and phrases.

Some participants also said physical protection—the ability to call upon others for protection at any time—was important, especially for young boys and men who had been bullied or grew up in tough environments.

Identity Fusion and Violence

In contrast to violent extremist and terrorist groups like ISIS operating in active war zones, DVE groups in the U.S. and elsewhere do not require members to take up arms. In some skinhead groups, street fighting is the norm; in some white extremist gangs and prison groups, group cohesion and defense are found where criminality, drug dealing, abuse, and violence are the norm. But some groups officially state fighting is only allowed in self-defense even while encouraging violence through their hate rhetoric.

Rank-and-file members are "armed" with flyers they're obligated to distribute, and must attend rallies, while others create social media propaganda. Still, despite many claims of being "non-violent" these groups often implicitly encourage and even at times celebrate street fighting, gun ownership, individual weapons training, engaging in violent acts and even lone wolf acts of terrorism.

In their 2018 study, Windisch and colleagues found that sense of cohesion and strong desire for belonging, over time, allows the group to redefine individual norms concerning violence, dispensing with an individual's own belief in favor of the group's violent ideology. Through sociological interviews with 89 members of white supremacist groups, the researchers found emotional and cognitive strategies were utilized to override initial hesitance to commit violence, create group coherence, so adherence to subcultural violent norms begins to override the social norms prohibiting violence.

Strategies included targeting vulnerable victims where fears of retaliation were minimized; participating with members supportive of violence; conducting clandestine attacks where one's identity was unlikely to be discovered.[127] This finding matches Scott Atran's theory of identity fusion in which he views terrorists and violent extremists as undergoing a process of fusing their identity with the violent identity of the group, something he argues is hard to undo.[128]

This phenomenon happened with our subjects. While most said they did not seek or join a group out of a sense of strong hatred, nor with the expectation or wish to engage in violence, many wound up engaging in violent acts. Even when leaders say they officially discouraged violence, hate rhetoric fueled it. Participating in fights, attacking others, or being attacked by those who oppose them were among the most commonly reported violent experiences in these groups (24). The NSM, which says it limited violence to self-defense, allowed weapons training in various chapters and sent armed border patrols to the Southwest.

In prison, some said survival seemed to be predicated on joining a white supremacist gang and once in they were violently punished by their own group if they failed to adhere to its rules or tried to quit. Those who joined street gangs were often those who faced bullying and joined for a sense of protection, but then engaged in violence once in the gang, with fights among rival gangs and groups whose membership was comprised of minorities commonly reported. However, members of less stereotypically violent hate groups chillingly admitted to stabbings, shootings, and more. Violence perpetrated by our interviewees included assaults on a Black man, a gay man, a female politician, and prison guards, as well as stabbing minorities. Oftentimes, members were drunk or hyped up on meth for quite some time before carrying out these acts of violence.

Antifa is a common bogeyman and target for white extremists. Fred Cook (NSM) noted the bonding effect of Antifa, "Worrying about Antifa always brought us closer; two extreme groups pushing against each other." Given the potential reciprocal radicalization occurring between far-left and far-right, all interviewees were asked if they had experiences with Antifa and to define how they identified others as Antifa. Most answered that Antifa were obvious by their counter protesting, being dressed in all black with bandanas over their faces and for their violence. Loosely organized, Antifa activists have been known to encourage and engage in violence against members of far-right groups, and occasionally police officers.[129] According to our respondents, as well as Antifa activists I have been able interview, an Antifa slogan is "Punch a Nazi in the Face" and six of our respondents said they got into fights with people they identified as Antifa.

Fred says Antifa would slash tires, break windows, and throw bottles of urine, and the cops would hold NSM back. "Then they'd find knives and guns on the Antifa guys, you'd see it in the news afterwards." Fred admits, however, his fights with Antifa were not as defensive as their group claimed, instead provoked by behaviors, verbal and otherwise. "When I was in NSM, I was in fights only when attacked, which would be often, if you wore swastika at rallies and meetings." TM Garret remembers an incident from the very first rally he attended in 1990 in Germany, at a large neo-Nazi march commemorating Hitler's co-chancellor Rudolf Hess. "I remember seeing some of our guys walking around with bloody bandages, thick like turbans around their heads. Antifa had thrown bricks at them."

Thirty-eight interviewees reported attending rallies, concerts, demonstrations, festivals, protests, and cross burnings. Organized public rallies of neo-Nazis often bring out counter-protestors, even Holocaust survivors and children of survivors who are retraumatized seeing Nazis in the streets. When protests and hate rhetoric receive press coverage, even more racial and ethnic minorities and Jews witness the extreme hatred directed their way.

RAHOWA: The Racial Holy War

The coming racial holy war, abbreviated RAHOWA, is represented across political and religious hate ideologies, new and old. RAHOWA calls on hate groups to prepare to win the race war at which time the "mud races" (Jews and people of color) and "race traitors" (Jews and white people who have intermarried, had mixed race children, helped nonwhites, or do not adhere to hate ideology), will be deported from Western white countries if not outright executed. White extremists will celebrate the "Day of the Rope", an ideology echoed by QAnon's "day of reckoning", with Q's forecasts for public hangings.

No date is set for RAHOWA, but Scott Shepard (NSM) repeats what I've heard from others, "They have been planning on racial war for years. We are closer than we've ever been." There's been no lack of deeply troubling and lethal hate-motivated attacks across the world meant to help catalyze it.

The 1995 Oklahoma City bombing killed 168 people, including 19 children and injured more than 680;[130] in 2011, 77 were killed in

Rahowa Patch

Norway by a hate-filled attacker;[131] in 2012, six members of the Sikh community were killed and four wounded in their Wisconsin house of worship (a seventh victim died of his wounds in 2020);[132] in 2015, nine Black worshippers were killed and one injured in a massacre at a Black church in Charleston, South Carolina;[133] in 2018, 11 Jews were killed and six wounded at a Pittsburgh synagogue;[134] 2019, in New Zealand, a lone shooter killed 51 and wounded 40 at a mosque during worship;[135] 2022, a young man live-streamed his massacre in a Buffalo, New York, grocery store that left 10 people dead. Most were Black. The manifesto he posted before the shooting, filled with racist and antisemitic messages, also referenced towns in New Jersey with large Orthodox Jewish populations.[136] A

July 4, 2022, parade in the predominantly Jewish Chicago suburb of
Highland Park, Illinois, erupted in tragedy when a 21-year-old murdered
seven and injured 30 by shooting into the crowd from a rooftop with
a semi-automatic. He, too, had posted racist and antisemitic material
online and had been known to the police. And many feel the January 6th
attack was meant to kick off RAHOWA.

Most of our 51 study participants were generally convinced of
an impending race war, with plenty of fantasies about how it would go
down.

Shane Johnson (KKK) told me, "You [would] have small cells
operating, like *Turner Diaries*, attack the government, world banking
system, eliminate the enemy." Timothy Zaal (White Aryan Resistance)
said plans were contained in texts white extremist generally turn to
for envisioning RAHOWA, *Turner Diaries*, *Siege*, *KD Rebel*. "You
just know to go to power plants, water treatment, internet, cell towers,
reservoirs, just standard stuff. Whole idea is leaderless resistance or now
accelerationism, it comes from *Siege*." Red (pseudonym, NSM) also
believed in a leaderless uprising. "Absolutely we were preparing, a lot of
us just had this notion, we'll just know. I thought instruction would have
come. Instruction was to remain loyal to your race." He also expected
hate groups would do "lots of recon" and take over infrastructure,
starting the 911 centers. "If you got control of 911, you control fire,
EMS, police." He was also an endorser of the Day of the Rope and ready
to participate in "mass lynchings, absolutely. At that point, I was ready
to die for the cause."

Fred Cook (NSM) told me when he was younger, there was
"always that feeling that there's going to be RAHOWA when enough
was exposed." People would spontaneously act *en masse*. "Blacks would
uprise and take over their own areas and whites, designated as their
areas, everyone [would] turn tribal. It would be us exposing the Jews,
they would be the most outed threat, so everyone would be going after
them. For a while in NSM, Jeff [Schoep] and I thought we should get

together with the Black nationalists. They want to separate, just as we do, we both see the same light."

JJ Chivers (NSM) who says he "always had a strategic mind," envisioned the coming race war as very bloody, but whites "had an advantage by many factors. We were more, we had more of an inherent ability as white people to be conquerors." They'd start underground first and strike as individual cell units, attack mainstream media, "that has to happen, assassinating key targets, wiping out propaganda outlets." He also saw different leaders serving different purposes. Jeff Schoep (NSM) was the charismatic leader who would be seen on the street, bring out the numbers, and recruit new people to the cause. Because he was good with words, William Pierce (author of *The Turner Diaries* and founder of the violent neo-Nazi National Alliance) would awaken people and make them conscious. He also said some leaders were just radical without a plan and not the ones to follow. "I was doing this event with this leader from Pennsylvania. When he got on stage, n-word that, n-word that, he was riling up angry white people but just hotheaded, no strategic plan for warfare, not qualified to orchestrate any race war."

Lauren Manning (Canadian skinhead) says believers thought tensions would grow enough to eventually lead to the race war from *The Turner Diaries*, but "it's a giant mindfuck. Never actually specified how it would ignite, everyone had their own variations of what it would look like." But it was a popular topic often discussed at every weekend party. "One aspect that the guys seemed to enjoy entertaining is hanging race traitors on lamp posts."

JJ (NSM) agrees and thought The Order had it right. Anyone who turned state's evidence, "should be tracked to the end of the earth and their head separated from their bodies. Yeah, execute them was my view. It's now a war." And when asked if he wanted to eradicate other races he recalls, "I wouldn't cry if people got genocided, but I didn't think we should eradicate this entire race. I grew up in a mixed area, all nationalities. I didn't really see it as something I'd initiate, but if someone decided to round them up and get rid of them…" Similarly, Raine, a female skinhead, says, "I thought there would be a race war, or riots or fighting or massive civil unrest. I never thought it would actually get [to the Day of the Rope], but if it would, in my teens, if I would have thought something could have set it off and followed through, I would have probably been involved."

Day of the Rope Meme

RAHOWA isn't limited to the U.S. Yonatan Langer, a former German neo-Nazi who changed his name after converting to Judaism, also thought a race war was on its way that would "correct all the democratic influence. It would be a cleansing of foreigners in the country—old idea you see all over the world—in Netherlands, France, Poland, Germany to clear the country of influences. Everyone goes back to his nation by choice or force. Wouldn't exclude killings, wouldn't exclude any actions."

Tony McAleer (Canadian skinhead) made sure he was armed and trained, "stockpiling guns and ammo, two assault rifles, shotgun, and a pistol. Everyone had them. We were waiting for the race war to come. A lot of it was fantasy, music posters of heroic German soldiers…an idealized masculinity, Norse gods, Vikings, war."

Greg Howell (an Iowa skinhead) says he knew it's a conspiracy theory but "I got sucked into it the more music I listened to, books I read, find[ing] confirmation bias in that." He saw himself as a soldier leading his friends "and because I was white, I was going to be the ultimate bad ass."

Jonathan Strayn (Aryan Brotherhood) says many different types of white extremists are actively getting ready for RAHOWA. "They 100 percent want it. They are waiting for the day it finally happens and they can create war." They train daily, with whatever weapons they can

Aryan Brotherhood Logo

get. "You always carry weapons, always supposed to be prepared if you are needed. If it kicks off, you always have your boots on, as they say." The goal is "to be separate and never have any contact with people who look different than they do or believe different than they do. It's all-out war; kill or be killed."

Ken Parker is a military veteran (KKK and NSM) and was a very successful recruiter for his groups by virtue of his military bearing, training, and experience. "We talked about it all the time. That was everyone's dream, yeah, let's have a racial war. If Hillary gets elected, it will ruin the country, let's have our racial war. Now with Biden, let's go." As for how it would turn out, "There wasn't a plan if we did win. It probably would have been modeled after Nazi Germany, concentration camps, talk of sending all the weirdos to California to hang with Nancy Pelosi, send them to all the bad cities Democrats ruined—we never had concrete plans—give them the crappy cities. If the time came, anyone full-blown in white supremacy, anyone would march people in the gas chamber and push the button. That's just the way it is. Klan would do any nonwhite, non-Christian, Blacks, Jews, homosexuals; NSM any homosexual, nonwhite, Jews, otherwise non-religious."

To be clear, race war ideation is not past tense which makes it all the more chilling, especially in light of January 6th and renewed calls for civil war after the Department of Justice issued an unprecedented search warrant for the FBI to search former President Trump's Florida resort, Mar-a-Lago, for highly classified documents. After the FBI executed the warrant, Trump's internet postings said his Florida home was "under siege, raided, and occupied." Extremists are heeding his words.

The radical right has plenty of conspiracy theories to motivate followers. Using decommissioned Walmart stores as re-education centers for the government to round up the far-right is among those that have been debunked. Our ICSVE research fellow, Wilson Warren, spent the summer of 2021 infiltrating QAnon and white supremacist forums and found a trove of similarly absurd claims. Thousands fervently claimed COVID-19 vaccinations are a government plot to control and even kill U.S. citizens. Others hold onto believing the federal government is rife with a cabal of liberal democrats and Jews dealing in pedophilia. Another conspiracy finds liberal politicians and Hollywood "elites" harvesting the blood of kidnapped and tortured children during Satanic rituals to extract adrenachrome and impart longevity.[137]

(Adrenochrome has made other fictional appearances in such movies as *A Clockwork Orange*, and Hunter S. Thompson's *Fear and Loathing in Las Vegas*. While adrenochrome is real, it's far less interesting. This chemical byproduct of adrenaline was once thought to trigger schizophrenia back in the 1950s. The science was debunked and adrenochrome today has limited medical application, mainly used to slow blood loss by promoting clotting in open wounds.)

RAHOWA remains the goal. Scott Shepard (NSM recruiter) says their military members "trained with weapons and paramilitary groups" in Alabama and when RAHOWA broke out, they would be instructed to "gather at several spots throughout the country" and "kill all the minorities, Jews, actually anyone who doesn't have their beliefs." They would wait for more orders with the "ultimate goal, take out people, murder, shoot them, blow them up…There's a lot of military people who are inside now, who had full white supremacy beliefs."

The rise of White Christian Nationalism whose adherents believe their moral basis and beliefs are correct for the entire country is also concerning as it is not just a threat to freedom of religion but is also in some cases fueling violent extremist movements. The fall before January 6th, Pentecostal far-right televangelist Rick Joyner told the PTL television audience that God has "seeded" the country with military veterans to head up Christian militias in preparation for civil war. He later assured the audience that most Americans' lives would not be all that impacted during this coming civil war because the militias would be focused on "inner cities" a clear dog whistle that the targets are communities of color, perhaps also a veiled reference to RAHOWA.[138]

Military & Police Recruitment

It bears repeating, a significant and disconcerting portion of the Capitol Building insurgency, and the most violent among them, were current and former military. We now know the rioters with military backgrounds were four times more likely to also be associated with violent extremist groups than the nonmilitary rioters.[139] Analysis shows 12 percent of the January 6th rioters charged with federal crimes as of this writing are veterans or active-duty military. Of that subgroup, 25 percent are commissioned officers and 44 percent had been deployed at least once, so they were trained in active warfare.[140] The depth of military engagement in DVE groups has left some of our interview subjects very alarmed, but not surprised, by the January 6 insurrection. Recruiting military and police has been a priority for anti-government militias and hate groups.

Jason Van Tatenhove recalls Trump's aide, Roger Stone, courting U.S.-based militias like the military-heavy Oath Keepers, and says his group intended to keep President Trump in power by any means necessary. "The Oath Keepers were absolutely attempting a coup," he told me.[141] Josh Pruitt (Proud Boys) says of his fellow rioters on Capitol Hill, "a lot are ex-military [who] just don't want our country taken over."

Readiness is crucial, making military and police engagement a priority. The military presence in DVE groups runs ominously deep.

In addition to the Oath Keepers, Jeff Schoep confirms NSM was increasingly focused on recruiting veterans and active-duty military. Scott Shepherd specifically recruited former military for the NSM's "stormtroopers", its security force. Both Jeff and Scott say the stormtroopers were more than 50 percent military and even their general membership was half military at times.

Scott says the KKK were also recruiting veterans, "these veterans have the best training in the world you can get. Who better to recruit? They would get weapons from military contacts." Shane Johnson, former Imperial Knight Hawk of the Indiana Ku Klux Klan, says 30 percent of his group were former military and recalls their vulnerabilities to recruitment, "They were looking for camaraderie from the military, looking for that brotherhood."

As KKK leader in Germany who later promoted white supremacy in the U.S., TM Garret says, "It was clear to me that recruiting skinheads and people with no or low education will lead nowhere. I created a policy of banning skinheads and open Neo-Nazis from membership, and recruiting educators, businesspeople, and especially members of military and law enforcement." TM adds, "Once the movement got to the point of revolution, we could not do it without the help of law enforcement or military."

TM's German group was particularly successful in recruiting police officers, eventually bringing in so many local police officers they created "a separate 'klavern' [local KKK unit] to keep their identities secret. TM describes them as an "internal secret police, the 'Klavaliers,' a group regular members did not know about…The goal was to organize paramilitary training camps." In just the past five years, there have been numerous discoveries of extremists in the German military. "We always believed that eventually there would be a race war and we needed the military to be on our side to take over the government. Reflecting on January 6th, TM says, "Imagine if a significant part of the military was with them."

Militia recruiters can also offer a substitute for the military. Timothy Zaal (White Aryan Resistance and Hammerskins) was rejected when he tried to join the military and joined the skinheads instead. "I thought it was my patriotic duty. If the military is not going to take me,

I'll join this other thing, they were very militaristic." A current leader in the KKK named Kevin (last name withheld), said he wanted to be in the military growing up but would not have passed the medical screening due to severe respiratory problems as a child. Similarly, Søren (NSM) said he knew his asthma and other medical conditions would prevent him from joining and being deployed to Iraq in the early 2000s. NSM's militarism attracted him: "We wore those crazy uniforms. It was actual brownshirts like Germany. Now I see they switched to black uniforms. Something about that appealed to me." NSM also used military terminology. "Everyone started as a private…There was some guy that had worked with George Lincoln Rockwell (former Navy commander and founder of the American Nazi Party) that was a colonel. That appealed to me."

Jason Van Tatenhove (Oath Keeper) makes it easy to visualize the exhilaration of training with Special Forces. "There was an allure to it, sometimes I'd be flown into work on Huey [helicopter] by a Vietnam vet," who had apparently bought a decommissioned helicopter. "[We were training with guys. I have pictures of me, videos of me flying into work all tacked out in a Huey. It's exciting and adventurous. The guys teaching the classes are the real deal. These are very serious and very intelligent." Extremists who would never make it in a real military got to play the warrior role. "You had the tactical guys driving the decked-out Hummer with everything, 5 to 10K of gear, but they were grossly overweight." Scott Shepard (NSM) also claims his group got "the most elite training" for free. "They had access to Stinger missiles, all kinds of high-powered military weapons."

For those who were eligible to join the military, white supremacists encouraged their ranks to do so and to be ready-in-place for a government takeover. As TM Garret tells it, "If we were someday going to take over the government, we needed people in place in the military and the police, and in high levels of government, so we worked hard to recruit them and to support our members to get to places of power."

A 2019 survey of 1,630 active-duty subscribers of *Military Times* found 36 percent of those responding saw evidence of white supremacist and racist ideologies in the military, a big increase from the still significant 22 percent found the year before.[142]

Viktoria, a German-born former member of the American white supremacist/Odinist group, *Wotansvolk*, describes an attempt to enlist in the U.S. Marine Corps: "Me and seven other people went to join the Marine Corps for combat training, access to resources, to get up the ranks. Two tried to get up to [earning the rank of] General." Viktoria was not admitted into the Marines, but she says five of her group were and a friend whom she helped got her a job as a security contractor, which allowed her to gain military and security knowledge.

Infiltrating the military also affects our allies. Dutch counter terrorism reported the threat of several hundred Dutch accelerationists, "In several of this movement's online networks, a fascination with weapons has been noted. There are concerns that individuals with this ideological background intend to join the armed forces or shooting clubs in order to gain experience with weapons."[143]

Maik Scheffler (German Hammerskin) describes secretive training his group received. "We definitely had advantages through those high-ranking military [members]. There were training camps almost like military camps, where we learned to handle weapons, fighting, and battle strategies…They also had contacts inside the military. Some were with mercenary experience, some had military experience in Bosnia."

Elisa Hategan (Canadian Heritage Front) recounts, "Everyone was encouraged to join the military to get free military training, particularly munitions. We had the Canadian Airborne Regiment in our group; we had Heritage members who were part of that unit…Some had put a swastika in their barracks in Somalia. There was another who

Canadian Heritage Front Logo

said he wanted to go to Somalia to kill [n-word]." (That regiment has since been disbanded.)

Military members also provide a sense of discipline and structure, qualities that are highly valued by violent extremist leaders. A DVE group cannot survive or achieve its goals if its ranks are full of rowdy young men only interested in drinking and picking fights. Indeed, such actions often undermine the group's reputation if they seek to present themselves as legitimate political organizations. In contrast to disorganized groups like the skinheads of the 1990s and early 2000s, or notoriously violent prison gangs like the Aryan Brotherhood, white supremacist groups with military members can paint themselves as orderly and rational, and thus less likely to be viewed by those they hope to recruit as violent or extremist.

Affiliating with disciplined active and veteran service members has many benefits. They help violent extremist leaders maintain their group's image as serious, respectable, and even patriotic. When faced with accusations of fighting against the government, these groups can point to their military-linked members, arguing these soldiers would never associate themselves with an unpatriotic or antigovernment organization. Violent extremist groups may hold up these members as symbols of their deeply patriotic support of the United States (or other Western country) defending their heritage from foreign "invaders."

In addition to imparting discipline, as well as tactical advice, weapons training, and helping evade detection and arrest,[144] sometimes the military provides the actual weapons. The Aryan Nations were supplied weapons by active-duty military across the U.S. in 2006. That same year, the U.S. military found evidence of white supremacists infiltrating their ranks when Aryan Nations graffiti showed up in Baghdad.[145] Raine (National Alliance) says they had active duty in their group and a lot of guys who came to their cookouts were veterans. Then she tells a revealing story about a guy "who came to our cookout.

Everyone got a weird vibe then it ended up in the news. He was trying to steal weapons from a base."

It's reasonable to question why professional military and police would join DVE groups. Jeff Schoep (NSM) says military members often resonated with the systems and sense of male brotherhood they lost after leaving the military. "They liked that we had ranks and they followed orders and were disciplined." Jason Van Tatenhove (Oath Keepers) recalls the group paying Special Forces to train members in survivalist skills. "They don't have anything to do. [In our group they can re-experience the] camaraderie of brotherhood and make decent money by doing classes for armchair warriors."

These groups are also a chance for veterans to continue fighting for a noble cause as defenders of America's heritage and culture under attack. This narrative can be effective, especially for those who were deployed to combat zones, telling them they can continue fighting for American values.

Veterans may also feel aggrieved toward the government for not offering them the physical, psychological, or vocational support they needed to succeed in civilian life, as was the case for former Iraq vet, Ryan Lo'Ree (Aryan Brotherhood), whose story is told in Chapter 5. Ken Parker (NSM), an 11-year U.S. Navy veteran, is also among those embittered. He faced a bad economy when he left the military and received no employment help. And having served during 9/11, he says he was already on his way to being radicalized. "I already had bad feelings about Muslims. Once you hate one group, it's easy to hate others." The dehumanization of the enemy he felt in the military was easily generalized to all Muslims then to other immigrants and non-Christian groups. The KKK and later the NSM offered him the lost sense of camaraderie and rank structure, while also respecting and valuing him for his military service and the skills he could impart to the group.

Keith Schneider (NSM security) says the majority of his "stormtroopers" had military experience and were "very resentful—the government is not doing everything it could, stabbed them in the back, put them in combat and turned their back. They are willing to join anything that is of a subversive nature."

For those struggling with posttraumatic stress disorder [PTSD] in particular, they may gravitate to "combat" arenas to make themselves feel more "normal". For example, the hyperarousal and hypervigilance that are common in PTSD can be more normalized when one feels he is still in a combat role. A continued command structure and semblance of order and a clear mission can offer feelings of safety and certainty, which can in turn assuage anxiety, hyperactivity, and other features of PTSD. DVE groups may offer a justification and an outlet for anger that is deeply felt but not easy to explain.[146] Likewise, a drinking culture may help keep posttraumatic flashbacks and nightmares at bay. The camaraderie and attachments may also help mitigate some aspects of PTSD, albeit for many, in a maladaptive manner.[147]

Jeff Schoep had believed the NSM would win a race war because a lot of their members had military training, because they were training others, and "mostly, we were so ideologically committed—that it was righteous and true—that there was no way to be defeated." Thankfully, the NSM was defeated as have been many others.

Which leads to this former U.S. Marine lance corporal's attempt to win a race war. Of the scores of cases of violent extremism inside the U.S. military in the past five years that ICSVE has identified from open-source information, this one may be the most unspeakable: Rapekrieg.[148]

Rapekrieg Logo

U.S. Marine Corps lance corporal Matthew Belanger helped create a vile neo-Nazi group that sought a white ethnostate by using rape as a weapon. The Rapekrieg group argued its rape ideology is necessary to exact revenge against other ethnic groups while cultivating "an entire culture of fear around the white man for the rest of time," according to court documents. An FBI affidavit says Belanger wrote, rape is "an extremely effective tool" to intimidate and control women. Rapekrieg sought to subdue and instill fear in its enemies to "increase the production of white children," and the group's manifesto also advocates for murder, torture, and attacks against perceived enemies of the white race with calls for the ultimate extermination of all Jews.

Rapekrieg Rape Feminists Meme

Belanger allegedly wrote the Rapekrieg manifesto, published in May 2020, while on his last assignment with the Marines, the 1st Battalion, 3rd Marine Regiment, 3rd Marine Division, stationed in Kaneohe Bay, Hawaii. In October 2020, the FBI and USMC searched Belanger's barracks and seized a laptop and two mobile phones. The FBI affidavit says they found "approximately 1,950 images, videos, and documents related to white power groups, Nazi literature, brutality towards the Jewish community, brutality towards women, rape, mass murderers, firearms, body armor, instructional documents relating to building explosives and/or illegal firearms, violent uncensored executions and/or rape, and communications related to illegally obtained firearms."

According to the affidavit, Belanger admitted to using the screen name Adolph Hitler while communicating to another member of Rapekrieg who used the screen name Joseph Goebbels. The two discussed attacking Jews and prosecutors say Belanger, allegedly writing under the screen

Rapekrieg Meme

name Hitler, wrote, "That fucking synagogue is going to get it." He and other members of Rapekrieg had talked about shooting up a synagogue then decided it would be better to attack and burn it down with Molotov cocktails. They did neither.

Belanger did not radicalize while in the military. He was a white supremacist before he enlisted in 2018; Rapekrieg and his violent extremism went undetected by recruiters.

Belanger was arrested in June 2022 and is currently behind bars for allegedly using a police officer as a straw man to purchase an assault rifle and pistol while still serving in the Marine Corps. Federal prosecutors urged the federal judge to deny bail upon his arrest as they feared he also planned to attack a synagogue on Long Island and engage in killings and rapes. He was discharged from the U.S. Marines for extremist activity.

From the military to the mainstream, we may indeed be closer to some form of RAHOWA than we think. We know people are being fed a radical array of conspiracy theories they are ready to swallow without question. Disinformation is spewed across the internet, by radical and far-right media, some mainstream media, and by politicians and their allies. White supremacists are connecting on the dark web; and lone wolves are live-streaming massacres for all the world to see. The dramatic rise in violent white extremism across our country poses a clear threat to the heart of our American experiment. The pandora's box of DVE has been opened. It needs to be taken very seriously and better understood—the ideologies, operational structures, and financing—if efforts to prevent, disengage, deradicalize, rehabilitate and reintegrate are to find success.

Antifa

In my research of violent extremism, I'm also trying to understand the other side of this coin, the extreme left antifascists who often seem to be a part of reciprocal radicalization. White supremacists seem to have a knee jerk hatred toward Antifa, whitewashing them as communists and anarchists, although they often can't describe Antifa with any precision. Who are they and what motivates them?

Antifa members are not easily interviewed (notably researcher Mark Bray has managed to do so.[149]) In the weeks finishing up this book, I happened upon an unexpected opportunity to interview five interconnected activists who identify as Antifa. They are 2 men and 3 women ranging in age from 24 to 31, all white from middle to upper middle-class

Antifa Logo

backgrounds. Because Antifa members rarely speak to the press or academics, I was quite pleased to have the opportunity to hear their side of the story.

They were very clear to state there is no organized group or ideology for Antifa, they are a broad political spectrum that includes communists, anarchists, democrats, and liberals. They all adhere to one unifying goal: stamp out fascism. From my first conversation with one of the five, I specifically requested to speak to those who endorse using violence to fight fascism. I was interested to learn when and how they justify using violence, how their violence may relate to reciprocal radicalization, and how effective their use of violence might be.

Antifa members, like white supremacists, see themselves standing up for their group and values, in this case freedom from fascist oppression, which most would agree is a good cause. They are willing to risk their own safety to do so. Speaking to Reuters, one Antifa activist explained her dedication, "We are prepared to put our bodies on the line in the event of police or fascist or racist violence. And it's really, like, a duty to humanity to do that, right?"[150]

What gets defined as fascism differed among the group and that concerned me, particularly in light of burgeoning anger among Antifa activists over the highly contentious and controversial strike down of Roe v. Wade. One person defined fascism as including "extreme nationalism, xenophobia, scapegoating, closing borders, and usually oppression of women or class of people." However, not all agreed with this definition and all five had differing views about when they would go to the streets, doxx, engage in property destruction, or undertake actual violence against a person.

As noted, those I interviewed were willing to use violence to fight fascism, although they all adamantly claim property destruction is not violence. All five endorsed the Antifa slogan, "Punch a Nazi in the face" though two of the women doubted they would actually do it. But another woman told me she had been in many street brawls with 3 Percenters and Proud Boys. She routinely heckles at counter protests, and in some cases frightening beatings from white supremacists resulted during or after the protests broke up. "I don't want them to feel comfortable in my community," she told me. Another young man admitted to routinely assaulting white supremacists. He's a big guy and said the assaults did not usually result in a fight, because the guy he hits goes down hard.

Seeing Oath Keepers and 3 Percenters show up at their rallies with automatic assault weapons strapped to their chests, Antifa activists

Three Percenter Logo

said they were beginning to obtain concealed gun permits for the "Black Block"—the Antifa protestors who typically wear all black, carry gas masks, cover their faces with black scarves, and carry umbrellas to protect themselves. "I need a gun in case one of these guys starts shooting," one told me. "I'm not going to let a massacre happen."

Alarmingly, all five individuals I spoke with also report arming themselves, out of fear for their personal safety not just at protests. One of the women who had been beaten, "stomped," and doxxed by white supremacists, fears for her safety at home now that her address has been published. Another Antifa activist worked in a gun shop in the southern Midwest and started collecting guns after overhearing too many extremists ask, "When can we start shooting the liberals?" All five cited self-defense and the desire to defend others who might be attacked by white supremacists as their reason for weaponizing. Their sentiment echoes what I heard when Antifa began weaponizing during Portland, Oregon protests in 2020.

Roe v. Wade had just been struck down at the time of these Antifa interviews and I was surprised to hear these activists include churches and crisis pregnancy centers (which sometimes pose as phony abortion clinics) as legitimate targets for property damage, including destruction, because they are against legal abortion and LGBTQ+ rights. The interviewees endorsed Jane's Revenge, an Antifa group

Jane's Revenge Logo

that threatened anti-abortion pregnancy centers and places of worship by defacing them with statements scrawled in red paint, "If abortions are not safe, neither are you."

It is notable if not concerning that some Antifa are broadening their definitions of fascism in this way following the fall of Roe v. Wade, targeting those with differing religious and political views they see taking away women's autonomy and freedoms.

These stances bring up several issues. Who gets to define what is fascist, what is not, and should individuals in society claim the right to become enforcers against what they individually define as fascism? Furthermore, is using violence the right approach and is it justifiable? In the U.S., we have the right to religious freedom, to free speech, even hate speech, though these five Antifa activists do not agree with the right to hate speech.

Scholars writing about authoritarianism note that the poles of extremism exist both on the left and the right and this is an example.

While it is a false equivalency to equate Antifa to white supremacists and hate groups—Antifa is not hating anyone based on race or ethnicity—they are working to stamp out fascism with some willing to use violence to do so. That violent extremists of any type believe they know what is right in Western democratic society and see the need to become the violent enforcers of their will rather than trust in our institutions to carry that burden, speaks to the frailty of democracy.

Escape Hate Counter Narrative Videos

You can watch many of those who were quoted in our *Escape Hate* study as well as those featured in this book telling their stories on our ICSVE YouTube Escape Hate playlist and www.EscapeHate.org and hear from former domestic violent extremists for yourself.

Chapter 10 - Hard Rocker of Hate

Strutting along the stage with his guitar in front of an audience of two thousand, thirty-year-old TM Garret snarled and belted the lyrics to his hate song, *We'll Stand up and Fight*, aimed at Jews and their so-called Zionist Occupied Government (ZOG):

> We scream it into your dirty faces with all of our anger.
> We're not gonna be oppressed.
> Just as you - we won't forget.
> You want to see us policed in a terror state.
> You value us like animals who are inferior to you.

His hate music pumped up the drunken and drugged crowds. The chorus:

> But we'll stand up and fight, just like others before us.
> Your Talmud won't help you then because we've got Odin and
>   Thor.
> And you will experience once again what a proud people is
>   about.
> We'll sweep you away from history, like the dirt on the streets.

TM had found his purpose. "We played all over Europe and even in the U.S., concerts of up to two thousand people," he tells me. "The audience was made up of aggressive skinheads and neo-Nazis, all very antisemitic and they were always drinking and fighting, and we pushed them into further aggression by the lyrics and the music, written and sung in both German and English."

TM was good at what he did. He wrote, performed, and recorded hundreds of original songs. Combining his musical abilities, his understanding of people, and his hate, he became a singer/songwriter then lead singer and guitar player with a group promoting Hate rock. Many of the skinheads and white supremacists we've interviewed talk about how powerful the music scene was in influencing them. Even long after they left, it remained hard to remove the hateful lyrics from their minds.

Hard to remove from the internet, too. TM is an extremism expert at ICSVE who helps me access and interview white supremacists and produce our counter narrative videos. He also runs Be the Change, an organization helping others exit extremist groups. Much to his shame, TM's songs are still for sale. He's been out of the hate movement for 20 years, but like so many, his past follows him. He can't take down his songs from the internet because he doesn't own the rights. So even though he has been a voice of peace and racial and religious harmony, his lyrics and voice still spew hate over the global internet. He knows this hate world well. He spent half his life in it.

When I read over his lyrics and listen to audio clips, I find TMs words are scary enough, but hearing him sing, backed up with the pumping heavy metal, he sounds totally terrifying. I feel a deep sense of threat resonating through my own body—and I'm not even Jewish—and I wonder how any Jew would feel hearing and seeing the hate his music is still able to ignite. His song entitled *RAHOWA* threatens to sweep Jews away with stormtroopers and screams of death to ZOG:

> *Fighting against treason, the traitors of our faith.*
> *Believe in the eternal flame of the pure white race.*
> *We haven't lost our struggle so far,*
> *So, fight with pride in the racial holy war!*

I hear TM scream out the chorus:

> *This is the racial holy war. RAHOWA!*
> *Hang the traitors of our race. RAHOWA!*

Fight for white survival. RAHOWA!
Declare the war to ZOG. RAHOWA!

The second verse invokes the German Third Reich and the Holocaust:

March against the enemy like Storm Troopers.
Watch out Jew scum! Yeah, back we strike!
Our time has come!
Revolution in our land!
White resistance! Smash the government!

I hear the chorus repeat and then a third verse warns Jews to flee:

When we start cleaning up our country, if you see us, better flee,
Because we will let you feel our hate. It's the way it's got to be.
Our sacrifice is more than life. We're the chosen ones.
Traitors will be hanging everywhere. When our work is done.
Death to ZOG! Death to ZOG! Death to ZOG!

Like all white supremacist ideology, there must be some darker forces working against whites rather than their own failure to succeed. Indeed, global forces are at work: globalization, accumulation of wealth by elites and the attrition of the middle class, social policies that don't deliver, educational systems that don't propel poorer people forward, a lack of jobs and low wages, corrupt politicians, and so on. In truth, a myriad of external factors may be holding down white people and all people, but a Jewish conspiracy designed to harm whites and elevate certain minorities isn't one of them.

TM was born in Germany and involved in hate groups from the late '80s to early 2000s. He first identified as a pagan, a heathenist, and an Odinist who hated Jews. He moved from embracing racial and ethnic hatred, to promoting neo-Nazism and fascism, then brought two KKK groups into Germany and promoted Christian Identity theories of white racial superiority, even creating an online magazine to spread these views. Like I said, he was good at what he did.

To bring his hate in from the fringe, in the early 2000s, he built a KKK movement with secret memberships in Germany, to recruit police officers, judges, politicians, and businessmen in an attempt to mainstream their groups away from the radical neo-Nazi and skinhead look. The ultimate goal was to put in place all the necessary personnel to take over the government. In recent years, the German population has been shocked to discover whole military units made up of white supremacists, and white supremacists who have infiltrated police units. One German officer is currently on trial for impersonating a Muslim immigrant while plotting false flag terror attacks on politicians while his group allegedly prepared for the collapse of the German government on "Day X."[151] This subversion, in part, dates back to TM's recruiting work.

TM is now forty-five years old and has lived in Mississippi for 12 years. We can't know it, but we are talking just weeks before the January 6th Capitol Hill attack.

"I was the kid in the corner you could push around. I was craving attention, to be somebody else," TM tells me during our formal interview for *Escape Hate*, starting as I always do with childhood. He tells me he was not a planned pregnancy but the result of his parents briefly getting back together before they divorced. With a huge gap between them, he was the youngest of four, growing up in a single parent home with a working mom who had a drinking problem. I hear sadness lacing his voice as he tells me about her. "She never passed out in a corner. She drank beer and cognac. She would start early in the evening and lock herself in her room after dinner. She hid it really good." Because she was not a raging alcoholic, in a way it created more confusion for him. "My mother was busy fighting her demons. I didn't know it, and I thought she didn't care. I thought no one cares about me."

He had a goofy haircut, thick glasses, and meningitis that left him with "a crooked face" due to paralysis. Poor, with a single mother, it added up to feeling strong social stigma. (His face has since healed.) Then his father died when TM was eight. "I had no father to take me to the German football matches. I got to watch on TV while everyone else's dads took them to the matches." He felt jealous of other kids whose fathers played sports with them and were home for family dinner after work.

TM was a smart kid and loved learning. But it didn't win him friends and soon he lost interest, didn't do homework, and was regularly missing school due to bullying. He thinks he may have been depressed. I try to imagine this handsome, well-built man as a bullied kid. Then the boys hit their early teen years and started proving their bad boy masculinity. TM was searching for his path forward and he found it.

Germany strongly suppresses anything glorifying the Third Reich and its antisemitic policies. TM was in history class, learning about World War II, the Nazis, Hitler, and the Third Reich. "There were the bad boys making offensive jokes, boys including me, cracking Islamophobic, antisemitic, homophobic jokes, but also about Hitler." The joking about Jews and Nazis made the other kids laugh, and that took away his pain and made TM a big guy, at least that's how it felt to him at age 13. But more than violating rules by joking around, he was beginning to embrace Hitler's guiding philosophy, National Socialism.

The boys in his class moved on "but I kept running with the National Socialism. They went back to normal, but I didn't have a normal to go back to, except to revert back to the boy in the corner that you can push around, and I wouldn't go back to that for anything." So, TM stepped things up. He turned his antisemitic jokes into a comic book.

A student took it and turned it into the principal. "Lord, I was in a heap of trouble. The principal asked, 'What do you think of Hitler? Didn't you know the Nazis were the bad guys?'"

"I answered, 'Yes, if they were good guys, these jokes don't work.'"

The principal asked him why he was a Nazi to which TM replied he didn't understand the question because Nazis had been gone since 1945 and he didn't know there were neo-Nazis. "So, I added, 'I can't be a Nazi, and I make fun of Hitler, too.'" From then on, he was stuck with the Nazi label.

Looking back with disappointment, TM says his principal's response pushed him further into racism instead of rescuing him from it. "They just assumed I was a Nazi and put this kid in a box. Label him, never open it again. That's a lost soul. That's like telling a child, 'You are bad. You are bad!' No matter what you do, you have no chance to prove you're not bad."

So, he embraced his newfound notoriety and it paid off. "I felt valued, kind of, and the bullying stopped. I thought it was respect, but it was most likely fear. No one wanted to pick a fight with a Nazi. I didn't care. I just kept running with that idea. It was better than nothing."

TM brandished his new identity, bragging about an apocryphal story of stabbing a Polish man. With another student, he took the lyrics from *My Fair Lady* dubbed in German and rewrote them "into antisemitic songs about gas chambers and killing Jews." That juvenile activity backfired during a weeklong field trip. A teacher found the lyrics. The fun evening activity was cancelled, and the class talked about antisemitism and Nazis instead. "Thanks to me. The class hated me for the wasted evening."

By eighth grade, TM's Nazi reputation was set in stone, and he began to learn the costs of embracing his hateful new identity. Every student went to the UK for a week with their English class and TM, who was a good English student, really wanted to go. His mother, though financially strapped, saved money so he could. Then a week before the trip, he was banned. Among his actions, he had stenciled Germany's 1937 border on a black jacket "to provoke, to say my identity, my only identity, is that I'm a proud German." He was banned from the trip and his troubles in school mounted. A classmate passed TM a note making fun of their principal, whose last name was Ziegler. The note said *Zieg Heil*. "I got caught with the note."

He was introduced to skinhead music at age 15, ironically by the same kid who had turned his antisemitic comics in to the principal. At the time, TM thought the skinheads were generally not racists, but nationalistic, proud Germans. He identified with the German skinhead music and message. With every new cassette tape, the music got more radical, and TM radicalized.

He found a skinhead group to join in 1989 but says it wasn't easy to break in. Clashes broke out by political leanings; ideology wasn't playing much of a role for him yet and he wasn't into violence (though he had become the school bully.) He was, however, into "swastikas, Seig Heil, etc., but to provoke against authority only." He recalls going to his first concert around that time. "The leader punched and threw another guy through a glass door. It was like out of a movie, and I thought, 'Dang that is some hard shit!'

TM graduated from high school and went on to college. It was his chance to go "back to normal then, but I didn't have a normal." He had a shaved head, wore camouflage pants, a t-shirt with a *Mr. Clean, We Keep it White* logo. "I arrived at school looking like that and I had all these people around me that didn't like it." So, he found a couple of other skinheads, ended up getting drunk with them, and didn't even check into his college dorm.

The skinhead uniform—shaved heads, Doc Martens boots, suspenders, and neo-Nazi and white power tattoos—is a lot more than a fashion statement. The Southern Poverty Law Center says, "Racist skinheads has long been among of the most violent-minded elements of the white power movement. Often referred to as the "shock troops" of the hoped-for white revolution." The movement flourished during the '80s, '90s and mid-2000s, "particularly through the lucrative, international hate music scene…The importance of music in growing the worldwide skinhead movement cannot be overstated."

William Pierce, the leader of the neo-Nazi National Alliance and author of *The Turner Diaries*, bought the hate-rock label, Resistance Records, which became a major force in the skinhead movement. Pierce rightly wrote in *The Turner Diaries,* "Music speaks to us at a deeper level than books or political rhetoric: Music speaks directly to the soul."[152]

In the U.S. as in Germany, skinheads showed up from Britain in the early '80s, first in the Midwest and Texas. They are now coast-to-coast and have been responsible for vicious hate crimes. Organized into small, mobile "crews," they act individually and without warning and pose a threat to law enforcement. Their assaults include arson; the murders of black men in Birmingham, Alabama and Arlington, Texas; and the actions of Wade Michael Page who played in several White Power bands until he massacred seven people in a Sikh temple in Oak Creek, Wisconsin in 2012.[153]

Skinheads are no longer recruiting in significant numbers in the U.S. White nationalist groups and militias are replacing them among younger recruits. Some of the skinhead movement's leaders have moved to other far-right groups, like the Proud Boys. Indeed, the Proud Boys, a much more mainstreamed and clean-cut group may be overtaking and appealing to young males who formerly would have joined the KKK or skinheads.

The attraction to violent extremism is local in flavor with current events almost always playing a role in pushing individuals deeper into the extremist trajectory. For TM, it was the Berlin Wall. "After the wall fell, the skinheads from East Germany were hardcore Nazis and the *Blood and Honor* movement from the UK had swept over to Germany to recruit Germans." Many apolitical skinheads gravitated to the far-right."

Then at 17, TM was introduced to the German neo-Nazi party. At first, he objected, "They just want to use us." But TM wound up joining and now it was all about the ideology: "Germany First." "We have to take care of immigration." "Keep Germany White." "Your [Nazi] grandfather was not a criminal; he was a war hero." "Don't believe the lies they tell you in school, here was the real ideology and substance." TM became a nationalist skinhead and got more connected with the neo-Nazis in 1991.

These groups have strong international ties. Propaganda, money, weapons, training, members—and music—flow and influence across borders and continents, linking individuals and groups in the U.S., Canada, UK, Europe, the Balkans, New Zealand, and Australia.

TM put his talents to use, and it was heady. "I felt like a rock star." At age 19, he was now a neo-Nazi singer/songwriter writing the music and messages they wanted to hear. Hate lyrics were in demand and his got harsher and harsher to please the audience. "I learned that when you write it and sing it every day, you radicalize yourself as well and start to believe it."

In 1998 he says he sold tens of thousands of records and liked to provoke skinhead subculture" They would get into fights with Turkish gangs and go to parts of town populated by immigrants to get attacked and then blame those groups for the violence. They even used injuries to their advantage. "One time a girl got hit over the head with a beer mug and one [skinhead] got stabbed. I got shot one time. We would use it, saying, 'Look how uncivilized, savage they are.' It justified what we believed in."

He played skinhead concerts every Friday, and neo-Nazi parties on Saturdays and Sundays. "It was about women and drinking and fighting for the skinheads. But for the Nazis, it was political," and the Nazis wanted TM for leadership. They told him to get rid of the skinhead look and appear clean cut instead, because "'We want to convince the people of revolution and get voted into Parliament.'" The Nazis saw the skinheads as expendable, the stormtroopers. "'When we don't need them anymore, just like how they were killed in Hitler's time and the leaders were assimilated to the SS, we will do the same with you guys. You will go to concentration camps. All your drinking and fun will be gone.'"

TM says he was at the height of his career in the white power skinhead movement but felt he now needed to make a choice about continuing as a skinhead or becoming a neo-Nazi leader. Then he met some followers while playing a concert at a neo-Nazi barbeque. They included an American and member of the KKK in Chicago. Though the KKK had existed in Germany since the 1920s, it wasn't operational. "This American was their Grand Dragon. I thought it was kind of cool and it was American!" Anything American had a fascination for Germans at that time, TM says, and especially for Nazis, "due to the First and Second [U.S.] Amendments (free speech and the right to bear arms.) Germans have strong hate laws, and weapons are much harder to get approved and we have to lock them down. In Germany, we have no gun and hunting culture, so only one percent have guns. Back in the day we had kings, barons, and sheriffs so there was no need to self-protect, but Germans loved that idea."

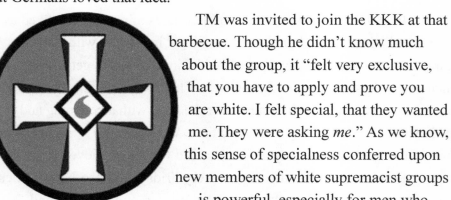

KKK Symbol

TM was invited to join the KKK at that barbecue. Though he didn't know much about the group, it "felt very exclusive, that you have to apply and prove you are white. I felt special, that they wanted me. They were asking *me*." As we know, this sense of specialness conferred upon new members of white supremacist groups is powerful, especially for men who like TM, didn't have a father, or were bullied in school, or lacked a positive identity since early childhood.

TM learned ideologies can differ a lot by national traits. "The American Nazis justified their racism with the Bible," referring to Christian Identity which plays a central role for many U.S.-based hate groups, including the KKK. German neo-Nazis justified themselves with politics and race but not Christianity. A neo-Nazi explained it to TM like this: "'Christianity is Judaism for non-Jews.' I thought that makes sense because Christianity is based on Judaism, and you can't be an antisemite and a Christian. To them Christianity is seen as weak, the idea that you beg on your knees for forgiveness. German neo-Nazis were more interested in Odinism, an old German religion. As an Odinist you die with your sword in your hand and go to Valhalla."

Once he joined the KKK, the neo-Nazis asked if he was not "a Christian nut job?'" He clashed with them and left and got in deeper with *Blood and Honor* which came out of the UK hate music scene. He wanted to figure out how to reignite the KKK in Germany which had pretty much died off since the 1920s, existing only in small, rival splinter groups. When TM asked the German KKK members how they squared the U.S. KKK's Christian beliefs with their members, they couldn't explain it. "I thought they were skinheads in bed sheets," TM says, as I almost spit out my coffee in laughter. "We have no ceremonies, just drinking. I almost regretted joining, then I thought, 'Why not make it what I want it to be?'"

TM translated the American KKK literature into German. But he wasn't sure what to do about Jesus. "He was Jewish, period. The KKK said, 'No, he was not.' Most KKK groups couldn't explain that and took quotes of the Bible out of context." TM says through Christian Id entity he adopted an "antisemitic, neo-Nazi's conspiracy theory that white Americans and Europeans are the ten lost tribes of Israel. I believed that Jews don't have a bloodline to God and are the devil, but whites kept the bloodline to God, they are still white. I worked it out for myself but had a hard time selling it to Germans who didn't identify as the lost tribes of Israel."

Conflict started between the German KKK groups. The American KKK made him an offer to come to Mississippi and "we'll make you a Grand Dragon for a new group in Germany.'" I imagine the heady thrill for TM, traveling internationally to be set up as a leader of an American-sanctioned group, building upon his successful career as an influencer through his hate music.

TM made the trip, returned to Germany with the intent to infiltrate society and government by recruiting judges, police officers, and of course the military. The advent of the internet "changed everything," TM says. From ISIS to white supremacism, the anonymity and the intimacy provided by the internet allows for quickly forming strong relationships that rapidly disseminate hateful ideologies. TM remarks on the accelerated pace of radicalization in today's world. "It took [me] 10 years from cracking a Holocaust joke to a becoming a full-blown antisemite...It can happen today in a week."

TM explains his aims. "We wanted [to recruit] judges, police officers, to get our ideas into society, and government, etc." Attempts by violent white supremacists to infiltrate government institutions are the same in the United States, Canada, Europe and elsewhere, as TM explains, "We always believed that eventually there would be a race war and we needed the military to be on our side to take over the government." Indeed, over just the past five years, there have been many discoveries of extremists in the German military.

Later, when reflecting on the January 6th Capitol Hill insurrection, TM says, "Imagine if a significant part of the military was with them." Indeed, the rioters with military backgrounds were four times more likely to also be associated with violent extremist groups than the nonmilitary rioters.[154] As Americans have grimly learned through the decades, it's dangerous and deadly to have military members part of violent domestic acts and is by no means limited to January 6th.

The internet is also the world's largest extremist bookstore. Germany outlaws white supremacist books so when they wanted books they had to smuggle them in from the U.S. or Denmark, risking being caught by customs. Now extremist books are a click away.

One of the outlawed books pushed in chat rooms during his time in Germany was *Protocols of the Elders of Zion*, which TM describes as "fake news made in Russia. But it was presented to me as the true blueprint made by Jews, proving that Jews are behind everything bad going on. I thought I found the Holy Grail and I can be a superhero defending my people. White people are under attack—not just the

Germans—Jews want to destroy the white people and take over the world. It makes sense, wow! What man doesn't want to be a superhero? Give me a cape!"

TM adopted chat room recruitment with a simple and straightforward strategy by appealing to the creation of a positive white male identity. "We would ask, 'Who in this room does not want to protect your people?'" He shares the view I have always taken in my more than 20 years of studying terrorists and violent extremists. No one joins a terrorist or violent extremist group unless they believe it will serve them in some way that meets a mix of needs, motivations, and vulnerabilities. Each mix is personally contextual, and the best recruiters find and focus on the specific needs of those they are recruiting.

In Germany, TM rose to KKK leadership and built what he calls "a parallel network" that successfully created a secret German KKK he hoped would take over the government when RAHOWA finally came into being. His group persisted for two years before they were discovered by the authorities in 2002. But in that brief time, he says his group recruited hundreds of police, businessmen, and started recruitment for politicians from different political parties "until the German government got us on the radar." An informant had reported they had police officers. Intelligence services approached all members, including TM, and "tried to threaten us. They said to me, 'If there is a violent act you will go to prison. You will be responsible. You are the leader.'" By then TM had three children. For some, a change of thinking happens when a child is born. But not for TM. "I was so proud of my three blonde, blue-eyed little Aryans, thinking I'm doing my duty to save the white race. Having children pushed me even further." But that doesn't mean TM was willing to risk prison. "I was afraid of prison. It's a scary place. I had to remove myself from the situation."

So, in 2002 while recruiting a police investigator, TM feared the situation was "so hot and I was so afraid of going to prison that I called another high-ranking member and said, 'I'm retiring. You are the new

Grand Dragon of the group and also take over the other realms of the
EU.'"

For many, it isn't so easy to renounce membership in a white
supremacist group. It means losing all one's friends, work relationships,
even family members, and livelihood. Often threats, reprisals and even
physical violence are perpetrated on those now seen as traitors. But TM
went quietly and didn't denounce the ideology. "I was still a racist at
the time and I was still hanging out with them." He continued to make
his living with mail order merchandise, KKK flags and patches, and he
repaired computers for the movement. "I knew that if I remove myself,
I'm unemployed, have nothing. I hung out for two more months."

It's also not so easy to psychologically remove oneself from
this world. "Being in those groups is a lot like being in an abusive
relationship—you are in an abusive relationship with an organization. You
realize at some point that this is not going to work, have doubts over and
over again, but who are you going to talk to? You are a hateful guy stuck
in your echo chamber, where they assure you of your doubts and that all is
okay; or you don't talk at all, and your doubts become a mountain. Some
work through it, but some take their doubts to their grave."

When TM started to leave behind his 15 years of white
supremacist identity, he stopped selling white supremacist paraphernalia
and repairing the members' computers and moved his family out
of town. He needed to find a place to live but it was a week before
Christmas and now he was unemployed and on welfare. He phoned an
ad for an apartment for rent and the man who answered the phone had a
Turkish accent. He was renting the second and third floors of the house
where he lived. The man didn't know what it was, but he could see TM
and his family were running from something. His future landlord told
him, "Everyone needs a chance.' I told him I repair computers, not that
I sell KKK flags." The man said he'd pay him to repair his computer. "I
was desperate. I needed to feed my kids—no food, no presents, and it's
Christmas."

A month before, he would not have stepped foot in this man's home, now he was in his living room helping fix an old computer and set up a new one. TM recalls, "He put out Turkish tea and pancakes. It was taking so long. It already bothered me that he is so nice all the time. For me love was for hippies. I was still a warrior, and I was convinced he was a terrorist. This was one year after 9/11."

Confusing thoughts were coursing through his head. He envisioned, as he describes it, "'He will slaughter me in my sleep! He is conspiring in the mosque to attack us.'" But reality was less dramatic. "He wanted me to eat so I did not want to offend. It was actually pretty good. But it was his house, and he was the terrorist. 'What did he put in the pancakes, blood? And he fixed it with his dirty Turkish fingers.'"

TM almost founded another KKK group during that time, but "I hesitated and knew it was wrong. Maybe it was already the influence with the landlord, and I had enough distance."

He recalls one day, being invited to dinner. "Sitting in his living room working on his computer you have a distance. But sitting in his kitchen with his wife and children, that's something you do with family or friends." The first course was a fish soup. TM didn't want to eat it. His internal voice started, "'He'll be offended, and it will escalate, and I can expose him...the terrorist, the Muslim. He's evil.'"

"'Himmet,' TM said, 'Sorry, I don't like fish soup.'" And then TM says he waited for the "tick, tick, tick. The bomb."

"Guess what happened? Nothing. His wife came and took the soup and put down the main course, chicken and fries, which I love, and I thought, 'Where is the falafel and couscous? This is food I eat.' I didn't expect for us to have much in common and then he is serving something so normal. Normal for me, I didn't expect it could be just as normal to him. And I started realizing that this wasn't the only thing we had in common. Things like his accent, his religion, the tone of his skin, they all became secondary. For months I had tried to rip that mask off his face, but I was not successful, because he didn't wear a mask. He always showed his true nature. He ripped my mask off, the mask I wore for years." The inner voice spoke one last time. "'But what about the other Muslims? Do they also eat chicken and fries, or little babies?' My hate was lying in front of me crumbled. I had to decide. The voice again, 'Dude, I hate Muslims. Why are you not hating me back? I'm a warrior. Come on, hate me back!'"

But his landlord did not hate. "He showed me something so crucial in my life—the compassion that I didn't receive as a child. The compassion that I didn't think I deserved at the time. The compassion that I thought I'd receive in the neo-Nazi movement and later I received it from the Turkish Muslim." TM's eyes moisten. "Today I know everyone deserves it, even at their lowest."

TM left the hate movement in Germany, but he kept silent about his past. "Shame and guilt. And fear of rejection. I was really afraid of rejection. If I told one of my new Muslim friends that I [had] wanted to kill them and wanted to send them to a concentration camp, I thought they'd turn their backs on me."

But the past finally caught up with him.

In 2012, TM says he got brutally outed by the media. "You have no say in it, no way to present yourself with your new life. No one wanted to know if I'm out or not, what I did in the interim. My world was lying in front of me, everything destroyed." He had not been in touch with ex-wife who had stayed in the movement longer than him, or his kids, in years. "I realized this country doesn't want me."

He moved to Memphis, Tennessee to start a record company, expecting the U.S. to be a melting pot. "I realized even this multiracial, multicultural melting pot doesn't exist, at least not here [in Memphis]. Instead, it is chosen segregation." He wanted to find out why. He no longer believed whites were superior. He got involved with Memphis' large Black community, like he'd done with the Turkish community in Germany. "I didn't know much about African Americans. Are some stereotypes true? I had to find out."

He made news again, but this time, "fortunately Americans love redemption, so I was not rejected again. A lot of people reached out and wanted to help."

During this time, TM was also connected to a program called *Exit Germany*, the second oldest extremist rehabilitation program in the world, founded by *Exit Sweden*. It has helped over 700 people disengage. Its sister organization, *Hayat,* works with jihadists.

The program helped him understand why he got into the movement and why he stayed in it so long. He became good friends with a former black gang member who became a pastor. Their similar reasons for joining, staying, and finally leaving helped him see patterns. Masculinity plays a big role, as do identity, respect, a purpose, a title. TM says, "It's what humans crave and that's what these groups give you."

TM had been a vocal Holocaust denier. In 2018, he had the opportunity to connect with the Jewish community for the first time when he visited the Museum of Tolerance at the Simon Wiesenthal Center in Los Angeles. TM told me the tour was very intense. "I can't even really express what I felt. I hadn't reflected on my past as an antisemite and Holocaust denier…The people I vilified the most were Jewish. I thought if I told them, they would turn [away] but it turned out the opposite." TM told the Simon Wiesenthal Center, which has a history of working with former white supremacists, "'I need to work with you guys. I need to do something.'" They made TM a campus speaker.

The campus work was a good education for him, and busted some stereotypes, too. When the Tree of Life Synagogue in Pittsburgh was attacked, he gave a lecture in Boston Hillel House, the international university student group. "I thought all Jews eat gefilte fish, wear black hats and have locks, but we had kosher pizza." He spoke at Appalachian State University in Boone, North Carolina, another hate crime location against Jews. Afterwards, they went to a little southern restaurant where he met students, including a redhead and a Black student. "I thought,

'They are Jews?' Stereotype—what does a Jew look like? I didn't expect what I saw.

Then there was the food.

"'What's on those biscuits?'" he asked the students.

"'That's ham,' they answered. I couldn't process it. I guarantee none of it's kosher. I was confused—what they looked like, how normal they were."

"'What the hell happened to kosher?' I asked."

The students explained there are different Jewish denominations and not all Jews keep kosher, and "I realized they are just as diverse as anyone, and—they also like chicken and fries," and TM laughs.

After speaking at many campuses and meeting Jewish students and Jewish organization leaders, experiencing family-centered holidays, Hannukah and Passover, TM wanted to learn about Yom Kippur, the holiest holiday for Jews. His inner voice bubbled up again, "'What, am I supposed to go knock on their door and say I'm the former Nazi, can I come for Yom Kippur?'"

That's actually kind of what happened. He met a local rabbi, explained his campus work and said he wanted to learn about Yom Kippur. It took several days for TM to hear back from the rabbi during which time he had given up hope. But the response came, "'You are welcome to join us for Yom Kippur. Looking forward to learning from you.' So, I went to Yom Kippur, the High Holiday in which Jews around the world ask God for forgiveness for their sins. Here you have a former Nazi on Yom Kippur sitting with Jews in the synagogue, also asking for forgiveness for his sins. What better day would there be for me to visit a synagogue for the first time?"

He also started to viscerally understand the threat Jews and others face, sitting in the crosshairs of DVE. "In the synagogue, I hadn't felt uncomfortable. But the next day, I thought, wait a minute. I was in a synagogue with a kippah, a skullcap, and I prayed like a Jew, looked like a Jew. If someone had come and shot people just because they are Jews,

I would have been dead. It was the first time in my life I realized what it's like to be unsafe because you are Jewish or Black. I felt really unsafe all of a sudden."

Over time, TM became close with the Jewish community in Memphis and decided their beliefs made sense to him. He converted and says his new community is extremely accepting and forgiving and supportive of his work to help others exit from violent extremist groups.

TM has words of caution for DVE recruits. "I know it feels valuable to feel respected. You get a title. It's most often fear that leads to hate, but it will consume you from inside. It is not very rewarding in the long run and makes a miserable life. Very often people in these movements end up in prison or dead." He concludes our formal research interview by telling me, "I left the true burden of living in fear and hate."

You can watch TM tell his story at www.EscapeHate.org

Chapter 11 - Welcome to the New and Improved Nazi Party

If one person can be credited with the growth of the neo-Nazi population in the U.S., it is the man I'm interviewing today, Jeff Schoep. Jeff is the 46-year-old charismatic former head of the National Socialist Movement (NSM). Under his leadership the NSM became the single largest neo-Nazi group in the United States. [155] Jeff was only 21 when he took over in 1994, changed its name from the American Nazi Party which was founded in 1959, and proceeded to preside for more than 20 years.[156]

It's October 2020, the month I start interviewing white supremacists and domestic violent extremists for *Escape Hate*. Jeff Schoep was a great place to start. Jeff has only been out of the domestic extremism world for less than two years and has decades of insider knowledge. Our nation is on the precipice of being consumed by a violent domestic event. We don't know what's to come, but you can feel trouble brewing in the air.

Under Jeff's guidance, NSM membership swelled into a powerful force that made its presence frequently felt through carefully staged protests, and plenty of media exposure—national and international. Their members memorably dressed in full-blown Nazi uniforms, wearing swastika armbands, and bearing billowing Nazi banners.[157] NSM's ideology and members openly idolized Adolf Hitler, describing him in NSM propaganda as "Our Fuhrer, the beloved Holy Father of our age … a visionary in every respect." NSM's propaganda said only heterosexual "pure-blood whites" should be allowed U.S. citizenship and all nonwhites should be deported, regardless of legal status. In April 2020, the NSM website read: "We demand that all non-Whites currently residing in America be required to leave the nation forthwith and return to their land of origin: peacefully or by force."[158] Because the U.S. Constitution was written by white men, they believed, "'It was intended for whites alone."[159] After the NSM instigated violence at a rally in Toledo, Ohio, Jeff blamed those his group had provoked into that violence, saying, "The Negro beasts proved our point for us."[160]

That is the man I have sitting across from me via Zoom, the first of my 51 interviews for *Escape Hate*. Jeff is a charismatic leader with impeccable timing. He was able to rise to national neo-Nazi prominence in 2004 due to the deaths of key leaders: William Pierce, who ran the neo-Nazi National Alliance died in 2002, and Richard Butler, who ran neo-Nazi Aryan Nations died in 2004. Additionally, Matthew Hale, the leader of the World Church of the Creator, was imprisoned in 2004 for soliciting the murder of a federal judge. Jeff had the national stage all to himself and he took it with aplomb.[161]

Membership ballooned under his leadership. The group created its own hate-rock music label, NSM88 Records, and in April 2007 purchased the now-popular white supremacist social networking site, New Saxon."[162] Recruitment included face-to-face recruiting at rallies and demonstrations where "White Power" was on full display and could appeal to those who wanted to feel strength in numbers around their whiteness. Leaflets preyed upon personal fears and failures, making full use of racist and antisemitic tropes. Jeff launched a Women's Division and a Skinhead Division and NSM's revamped website was offered a robust entry point for many, featuring a newsletter, downloadable leaflets, and field reports from NSM chapters across the country.

Jeff also strategically adapted as necessary. Demonstrating in Nazi uniforms gained the group notoriety and helped draw media and increase membership, but that tactic also began to bring public ridicule. In 2007, NSM national and state chapter leaders voted at the group's national congress to switch to "more militant looking" black battle dress uniforms (BDUs).[163] Jeff further mainstreamed the movement

by changing the group's symbol from a
swastika to an Odal rune, [164] an ancient Norse
mythology symbol adopted by neo-Nazis
to signify a white heritage of strength and
heroism.

National Socialist Movement
Updated Logo

The Southern Poverty Law Center,
SPLC, also credits Jeff's relatively young age
for his ability to attract a younger generation
of neo-Nazis. "Under Schoep's leadership,
the NSM set up a unit specifically focused on
recruiting teens called Youth Corps where 14-
to 17-year-olds were taught military skills and
how to become more effective warriors."[165]

Jeff tells me the youth aspect of his early recruitment strategy
was more nuanced. "It wasn't just random kids off the street. They had
to have signed parental permission." Therefore, he says, most youth
involved were children of NSM members. He later disbanded the Viking
Youth Corps and raised the age of membership to 18. "As a father I
thought about what if the communists tried to recruit one of my kids,
how would I react? The answer in my mind back then would have been,
I will find whoever recruited my children and they would regret it.
Thinking of that possibility made me rethink recruiting someone else's
children. Like the old saying from the Bible, do unto others as you
would have them do unto you."

Though the NSM claimed to be a strictly non-violent
organization, Jeff was concerned about minors getting hurt during
violence that frequently broke out. "We had experienced plenty of
vicious violence from fights with ARA [Anti-Racist Activists Network].
For example, a skinhead girl who was pregnant was attacked by ARA
when she was out alone, and she was beaten and kicked in her stomach
by them. So, after some experiences like that we knew that our women
and children were fair game to be targeted by Antifa," Jeff asserts.

Jeff Schoep Speaking at an NSM Rally

Since 2015, the NSM sought to reinvigorate itself by forming coalitions with other white power groups, a strategy that eventually landed the NSM in the center of the deadly August 2017 "Unite the Right" riot in Charlottesville, Virginia, causing many members to exit the group.[166] NSM's membership has continued to dwindle since, and Jeff at the time of our interview was a defendant in the *Sines v. Kessler* federal civil lawsuit, which seeks to hold responsible those who planned and promoted the deadly rally which killed Heather Heyer.[167] Civil lawsuits of this type are increasingly being used to hold militias and white supremacist groups responsible while also causing them to shut down.

Jeff left the NSM in 2019 and has since founded a nonprofit, *Beyond Barriers,* which works to prevent white supremacism and helps white supremacists exit the movement.

Always assuming one's roots offer many clues to later behaviors and life choices; we start our interview with childhood. I've heard a lot of horrific childhood stories ranging from extreme neglect to sexual assault; parents imprisoned and kids growing up in drug dens. In Jeff's case, his upbringing doesn't exhibit that kind of overt trauma. Still, family played a foundational role.

His mother is from Germany and his parents met when Jeff's father was stationed there with the U.S. Army. Jeff grew up in rural Minnesota. It was a white world. "In fourth grade I had to wrestle a Black kid. It was first time I touched a Black person." (That child had been adopted by an all-white family.)

Jeff's German military family history loomed large for him. His German maternal grandfather was his hero, though he'd fought for the Nazis. "He was an alpha male personality, bigger than life type of guy. I don't think he was a [Nazi] party member; he was in the German army and captured." A great uncle was a German General and taken to Stalingrad. Other uncles also fought in World War II, including one Jeff stayed with on summer visits to Germany as a teen.

Jeff became fascinated with the history of World War II, starting in grade school, checking books out of the library and watching PBS documentaries. "I thought I might find my grandfather in them." Jeff's grandfather, an engineer who immigrated to the U.S., didn't like to talk about the war. Jeff recalls his grandmother telling him to not ask his grandfather about it as it upset him. Secrecy and hidden family myths are nearly always sensed by children, usually captivating them and carrying more power because they are "forbidden."

On his teenage visits to Germany, Jeff elected to stay with his great uncle, the German General, rather than cousins his age, a German war hero in Jeff's young eyes. "I knew his face was blown off by a tank attack by the allies in Ardennes, in the Battle of the Bulge," his voice still filling with excitement and admiration. When his war hero uncle appeared, Jeff recalls through teenage eyes, "He looked like he owned the place."

I know from being around military and high-level diplomats that high status often does cause people to carry themselves differently and people around them feel it. Jeff, enthralled by the family war histories and sense of glory, sounds like a youth impressed by manliness and valor, trying to figure out how to find that for himself, to become like his grandfather and uncles.

By age 15, he knew about Nazi ideology and wanted to meet up with the skinheads in Germany, but a cousin warned him off, fearing he'd get beat up, "They'll notice you don't speak fluent German. Some don't like any who aren't from here." That stopped Jeff from approaching, but not his continued fascination. At age 16, he got his hands on a copy of *Mein Kampf.* "It was a hard read. It was all the politics of that time. I was underlining things. It felt very intellectual. I only read a couple of pages at a time. It was the rabbit hole I went down that I wish I never would have," he now says, swallowing hard. He's clearly a proud man; I don't think remorse comes easily to him.

In Germany, his uncle's rules were lax and when he returned home, "I just screwed it up," he admits. "I was out of control." Jeff loved music, and his plan was to become a disc jockey in college. That never materialized. Though smart and in accelerated classes, he was not motivated and started skipping high school. Eventually his grades took a plunge, and he was kicked out. He did finish high school in an alternative learning center and notes with pride, "I breezed through school and graduated before the rest of my class of the school that I got thrown out of." He says he returned to apologize—and to taunt his classmates for having graduated before them. "I was being a smart ass."

He went from being kicked out of school to being kicked out of his home "because I was not behaving." Things must have gotten quite out of control. Jeff tells me his father even sold his motorcycle, "They were afraid I'd take it and crash."

Jeff does not blame his family for his shift into hate. At age 16, he moved to St. Cloud, a mid-size city in Minnesota, where he ran into National Alliance members [a now defunct Nazi group] and was reading as much as he could about the movement. To my dismay, he tells me, he found a glossary written by a sociologist that listed all the DVE organizations active at the time, "skinhead-Christian Identity, Klan, skinhead-Nazi. I wrote to them all. That's actually how I connected with the movement." I am horrified it was an academic's information that helped lead to his entry into the white supremacist world, and that is the reason no direct links to extremists' materials are listed in the references of this book.

Though still a teenager, by now Jeff was emancipated from his parents, entrepreneurial, and independence came naturally to him. Before he turned 18, he was interviewing a range of hate groups to join. An out-of-state Christian Identity group invited him to meet up at the State Fair in St. Paul, a huge annual and all-American tradition in Minnesota. Jeff says from the look of him, they thought he was a Satanist. "I had dyed black hair, earrings," he tells me. "My passion and my dream, besides this garbage, I wanted to be a rock star. I lettered in choir. I had long hair. I sang in a hair band." Though the Christian Identity folks were shocked by his appearance, Jeff recalls an 80-year-old woman among them. She handed him a list of white supremacist groups local to Minnesota.

"I met all of them. I didn't think much of the Klan. The skinheads and bands were fun, but immature. You would think that at that age, when I'm meeting with the different groups, that I'd go with the skinheads because they had bands and everything, but instead I was more wanting to go to George Lincoln Rockwell."

George Lincoln Rockwell is an extraordinary figure in U.S. extremist history. A former Navy commander who had fought against fascism, he later became convinced of its ideology. He became a political activist and in 1959, founded the American Nazi Party. Rockwell was a flamboyant and media-savvy character, who staged swastika-draped demonstrations on the National Mall in Washington D.C., called for gassing "communist Jews," and in his later years coined the term "white power."[168]

Always a history buff, Jeff resonated with the historical ties of the American Nazi Party and joined the National Socialist American Workers Freedom Movement which sprang from the American Nazi Party after Rockwell was executed by one of his protégés. Jeff would one day rename it the National Socialist Movement, NSM. He'd grow its ranks by practicing a big-tent policy in which the group welcomed members of other neo-Nazi groups. As a result of his leadership, the NSM became the largest membership-based neo-Nazi group in the U.S. throughout the 2000s and into the following decade.

"I was highly active. I rose up through the ranks pretty fast," Jeff recounts of his early days. "I became the national leader in a few years. It was in two or three states. I turned it into a national movement," he says with pride filling his voice. By 2009, the group had 61 chapters in 35 states.[169]

"I was all about facts," Jeff continues. He was still avidly reading and researching when he came across writings on Holocaust revisionism. "If they are lying about the Holocaust," he thought, "They are lying about other things. I found these so-called truths and was spreading the word." To justify how he began to believe and spread lies, he tells me, "You do hear different numbers that support Holocaust denial."

Jeff believed he "was going to save my country and race, that I was a patriot and that it was a noble thing." He even says these movements are not about hate. "My experience in that movement is that 90 percent are not in it because they hate everyone. There is hate there, but that's not the driving motivating factor."

"Then what do you think it was?" I ask.

"For me, it's the historical connection, being interested in politics for such a long time. I spoke in the Republican regional convention at age 18 and I went to the state convention, to disrupt it, in '92...That was my first public speech. David Duke was running, but not on the ballot. Pat Buchanan was on the ballot." Much later, Keith Schneider, Jeff's former head of NSM's stormtroopers, will be put forward as a presidential candidate, so clearly, the leaders of the NSM had lofty political ambitions.

"Were you looking to restore your family honor?" I ask, wondering how a young boy makes sense out of resonating with the manliness and valor of war hero relatives who fought on the wrong side of history.

"In the war the victors write the history," Jeff responds. "For me, probably hearing some of the stories of the suffering that happened to my grandmother losing her home, put on a train car—same train cars that they put the Jews on—starving. Hearing some of those stories, it was a way to psychologically right those wrongs, or perceived injustices." It is true, many Germans became refugees in what remained of Germany after the war. "One of her memories," Jeff recalls, "was about being loaded onto train cars in Prussia and how a chicken bone was being passed around the train car because there was nothing to eat."

Yet Jeff's grandparents were against his radicalization. "They'd see me on the news because I was highly visible. We were on the media a lot. My grandmother had seen me on *60 Minutes*. My grandfather said, 'They are going to lock you up or they're going to kill you.'"

"I said to him, something to the effect of, 'You might be okay with living on your knees like a coward. I'd rather live a day as a lion than a life as a lamb.'"

He used bravado to justify his actions with his grandfather, but with his parents, his involvement came at a cost. "My parents knew because when I first got involved, I wanted to tell everyone and recruit everyone. It was really stupid to think I could recruit my parents. But I was in this mindset of, 'This is what I learned, and this is the truth.' I was completely an ideologue, dedicated to that movement." For some time, his family would not speak to him, and Jeff would later pass that lesson onto NSM members, telling them to avoid talking politics with their families.

Now looking down in shame, he says his involvement "cost my family dearly." His mother, who was an attorney, was up for a judgeship. The governor stopped it, saying, "'Your father was in the German army and your son is in the Nazi party. You're not fit to be a judge in this state.' It destroyed her dream."

I return to Jeff's own journey to hate. "If you didn't join over hate, how did you become a racist and a hater?"

"The hate was developed in the movement, at age 19." Jeff's trajectory is similar to most others I have interviewed who say they were taught to hate by the groups they joined, rather than joined the groups because they hated. Jeff says only a quarter of those who join are motivated to do so by actual hatred. The hate greatly intensifies once inside and is funneled toward a particular group or groups. The racial superiority claimed for whites, and the hatred toward others, is the glue that binds the group together. Hate, one white supremacist told me, is a powerful force and still not totally understood.

Jeff tells me a lot of people would say he is not a racist. As TM Garret explains, claims of being racist are countered with, "I am not a racist. A racist hates other races. I am a racialist. A racialist is someone who loves their own race. I want the other races to stay pure as well. There's no hate in that." In 2007, Jeff is quoted, "You take a German Shepherd and mix him with a Golden Retriever, you have a worthless animal that nobody wants and that isn't worth anything if you're trying to breed him or sell him… These degenerates that allow their children to race mix and this sort of thing, they're destroying the bloodlines of both races."[170]

In the NSM, hate is squarely focused on Jews. Jeff says, "It was so bad in the movement that you stub your toe, and you'd say, 'Oh that's the Jews!' We'd say that for everything. The Jews were behind everything. They were our absolute bogeyman." The antisemitism he promoted provided especially long-lasting glue for the group and for him personally.

As he began to part from the NSM in 2019, he says meeting people of different cultures and becoming friends with people of different races helped him exit. However, "For me, the antisemitism was the hardest part to let go."

"Did you know any Jews?" I ask.

He didn't.

"I automatically assumed they were all evil. I wouldn't have anything to do with them."

"Did you enjoy making others fear?" I ask.

"That goes against my morals," Jeff responds. "I wanted my enemies to fear, but not the average person."

"Jews?"

"Yes, the Jews were the enemies. They shouldn't have been. The Jews were the enemy, the fault of everything. The movement wouldn't try to scare or victimize children. I wouldn't have taken pride in that. But there wasn't a lot of empathy for bad things that should happen to Jewish people." Jeff reflects.

"Did you promote attacks on Jews?"

"No, that would have been illegal." Then referring to the Nazi propagandist Joseph Goebbels, "'We'll stay legal to the end.' If there was civil or race war, we would engage. It was important to stay legal because otherwise it was bad for the group."

"How about celebrating attacks?"

"Once in California, the guys protested outside a synagogue, but I thought it was not a good idea. I thought messing around a house of worship wasn't cool; not enough to stop it, but I didn't like it."

Fred Cook, who rose to become Jeff's chief of staff, like most who joined the NSM, recalls having no natural hatred toward Jews and instead being taught to hate them. In fact, he says he was initially puzzled and would ask why Jews were to be hated. The standard answer was, "Because the Jews control everything." But Jeff would tell them, it was because Jews "'have preferential world treatment. They can do as

they wish in Palestine, a list of grievances, this is how it's connected.'"
It makes sense when you are looking for something." Fred recalls of the
desire to belong. He read and researched, "It's like living in a bubble,
there's a lot of information and disinformation."

Jeff says he was in the business of selling that NSM ideology.
He made his living in retail, selling hate music and Nazi paraphernalia
like t-shirts, patches, etc. "I ran an ideologically aligned business. That
record label became the largest of its kind," he says proudly, coming
off more like a corporate executive, still disconcertingly proud of his
accomplishments made on behalf of hate.

He also wore that ideology proudly, with the intent to intimidate.
"I looked and dressed like a skinhead, flight jacket and swastikas, so
[minorities] steered clear of me." Like many extremists, he also tattooed
his body, but says, "I was smart enough not to get swastikas. I wore my
jacket with swastikas. You can't cover it up if you tattoo yourself on
your face or fingers." Though he says at the time "I thought it was cool,
but something told me, 'Don't do it.'" (When Jeff left the NSM in 2019,
he was living in Detroit and the lack of visible markings likely made it
easier for him get out of the movement.)

Jeff was also clear about the mission of the NSM. "To have a
white homeland, an NSM state, and be separate from other races." They
fantasized about race war. "I would say publicly, I didn't want a race
war, but I thought if there was one, we would just massacre people. Most
[of us] had firearms."

"Did you train for it?" I ask.

"A lot of guys had military training," but he says it was their
ideologic commitment that was their real strength. They'd fight with "the
anarchists, leftists, or communists, it could be ratios of one to 10, but
we'd win because they were not ideologically committed to their goals,"
and he again puffs up a bit with recalled pride.

The NSM is one group that was careful to stay on the right
side of the law, though at times that line feels gray. They were adept at

instigating verbal racism and physical violence they publicly disavowed. After a planned march through a Black neighborhood in Toledo, Ohio, the SPLC described the December 2005 rally as the "best example of the NSM's provocative rallies" which "sparked unrest by residents and counter protesters." That unrest cost Toledo more than $336,000, but NSM's members were not held liable for any damage and escaped the violence that broke out in response.[171] (It's also the rally where Jeff labeled Black people "beasts.") The NSM also regularly staged events with the Klan; and the Klan and skinheads often joined their demonstrations. Both had few restrictions. Jeff insists the NSM always kept clear of the law. "I was in 27 years total. In 27 years of rallies, not once, including in Charlottesville, was anyone from NSM arrested for violence. They were arrested on their own for stupidities over the years, but at events our rules were so strict, not one was arrested. We would fight only in self-defense."

When I ask about skirmishes with Antifa and other counter protesters, Jeff claims the NSM never started the violence. "Antifa would attack us. Typically, they like to throw rocks and bottles and bricks, sometimes weapons" and he recalls a particular incident in New Jersey, sometime around 2010. "Antifa attacked us with knives and hammers. I hit someone with a chair out there in self-defense. The guys wanted to fight but were not allowed to start it."

"They would show wherever we were," says former NSM member, Keith Schneider. Now 70-years-old, Keith is Jeff's former bodyguard and was in charge of NSM's stormtroopers. "We never got arrested. We did everything legal. They were carrying mace, brass knuckles, a bludgeon. They would get arrested. They were always armed." He says he and Jeff organized NSM activities "actually working with law enforcement" and demanded their members follow NSM nonviolent policies. He also recalled a specific confrontation, this one in Pennsylvania where Jeff was maced in the eyes. "Police showed up and thought Nazis would be the problem, but five ARA [Anti

Racist Action Network] of the antiracist group got arrested. We were fully cooperative. Why wouldn't we be?" Keith recalls. "I'm a retired lawman."

Yet Jeff clearly understood the value of confrontation. Police would put up barricades to separate groups but "the guys liked to fight." When fights broke out, Jeff knew they made useful propaganda. He would have members film violence with counter protestors and post it on the NSM website to attract new members. "When we put out the video, they'd come to the next [confrontation]. They wanted the opportunity to take part."

If that sounds familiar, "You are going to find a lot of parallels," Jeff says about my research with hundreds of militant jihadists. "I didn't realize until I was in for a long time, but the social structures and driving factors have a lot of similarities." He also points to religion's role, to a certain extent, and points to NSM's Christian Identity faction and the FBI's concerns. "Back in those days they [the FBI] said they were the most dangerous because they believed God was on their side. It's like a jihadist, if ISIS justifies chopping someone's head, it's the will of God and all that."

"I was Christian Identity for a little while," Jeff adds "but Christianity didn't click for me."[172] NSM was oddly religiously diverse. "Forty to 45 percent were Christian; 40 percent were pagans, Odinists [aligned with Norse mythology]; five to 10 percent were other—some Muslims, Buddhists, a couple of Satanists, Creativity—where you are your own God, and general atheists."

"You had Muslims and Buddhists in the NSM?" I ask, amazed to hear it.

"Muslims and Buddhists, if they were white, we let them in."

Religion also proved to be contentious. Christians wanted to be rid of the pagans and the pagans wanted to be rid of the Christians. Due to the divisiveness among the majority groups, Jeff declared, 'Religion is for home, church and family, and not to be pushed or proselytized.'"

Pagan or Christian, those internal conflicts were not the ideology that binds. It was fear.

So, I ask Jeff, "What did you fear about minorities and Jews, really?"

"I don't like the word fear. I see myself as fairly fearless," he responds. But he certainly used fear to incite others into action. Fear was "a mitigating and driving factor. Whites are going to be extinct. Other races are going to take out their vengeance on whites for past injustices like slavery. We'd use propaganda messaging like when Blacks asked for reparations. For us slavery was an injustice, but we didn't have to repay. The Klan was pro-slavery, but I never was." He called on those who were enslaved to rebel. The NSM was sure to publicize Black crimes against whites in South Africa following the downfall of Apartheid. The fearmongering was clear: The same could happen here.

Which leads to what has to be the most surprising partnership meant to further NSM's goal of a white homeland: join forces with Black nationalists. As Jeff's deputy, William Trull tells, it, "They want to separate just as we do. We both see the same light. We started working together." Black nationalists invited Jeff to be a guest speaker at their events. Jeff says NSM leaders believed Blacks would up-rise and take areas "that whites designated as their areas. Everyone would turn tribal. It would be us exposing the Jews…so everyone would be going after them."

As for what that white homeland would look like, "We felt the U.S. would Balkanize at some point. Blacks would get part of it and mixed peoples, and there would be a white homeland somewhere."

In August 2013, a 61-year-old neo-Nazi named Paul Craig Cobb decided to create that white homeland, a white ethno-state in the small town of Leith, North Dakota, population 19. Acting upon H. Michael Barrett's 2001 proposal called *Pioneer Little Europe,* which makes the case for white nationalist community-building, Cobb, a member of the Church of the Creator, donated or sold land for pennies to the leaders of several white nationalist and neo-Nazi groups, including the NSM.[173]

I will later interview one of the main recruiters for *Pioneer Little Europe*, Scott Earnest, who holds contempt for the type of people applying to live there. "I would meet them to see if they were decent. White nationalists are the worst people in the world. I learned that really well talking to them." Scott had of course initially believed in *Pioneer Little Europe* and joined for the sense of community and belonging I so often hear longed for in our sample. However, reality was quite different, "I started to realize how horrible it was. They were having Hitler movies in the library basement, fire drops, in your face stuff, all stuff I opposed." Scott, who was active on the once popular white supremacists message board, *StormFront,* says he (like Jeff) was trying to mainstream the movement and make white nationals acceptable, "but I was worse than a Hitler lover, 1488, because I made it more acceptable to be horrible and that's arguably worse."

In 2013, Jeff told the *New York Times*, "People should move and get the process going. It gives us a base of support for elections and things like that." Soon after, Jeff arrived in Leith to plant Nazi flags on Cobb's property, flanked by a dozen or so NSM members. Two months later, however, Cobb and 29-year-old white nationalist Kynan Dutton were arrested on four counts of felony terrorizing when acting as a "safety patrol." They were accused of threatening a number of Leith residents.[174] Jeff returned to North Dakota to support Cobb and Dutton, though by February 2014, Cobb pleaded guilty to one count of felony terrorizing and five counts of misdemeanor menacing.[175] The project failed.[176]

Jeff also turned the NSM's attention to the U.S. southern border. A growing number of the NSM's efforts and protests targeted immigrants, beginning in the mid-to-late 2000s and extending into the 2010s. Keith Schneider recalls trouble on the California and Arizona border with Mexico and sheriff's deputies and police requesting but unable to get needed assistance from state capitals and the National Guard. "Lawmen were alone without any type of support."

Always looking to the Third Reich for guidance, Keith explains, "When Hitler became the Chancellor and Goring was appointed the Ministry of Interior, he addressed crime in the cities. He [ordered], 'Get your stormtroopers to every police district. We need them as reserve units to the police.' Stormtroopers assisted the police. It worked back then; it can work today. So, I ordered my stormtroopers and all who were permitted to carry firearms to get involved as deputies and give any help they could. At least they'd have fully armed men ready to assist. [The sheriffs and police] accepted that help from the stormtroopers. We had five in some locations, more than 20 in others. They would walk the border perimeters, working against drug cartels. The police welcomed and were very happy for the help." (I'll add here, not everyone agrees with that recounting.)

No matter where the truth lies, putting their members on patrol of the southern border burnished the image of the NSM as protecting the United States from unwelcome immigrants. Among the leaders of these patrols was a former NSM member, 39-year-old J.T. Ready, later reported to have shot himself and four others in a brutal murder-suicide. (The victims included Ready's girlfriend, his girlfriend's daughter and boyfriend, and their 15-month-old child.) At the time of the shooting, Ready had been running for sheriff of Pinal County in Arizona with the appeal to the county's residents that they were "under constant threat of encountering the horrific reality of terrible violence associated with illegal immigration." The Bureau of Alcohol, Tobacco, Firearms and Explosives investigators found ammunition, weaponry, explosives, and smoke grenades at Ready's home.[177] He was clearly prepared for violence, if not war.

In his later years as leader, Jeff's NSM messaging focused on dehumanization. "Whites are being dehumanized and the left is dehumanizing us," Jeff would say. "I said it to the press: 'A Nazi is talking about dehumanization.' I spent my entire life dehumanizing other groups, but I felt whites were being dehumanized. I couldn't see that I was doing it. That's karma. When you are involved, you don't see yourself as an extremist. You see yourself doing something noble and right." The irony is not lost on him.

You can watch Jeff tell his story at www.EscapeHate.org

Chapter 12 - Leadership and Loyalty Through the Prism of Hate

Jeff Schoep is a study in leadership through the prism of hate. He rebranded and brought the former American Nazi Party to national popularity and prominence as the National Socialist Movement, NSM. "I didn't pretend I knew everything, I never thought about myself as a dictator, but my friend [later] said that I was a benevolent dictator."

In most violent extremist groups, the leader is someone with personal charisma who knows how to play to the needs of those who join the group, making them feel significant, that they have purpose and belong. Leaders often are those who do not commit the heinous acts of violence these groups are known for. Instead, they act as inciters, standing back, maybe even condemning violence as a policy, but encouraging it on a personal basis.[178] Jeff was all these things.

I have interviewed 12 members of the NSM, thus far, many from Jeff's circle of loyal commanders. Some followed him out of the movement when he left in 2019. Some now work with him at *Beyond Barriers,* the project he founded in January 2020 to help white supremacists and other extremists exit from hate groups and prevent new members from joining. Talking to them underlined their adulation. Many members I interviewed, both men and women, revered and worked hard for him, putting in long hours and often ignoring family and sacrificing leisure time to serve the organization and Jeff.

Jeff ran the group as a capable executive. He was charismatic and rewarded those who put in those long hours, with attention and care, and routed out troublemakers and those likely to get the group on the wrong side of the law. Members were very proud of promotions, which encouraged them to give even more hours. He was also a confidante and advisor to many. In return, a group of men (and a few women) rose to become Jeff's loyal leadership circle. Many stand with him to this day.

William Trull, one of Jeff's deputies, told me," A lot of guys saw Jeff as the President of the United States. "Jeff is a smart man," says Keith Schneider, who like many former NSM members remains loyal; and in Keith's case, even after doing an about face and marrying a Black nurse named Catherine, who cared for him during a bout with cancer. "I've told Jeff on a number of times, 'You and I were in the movement. I was your bodyguard. I'm still your bodyguard if needed.' Catherine is crazy about him," Keith adds.

William Trull says he was influenced to join NSM by Jeff's videos, rallies, and protests on YouTube and tried to join when he was just 16. (He had to wait until he was 18 due to the NSM's age restrictions.) He recalls Jeff's strong leadership, "Jeff was very strict: no racial slurs, stick to the facts about how the government is being ran. That kind of made me realize—at least I felt then—maybe this is not a racist organization?" William still defends the NSM, "It wasn't until I became a high-ranking member that I saw a broader picture. It was not the organization, but the people who were racists."

Yet Jeff's inspiration was guided by their Führer—the Führer. For example, he understood the power of an oath due to the Third Reich. "When they asked guys from the [German] SS, 'Why did you carry out this order?', in the military you don't have a choice. In time of war, you get shot. They expected them to say that I was following orders." Jeff also understood the power of being called upon to uphold that oath. "Your oath was your honor. If you broke it, you weren't a man. I felt that was important, to have that honor and nobility, and you keep your word on things, the way I was raised." Recall Jeff's adulation of his own, his uncles who served as military leaders under Hitler during WWII.

William Trull, a volunteer firefighter, devoted much of his life to the NSM. He would spend six to seven hours a day with NSM, sometimes even while at work. "It was a full-time job." He says there were a lot of firefighters and EMTs in the NSM and he created a squad and a personnel medical team for which he provided firefighter training. He also worked himself up to providing "close protection" for their commander-in-chief as a member of a high-ranking security squad. Even his personal life aligned with the movement. William would only date women with the same views as his and a partner had to be aligned with the sacrifices he was making as a regional leader in the movement.

Fighting was not a part of his work, he says, but that caveat always seems to come with a "but." His security work looked out for Antifa and others willing to do property damage where NSM was staying. "There were a lot of members looking for a fight. That's what they thrived off of." William says he had some law enforcement training and his priority was protecting his leader "versus being a fighter. I was in a flight situation. If cornered, I would fight, but only if cornered."

William sounds like he adored Jeff, and Jeff in turn often gave William full authority to handle troublesome situations in his region. Sounding a lot like Keith, "He was my friend and my commander," William recalls. "We clicked."

Søren, (not his real name), now 39 and a former NSM member, recalls Jeff as "an intelligent and good person, deep down." Before joining NSM, Søren did his homework, researching various white supremacy groups. Søren had wanted to be in the U.S. military but was precluded from serving due to health issues. The NSM resonated with him. From the membership packet he received in the mail from Jeff, to being connected to "the unit from my area. It used military terminology. Everyone started as a private under your unit leader." (Recall George Lincoln Rockwell, the Navy commander, founded the American Nazi Party and established its so-called military ranks.) Søren fondly recalls his rise in the ranks. "I was working hard. Some higher-ups reported to Jeff that I was doing a good job. He sent me an e-mail with a promotion. You get a certificate in the mail. That was kind of cool and exciting." Embarrassment filling his face, "It sounds silly now."

Fred Cook, another Jeff devotee, says he moved through the ranks very quickly to Chief of Staff. Fred also recalls working hard. "I organized rallies, which caused absolute terror. I remember seeing Holocaust survivors screaming, pointing at their numbers on their forearms; gays counter-protesting." In a haze of irony, Fred says, "I remember thinking all these people hate you," and like Jeff, failing at the time to recognize that they, the NSM, were the haters. "You don't realize it could be because you are Nazis. You overlook that," Fred says. (In a turn of events I've seen before, after Fred left the NSM, through DNA testing he found out he is not "pure white," but in fact Jewish, an identity he now embraces rather than reviles.)

"It's cult-like," Jeff now admits. Indeed, as Steve Hassan, one of the foremost experts on cults and undue influence explains, cults are any group that requires you to give up your freedom of mind. Hassan developed an assessment tool to describe the specific methods cults use to recruit and maintain control over people. His BITE Model assesses the level of undue influence an organization has by weighing how and how much a group is able to control a member's Behaviors, Information, Thoughts, and Emotions.[179] I would add, when cults engage in disinformation to Behaviors, Information, Thoughts, and Emotions, they often learn the best lies have some truth in them, making them harder to reject. So, for example, Jeff might reference a Black person as "not too bad" or "one of the good ones" to make excuses for a decent non-white person. Other times, he'd use racism to outright agitate and manipulate followers. "Sometimes, I'd pick a Mexican restaurant because I knew it would fire up certain people that didn't like that."

"Why did you want to agitate them?" I ask.

"I liked the food," Jeff replies, eyes lighting up with mischief. "I knew certain people would act up and I could tease about it."

Comparing his brand of loyalty to the violent repercussions that came with groups like the Aryan Brotherhood, I ask Jeff if he tolerated dissent. Jeff responds this way, "You can leave a group like the NSM and not have to worry about any backlash. But speaking out against them can lead to threats." He said they "self-policed" and would punish or throw out members who did not abide by NSM group policies, such as treating women with respect, not using drugs, and not engaging in overt violence. "We didn't call the police. If we found guys with drugs, or a guy beating his wife, they would be beaten. Smoking weed privately, okay." If they found drugs at a party, they'd flush them. He recalls, "One time we were at this event and the guy punched his girlfriend in the car. I told the cops, 'We'll take care of this. You can leave.'" The cops "figured out what was going to happen."

"Who were the enforcers?" I ask.

"It could be anybody. I sometimes hit them myself." Jeff tells me he's long had a streak of justice. He'd stand up for bullied kids in school. He once witnessed a purse-snatching in town—slammed on his brakes, jumped out of his car "and went and took care of it. What shocked me about it was that it was just natural." The victim was white, the would-be robber was Black, "but if white I would have done the same thing."

"So, you are a stand-up guy for your own people?" I ask.

"I don't know if I would have stood up for another race. I have to think on that," Jeff says, shame briefly flitting across his face as he understands the point of my question.

In his treatment of women, Jeff's leadership was certainly unique among white supremacists. Many NSM interviewees told me how strategic Jeff was in working to mainstream the group and having women involved was part of it.

"In the NSM women were allowed leadership positions," he says smiling brightly, once again looking more like the proud company executive with forward leaning social policies than the former leader of a hate group. NSM had female regional directors and his current and very capable deputy, Acacia Dietz, at *Beyond Barriers* ran NSM's propaganda department.

"We wanted women in, and we wanted to make it palatable. We thought the Alt-Right must be homosexual. They hate women. Something wrong with these guys," he tells me. "The Alt-Right is so anti-female. I didn't like the Alt-Right [even] when we were in the movement." In Charlottesville, Jeff says the Alt-Right chanted "White *shariah* now." He shakes his head, "I was amazed. There are memes about raping women, subjugating women. It's very, very strange."

Janet Louise (a pseudonym), who was raped by a Mexican friend in high school, said the group's application process to join gave her confidence in the group. They conducted a background check and had an introductory membership packet that included a CD with speeches and a music CD from Jeff's music label. She showed me an NSM CD called *Built for War*, with titles like *I Hate Niggers*. Defending her leader, she says, "I never heard that [n-word] out of his mouth, not once. He might have used the term, but I never heard it. I really respected him. I expected him to be this hate-mongering leader, but he was the opposite."

She met Jeff at her first rally, in North Dakota. She didn't know what to expect and says the events became "like a family reunion. I lived for that. I wanted friends. I wanted something to do. I wanted to belong to something, to stand for something." Jeff and the NSM provided her that, alongside a sense of protection—surrounding her with strong and aggressive white men who were told to protect their white "sisters."

Janet Louise also regularly turned to Jeff for personal support. "He's like my counselor," and recalls him patiently listening to her concerns when she started losing friends because she was in a hate group.

She was another member seemingly blind to the fact she had become the hater. She'd see anti-NSM activists and wonder, "Why are these people so angry and hateful? Why do you hate us?" She recalls confusion, but no guilt. "I loved every second of every hour I spent working," on behalf of the NSM. "[Jeff] was a big part of it. I also loved the camaraderie, something I believed in. There was a point I was only around white people. I believed you should only be with white people."

Jeff would "hold his shoulders back, and he'd put his head high because that states dominance and power. And when people see that in a leader, they think, 'That's who I want to be following.'" By emulating Jeff, she felt able to regain her sense of agency and self-esteem. "Then they did the *Sieg Heil* with the flags over him. There's no greater sense of power than that," she recalls. "The feeling of, I'm a Nazi, today, it's pretty empowering. You can get drunk on your own love and power."

Janet Louise exited NSM because Jeff did (though she does not seem to have fully left the movement.) "I'm loyal to Jeff. We are extremely close. He's crazy. I love him. He's just awesome." Jeff may also have been a bit of a ladies' man, not something I explore with him. He has been married twice, both times while in NSM. He told me he dated a lot of different women over the years, not all in the movement. But in the last 10 to 12 years, he says he dated more than in his entire life. "In those years, some would say, 'This is like a cult.' They'd go with me to support me, but not the movement. I kept wondering why they would say that."

Jeff's longevity in the world of hate is impressive. "How do you think you lasted so long as the leader in the NSM?" I ask him, knowing it was a cutthroat group of mostly angry men.

"Because I brought so many people in," he answers.

Jeff Schoep Speaking

In essence he had his own "army" brought in by a lot of recruitment techniques. He lists his public speaking, propaganda, hate music; NSM developed first-person shooter video games; they utilized radio, podcasting, rallies, spoken word at rallies, leaflets.

In sum, "That I was able to stay as the head of that organization for so long, that's a major feat."

Chapter 13 - Neo-Nazi Women

Though toxic masculinity is a common thread among hate groups, it isn't only men who get drawn into white hate. Though reasons for engagement in DVE generally differ for women and men. Meet three very different women who entered hate.

Recall Janet Louise (a pseudonym) was raped in high school by a trusted friend who was Hispanic. As she told me, "I don't like Mexican men. They gave me the creeps." NSM offered her a warm and confirming welcome when she was willing to make her new identity all about being white. In NSM she felt the protection, acceptance, loyalty, and respect she craved. NSM directed her hate and made her feel she could still become the person and professional she wanted to be. She was responsible for membership in several states and later helped produce a radio show. She says she enjoyed choosing the topics, writing, and research. "We picked apart *Mein Kampf.* That's our Bible. We'd find three to five passages that we'd talk about. That was fun."

"I was a true believer," and adds, "I'm still a sergeant," though she also told me she had left the NSM when Jeff Schoep did. During our interview, she showed me an SS flag she bought from the paraphernalia business Jeff owned. "It means being secure and having someone with you at all times," seemingly still in awe of the SS. "This copy of *Mein Kampf* is really rare," she continues. "I've tabbed it out, from when we did our talk shows. It's the first English translation." She also shows me the CD mailed to her when she first joined the NSM and she reads off disturbing titles. "I don't like it," she says, scrunching up her nose in disgust. "I used to

Mein Kampf Book Cover

worship that CD, but I don't anymore." She also tells me, if you want to be hate-filled and feel good about it, "it makes you feel, 'Oh yeah, I'm this and I really do hate them.'"

NSM is the rare DVE group that offered women leadership roles. Reflecting on how the traumatic rape had cratered her high school studies and plans to continue onto university, Janet Louise says her work at NSM "felt revitalizing, like I was doing something, like I had a purpose." She says she worked day and night and loved hosting the radio program. "It feels great to be a local little star."

Forty-two-year-old Veronica, nicknamed Ronny, had a very different experience in her world of neo-Nazi skinheads. Racist skinheads have always promoted hate and violence and today's skinheads remain a violent, misogynistic, racist, and antisemitic subculture, global in scope, who have come a long way from their start as the neighborhood-based, anti-hippie counterculture in 1960s working-class London.[180]

Ronny is a pretty, dark haired woman, with a playful smile that lights up her face as she talks. She looks far younger than her age and it's easy to imagine her as an energetic, hard-to-control teen. Which she was.

She started smoking pot around 12 and would run wild with her best friend, Jessica. "We met in third grade and did everything together." On one of their "adventures," she told a punk rocker she was 16 and had run away from home. The 19-year-old took her in but warned, "You have to be really careful out there." They weren't. They started dropping acid at 13. Ronny's dad tried to curtail her wild behavior, then she thinks he gave up. "I was uncontrollable."

Ronny's tumultuous life started with young military parents. Her mom got pregnant at 18, her dad was 23. Ronny's grandparents insisted the young couple get married. "They gave it a good try," Ronny says. They got divorced when she was 11 and her younger sister was seven. Hearing her childhood story, you can feel her slow decline into hate.

She was born in Iceland where her father was stationed, then they moved to a small town in Germany where she recalls wonderful memories. "Our family was together, me and my sister, in a beautiful place. All my memories there are happy," then adds, "Except for kindergarten." Thinking it would be a good experience, her mother enrolled her in an immersive German program (she did not speak German.) She found a tough culture among kids who would "run you over and then make fun of you because you are a sissy." Ronny was picked on and beat up. She hated school and started to hate social situations. The situation "was sink or swim. I sunk."

By second grade they were back in the U.S., in the Southwest where her important developmental years continued to get harder. She was teased about needing to wear a bra in second grade, which can have lasting body image impact on girls. She tested into the gifted program in third grade and says that was the first time she was around students smarter than her, which made her feel inadequate. As many kids do, she engaged in avoidance and described being with kids to whom she couldn't relate as "boring," and would pretend to be sick to get out of going to school.

Then her dad went to the Gulf War for seven months, creating a stressful time for the family. And messy. Her mom cheated with a friend of her father's (they'd eventually marry), and as her parents' marriage broke up, Ronny was furious at her mother. She lived with her dad who became reclusive, leaving the daughters to fend for themselves. Her relationship with her father devolved into anger and name-calling. She recalls packing a bag and going "downtown and hung out for two weeks, got drunk and did drugs and had a great time." Then her dad started dating a friend of her mother's. She was bipolar and added to a tumultuous homelife.

Ronny dropped out of the gifted program in 7th grade, a tough year for most adolescents, and the bullying increased. "These Mexican girls who were very beautiful and popular in school, for some reason in 7th grade they laughed at me for the cowboy boots I was wearing. They'd wait for me at the bus and surround me and throw things at me and laugh at me. It was scary, intimidating and humiliating, I was only 90 pounds, 4'11". That's when I got into racism."

Ronny says she was primed for white supremacy by her parents' origins. Her parents were from the South. "It was heritage, rebel flags. My dad was racist, so it was easy for me to transition." White power started planting its roots. She and her best friend met a boy whose mother was dying of cancer. Unsupervised, they started skipping school and hanging out at his house, filled with rebel flags and swastikas. She says it further fueled her "fuck Mexicans" attitude. "We'd smoke weed and drink alcohol and take their four-wheeler out into the desert. I was thinking white power was cool." But her school principal did not.

At that time there were "slam books" floating around schools. Students were asked to answer inappropriate questions, like what would you do to your worst enemy? "I wrote something horrible," and I see her recoil in hindsight. "I didn't even think about it when I wrote it down." Ronny told me she wrote, "'I would hang a nigger in a tree.' It's really horrible to say something like that. It's disgusting." A fellow student saw her comment and told some popular Black kids about it. Ronny says she was already unpopular and counterculture and now these hateful words started circulating around school, "'Ronny is a Nazi. We are going to kill her.'"

The principal had her meet a Black counselor. She recalls him telling her, "'I read this and expected to see a monster, but you are a pretty, white girl. Why would you write this?'" (I think to myself, many monsters are externally beautiful. Being pretty doesn't preclude her being one.) Like most kids who get caught posturing with white supremacy at a young age, Ronny had no good answers when confronted. She couldn't articulate she'd been bullied, had a chaotic home life, was acting out with drugs and alcohol, and was scared; or that her aggressive and hateful expressions were her ways of dealing with the pain and fears.

The counselor ordered the girls who'd threatened her to leave her alone. Ronny was relieved but says, "I really needed way more help. That is the only time someone stepped in. He should have said, 'Racism is wrong and let's talk about why'...I wish [the school] had the resources to follow up and look into why."

Ronny slipped through what could have been a safety net. Her story is common. The school missed an important opportunity to intervene, to learn what was going on with her, and try to stop her downward spiral into hate while she was so impressionable. In many cases, school administrators will simply choose to expel students, pushing them further into the arms of those who have been radicalizing them.

TM Garret laments, like Ronny, he was one of those kids and his young experience came at a deep cost to both him and society. Losing his father at a young age, he says his expression of pain could have been redirected had his school been more attuned. Instead, he became exactly what they feared he already was, a neo-Nazi, and he went on live up to the label and eventually launch his own branch of the KKK in Germany. For the past two decades, TM has been applying the lessons too many school administrators have yet to learn, helping youth resist recruitment and exit hate.

In high school Ronny met kids who were racist punks who in turn introduced her to a racist skinhead named Robert, recently released from jail, who was trying to recruit kids. "He was a grown-ass man. He was gross looking. He had to be 30-something. I was 14." Ronny says he was always hitting on her. They'd get drunk and he would challenge her football player boyfriend and his friends "to fight him to get strong." She recalls, "My boyfriend didn't want to. Robert was like, 'Hit me! Hit me!' My boyfriend knocked him out and Robert pissed himself because he was drunk." Twisting her hair around her finger as she continues, "But his influence, the ideology, was there."

Robert told them about Hitler and would read from *Mein Kampf*. I cringe as she tells me she started carving swastikas in her skin. "It was so stupid, but we thought he was a cool grown-up that would teach us and wanted to hang out with us. He taught us why white people were better, that it was our heritage."

Home life got rougher. Ronny's father and bipolar girlfriend decided to move to Berkeley, California. Ronny was excited to move. But her parents got in a fight that blew up and Ronny says she got the blame. Tempers flared and her father hit her in the face. "I fell backwards. They threw me out the door and locked the door." Ronny's mother, who was waiting for her outside "went berserk." That was the last time she saw her father during high school. She was 14.

Ronny threatened to drop out of school after ninth grade, but her parents enrolled her in an alternative high school that she "really loved" and eyes light up with that memory. It was creative and she felt the teachers really cared about kids. She graduated early with a 4.0. I nod, thinking, okay, finally someone gets it right in her life.

At age 16, her mother and stepfather were transferred to Arkansas. Ronny refused to leave her friends and the alternative school, so her parents let her move in with a girl friend from the school. She says they were a very nice family, yet she continued to get more entrenched in white power ideology.

Upon graduation, Ronny had no plan and after a one-year scholarship to a community college depleted, she couldn't afford to continue. She decided her only future was to move back to Germany with her hard-partying childhood friend, Jessica, where the plan was to find husbands and live in Europe.

In Germany they got into the underground scene, did drugs, partied "like crazy" and met all kinds of people there. "Sadly, those Germans were totally racist still, totally into Hitler. I thought that was awesome. I remember Jessica would argue, 'You guys lost the war! Why are you hanging on to this?'" Ronny's German husband didn't materialize, and at 18 and flat broke, she moved in with her mother in Arkansas where she says, "Everyone is racist. It's a common belief."

As Ronny moved from place-to-place, she would tap into the vast network of like-minded people on the internet. Her extremists of choice were homegrown neo-Nazi skinheads. From jobs in record stores, bars, and strip clubs, she would find the skinheads in the city she was in, and they would protect her. "I thought these guys are so tough and hot, that they can protect you. I had been bullied all my life." Other women I've interviewed also voice this sense of protection. These violent guys offer women and girls a sense of safety, often while also exploiting them, and the women in turn support the guys in picking on the minority groups they have learned to hate.

I'm curious if Ronny was a fighter. Some women do fight, and they can be vicious. Ronny laughs. "I have never been in an actual fist fight." But she says the skinheads are extremely aggressive and surround themselves with violence. "If they can't find someone to pick a fight with, they will just fight each other. It was every night. They are drinking and bored, and they look for someone to fight." Many have told me about the addictive quality of skinhead aggression, getting hooked on the constant adrenaline rush provided by fighting. Others have told me, "If you are poor, you can't join a club where you can fight, so you find it on the streets."

"Were they good to you?" I ask. Skinheads in general are not respectful of women. I've learned from others; most women are not considered real members but merely the girlfriend or wife of whichever skinhead they are currently with. Some are passed around for short sexual exploits. Ronny is very pretty, and I imagine many of these skinheads would have wanted her for their girlfriend. "They were [good to me]," Ronny answers, "I saw plenty of them treat their girlfriends badly; hit them and be emotionally abusive. I didn't experience that with any of them although I still grapple a lot with internalized misogyny," and admits, "I hated girls. It was always girls who bullied me. I would always go to the guys, and they always loved me." She offers her succinct explanation: "I had big boobs, would drink beer, and listen to them." But she says she "was not 100 percent down with the skinheads. They wanted to continue the white race and have babies." She was not looking to be a breeder, the role often assigned to women.

Now 21, Ronny reconnected with her father and joined him in South Carolina where she met up with more skinheads. She says, "It's totally normal to be a white supremacist there," and she found a gang of ex-skinheads to hang out with, "the toughest guys around and they were my best friends." Her best friend, Jessica, had gotten married and moved to the UK, "so I was so lost. She made it and I didn't."

Ronny went through a series of "low-wage shit jobs" she says, and working as a waitress and bartender in a strip club "certainly people tried to coerce me into doing things I didn't want to do. I did see that in young girls, with drugs and overdoses." She adds, "You have to have a very strong mind to work in a place like that, but I don't see it as inherently a bad thing. But I do wish so many didn't do it out of desperation."

Not surprisingly, Ronny found herself in an abusive relationship. It would be this relationship that would start to create doubt in the hate she was holding. He was popular and good-looking and "very emotionally abusive." Ronny of course felt lucky to be with him. He was cheating which led to a "very tumultuous relationship with screaming and fighting, breaking up and getting back together and 'I'm going to kill myself without you'—from him or me." She finally learned that he was bisexual, "more gay than straight. It was over a year in when he told me. I had to accept it."

That pushed her to open her eyes to some of her beliefs, like homophobia. "Before I thought it was disgusting, but I started becoming accepting of that." Other ideologies started falling away, like her racist attitude toward Black people. She began to see that some of the societal roots of her discontent had nothing to do with race and now in her mid-20s, asked herself why she could not save money or buy a house. "It's not because Black and Mexican people take a job from me. It's because

people don't pay you enough. Then it snowballed. I realized the beliefs
that I have believed my whole life were stupid and didn't make sense."

Her skinhead relationships started to deteriorate. Ronny got
married which caused a rift with the skinhead men who didn't appreciate
an outsider taking her away. He was an alcoholic. The marriage lasted
five years. With a new daughter, Ronny knew she needed out. She
moved back to Arkansas and in with her mother. "That's when I realized
how hostile this country is to single moms and moms in general." She
looks back at this time with frustration, "They wouldn't hire anyone
fulltime [to avoid paying benefits]. The town was five thousand people,
all white. You couldn't admit you were liberal. People would openly call
Obama racial slurs. Everyone had rebel flags. Everybody had a gun."
Having previously lived it, she realized this wasn't how she wanted to
raise her daughter.

White supremacy ideology fell apart. Her turning point "was
realizing what was preventing me from getting ahead—the whole
system." And that system is unfair to all.

"I have literally never been beaten out for a job by a person of
another race. I never worked with any Blacks and Mexicans. Where are
all of these minorities stealing our jobs? Once I realized that, I knew
these people are in the same fucking boat with me, but it's worse. They
are paid less. We should be on their side. Why are we hating them?"
She recognized Blacks and Hispanics were having the same struggle
"as me, as a poor white person. History in this country is built on the
backs of Black people kidnapped to work for free not that long ago,
and then in my parents' lifetime they are still treated badly. The people
at the top of the economic system, it works out for them. That's how I
see it." And adds, "I don't see how Black people couldn't hate white
people."

She tells me she voted for Obama. Coming from a former white
supremacist skinhead, this admission is huge. When Ronny's dad moved
to Oregon, she jumped at the chance to join him. She reconnected with

an old high school flame who drew her into workers' right and other causes. They married and merged families.

Ronny credits her husband for her transformation and exit from white supremacism. "Although I'm not quite there with the misogyny," she admits. "I still sometimes think other women are stupid bitches and I hate mom culture…Then I had a daughter and I realized how hateful and hard the world is. I have to make the world better for her."

Ronny is now an activist. She has joined protests with Black Lives Matter, the 15 Now movement [$15 minimum wage in Seattle] and is the board chair of Family Forward which helped win paid family leave for the state of Washington. "I'm super proud of that…Our next big fight is for childcare."

She also sees her own family history differently now. Her parents were born and raised at a time when Black people couldn't come into white institutions. Her father was part of desegregation bussing policies "where he was beat up by Black guys. That's all he can see. He can't get past those experiences in his life." Hate is a powerful force.

When I ask her what warning she might want to convey, her focus is on children. Kids get involved with extremism out of boredom, she says, when parents don't have the money to get kids into activities, or they work all the time and "you are looking for someone to show you this is the way of the world." Kids need support and "any kind of gang situation, it feels like it's a family, but it's not. It's a bunch of broken people coming together to try to feel stronger, but they can also turn on you at the drop of anything."

She agrees to be a part of our counter narrative project but pushes back against the white supremacist label. "'Nazi punk' is how I would describe myself." I don't argue with her, although in truth, is there any better descriptor for a Nazi than white supremacist?

You can watch Janet Louise and Veronica tell their stories at www.EscapeHate.org.

Chapter 14 - The Nexus of My Hate

Meet Phoebe Rose. She spews anger. "I became very angry, very aggressive, very violent, I drank a lot, didn't care. That is the nexus of my hate, because I hated society itself from that point on." Phoebe is 31, British, and a victim of a sexual assault, a traumatic experience that set her on a trajectory of hate and propelled her into being a powerful propagandist for the English Defense League (EDL), a British hate group dedicated to eradicating Muslims from the United Kingdom.

Phoebe is sitting in a wood paneled room that looks a bit like a sauna when seen through Zoom. She looks relaxed. She is tall, wearing a navy striped dress. Her dark hair is long and frames a pretty face as she speaks. Yet almost immediately I sense something is different. Her limbs are long for a woman and her choice of words and humor strike me as a British male. I begin to wonder if she's transgender and as that train of thought fires off a flurry of questions in my head, I wonder if I can ask them or if it's better to not pursue questions about her gender identity.

I begin our interview with her upbringing. It doesn't take long to find out where trouble began.

"My father was a bastard," Phoebe is quick to say when I ask if she came from a happy home. "He and I have a peculiar relationship." She says he was physically and emotionally abusive only to her, not her brother or mother. "He never understood me. I never fit the narrative he wanted. He couldn't handle me knowing more than him. Any defiance, any individuality, anything not what he expected, was problematic to him. He always viewed me as not successful enough for him; not stereotypical for him; he couldn't control me. Those three things worked in tandem."

Phoebe describes her family as typical middle class. "My father was a sparky," British parlance for an electrician. The family was religious, and the kids were privately educated in "high Anglicanism, in

Christian schools," experiences often reserved for the higher classes in the UK.

Phoebe says she was always close to her mother growing up, but when her parents split, her mother did not process the divorce well, "she had become a very toxic person," and Phoebe cut off all communication. It was about the time Phoebe was off to university. "Then when I finished university, she said, 'You weren't here so I didn't think it affected you at all.' The family that had existed had disappeared. That level of blindness!" Phoebe declares.

Phoebe graduated, and jobless, she moved home with her now divorced mother. "When I was back with my mother, it was as if she had become my father," Phoebe explains. "She was never physically abusive but verbally abusive."

I feel sure the abuse was about gender identity alongside other issues but decide not to venture into that topic, at least not yet, asking instead how Phoebe did in school.

"I was one of those persons that went to university that shouldn't have," and Phoebe's voice gets agitated. "I am a very intelligent person, but I don't test well." At age 25, she found out she is autistic. "I am in the lowest five percent of reading speed. No one picked up on this disparity. I passed all my A-Levels," referencing the challenging UK high school competency tests that open and close doors to different majors in British universities.

I'm not surprised to hear about reading issues. Traumatized and abused kids often have difficulty concentrating. Their brains are busy scanning their environment, trying to detect, avoid, and brace for the next round of abuse. They usually live in a constant state of heightened physical alertness. Very intelligent kids who have been abused can come across as learning disabled if evaluated out of the context of what they are enduring.

Turning to early schooling, Phoebe acknowledges school can be a reprieve from a dangerous home, but not for her. "You don't get an escape. School isn't the escape." I feel a deep sadness listening to that. The abuse just kept on coming. "Race doesn't play the same dynamic as it does in the U.S. Racism is even with people who look the same." Phoebe explains, "I don't come from the right class." She says she was bullied because her father came from a working-class background in the 1960s and was working his way up the class ladder. However, Phoebe viewed herself as middle class, so school dynamics were confusing for her. She couldn't understand who would want to be friends and who would not.

Church was her escape. "I could find people I had a common bond with. I was actively taking part in the services as an acolyte at the chapel. It gave me a sense of no longer being the outsider." I nod but wonder how long that lasted if she is transgender.

"You felt appreciated?" I ask.

Phoebe affirms, then reveals, "When you are nerdy, and a not very conforming male presenting person, there are a lot of expectations on you."

I breathe a sigh of relief to have that out in the open.

"I started a social transition around the age of 15," she tells me, in response to my questions about when she first comprehended her gender. "He didn't like it at all," not surprising, when I ask about her father's reaction. I ask if her gender identity is why her mother and father were abusive to her and Phoebe confirms.

Phoebe describes her early attempt to come to grips with being transgender. She first saw a medical practitioner in 2004 at age 15. Her parents didn't know. "It was a much more hostile landscape than now. The doctor referred me to a psychiatrist telling me, 'I don't know how to deal with this.'"

"You were made to feel that you're sick?" I ask, aware of the prevailing psychiatric approaches to transgender people during that time.

The psychiatrist "was an odd experience, a lovely woman, clearly out of her depth." Phoebe's attempts at social transition lasted for two years, "then I thought, I'll give this being a bloke thing a try. Which is why at university I tried to be the man." She left Christianity and got involved in a political party at university and tells me she fell in love with a Jewish woman, converted to Judaism, and nearly married. Her fiancé (perhaps sensing the underlying issues?) instead had an affair and got pregnant.

"I was at university, and I was in the Army," Phoebe informs me, implying it was a concurrent assignment. "That ended in tears, with a court martial. It was a medical discharge, honorable, not based on trans. I was trying to suppress it at that point, but it was manifesting in other mental well-being: drinking far too much, depressed, workaholic due to too much university work." Phoebe was not functioning well, and it seems the military gave her a break, discharging her from service without penalty or dishonor. "I thought, 'Fuck it!'" and she started her "re-transition." Phoebe "kept the Judaism from that relationship" and as for the social transition, "this time it stuck."

Phoebe began working for social services that provided housing for young asylum seekers, ages 15-25. And as she tells me about her job she breaks into an unexpected rant. "Most people see the people in those kinds of jobs as wet white, leftist looney, humanitarian ass wipes who let every Tom, Dick and Harry in, who like open borders. But I saw them [asylum seekers] as taking the piss out of the country. They [the asylum seekers] turn out to be drug dealers, steal welfare money, are not interested in contributing anything, only interested in a free ride. They turn out to be criminals. I enjoyed helping the genuine ones, but those ones wanted to go back, never wanted to be here in the first place."

An asylum seeker is a legal designation for someone who has arrived in a country and asked for political asylum because they cannot live safely in their home countries. Asylum seekers are not economic migrants, though many face dire economic conditions. In the UK, they remain in limbo until their case is decided and they are either granted refugee status and permitted to stay or denied and sent back. Of course, there are people who game the immigration system. Phoebe's job dealt with sorting through the flood of asylum seekers to the UK from Eretria, Sudan, Iraq, Syria, Afghanistan, and Somalia.

Phoebe softens her tone. "We are talking places of abject poverty," now with clear compassion in her voice. However, that compassion is also tinged with anger over some she believes are gaming the system. With broad strokes she points to "the Albanian Muslim men were trying to take the piss out of the system. Afghanis came to the UK to be pedophiles. They were lying about their age saying they were children when they weren't. We would see schoolgirls going into this 40-year-old's place. But social services would do an age assessment and say he was 17! Afghanis are fanatics. That's why they were so hard to conquer militarily because they are fanatics."

Phoebe says this job led to the start of her distrust of humanity in general. "As a trans person, I never trusted the government or any authority in my life." In fact, her extreme distrust of authority has a deeply violent source, but I don't know that yet.

Phoebe decided to transition physically and flew to Thailand for gender affirmation surgery. The trip to Thailand changed her life in more ways than she would imagine. Phoebe fell in love and started falling for violent extremism. She met an American girl with a "very troubled background," there for the same surgery. "She was the most intelligent person I have ever encountered in my life. She started to radicalize me into the extreme right. That is the relationship that changed everything."

Slowly she introduced Phoebe to Canadian white nationalists. Among them, Stefan Molyneux, who Phoebe says, was "part of the nouveau right white nationalists. He calls himself a philosopher. He is not a philosopher." Molyneux promotes scientific racism and eugenics based on pseudo-scientific sources. According to the SPLC, he has "encouraged thousands of people to adopt his belief in biological determinism, social Darwinism and non-white racial inferiority." With a following of some 650,000 people on YouTube, he is described as "an effective communicator within the racist 'alt-right' and pro-Trump ranks." YouTube banned Molyneux in June 2020.[181]

Phoebe says her American counterpart "started dripping me his work. It was race and IQ, a lot of ethnic disparities in crime rates, country development, and so on. We were in a long-distance relationship, and I was consuming more and more of this." Phoebe started looking for people locally to explore these ideas further and found people online. "They asked, 'Would you fancy coming to the pub and we'll chat there?' I went."

It was 2016 and Phoebe says, for the first time she found someone interested in her just for being herself. The man she met with didn't care she was Jewish, trans, or in a same-sex relationship. He just wanted to talk issues. "It was wonderful. I had a friend! We decided to meet again, and he brought others." The others were members of the English Defence League (EDL) and "shared the belief and goal that I did. It wasn't misogynistic, transphobic, or antisemitic. It wanted what I wanted—Muslims out of Britain."

The EDL showed up in the UK in 2009, and frequent street demonstrations across the country helped quickly grow its ranks into the thousands. The EDL claimed to be a human rights organization standing up for the white working class and raising legitimate concerns about radical Islam. Its slogan was "Not racist, not violent, just no longer silent" but its supporters were primarily loud racists and Islamophobes who liked to provoke. For the UK, the far-right had not seemed so animated in decades although when the EDL's leader Tommy Robinson left the group in 2013 it began a rapid demise, necessitating new tactics, although its members continue on even today.[182]

"It didn't matter if you were Black and Christian, you were welcome—or trannie—   English Defence League Logo in the EDL. Just Muslims out. The common goal was to eliminate Islam from this country, to eliminate the scourge that is Islam that is destroying the values of Britain." Phoebe easily floats into her former propaganda role, wagging her finger as she lectures. It's scary watching how easily she slips back into her propagandist role. She put the voice in "no longer silent."

As she talks, I can sense the high and happiness she found in people who appreciated her for who she was and what she believed. Heady with finding friendship, and that belonging, sense of significance, purpose, and dignity, she went all in.

"The English Defence League wanted England for the English and I wanted Israel for the Jews. Who is in the way? The dirty stinking Muslims." Pausing, Phoebe reflects, "People have said, 'But you were a convert?' Yes, but that was one of the reasons why I was as I was—the zeal of the convert."

Phoebe recognized she needed to leave her work with asylum seekers and in 2017 returned to university to study law. She also continued on her path from radicalization to violent extremism. She attended EDL rallies and figured out how to avoid arrest. Then Phoebe found herself center stage with the EDL.

Her strong speaking skills got noticed and she was invited to address an event. "I got a rush. Someone gave me a microphone and gave me the stage. I had them in the palm of my hand," Phoebe says, holding out her palm and she takes a deep inhale from it as though she's inhaling a drug. "I didn't need a script, I knew what I was going to say, how to get them going. By the end of it they were all standing and cheering. They had come to listen to people, but I don't think they expected a 20-something Jewish, white, trans-girl to steal it. There were people saying, 'I couldn't give a shit that you are Jewish. I couldn't give a shit that you are a trannie. I couldn't give a shit that you are a third younger than me. You know the problems of this country. It's them! Those stinking *jihadi* men who come to rape, blow up places, to murder our children! They are the enemies, and you get that!'"

It was the validation she'd been seeking. "I had one person tell me, 'You are Britain's Marine Le Pen. You are the savior of this country, what we have been looking for, and you don't look like us.'"

Being transgender even came in handy for the cause. At a rally she was pulled aside and asked for help in identifying counter protester leadership. "We have these cunts down the road who want to wreak havoc on us, counter protestors, Antifa and so on. We know they are a disorganized mob, controlled by one or two, but we don't know who they are.'" Phoebe delighted in the task of becoming the group's spy who crossed enemy lines. She sat in a café, unsuspected, and was able to identify the leaders planning to cross the police line. The leaders were stopped and "the counter protest was meaningless without them."

Her stature in the movement grew and it fed her ego needs. She could analyze crowds, rally people with hate speeches, and direct violence without participating in it. The police couldn't touch her "because of who I am. They didn't want to arrest a Jewish trans-woman…That was lovely. They were scared of me. The police, the people I'm supposed to be scared of, are scared of me!" But she gets serious again as she tells me they have a file on her. "I requested it, but most is blacked out. Police officers were assigned to just me." She seems to brag despite her concern.

Her motivational speeches were meant to recruit, calling on people to defend their country, which she filled with propaganda: "Stop it from being overrun, from being turned into a *jihadi* state. Don't make your mother walk down the street in a *burka*. Don't be forced to grow a beard. British freedoms mean I can see my wife's face. Don't let those rats take that away from you. Don't let them destroy the freedoms of this country. Don't let them turn Britain into Afghanistan in Europe."

Phoebe saw herself as the British analogue of Alex Jones, the right-wing American propagandist, radio show host, and owner of the

conspiratorial website *Info Wars*. The SPLC
has described Alex Jones as "the most
prolific conspiracy theorist in contemporary
America."[183] She now chides herself. "It's
absurd," she says. "It was like I was the
mouth of Alex Jones! I believed it at the
time."

InfoWars Logo

    A question I ask everyone is whether
their group had a practice of recruiting police
and military and if so, what role these persons played. Phoebe answers,
"they weren't insignificant," then rolls off a long litany of how they
helped: "They offered tactics training on how to avoid the police, how
to corral a crowd, how to have a fight and not get caught, how to defend
yourself, that if you start picking up weapons that's a problem, doing
graffiti is a problem, don't pick up a gun, knife or can of spray paint,
they can put you in prison, prosecute you. Stick to the streets, to rhetoric.
Keep fights away from the rally and only with counter protesters and
make sure the police are in the middle, and how to defend yourself.
Some would provide protection for more valuable members. I had
at least two [active-duty EDL] police officers who were at the rallies
protecting me on either side of the stage. The military guys would blend
in very well and keep order amongst the people in the rallies. They were
on our side, and we had respect for them."

    As she speaks, I'm surprised she ever left the EDL. This group
powerfully met needs for validation and gave her an outlet for an intense
anger. They gave her a literal stage and let her reign over it.

    "It was oh so much fun," she tells me, obviously reveling in the
attention and power. Then for a moment, interrupting her thoughts, she
hints "there were other events in my life that precipitated my exiting" but
then continues the nostalgia about how much the people she associated
with wanted to listen to her; the wonderful affairs with married men; the
long-distance relationship she was still in with the American woman,

who told her, 'We are an ocean away. Go enjoy yourself!' As I watch Phoebe pretending to be in a drug induced high, I don't doubt it felt exactly like that.

"It still feels relaxing," she admits, beginning to return from her past.

"It was meeting all your needs for belonging, making you feel powerful respected and desired?" I ask, seeing clearly that was the case.

"Hmm" she answers, still enjoying the remembered buzz of it all.

But her world finally started to unravel, starting with a series of family deaths in 2018. Her grandmother's death really hit her hard. "She was one of the only family members that accepted me, was nice to me, kind to me." That death started an internal wake-up call. She understood the EDL didn't care for her like her grandmother had, they only cared about what she could do for them. It was a heady but poor substitute for family. And she was learning that outside the EDL bubble she wasn't respected or cared for. She was reviled.

Her long-distance girlfriend could not handle "how I had been mourning" and for the very first time, Phoebe ended a relationship. It was March 2019. Then in April 2019, her step-grandmother died. July 2019, her grandfather died. November 2019, she contracted MRSA [Methicillin-Resistant Staphylococcus Aureus infection], had stage 2 sepsis and spent seven days in the hospital. Four traumatic events happened within twelve months, then in March 2020 "the world shut down and that changed my life." Phoebe has asthma and COVID-19 classified her as "vulnerable" by the UK government. She was not allowed to leave her home.

"Late April [2020], one day everything hit me like a brick wall." Isolation gave Phoebe a chance to slow down and begin an awakening about her role as a hate leader. "I went into a state of physical illness because of it. I never believed people who said psychological events can manifest as physical trauma. Jesus they can. I realized I was at rock bottom. I was a mess of a human being. I started to reevaluate myself and I stopped engaging with everything. Absolutely everything. Then I took stock of things."

One of the things she may have been forced to "take stock of" during this period is the violent source of so much of her anger. "There is one event that I haven't mentioned, that happened in 2014. It's very difficult to mention—the nexus of my hate."

Phoebe draws a deep breath as she musters courage to delve into her story. Now speaking as a trauma survivor with the familiar fragmented memories, Phoebe says, "I've pieced together a lot of this over a long period of time. Some of this may be my brain filling in the gaps, some genuine. I was in Scotland, at a political party conference, and I was date raped by someone I considered to be a friend. It gets darker than that because nobody gave a shit."

Phoebe goes on to detail a gruesome date rape after a drug had been slipped into her drink. "I remember the very last thing said to me, and these words have always haunted me to the present day. It was: 'I am a millionaire. You can tell whoever you like. Nothing will ever happen to me.'"

Phoebe did go to the police but concerns about how she would be dealt with by authorities as a trans woman made her back off from reporting the incident. Returning to England, when she tried to get help from support services she was told if she came for help, they were mandated to report the crime. "I wasn't prepared to do it."

She then called a private therapist and left a message asking for help and was amazed to get back a message refusing to treat her, "'because I know who you are; I know what you do and who you associate with; and I don't want you associating with me.'"

Phoebe tells me, "I have never been able to sit with a therapist and talk about this, so I have pieced it together myself. I am not unfamiliar with the techniques having worked with asylum seekers, as some had genuine trauma." As with many untreated trauma survivors,

Phoebe's hurt manifested in multiple ways—anger, aggression, violence—and the EDL capitalized on it.

"Did you feel used by the EDL?" I ask.

"I didn't feel used. I knew what I was doing. I knew exactly what I was doing. I take full responsibility for my actions." She explains her actions like this, "When you have large-scale media organizations platforming people who want every Tom, Dick, and Harry to come in, and saying white people are born racist and responsible for people of the past, that's a problem. Yes, slavery is wrong, racism is wrong, racial injustice is wrong, but guess what? I'm not responsible for that."

She still loves the stage. "I find that getting on stage, standing in front of people being all dressed up with the makeup on, a good outfit, and some guitars behind me, and drums behind me, and the house lights are coming up, and I stand there and hold the microphone, and everyone is waiting for me. I enjoy that—to rock out. They are there to see me and the people behind me. No matter if I dance around like a lunatic. It's a lot of fun. That's how I get a natural high. If you enjoy a crowd, you enjoy a crowd…It might sound like an ego the size of Jupiter, but it's not a bad thing if you use it positively. Find your outlet."

As I listen, I still think how hard it must be, not just leaving behind her outlet for deep hurt and anger, and need for adulation, but to leave that sense of raw power behind—her extremist rhetoric, how good she was at it, and how she was able to galvanize whole crowds into violent action. She realizes the power. "I know that I am a dangerous human being if I want to be. I was weaponizing words."

Leaving behind this kind of power is a serious issue that follows charismatic influencers when they exit far-right movements. The rewards they had in their movements are hard to replace out in the real world, where they may find themselves despised for their former words and actions. It's not easy to find new ways to channel their gifts into socially acceptable means of succeeding outside their hate movements.

"What can replace that?"

"I may not be able to recapture it in its entirety. Now, I'm a different kind of activist." Phoebe left religion entirely and is now active in atheist circles and transgender rights. She's a big Twitter fan where she can argue but not break the law, doxx, or threaten people. "The law doesn't like that, and Twitter doesn't like it either."

I ask Phoebe how she deals with her anger. Many people have grievances. She channels her energy into debates, playing football (soccer), and singing death metal, heavy metal, heavy rock. "It gets the anger out." She says people need to find outlets that are not destructive to find sustainable belonging, community, and personal empowerment. She advises it has to be "something that will make you feel satisfied at the end of the day. Don't let the hate, or the pain be the driver."

She goes on and I again see the former inspirational speaker take the stage: "You only get one life, one chance, one opportunity, one way forward, and you should try to make tomorrow a better today. Don't rip society apart at the seams because society will rip you apart. The hate is temporary. Self-empowerment can be forever and that's what you need. It may be tempting to say to yourself, blame others—it's everyone else's fault—but at the end of the day the only person in charge of your life is you. You may have difficult surroundings, pain, trauma, but at the end of the day they are yours. Own them. Don't let them own you. Today will be hard, but it's supposed to be. It means you are working. Today being slightly difficult means tomorrow will be easier. A painful today means it was a painful yesterday, not a painful tomorrow. Do what you want to do for you, not for others, not against you. Do it for you. If you do that, then your tomorrow will be yours and not somebody else's…Don't think that other people control your life. At the end of the day the only person in control of your life, the only person you need to be answerable to is you. Other people are responsible to themselves. You are responsible to you. So don't let someone else control your life. Own your own life and be responsible to yourself. Selfishness is not always a dirty word."

After that flowery speech, I ask Phoebe if she still feels the same about immigrants, particularly the ones who are not legitimate asylum seekers.

"Deport the fuckers," she says without hesitation. "I don't care if you are coming from a country that won't take you back. If you are disqualified from entering this country for any reason, just because you came to the UK border, we don't have to roll out the red carpet for you. The UK taxpayers are not here to fund your lifestyle. If you are a criminal coming from another country to be a criminal in this one you are not welcome." She laughs as she realizes she still has all the old rhetoric intact.

"Do you have Muslim friends now?" I ask.

"Not actively. I do find it a struggle. It is difficult to eliminate that kind of prejudice."

It's an honest answer.

"And what do you believe now about the genuine asylum seekers?" I ask.

"I started seeing the individual again," she answers. "When I was in the EDL, I stopped seeing the individual…Yes, the individual criminal who comes here to be a criminal in the UK should be stopped, but the person standing behind them in the queue who is not a criminal, and not coming to be a criminal, should not be treated the same as the criminal."

I wonder how she now views the EDL.

"I view the EDL as an indictment of the political situation in this country and on society at large," she answers. "It didn't spring up overnight because a few lunatics decided. A lot of people in a lot of parts of the UK have felt disenfranchised for a long time. Why did Britain leave the EU?" She then turns to the elites who lead the UK and "don't have an idea of living in poverty, mocking them, 'You have to make sacrifices while I'm a multi-millionaire with money coming out of my backside.'"

I'm reminded of her rapist. "I am a millionaire. You can tell whoever you like. Nothing will ever happen to me." I leave the interview with a profound sense of sadness and reaffirmation that traumatic experiences can have a deep effect on those who experience them and become catalysts to pass on more hate and violence to others.

Chapter 15 - Addicted to the Klan

I'm a bit mind-boggled by the incongruous sight in front of me: His tall angular body lounging against a big brass headboard, surrounded by a whole lot of pink florals. As I try to filter out the wallpaper and comforter and focus on Greg and his membership in the Ku Klux Klan, I remind myself this is COVID and I'm doing interviews any way I can. It turns out Greg (not his real name) is talking to me via Zoom from his mother's bedroom while she's away in Florida. Still, this bizarre juxtaposition takes me a moment to adjust—the pink, his lightly bearded face, and his current membership in a hate group, all simultaneously coming at me. "I am not antisemitic," the 38-year-old is telling me. Unlike many white nationalists I've interviewed, Greg is not a former but an active member of the KKK.

"I had a happy childhood. I had wonderful grandparents. People had it lot worse than me," he tells me, but his handsome face, strained and twitching, suggests a different truth.

His mother got pregnant with him, married and divorced a year later. Greg did know his father and defends his mother, telling me she couldn't get back on her on feet. "She had her own issues. My mother has been married five times," and adds, "I still live with my mother." Then his eyebrows furrow as he recalls his confusing and chaotic, revolving door of father figures: "My brother's father had a drug problem. She left him, met my father, left my father, reconnected with my brother's father, then married somebody else, then my brother's father came back, my mother divorced her husband, went back to him. I think she harbored feelings for him all along," Greg's concludes. His eyes are downcast, and he looks sad. Greg says his stepfather eventually went back to drugs and my mother left him for good, and they moved in with her parents. "He got himself killed by the police. I didn't know that. She said he died of smoking. I wasn't aware of the drugs. I was only seven."

Greg does remember being afraid. "He was very angry. Looking back now, he wasn't a healthy guy," and now anger tinges his voice. "He was a born-again Christian. If you were bad, he would spank you." Greg says he grew up with a lot of fear and guilt. He paid another price for the unstable home. He was a good kid and decent in school, but he was put in special ed classes.

"You don't seem like a special education student," I comment. "Were you hyperactive or acting out somehow in the classroom?"

Greg shakes his head no. "I was a pretty good student. I liked history a lot. I was bad at math and sciences, and I was always insecure." He then adds his current psychiatrist says he should have never been in special education. I reflect on the fact he has a psychiatrist but say nothing about it. Listening, I have to agree. Greg seems very bright and self-aware.

It was during sixth and seventh grade, studying the Civil War, when Greg says he "fell in love with the Confederacy" and first learned about, and became infatuated with, the KKK. Because he was afraid of the bullies, he felt "a sense of power—hoods on, and fires—for kids it comes off, like powerful. Maybe it was just me compensating for my own fears," his face now looks anxious. "I didn't do good with bullies. I was always afraid of other people—intimidating kids." He describes himself as a "very sensitive kid."

"I printed out posters of them," Greg smiles weakly at the memory of his youthful admiration for the KKK, and is quick to add in his defense, "I wasn't a hateful person." He likens his veneration of the KKK to how white kids his age put up posters of Black rappers and identify with them as powerful figures. "The Klan was a counterbalance." Greg again references his feeling of powerlessness amongst these kids he perceived as tough.

Though Greg was a big admirer of the Klan as a teen, he didn't join until he was well into adulthood, and it was the one consistent male figure in his life who reintroduced him to the Klan years later. His grandfather.

Greg's mother was drinking and changing partners every few years, and they were on food stamps. He and his mother lived on and off with his grandparents for many years. "Thank God for her parents," he says, eyes brightening. "With them there was some stability."

Though Greg says he never saw his grandfather as a father figure, he found him loving and "manly in some ways." Grandparents often fill the parental gap. "Looking back, that was a very dysfunctional period." Greg sounds sour. Up to now, he has taken great pains not to blame his mother too much for her struggles and failures in his life, but now he does so, very gently placing some of the blame where it belongs. "She made a mistake. Getting back with my brother's father and putting me in special ed was not right."

I ask Greg about his dating life and if he had girlfriends growing up. "Not at all." He looks sheepish. "It's still an issue to me." He says he didn't really try to start dating until he was 26, going to nightclubs and dating sites. His anxiety always got in the way. "'Til this day, I haven't had a real girlfriend," his voice trailing off, "I am a hopeless romantic."

Greg offers further perspective. He says he has an addictive personality and has become addicted to "chat rooms, chatting, love addiction with girls. I'd get these unhealthy attachments to girls, too emotionally attached. Where it was unhealthy." He concludes, "I believe in romance and chivalry."

I ask Greg about the themes I'm hearing: Do I belong? Am I protected? Am I worthwhile? A pained expression flashes across his face and a catch enters his voice. "I never had someone to protect me really. My psychiatrist said not having a healthy father figure, having a mother who coddled you, I never got that manly growing up. I was told that I felt abandoned, like in those primitive years, I don't know," his voice trails off again.

To lack a role model of the same gender is a big vacuum for a growing up and like many young men, Greg went searching to fill that vacuum. He found it. His grandfather found a KKK card in the local library inviting people to join. Remembering Greg's youthful infatuation with them, he gave the card to Greg at a time of personal, as well as national, confusion.

Greg had been on disability for six to seven years for obsessive-compulsive disorder (OCD) which went into overdrive during periods of distress, something he suffered from since childhood. He wasn't working and with this invitation presented by his grandfather, and now an adult, he was once again enthralled with what the KKK might have to offer him.

"I knew it wasn't true what I was writing," he says of his application to join the KKK. He found himself at the library on the computer with his finger undecidedly hovering over the enter key. "Press it. Don't press it. I decided to press it even though it wasn't right and true. I pressed it."

Then, Greg says, Donald Trump came on the scene in 2015. Indeed, Trump was putting forth that sense of empowerment to disenfranchised white men with his *Make America Great Again* campaign rhetoric to restore a misperceived and idealized past. Greg recalls news stations talking about the Klan supporting Trump's presidency. "He can't control who supports him." But Greg liked the novelty of Klan groups thinking they were like Trump and he thought, "If I vote for him, let it be for my tribe, because I'm white." Greg is quick to add, "I didn't believe in the ideology." Greg found himself moving in and out of different Klan groups, sometimes voluntarily, sometimes not.

It should be noted, the KKK is no longer centrally controlled after having been broken up by successful legal challenges. It is now made up of many different local chapters called klaverns, each specifically labeled, such as the United Klans of Alabama of the KKK, or the Mississippi White Knights of the KKK. The largest klaverns reportedly have no more than 50 to 100 active members, and most have fewer than 25. Many of these klaverns claim to be reviving the original

KKK, while others are in deep
competition with each other. The
Anti-Defamation League reports, as
of June 2017, the organized Ku Klux
Klan movement in the U.S. consisted
of just over 40 active Klan groups,
a slight increase from 2016. An
estimated 3000 members and
unaffiliated people "identify with

Ku Klux Klan Flag

Klan ideology" and notably, more than half of the existing Klan groups
formed between 2015-2017.[184]

Smiling weakly and shaking his head, "I heard disturbing
things." Klan members sensed his doubts. "They kicked me out
thinking I was a reporter, then let me back it. Then I left it, but it was an
addiction." He in fact joined and left a revolving door of Klan groups,
often for disagreeing about their ideology, yet he kept returning, and kept
getting kicked out or kept leaving.

I ask Greg if he ever engaged in any violence or arms training in
these white supremacist groups.

"I have not engaged in any violence," Greg answers. "They are
law abiding, but I'd rather not say [about weapons training]."

"What about RAHOWA, were you taught about that? Did you
make any preparations for it?"

"Racial holy war," Greg says, spelling it out. "Some of them do
believe that. I don't believe that."

In spring of 2017, with yet another Klan group, he attended a
rally in Philadelphia. The Klan and the NSM often held joint events,
which was the case in Philadelphia. Greg met Jeff Schoep there. "He was
like a celebrity." For Greg, all of Jeff's pomp—the black shirt and black
suit, sunglasses, flanked by bodyguards—left him enthralled.

After Philadelphia, he got himself kicked out of the Klan again.
This time, "I was disrespectful to a Klansman's wife," his eyes darting

downward. "I was very inappropriate. A lot of my issues were coming up. I felt very alone. I wanted a girlfriend. I think I wanted to leave, too. I kind of sabotaged myself."

True to his obsession, Greg went back time and again. He also joined the NSM "but then a documentary said horrible things about Jewish people so I left that." He contacted other groups and ended up not joining. Then he says, Spring 2020, he contacted a group and "this time I was serious." He said he was going to learn from his mistakes, stop being sensitive, "doing the work, being a real soldier." And he was "doing fantastic. But not being a true believer, God ugh, I was going to go to their rally, but I didn't go for moral reasons." As he frowns at his repeated failures to succeed in the Klan, I reflect that this is the least racist and hate-filled white supremacist I've interviewed thus far. Yet he seems to be seriously committed to somehow making it in the Klan. Why? What is the Klan offering him?

"Every time I would leave [the KKK], I'd feel empty and bored, like I made a mistake. I felt miserable." He contacted yet another Klan. "I guess I asked too many questions. They ghosted me. I was never ghosted before. Usually they tell you." Greg looks genuinely forlorn. "I ended up reaching out to this new group in December. They let me in."

"It sounds like you need people, need to belong with others," I comment. "Did you ever think of joining a less hateful group?" still wondering what about the Klan in particular has him hooked.

"Yes," he answers. "I do love Buddhism. I found it in 2012 or 2013. It showed me a practical psychological way to look at things, how we get attached to things. It's okay to just be you. You are enough. You don't need symbols or flags or a costume or titles. I'm trying to learn [that] when I get these feelings of emptiness or boredom."

A pained expression again crosses his face. "I've used the 'n' word, even though I wouldn't say it in person. I'm guilty. That's their culture, I'm guilty of trying to fit in." He tells me he doesn't believe what they believe, and the Klan world is not who he is. "I'm in it for very materialistic reasons." I assume he's not actually gaining material advantages.

"That I'm in the KKK organization, having that title, belonging to this organization and that's my title—like a name brand, like a materialistic belonging. It looks good on paper," he explains, although he doesn't really seem convinced by his own words. "The weird thing is it became like an addiction."

"None of us were meant to be alone in life, Greg. It's human to need to belong and be attached to others, to find a sense of protection and comfort in that. We're a social species," I reflect back to him. "You need to belong somewhere and probably have a real relationship, too. You sound very alone in life without a partner or a family of your own, no?"

He tells me about limited, failed attempts to date online. I ask him about finding a Buddhist group to join. He nods but then references an article he read about a Proud Boy. "It's hard to compete with extremist narratives, that author said. Non-violent movements don't offer a thrill. It gives the brain oxytocin." (Dopamine and adrenalin are released with danger and thrills; oxytocin more often comes with attachment and belonging.)

"With the Klan group, they offer something these peaceful movements don't offer, a thrill maybe?" Greg asks.

"You mean there's something to the hate and violence that the Klan may offer you more than just protection, maybe also an outlet for rage, or a sense of manliness?" I ask.

"Yes, a Buddhist group won't offer that," Greg says nodding. "That thrill, that manliness, that toughness…" and his voice fades. He looks both conflicted and sad. "I've burned all the bridges I could burn with all the Klan groups I could find."

"How do you handle that, being kicked out so many times?" I ask. And with that question, we get to the heart of the matter, and why the Klan appeals to Greg. He again mentions his psychiatrist and that he has a personality disorder, OCD, obsessive compulsive disorder. He describes it as the inability to let something go. Especially if he's offended or upset, "I can't stop thinking about it."

It began with his stepfather (his brother's father.) "He was a born-again Christian. I had a homosexual experience. I had a few of them," his eyes look earnestly into the screen as he begins to open up. "One of them was with my brother's father's son from another woman. They were my stepbrothers and sister. They would come and visit. I had sexual encounters with both of them."

"How old were they and how old were you?" I ask, my voice gentle and conveying acceptance as I try to gauge if this was full blown sexual abuse or more normative childhood sexual play.

"I was seven years old. She was older, nine or 10, and he was seven or eight, and then I had a homosexual thing with one of my friend's brothers. He was 10. I was seven or eight. I don't know if it was molestation. The boys bother me, the homosexuality in that, and him [my stepdad] telling us that was wrong. I had this guilt with that, the guilt obsession, me feeling so guilty, what I did was horrible, that I did this homosexuality. That was my first [obsessive thought pattern] ever, mentally destroying me. Until I told my mother I felt better. That's when it [the OCD] all started, around the same age."

"How did your mother respond?" I ask, hoping she was accepting.

"She was kind. Then later on she came and said, if you ever did that again, she would beat me."

"She did the best she could." Greg is still trying to defend her.

"So, your stepdad was the judgmental one, the one who instilled the deep sense of guilt and anxiety?" I ask.

"Quite frankly I think he was a bastard." Greg's voice suddenly fills with anger and bitterness for the first time in our conversation. "That whole period was an unhealthy and screwy period; sexual experiences, the guilt, and obsessing about that."

I'm realizing that in Greg's case, the hate groups are an obsession covering for his emotional pain that likely includes guilt over the early sexual experimentation, and likely some self-doubt about his sexual orientation, in addition to issues of power and belonging. The Klan requires members to renounce homosexuality, a possible vulnerability for him.

Greg has been so careful not to blame others but now his full anger lands on his stepfather and even spills over a bit to his mother who he admits had "man issues." "Even now, she's a full-blown alcoholic. She is not doing well. She is in Florida for a month."

I ask Greg about joining an Al Anon group where support is central, and he tells me he was part of a 12-step program for eating disorders. He binged, gained and lost weight, and paid the price with a damaged digestive system. I ask about mixed martial arts, a place some former members of hate groups find satisfying. Greg's face lights up as he tells me he recently watched some boxing lessons. "It was a Black guy. I was enjoying it, seeing that. That was pretty cool." I can't help but note it's a Black man he sees holding a possible solution.

"It doesn't seem you belong with the Klan," I say, smiling softly. I still don't comprehend that the Klan is a name brand for him and belonging to it brands him pure, white, manly, powerful, and perhaps most important to assuaging his guilt—straight.

"Yes, what is the end game here?" Greg agrees and tells me he feels triggered when the Klan is in the news."

"What exactly are these triggers?"

"On the news, if white supremacism, the Klan, or accusations get brought up, it triggers me. I get pulled into something in my mind that is so appealing to me."

Greg is describing how his obsessive thoughts get fired up. This neural mechanism is a distraction to cover over deeper feelings of anxiety.

"Tell me again, when you first heard about the Klan?" as I now see the pieces start to fall in line.

"11 years old."

"Right after the disturbing sexual relationships?" I suggest to him his childhood encounters sound like normal sexual play.

Greg nods, letting me in on the anxiety.

"And then you learn about this group that is strong, powerful, and seeking racial purity, that can be your obsessive distraction from the guilty obsessions?" I ask.

"To me it was this strength of being in a hood," Greg answers. "I loved the Klan. They were awesome. I do feel sort of guilty over the 10-year-old encounter," he adds, making the connection himself without even realizing it.

After a bit more conversation, I decide to back off as I'm not Greg's psychologist, and this is a research interview not a therapy session. Often a research interview will include the same questions and reflections I might ask in a therapy setting, as many questions and statements I make may help the research subject be more reflective, more self-aware, and also correct me if I'm wrong about the assumptions I'm making as a psychologist listening to their story. Greg has a psychiatrist with whom he's happy and he can do that work in his own time with his own psychiatrist.

"Is there anything else you want to tell me?" I ask.

"I don't believe in the ideology," Greg repeats.

To wind us down I ask him about the oversized silver rings he's wearing, wondering if they are white power symbols I can't identify and have failed to notice up to now.

"Oh, this one is a Harley Davidson ring. This here is a skull ring. This one says FTW, Fuck the World. I'm a biker, a new rider," Greg explains.

"Ever think about joining a biker group?" I ask, although I realize as soon as I've said it that might be a world of trouble of its own.

"Yes, I've considered it," Greg says smiling.

We end the interview and I tell Greg if there's anything we've talked about that later upsets him, he can contact me to talk it over. I thank him for being so honest. He seems fine, even satisfied about spending over two hours talking and not facing negative judgment.

Greg doesn't call but he does email me about a week later:

> Hi Anne, Hope all is well. Just letting you know I left the group! I'm out and free. Your zoom session did help. Thank you for the insights you provided. And, when you had asked me if I had anything more I wanted to share, I forgot to mention the part of having the burden of keeping all that a secret from my friends and family, living a double-life. That did weigh heavily and was a mind-messer. The idea of them finding out about any of that... too scary for me to think about. Other than my psychiatrist, I never shared any of that with anybody.
>
> You also put in perspective of me turning to those groups to run away from my problems and such. That truly helped. Before I left, I had to keep telling myself, that after leaving, life's problems wouldn't be cured and gone, that I still have to cope and get through stuff. Any "group" I should "join" should be an Al-Anon meeting, as you suggested. Anyway, just updating you, and thanking you again.

I was aware it was a pretty intense interview, but I hadn't meant to make an intervention. That said, reading the email, I smile and hope it sticks.

Chapter 16 - Raised by the Klan

"It was basically me, cousins, and people I called cousins that were not my cousins. We considered the Klan my family. My uncles were also in it, real cousins affiliated. It was just all Klan."

I'm about to have a pretty blunt and chilling conversation with someone born into the KKK. Shane Johnson, now 30 and a born-again preacher, has come a long way from how he grew up, extremely poor and all Klan all the time. "We lived it, breathed it, ate it. Everything was conspiracy, paranoia, always talk of the FBI listening to us, drugs and alcohol, a whole lot of fights." His father was in and out of jail for minor offenses but also did six years for involuntary manslaughter. "Then they got smarter," he says of both his father and the Klan, which grew more careful about openly violating the law.

Infighting among local KKK groups, known as klaverns, was a regular occurrence yet his father's commitment to the KKK never wavered. Klan groups would grow and contract with infighting that split them, accusing each other of not being real Klan. "It's unreal how it happens so many times, but my dad was always there." Shane says his family's reputation was built around his father. "So here I come following in his footsteps. Every kid wants to make his dad proud."

Shane's father didn't agree with authority or racial mixing and was heavy into anti-government conspiracies. He homeschooled Shane until the sixth grade then declared the curriculum was propaganda, based on brainwashing. Shane also went to public school for a bit, but "when I refused to sit with a Black kid at breakfast, they called my dad originally. But he went on a tirade." The school also called child protective services, but "I was never taken or nothing. God knows I should have been. They'd come around often, but he knew his rights, his constitutional rights, really well." The Klan taught its members what their rights were, including rights to privacy. "The cops didn't want to deal with him. He'd go into jailhouse lawyer mode and was a hassle."

Shane draws a vivid picture of his father. "He would drink Calvert's Whisky. He was this 300-pound workout guy with a long beard and long red hair. He'd chug it out of the bottle and follow it up with Hot Damn [cinnamon schnapps]. He was a different breed. He grew up in a chicken coop that they turned into a house in Kentucky, grew up with a lot of brothers, all Klan."

Knowing Klan groups today are generally Christian, I ask Shane if he grew up with religion. Christianity is a sticking point with white supremacist groups who reject Jesus because he was Jewish. I wonder how his family handled that issue.

"People think of Klan with cross lightings and robes, but throughout the week it was teaching Christian Identity and wild conspiracy theories of Jews controlling the government."

When I ask him to elaborate, he launches into dual seed doctrine. "My beliefs are that we are the chosen race of God. He died for our sins. Jesus called the Jews the spawn of the devil. They were literally the children of Satan. Nonwhites were beasts of the field in Genesis. When Eve took the apple, she had sex with Satan and had Cain, who killed Abel." Shane now says, "It's a wicked, wicked belief, but I didn't know. That's all I really knew." He believed he was involved in a noble cause: the fight between good and evil.

Fully indoctrinated into deep hate at a very young age, and groomed for KKK leadership, I wondered how far he would have taken violence. "Were you taught to kill?" I ask.

"Definitely taught, but I wouldn't get my hands dirty. They groomed me to speak well," then he returns to my question. His answer is unnerving. "I would have killed easily. It would be like killing a dog. I might feel bad at first, but a dog has no soul. These people [Jews and minorities] don't have souls." He says they celebrated murders of people of other races. It was encouraged. "I never told anyone to do it. I watched what I said," to stay clear of the law. "I didn't want to get RICO charges [laws targeting organized crime] but it wasn't frowned upon."

Shane grew up understanding his quest for personal significance would be answered by how well he filled his father's KKK footsteps. All his talents turned toward serving hate. He was studying everyday— politics, immigration—and how to use these issues to make white people feel they are under threat. Shane's education was unusual to say the least. He read George Lincoln Rockwell, *The Turner Diaries*, *Mein Kampf.* He would listen to extremist interviews, how leaders carried themselves and debated. "Even David Duke—I studied the way he handled himself."

When Shane was a teen, his Klan broke off from the other klaverns focused on loud protests at government buildings and went underground, focused on private rallies, cross lightings, and ceremonies. He was 13 or 14 when they started pushing him to recruit.

An argument for inoculating vulnerable youth against recruiters is to teach them about extremist and terrorist ideologies well before they encounter recruiters, like Shane, online or face-to-face. The recruiter's power over a naïve or hurting individual is the emotional appeal that can unwittingly seep in without the needy target recognizing some very serious logical holes in the propaganda. All violent political groups and movements capitalize on social grievances. Recruiters will heighten emotions with graphic photos and video, as well as conversations that feed those grievances with fears and conspiracies. If at-risk youth are pre-exposed to the false arguments and logical fallacies in a controlled setting, and not a heightened emotional state that increases irrational thinking, they are better prepared to keep their critical thinking skills active and not succumb to being manipulated.

Shane says their recruiting is now 100 percent online with anything-goes sites like 4chan, accessible to anyone. He recruited on Stormfront, the oldest and one of the largest white supremacist websites. Stormfront's logo has become a universal and generic symbol of hate for all white supremacists, whether or not they are associated with

Stormfront.[185] The logo consists of a squarish Celtic Cross encircled with the words "White Pride World Wide". Stormfront was created in 1995 by Florida-based white supremacist, Don Black.

Stormfront Logo and Slogan

Shane was well-prepared to recruit effectively. The Klan prides itself on being a Christian organization and Shane knew how to respond to legitimate questions from those they wanted to recruit. When asked, "How can you be Christian if you hate people?" His response, "White pride is not the hate of other races. It's love of our own race." He got questions about the cross burnings featured in most anti-Klan propaganda. "We said we light crosses to light the way of Christ." Shane worked up answers for most challenges, making it "easy to recruit from there."

There was plenty of drinking and drugs and as for RAHOWA "at 16 I was like, 'Let's get this thing started!'" Violence became a kind of game. "I guess [I fought] to dominate other people," he tells me. "I had no emotion. It was just something I had to do." He says from age 16, he was going into bars and fighting. At concerts, they'd get into mosh pits where they'd encounter SHARPS [Skin Heads Against Racist Prejudice] and Antifa. Fighting them was like a sport and he liked winning.

Skinheads Against Racial Prejudice Logo

"Did you get a high off it?" I ask. Some white supremacists have described to me the adrenaline from fighting provides an addictive rush of pleasure.

"Yeah, you could say that," he answers, but it doesn't sound like the same neurological rush of pleasure, the dopamine hit, that some skinheads have described. "I felt a sense of accomplishment. It was doing something for my race, in my eyes."

Skinheads became a source for recruitment. Combat 18, Aryan H Brigade, and the Hammerskins were all active groups in Shane's area. Though he says the Klan didn't mingle with them, he did and started to push his propaganda against their propaganda. They were pagan and he'd debate religion. "I'd come in with Christian Identity. They'd say, 'You worship a dead Jew on a stick.' I'd argue and hold my own." He'd sit with whoever was in charge and invite them to "drop your path and join with us and we'll give you a position." Shane says he was effective. "That got us our numbers."

And it got Shane promoted. "When I turned 18, they made me Grand Dragon over Indiana," pride filling his voice even now. "I started popping up klaverns all over the state." His strategy was to bring the skinheads into his Klan structure and together prepare to kick off RAHOWA. "I didn't target rich people. I targeted the projects and trailer parks telling them, 'You are in this situation because these people are evil.'" Shane believed in a popular uprising of poor whites. "Once the information got spread by spewing propaganda, my idea was, once people start seeing that the Jews are in control," RAHOWA would begin.

If RAHOWA did kick off, he envisioned the second coming of Christ, Armageddon. "We would eliminate all the races, and white people who were not Judeo-Christian, and race traitors, anyone who wasn't one of us. Honestly, I didn't like most white people. I didn't believe that they were saved if they were not just like us. That there were churches calling Jesus a Jew? In my belief he was not."

I find it interesting that both militant jihadists, like ISIS and al Qaeda, and white supremacists alike, adhere to an apocalyptic vision of the future in which the unbelievers, defined by them, are destroyed with God's help, while they are elevated to positions of power in a future utopic world that arises according to their expectations.

"You have small cells operating," Shane continues. "Like *Turner Diaries*. They attack the government, the world banking system, eliminate the enemy." It's amazing how a piece of fiction can hold such influence, clearly hitting a nerve again and again.

"What about the Day of the Rope? Executing people, was that something you bought into?"

"Yeah, I was all for other races dying," Shane answers bluntly. "All through the Christian Identity teachings we wanted to be the only race on Earth, and we blamed all our problems on them. Be it through RAHOWA or random acts of violence, it didn't matter. We wanted them eliminated."

Shane also echoes what others have told me about engaging the military. They also targeted former military for recruitment, and he estimates 30 percent of his klavern were ex-military. They showed up at rallies in full camo and wanted to appear like an anti-government militia. He describes them as not necessarily racist, but militants focused on government conspiracy. They believed the Jews controlled the banking system, all major government, media, and pushed dangerous practices like interracial dating through movies. Like others, Shane references the fictitious ZOG [Zionist Occupied Government].

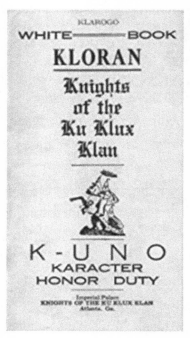

Given the military presence, I ask if they trained with weapons. They did, and they were armed. However, Shane says he took care to stay out of that limelight. If they made videos of shooting in the field, he says, the FBI would get involved. Some KKK members weren't as smart. "One guy got nine years. I took the picture. Klan robe, gun, tattoos. He was a felon and got it for felony possession of a gun. He got his door kicked down." I've been told by other interviewees the FBI regularly questions white supremacist

KKK Kloran Book Cover

leaders about threats and potential illegal activities. It appears the FBI as well as other domestic intelligence and policing groups scour the internet and may intercept messages signaling imminent violence as well as those between those on suspect lists.

The Klan has an articulated structure and established hierarchy. As Shane explained to me, the Kloran is the Klan's constitution and bylaws, created by William Simmons in the 1920s. He was a Freemason. They have codes and handshakes and instructions on how to organize a klavern. "They test you on it. You get the other books. It's not anything complicated. I mastered all of them by the time I was 10-years-old." I'm reminded of Søren, another white supremacist, who said being introduced to the racist texts, writings, and conspiracy theories made him feel he had "special knowledge," and educating himself in racism made him feel he was joining an elite club of sorts.

Ultimately Shane rose to the level of Imperial Knight Hawk in the KKK, the rank of the highest security officer, and along with it, his sense of belonging and significance increased as well. "Where can you take a guy from a trailer park and then he's a Grand Dragon and people are listening to you?" Shane asks, smiling widely. "A lot of these guys haven't accomplished anything. They have nothing to take pride in, except 'I'm white.' This is an accomplishment? And there's titles, and robes, mystique, and intimidation, hundreds of years old fraternal brotherhood. There's no other point. They just want to be a part of something." Shane also explains, "It's easier to believe that there is a spawn of Satan than to get up and fix your situation. It has to be a conspiracy. 'I'm not on food stamps because I'm too lazy and ignorant to get a job. It's because it's a conspiracy to bring the whites down.'"

But if people begin to really believe their own cause is noble, they are more likely to progress to carrying out violence, even RAHOWA. "I don't know if I was really foolish enough to believe it," echoing the more realistic white supremacists I've interviewed about

RAHOWA, "but it's what I wanted." Shane recruited to get the war started and he believed none of them would be killed.

"If you ask me, 'Will they ever do it?' No. [The KKK] are not organized enough, but they want to thrive on that image." With that, Shane shakes his head and laughs at his former compatriots. "No man, you are talking about a bunch of poor, fat hillbillies that never amounted to anything, spewing propaganda and blaming all their failures to everyone else." Similarly, while some white supremacists are savvy and know how to push their ideas into mainstream culture, KKK leader TM Garret says a lot of the KKK he knew were "unemployed toothless drunks in trailer parks."

Shane is frustrated by current media depictions of the KKK, news and Hollywood images of an organized and powerful force, lighting crosses and plotting to kill people, "It's not that at all. Our government has done a pretty good job of ending that reign." His reality was of a "small handful of failures" who spewed propaganda and tried to get members do what they want, "break into cars, steal the console, so they could get beer, or rob vending machines for their beer money."

As Shane got older, he went on night rides to spread flyers, get into fights, commit petty theft. It earned him quite a few run-ins with the law. After his father died, a very violent episode nearly landed him in prison. He got drunk and high on Adderall and tied padlocks to bandanas. "We went to a concert and were attacking everyone. I don't remember much." They attacked members of a Black gang. Shane received eight months house arrest for racial intimidation. The judge ordered Shane to disengage from his group, a process that can sometimes lead to spontaneous deradicalization, or seeking out or being mandated into a formal program to deradicalize. Forced separation opened an opportunity for Shane to explore other ideas and ways of thinking. "I had a little pink Toshiba laptop with a cracked screen. I would sit and study—Bill Maher, liberals. I found myself agreeing with some of the stuff they would say. A change started to happen."

Shane's future wife (girlfriend at this time) also played an instrumental role. When she overheard a particularly offensive rant between Shane and a KKK member, she said, "'Let me get this straight. If you could kill a Black baby and get away with it, would you?'"

"I answered, 'Of course I would.'"

"She said, 'Okay' and turned the radio back up. Then it entered my mind of actually doing what I said I would, and I realized, 'No! Ain't no way I would do that!'" And that started a downward spiral in my mind." Shane started to question who he was and why it bothered him. It also made him double down and commit the violent assault at the concert which landed him in house arrest.

This process in Shane's mind illustrates two important points. One, when cognitive dissonance occurs, that is, when one's strongly held beliefs are challenged, it can reinforce those beliefs. Likewise, it shows how spontaneous deradicalization occurs, a concept I identified in ISIS cadres who I saw turning away from ISIS after reflecting upon and comparing their negative experiences in the group with one another, this occurring in Syrian prisons and camps without any formal program in place. For example, a highly radicalized Belgian told me, *"Coming to ISIS was the best deradicalization I could have."*[186] For any type of ideologically driven extremism, in prisons or out, small challenges can add up and create internal questioning. Then, even without any formal deradicalization program in place, the individual slowly (even sometimes dramatically) begins to give up strongly held beliefs they come to understand are wrong. We believe that's why it is important for groups like ours to create and distribute counter narratives of white supremacists telling their own stories in their own words to begin to shake other white supremacists' beliefs in what they have come to embrace.

Shane resolved to "look into the other side, without my dad in my ear." It took isolation from his former extremist friends, but Shane made his way out over the course of eight months. "I made my mind up. I wanted out. It wasn't what I thought."

When Shane was released from house arrest, his friends threw a party for him, but he skipped town. He went to Evansville, Indiana, and moved in with a Mexican guy he had met online. This man was part of a Democratic Socialist site Shane was on. Shane says they would debate for hours and when Shane told him about his situation, the man opened up his home to him. I smile as I hear, yet again from a white supremacist, that it is a member of a group he used to despise and wanted to destroy, who aids the way out of the hate movement.

But Shane made the mistake of returning a week later for his things. "Eight guys, 16 fists, and 16 feet." Shane was jumped by his former KKK allies and despite his nickname being Punchy, he went down hard. He wound up in the hospital for two weeks. "They wanted my robe."

All he knew and all he had was the KKK. His arms and body were covered in tattoos. He had no money, no education, and a criminal record. He didn't know what to do. So he stayed in Evansville and in another unexpected turn of events, when Bernie Sanders started his campaign for president, his new Hispanic friend began campaigning door-to-door and Shane started going with him.

"I was wearing a tattoo with nuts and bolts on my neck, saying, 'Hey, vote in this Jewish guy for President.' People started recognizing who I was because I couldn't keep wearing a turtleneck in 90 degrees heat. News covered the story, 'Former Klan guy is now working with the Democrats.' Then my life went to hell quickly after that. That's when I went on my media binge."

Like other former extremists, from militant jihadists to white supremacists, Shane jumped into a media circus way before he was ready. Still trying to meet needs for significance, dignity, belonging, and purpose, it's easy to see why people fall for media attention. (Note: ICSVE carefully vets our interviewees before inviting them to be part of our counter narrative program and we offer them complete anonymity if they wish.)

"It made a great story," Shane says of his media blitz. "This guy who faces down the Klan, who fights them back in his own hometown, and not scared of them. It was the spin, but reality was, I had a lot of issues. I needed therapy, and I wasn't sure what I believed anyway. I went from extreme far-right to extreme far-left, and drugs. I got on drugs really bad. The journalists would give them to me," Shane adds.

I'm shocked, though not completely, to learn some reality TV show staff (not journalists as he calls them), might be willing to do this. He alleges they gave him Adderall and meth to make him look and speak better on camera. "We'd go for 16 grueling hours. They would sit me down in front of people in the Klan, or victims. Here I'm strung out of my mind, lashing out at these people. They made me go visit my dad's grave. I wasn't ready for that. I didn't sleep the night before, so they gave me Adderall. They were making me out to be a hero and I was eating it up. They were flying me around, putting me in the nicest hotels ever, but I was just a strung-out little idiot being a puppet for these guys, angling it back to Trump."

Though he brought his Klan skills with him, and it translated well on camera, no one who has just exited any type of extremism is equipped for this kind of attention, and Shane was no exception. He says he was on eight to 10 grams of meth a day and weighed 130 pounds. "They [reality TV staff] are wicked people, all about ratings...I was just being used. It led to a bad drug addiction."

Shane also wound up on the cover of the progressive newsmagazine, *Mother Jones*. In the article, Shane is described as having been on significant drug and alcohol benders while in the Klan.[187] Recalling he'd been under the influence of Adderall during the violent attack that landed him in house arrest, I ask him directly about his early drug use. He tells me he would "dabble in them because of the life I was in, but I wasn't using big time because I didn't have the money. But on TV, they'd hand you money. I was strung out and getting glory for it. 'I'm going to have my own reality show!'"

Shane was spiraling out of control and his life unraveled. His wife left him and took their young son. He attempted suicide.

"I was up for 13 days straight. I attempted to hang myself from a gas station bathroom." He was taken to a state hospital where he told them, "I'm not mentally insane, just a drug addict." He was held for three days, then he says the nurses found out who he was. "I remember they printed off the *Mother Jones* cover and had me signing it. They let me out, but I left from them and snorted a line of dope thinking 'this will never change. They enjoy me being this guy.'"

Shane is now a believer, and in his world, God performs amazing miracles, one of which was to save him. But not without one more test.

"God sent an old man down who invited me to a Bible revival in Tennessee. I had declared myself an atheist. It was the liberal thing to do, and religion had its downfall," Shane explains. But like most drug addicts, Shane was more than willing to lie and manipulate to get what he wanted, and he wanted his family back. "I thought if I tell my wife I'm going to church, she'll come back." Instead, she joined him, and he got her back on drugs, then on the drive down Shane was arrested. His wife went on to the tent revival, got baptized and saved, and the old man who had invited him bailed him out. "I felt the conviction and got baptized and I started living for God…I never left."

Some white supremacists tell related stories, moving from white extremism to an authoritarian type of Christianity or joining leftist movements where some continue to endorse violence. Shane, it seems, made a fundamental change in his life.

He says he broke TV contracts and "I started focusing on me, and my family. I started serving God. The month I got saved, I started preaching." Given he'd already been preaching KKK so-to-speak, this was not that big of a shift. He says others stepped up to help him with a place to stay, a car, his bills, and seminary tuition. He stayed clean, got his high school diploma, and graduated as a chaplain and pastor of ministries. "It took a lot of prayer and fasting" to be able to read the

Bible and not automatically revert to hate propaganda, words that echo Kerry Noble, also heavily indoctrinated into Christian Identity. Kerry told me it took years to cleanse his mind of Christian Identity and to be able to read the Bible normally again.

"That's what I do," Shane says, beaming with pride. Part of me cynically wonders if all that Shane describes here is real, but another part accepts when anyone is shown genuine support, love, and compassion, fundamental and enduring changes can occur.

Today Shane evangelizes in jails and prisons. Since overhauling his own life, Shane started *Where God Leads Correctional Ministry* and trains others to be chaplains to the prison population he is serving. His ministry has a Facebook page with videos showing "another soul saved," drug addicted inmates who came to Jesus.[188]

Shane's current area of ministry is getting jailed inmates into drug rehabilitation programs. He believes when guys are on drugs, they don't need to be punished, they need to be rehabilitated and prisons alone don't work. His preaching offers a comprehensive and supportive approach for inmates with repeat drug charges and probation violations. "I can't say, 'Good job! You got saved! Have fun!'" He started working with a rehab center and says he approached a district attorney's office in Indiana, asking for his guys to get a second chance, and offering his rehabilitation ministry as a free 12-month program as an option. If the inmate completes the program, he says the DA has agreed to drop charges.

One of the men Shane has helped is a former Aryan Brotherhood member, who like Klayton Bindon, has hate tattooed across his face— "white power" in bold letters. "Says a lot about a guy that will quit while still in there," Shane says of the "blood in blood out gang mentality." I recall Sean Gillespie telling me he was brutally beaten with padlocks when he quit the Aryan Brotherhood while in prison. Exiting hate is never easy.

"I was raised to have a hardened heart. Not to have feelings, not to show remorse for things, stuff like that," Shane says. "I was raised in hate. Hate is a heck of a thing. No neurologist will ever be able to explain exactly what hate is. It consumes you. It's like a drug. You can justify a lot of things with it, blame everybody else. It gives you a false sense of reason." Then he tells me, "This is my first sober interview," which makes me laugh. "I don't smoke, I don't do drugs, I don't do anything," and he complains the Southern cooking at the church he joined has led to a big weight gain as he gave up everything but eating.

But he is still marked. "Do any of your tattoos interfere with your life now?" I wonder.

"Whatever was showing I had to cover," he explains. In a demonstration, MTV covered a swastika on his neck and TM Garret helped him cover another racist tattoo. But the rest he left. "Sometimes I think about covering them. I don't want my son to see it," and momentary shame crosses his face. Then he reassures himself with his belief in Christian redemption. "I'm covered by the blood [of Jesus]. I tell people if you can see these tattoos, the altar is open. If you are judging me, you need to come hit the altar."

He shares advice for someone sitting behind a keyboard intrigued by white supremacism: "It is not what you think it is. It's not cool, not mysterious, not dark, not the answer to the problem. No one joins this unless there's a problem." People are tempted to accept answers that come with big conspiracies he warns, "Watch what comes into your mind. It's dangerous. It will open the door for them to plant seeds of hate and racism in your life, to create a life of lies, a life of addiction with no camaraderie, no brotherhood. The biggest thing I learned is it's a lie. They use you."

Then, the preacher takes over. "I hate to put rap down, but heavy metal rap [is about] murder, fornication, and adultery. That's not what it takes to become a man...A tough guy is someone who loves, has patience, stands on the word of God, carries himself with character, and imitates Christ. That is what a real man is...You can't play games with the devil. He's a cheater. He will win."

Shane advises, "If you want to join something, join a church. If you want to be on mission, open your Bible. You have been called and commissioned for a purpose—to make disciples of all nations, as the King says. If you want to belong to something, belong to God's kingdom not the devil's kingdom. The Klan and all the rest is the devil's kingdom."

"I have lived that life it's not a good one."

You can watch Shane tell his story at www.EscapeHate.org

Chapter 17 - The Euphoria of Hate

"That's a powerful feeling to think God has a mission for you," I say.

"I don't have fancy words to put it in. I know what I felt and how powerful it felt. It was a spiritual journey to hurt other people from other races," Benji tells me. "That's how serious and misleading this stuff is, it really can get a person to believe they are on a spiritual journey."

June 2015, white supremacist Dylann Roof was welcomed into the Emanuel AME Church of Charleston, South Carolina, by an unsuspecting Bible study group of African Americans. He sat quietly until the final prayer. Then he took out a gun and massacred nine people and injured one, so one person would be left to tell his horrific tale. RAHOWA isn't just hyperbole, it's a goal, and Roof wanted to kick it off. His ruthless killings were later celebrated and are still referenced by white supremacists throughout the U.S. and beyond, including in memes lauding his violent actions. Two years later, another South Carolinian, this time a member of the KKK, was arrested for wanting to emulate Roof's attack, aiming his sights on a synagogue. His name is Benjamin McDowell.

Benji apparently radicalized while serving an earlier three-year sentence for a third-degree burglary conviction. By then he had earned a wide-ranging rap sheet, charged on six other occasions for crimes including malicious injury to animals, assault, violent second-degree burglary, littering, and possession of marijuana. In prison, he affiliated with a hate group known as the White Supremacy Extremists and has the hate tattoos to prove it. But it was after a series of Facebook posts were flagged that he was brought to the attention of the

Dylann Roof Meme

Dylann Roof Meme on Shirt

FBI as a potential violent extremist. In these posts, he praised Roof's attack, ranted against Jews, and made threats against Temple Emanu-El, a Jewish synagogue in Myrtle Beach, South Carolina, according to the FBI's field office in Columbia, South Carolina.[189]

His wasn't a random Facebook rant. Because he was now a known criminal with verified white supremacist affiliations, McDowell was considered by the FBI to be dangerous and capable of carrying out his threats. When the FBI deems an individual meets strict criteria for being at risk of launching a violent extremist attack, they may organize a sting operation, which they did in the case of Benjamin McDowell. Benji would learn, much later, it was a most unexpected insider who turned him in.

It's now March of 2021 and Benji, recently released from prison, has agreed to meet me in his therapist's office via zoom. Although there's a smart, modern looking background behind him, I can immediately tell from the way he speaks he is from less privileged circumstances and perhaps less intelligent or less educated than most. His Southern upbringing leaves him politely addressing me with frequent and respectful ma'ams as he replies to our informed consent procedures. Now 33 years old, he still seems very compliant and almost childlike as he relates to me, which makes me feel protective and wanting to be extra careful to do no harm. Throughout this interview I have the feeling I'm talking to a hurt little boy inside a man's body who's capable of doing real harm. Reciting his history with little emotion and as if it happened to someone else, he tells me matter-of-factly he's been broken and lost his whole life, plagued by generations of poor choices.

He is the only child born of an unhappy marriage and an absentee father. "He used to go to the drag strip and race motorcycles," Benji tells me. "He was, from birth on, with this other woman. He was not mature, not embracing the family relationship. He was with her on the racetrack while I was being born."

Benji says his mother found another man when he was nine, and another poor choice. There was plenty of drinking and trouble, and he did not treat her well. In his teens, Benji's mother was diagnosed with cancer which would eventually take her life. As his mother got increasingly sicker, his stepfather "started acting funny. They divorced. He married someone else. He was maybe cheating on her while she was sick." Again, I'm struck. Benji sounds much more like a young boy talking about things he doesn't fully comprehend, not a man in his 30s. He looks forlorn.

Similarly, his grandparents, always present in his life, divorced when he was young, and his grandfather was abusive. He cites a lot of chaos through childhood, "it was overwhelming," and even now he looks bewildered by it. "Why was I born into all this nonsense?" he asks, the first time I feel him expressing the genuine pain of the child he is describing.

It looks to me like Benji has been trying to sort through this chaos with his therapist but is still dissociated on an emotional level, protecting himself as he likely did as a child. In court documents, a behavioral specialist wrote he functions socially and emotionally as a nine- or 10-year-old.[190] I see it differently, like there is an emotionally numb and detached man who is polite and smart enough to articulate what he's discussed in therapy, often parroting the words of his therapist during our interview. But he's confused by what he can now put into words and perhaps still not fully feel, including the pain of that inner child.

I ask about school and his face brightens a bit, but then says it was also a struggle. He says he had a learning disability and was placed in special ed; and he received mental health counseling in school because he felt overwhelmed. Someone tutored him which got him to a

9th grade reading level. But for her, he says, "I wouldn't be able to read like I do." The irony is not lost on me that his reading ability, without critical thinking skills alongside a lot of hurt and anger, helped lead him into deep trouble as an adult.

"How were you overwhelmed, what mental health issues did you have?" I ask, hoping he can explain.

"Defiant stuff, maybe," he replies, clearly unsure. "Not emotionally supportive parents, not having the healthy relationship I deserved as a young child and that they deserved." I feel I'm again hearing him parrot psychologist's concepts he can articulate but not fully grasp. "Not structured the way it should be."

Children who grow up in chaotic and abusive homes often lack a coherent sense of self, and are sometimes hyperactive, dissociative, or unable to concentrate. I wonder which it is in his case, a true intellectual deficit or a need for help in regulating his emotions, which created the sense of incoherency in his young life, which I am intuiting now.

Benji did graduate from high school but has had difficulty keeping a job. Again, he says he'd feel overwhelmed, have a hard time concentrating, get frustrated and quit. The hard time concentrating often goes with trauma histories. He started to ask himself why labels had been placed on him and why he'd grown up with such instability that led to his inability to make healthy choices. Again, parroting but I now also hear some genuine anger.

When I ask about dating and relationships, Benji says, he "had companionships off and on with all this going in my life. I didn't really know..." and his voice trails off in what feels like sadness and confusion. He found it hard to stay in a relationship. "My grandfather beat on his wife. My mom picked a husband that didn't stay faithful to her, so when I started dating, I picked bad actors. I wasn't trained for what kind of values to look for."

"Did you start partying? Drinking or doing drugs?" and I'm not surprised by his answer.

"I was partying and not connected to life at all." Indeed. That is exactly what I'm feeling, a strong sense of disconnection. "I was deviant and young and let all that pain and sorrow come out in a negative way... hanging around knuckleheads and bad people, making bad choices instead of saying, 'I have these learning issues. I'm just as good as anyone else.'"

But Benji sounds so numb that I would call what he is telling me a "canned" story. He can intellectually verbalize but does so with no emotional connection, a childlike recitation of his situation. It is heartbreaking in a way. His robotic numbness shouts at me. "I didn't have no inspiration, no hope. I just felt all these terrible things happen to me. No hope. I didn't care less if I live or died. Nothing matters in my life."

He also grew up with a strong dose of racism. He says if he was treated well, he would treat others well, no matter skin color; however, his grandfather would say, "you never saw a successful Black person." He says he did not grow up with white supremacy ideology, yet, "I would never mistreat anyone from another race, but being from the South, I had these preconceived ideas that white people are better. Just being born in the South it made me susceptible to get involved in that stuff and I had an unstable environment growing up."

In his simple words, I hear Benji summing up a part of our *Escape Hate* research findings. In the U.S., those who grew up in the South in racist environments appear far more susceptible to accepting extremist white supremacist claims. Similarly, those from tough environments—bullying, economic hardship, family abuse, broken homes, or where addiction reigned, are also preyed upon by hate groups who help broken people feel they belong and are even loved. This counterfeit love exploits and manipulates people into fusing with the violent aims of the group. As Benji explains, "They don't take people who are successful, who embrace life in a positive manner. They take broken-hearted people who never had a father; people it's easy to show a little bit of love, even though it's fake love, and you open up and wind up thinking they are your true family. They show you love, and you end up doing bad things for these people. They use you."

Benji then details for me the would-be hate crime for which he was arrested, and his shock at being betrayed by an ally. The seed of racism in him, as he calls it, had been planted. He started to read up on supremacist ideologies. Then he met a guy going to a rally of the United Klans of Alabama.

Benji was about to become a very active member of the Ku Klux Klan.

"Being a person born in the South," Benji restates, "and not having hatred for others, but a little bit in me, I done went to a Klan rally." He says the journey into the Klan starts by meeting the people and feeling their embrace. At the Saturday afternoon rally he joined 200 people in a field, partying and getting to know one another. "They don't start out burning flags and screaming white power! It starts out it's not so bad. It's okay to be proud of who you are." He joined the KKK that night. "I went through the whole ceremony with lighting the cross. That night really changed me, having all these people, after lacking support. At the time, I felt like this is where I belong. It blew me away. I never had those feelings." In hindsight, he says their "love" was "a negative light, destructive and unhealthy, but I felt like I was loved, and belonged. It felt beautiful."

The inevitable followed. Their ideology taught him, "We are superior, other races are subhuman." He started studying Christian Identity. He calls it "the Christian version of being racist." They cherry-pick scripture and manipulate the Bible, "and when it's strong and planted in your heart, [they show you] videos of Black people attacking whites. They grow and grow this seed. They want it to grow into a big tree: you're superior, white power, and all that nonsense."

Growing up, he had been taught, "The Jews are God's chosen people and learning from the Bible is all I ever knew. I never knew these lies that they run the banking system. [The Klan] were up there burning Jewish flags and Black Panther flags. These were Jewish things I never knew until I knew these guys. They showed me in the Bible that Jews are the seed of Satan. When they showed me that, the first thing that popped in my mind was that I thought all Jews were Satan from that one scripture they were misusing."

Once inducted in the Klan, Benji says you learn on your own all the history you can—Hitler, Germany, the Civil War and adds, "there is nothing beautiful or positive in it. It leads to either the grave or prison."

For Benji it would lead to prison.

Benji says he felt the group began to burden him with the obligation of creating a white nation, kicking off a race war, and more. "I really believed God wanted me to go out and hurt these people just for Him. I thought God was telling me to do this, that I was God's warrior." Benji almost speaks like a schizophrenic who hears voices instructing him to harm others. Yet his are not the delusions of a mentally ill person but the ideological indoctrination by a hate group that manipulates with religion. He tells me, completely matter-of-factly, "I wanted to be a warrior, a hero to save the world, to get the other races off the planet." ISIS, al Qaeda, Klan, or otherwise, it's the same process and same end result—destruction to self and others.

Benji almost sounds like the jihadist suicide bombers I've spoken with, who begin to dissociate and enter a euphoric state as they contemplate taking their own lives to kill others.[191] I think of sitting in an Israeli prison with a young woman who told me she waited six long weeks to be called on to carry out the first female suicide bombing by a Palestinian. My Israeli colleague, Yoram Schweitzer, who facilitated these prison interviews for me, didn't believe a human being could tolerate that level of distress, waiting to be called to explode oneself at any moment. But I knew she was telling us the truth.

The mind can split off certain experiences and replace fear with euphoria and a determination to kill and die. As she explained to us what that waiting period was like for her, she described feeling an overwhelming euphoria—floating above it all, saying internal goodbyes to her family members, as she truly believed she was already sensing a taste of Paradise to come. She, like other would-be suicide bombers I've interviewed, and others have reported in the news, slipped into a dissociative ecstasy as she contemplated taking her own life in service of Allah and her people.[192]

This euphoria is probably mediated by the same endogenous endorphins our brains deliver whenever we face serious physical pain such as starvation, or an injury when we must keep running. Endorphins give us the ability to bypass the pain signals, or in the case of committing suicide, the self-preservation signals that would normally stop us from going forward. This young Palestinian woman admitted she actually got high recounting this period in her life, prompting me to ask if she had been drunk or using drugs at the time. "No," she replied, shocked, "This is what I felt each day, all day long" living on the thoughts of going to Paradise by pushing the button on her suicide bomb.[193]

Not only do captured jihadist suicide bombers report these feelings of euphoria, those who send them on their suicide missions have described this feeling as well. Zakaria Zuebedi, a former Palestinian who handled suicide bombers and was himself a fighter, got excited when I explained the idea of dissociation in trauma victims, because he had experienced it, too. When I compared his feeling to a fighter's mentality of defying death to return to fight another day, Zuebedi told me he could resonate with both brain states as he had entered both many times.[194]

As a "thought experiment," I conducted a roleplay with 30 students in Belgium from various nationalities, all of whom knew very little about the Palestinian/Israeli conflict and suicide bombings. We suggested imagining living a basic Palestinian life in the West Bank during the second intifada, while asking them to take on the role of a suicide bomber who had been caught before carrying out the mission.

We asked them to recount what it had felt like to put on their suicide vest as they constructed their roles in fantasy. At least half the students reported feeling they'd entered a dissociative state that took on various facets of experience. One young woman reported floating over her body; some spoke of a feeling of bliss; others of feeling all-powerful. Indeed, contemplating one's suicide even when couched in zealous faith can turn on such terror that it is compensated for by a cascade of what I think must be endorphins in the brain that make it possible to jump over our normal self-preservation instincts.[195]

Benji was feeling it all: "It felt so powerful. I didn't care if I died. I was invincible. God wanted me to do this, nothing would happen to me." He had overwhelming feelings of being on a holy mission and the corresponding neurobiological state-of-being. He could not separate out this religious zeal as a hero for God and an ordained warrior for his race, from the feelings of purpose and joy those thoughts gave him. This powerful combination propelled him forward despite the likelihood he'd die carrying out his mission. "By exposing myself daily to this hate, and all this ideology, it consumed my life and who I was as a human being. It brung me to a very negative place in my life." He hadn't gotten to this state alone.

"I got to the point where I believed this so much, I contacted the Imperial Wizard to do an act on a Jewish synagogue. Prior to this I didn't have any representation of who Jewish people are…I only knew what hate-filled people were telling me to believe." Benji tells me he was "hate-fueled" when I ask how he imagined his plan to attack the synagogue would go down. "That's the reason I purchased the firearm. I don't know if I would have taken the action to do it. I was talking about it, but who knows? The fire was lit, and it was burning out of control, but I don't know." Benji's face clouds over in pain and adds, "I'm thankful for the FBI picking me up."

My view is Benji would have gone through with his plan to shoot up a synagogue if he hadn't been intercepted by the FBI. What is exiting this life compared to the future glory of being in the presence of a God for whom he was a heroic warrior come to claim his rewards?

"Did you play it out ahead of time in your mind?" I ask, knowing the Norwegian mass shooter, Anders Breivik, for example, had watched videos to help him overcome his natural disdain for killing women and children.

"No, I never got to that point. There was no planning for me. I thought I'd go in there and start shooting. That was kind of what my idea was, when you do this."

"And how would it end for you?"

"Making a name for myself. I was supposed to show, 'Hey I'm brave, I'm strong.' I'm supposed to do this for my culture, my race."

When Benji says he wanted to harm Jews, his motivation is likely not just due to the hate he had been taught, but also likely springs from the deep hurt he held inside from all who failed him all his life. The well of pain inside could be easily manipulated by groups like the Klan who fanned that hurt into flames of anger and hatred directed toward someone totally unrelated to the original harm. Lashing out felt right.

Benji also believed he had the approval of his Imperial Wizard. "He was telling me Jewish people control the world and the banking system. And there's so much on the internet. There are lies and negative conspiracy theories, all false but so easy to believe, and they cause destructive terror on people who don't deserve it. Telling people these people are controlling the world..." his voice trails off.

After reassuring himself of his new beliefs that Jews are not the enemy, telling me, "They all have blood, all as good as us," he continues his story. And here is where an unexpected betrayal would play out and shake Benji to his core. Here's how the FBI sting went down.

McDowell told his Imperial Wizard of his wish to emulate Dylann Roof and attack a South Carolina synagogue. The Imperial Wizard sent him to a Facebook contact who "handled problems for the Aryan Nations," meaning someone who could procure the necessary weapons. However, it turns out this online "problem solver" was in fact an FBI agent. Reaching out to the agent via instant message on Facebook, McDowell incriminated himself with his request for help to obtain an "iron" (code word for a firearm), according to testimony against him in court. After weeks of meetings with the undercover FBI agent, according to a court affidavit by the agent, McDowell said he wanted to purchase a gun and complained about other white supremacists, "stating that screaming 'White Power' was not getting the job done.'" He allegedly expressed his desire to commit a terrorist act, telling the agent, "I seen what Dylann Roof did and in my heart, I reckon I got a little bit of hatred...I want to do that shit." According to press reports, McDowell also told the FBI agent he planned to attack somewhere in the name of white power and write on the building "in the spirit of Dylann Roof."[196]

Bringing the sting operation to its conclusion, the FBI agent agreed to pick up McDowell at his mother's house and drive to his grandfather's home to borrow money to buy the gun. McDowell then made the purchase and was arrested before he could carry out his plan. He was charged with possession of a firearm, illegal for him as a felon. He was sentenced to 33 months in prison as a result.

The informant was his KKK Imperial Wizard, the same man who, according to Benji, was encouraging him into violence. Terrorist inciters don't need to get their hands dirty. They can spew hatred while claiming to decry violence by filling the heads of the people around them with a violent ideology and inciting them into violent actions while staying clean.[197] Jeff Schoep and other leaders in the NSM recall visits and threats from the FBI, compelling them to cooperate and turn in violent individuals in their groups or be held responsible. TM Garret recalls similar visits from German security officials.

Benji now says, "God's plan was to let me get to the point where my life was saved and rescue me by the FBI." But he was extremely confused. Indeed, he thought he was an empowered white supremacist when he found himself in hand cuffs. "You are on your way to the Imperial Wizard's house—and arrested?!"

He pieced the story together much later, some of it from news articles and court documents. The Imperial Wizard had called the FBI to turn him in. The Imperial Wizard took him to the motel to meet the undercover agent where he eventually bought a firearm, thinking the agent was from the Aryan Nations. The gun was an incapacitated weapon. The agent supplied him with ammunition and Benji was arrested in the motel parking lot. In the meeting with the undercover agent, Benji says, "I said things supporting Dylann Roof. I said all kind of stuff. I have no desire to really repeat those things. They don't exist in my heart anymore; I had a lot of violent things," and I decide not to push him further.

I do ask Benji if the FBI undercover agent encouraged him. While I know that is strictly prohibited and would be considered entrapment, it remains an important issue in considering what may motivate a person into action. In my lethal cocktail of terrorism theory, I place providing social support equal to the group, its ideology, and individual vulnerabilities and motivations, the four necessary factors for making a terrorist.[198] So when an undercover agent shows up interested in what someone has said or posted on social media, they may be inadvertently providing social support that can tip the balance into becoming an actual terrorist.

"I don't really remember his saying great job, this is what you should do," Benji responds as I expected, but he says the undercover's body language conveyed something else. "He was kind of supportive in a way, supportive just enough to get information, to see how destructive and what I was willing to do. He didn't speak a lot, just letting me speak, saying all these violent things. Making me comfortable to attain these weapons, whatever I wanted."

I'm glad to hear he was not encouraged, as for me this gray area is worrisome, whether applied to terrorists like ISIS or white supremacists who might become violent like Benji. Law enforcement should never encourage vulnerable people. Aside from it being unfair, if left to their own devices, they could readily enact violence or engage in other self-destruction.

In prison, Benji was seen as a kind of star. Though the white supremacist prison gang, Aryan Brotherhood, wasn't inside, other white supremacists were and they knew who he was from stories on CNN and other news outlets. "They look at me as a prisoner of war, getting arrested for my race."

"You were looked upon as a hero?"

"To them I was," Benji responds. "To me, I was broken, confused."

Benji says one of the biggest factors that helped him find his way out of hate was being set up and being betrayed. "It shook me to my core and made me realize this stuff is false" even if the organization is real. No matter what, he said one will be betrayed, "If you go to prison, they are going to forget about you. Just because you get in an organization— you might not be set up by the FBI—but anything can happen." He calls hate organizations "a sickness in our world. I'm so thankful to escape it and embrace life."

Benji says he is horrified about standing on the brink of murdering innocent people. He is profoundly disturbed that he sold his soul to a group that really didn't care about him and sold him to the FBI while simultaneously assisting his steps toward becoming a race warrior. But again, as he rattles off his feelings, I feel like he doesn't really emotionally comprehend all he's saying:

"I'm so thankful that I didn't hurt anyone. No one has to look at anyone in a casket. My family doesn't have to have me in a federal prison. I didn't think about, I am going to get in trouble. There was so much hate in me I didn't really care if I lived or died. So much hate in me would override any positivity, anything good for us. I had no respect for the rule of law. I was so radical. I could care less. I was out of control. I was at my end of the rope. I'm so thankful I got caught before anyone was hurt. I'm so thankful to just be free and to talk to people. What I'm doing now is just as powerful than going in any place and hurting people." He broadens out, "We need people to embrace humanity, I'm looking for a time when there are no more children raped, no more wives abused by their husbands...I'm thankful for all these groups, women's rights, and different groups that speak out about real issues, positivity in life."

I now wonder how much his act of killing might have, in his mind, given him a heroic exit from life. I decide to dig a bit more and I ask if he's ever actually been suicidal. And he says very much so, from age 12 into his 20s.

"You were hurt as a boy?" I ask.

"No," he denies, although he started our interview telling me he had no father figure and his mother died of cancer.

I ask him about his criminal history. "My first arrest was at 17 for criminal stuff, stealing. I was 28 or 29 when I arrested by the FBI."

"Where you suicidal then?"

"Yes, very much so," and I feel Benji open up a bit as he refers to the pain in his childhood. "It was easy for me to get in these hate groups. It happens to kids now. They get involved in these gangs. It's easy because they pick people who struggle."

Dr. Charles Conant, a behavioral specialist who has known Benji for years, is the expert who concluded "socially and emotionally, he functions as a nine- or ten-year-old." He wrote in a letter to the court that he hoped Benji could get "mental health treatment in a therapeutic environment" while incarcerated.[199]

"Did you get counseling in prison?" I ask. He did not.

"I don't think counseling would have hurt, but I didn't need some Ph.D.," he responds. "I had to go through this struggle myself." He says he needed to find the human within and break down his mindset that everyone is the enemy which he'd had since childhood, even his family.

"Even five years ago I'd ask God, 'Why did you put me here?' I couldn't comprehend it, 'Why do I exist?'"

His says he now has more to live for than field rallies and burning flags, and a number of people deserve credit for helping Benji get to this point. In addition to Benji's counselor, Jeff Schoep and TM Garett check in on Benji, and TM is helping with tattoo removal. Benji underscores the power of having these images on his body and says the tattoos weren't a problem in dealing with others, they were a problem dealing with himself. Removing them, he has felt his identity shift, it's "sealed the deal, that's not you anymore." I see the evidence, in people like Benji, that TM's *Erasing the Hate* tattoo removal project has impact. Benji thinks the impact of tattoos needs to be better understood, and like others have told me, more assistance should be available for their removal.

Several Jewish leaders have also come to Benji's assistance. One rabbi in particular has spent hours on the phone with him and he's been able to open up to her and find support without judgment. "I'm still learning Jewish," he tells me, making me almost burst in laughter. I'm not exactly sure what he means, and I don't ask. "This lady checks on me often. I'm very blessed."

Benji also credits advice he received from an older white supremacist he met in prison, incarcerated since 1987. "He said, 'You really wasted your life. Look kid, when you go home, find someone to love. Find passion in life. Do great things, instead of destructive.' Having a male figure tell me, in certain ways that his life was negative, he did help."

Thanks to valuable outside support, Benji is at least making tangible changes. And he seems to embrace a future. Yet my guess is Benji has a hole in his heart that may never be filled. He won't likely become a hater again, but he doesn't seem healed either. I'm not his therapist so I'm not going to question him or dig too deeply beneath the surface. But he still needs a whole lot more healing. Hate is a complex thing and it's definitely a response to deep pain.

"With all the pain and sorrow I was exposed to as a child I would have made bad choices. I would still come to the end of the road of some bad negativity. I'm sure something would have transpired, all this pain and confusion holding in me," Benji answers insightfully. Maybe Benji has gotten to the core of his hurt and maybe he is healing. It's hard to tell.

You can watch Benji tell his story at www.EscapeHate.org

Chapter 18 - Exiting Hate
(and How We Can Help)

"You don't only need to get your head out of the hate—you also need to get the hate out of your head. And that takes a while. That's why radicalized people need professional help."

- TM Garret

When a violent jihadist in London was released from a prison-based deradicalization program only to carry out a murderous rampage, in addition to failures of other programs, many declared deradicalization an invalidated practice.[200] In the field of violent extremism research, there is significant disagreement about whether only disengagement, and not deradicalization, is possible.

Disengagement means leaving a group and separating from its membership, which can occur with imprisonment or by simply walking away. Not everyone in a hate group is necessarily ideologically radicalized, thus disengagement may be enough.

Deradicalization means changing one's thinking to relinquish the extremist ideology and commitment to violence. The disagreement centers around the challenges in getting someone to end their fusion with a terrorist or violent ideology and group, and the failures of some deradicalization programs. .[201]

Because radicalization involves changing minds by convincing someone of the righteousness and need for violent action, so too, does deradicalization. Which means understanding the motivations and influences for why people join hate groups and how they become radicalized is vital, as is understanding why and how the mechanisms work that help individuals successfully deradicalize from violent extremism.[202]

I know deradicalization is possible. I've seen it work. I helped design and create the *Detainee Rehabilitation Program* for the U.S. Department of Defense in camps Bucca and Cropper in Iraq, a deradicalization program to deal with the 20,000+ detainees and 800 juveniles held by U.S. forces. We worked with ideologically indoctrinated al Qaeda members with blood on their hands, who began to understand their murders were not carried out "in the path of Allah."[203] We used a combined approach of addressing the grievances and psychological traumas the individual held, alongside helping them understand al Qaeda does not accurately represent Islam. This dual approach helped al Qaeda detainees drop their support for terrorism and redirect into nonviolent ways to address their concerns.[204] Unfortunately, General Stone who oversaw the program did not address it to the hardcore al Qaeda detainees, many who later became ISIS. Likewise, it was hard to measure programmatic successes given the massive releases that happened during the Awakening movement in which Sunni tribes received their imprisoned sons back and were strengthened to work alongside the U.S. forces to drive out al Qaeda. General Stone claimed success in that there was very little recidivism among those who took part in the shortened program and were released, but one could argue that al Qaeda was falling out of power at the time and not getting rearrested did not mean these individuals didn't return to terrorist ideologies, as many of the Camp Bucca detainees did later join ISIS.

When it came to ISIS, we found that 29 percent of ISIS members I interviewed (most were held in prisons in Iraq and Syria) had spontaneously deradicalized without being exposed to any program to support the deradicalization process. It was ISIS's grievous brutality, corruption, and un-Islamic practices that pushed many to part with the group and give up the extremist *takfeeri* ideology that had been deeply drilled into them. As one woman stated, "I didn't need a deradicalization program. ISIS was the best deradicalization program!"[205] Deradicalization in these detainees was real and involved disillusionment and denouncing of their former group, but few made it all the way through to expressing concern and repentance for those they had hurt. Their deradicalization was more about realizing the group had been bad for them personally as well as hurtful to many others, without their getting to the point of taking personal responsibility for having harmed others as well.

While spontaneous deradicalization does occur, more often a lot of support is needed and far too few exit programs exist. Among our sample of 51 domestic violent extremists, only a few had the opportunity to participate in a formal deradicalization program.

Cognitive behavioral therapy is an evidence-based and proven method of changing minds.[206] This technique can be adapted for violent extremism. But it takes skill, an ability to create rapport with terrorists and violent extremists, knowledge about the varied groups and ideologies, and the ability to offer various incentives and support for the losses incurred when giving up a group and ideology. It also takes finding a therapist not fearful of or repulsed by the violent extremist, access to that therapist plus costs of treatment. So, it's not surprising, a recent RAND Corporation report based on a series of interviews with former extremists and their family members, found the difficulty accessing mental health care was a barrier to deradicalization.[207]

Only a few of our 51 interviewees mentioned psychotherapy being available and many noted traditional psychotherapy either was not within their means or would be unlikely to help because they needed much more support than the one or two hours a week available in a traditional psychotherapy schedule. They felt they required intensive conversations and support on multiple levels for crises more unique to them. For example, crises often occur late at night; they face issues like being suddenly unemployed after being doxxed; or involve probation officers or hearings in the criminal justice system.

This underlines why the informal counseling provided by Jeff Schoep's *Beyond Barriers*, TM's *Be the Change,* Germany's *EXIT* program, and many other programs run by former members of extremist groups, are necessary. Extremists are not people who generally have the resources or willingness to go see a psychologist or social worker and even if they did, they may encounter mental health workers who fear them, or counselors who have no idea how extremist groups operate and lack useful advice to assist in exiting.

Likewise, these members have so many doubts and so few relationships outside their hate groups they may require many hours of group support and guidance to successfully exit, something most professional counselors do not have time to give. Only then might they be ready for the traditional limits of a psychotherapy relationship. To successfully exit, extremists may need something more akin to a competing network of extremely supportive friendships and open homes to visit. As Jesse Morton, a former militant jihadist, often stated, "It takes a network to fight a network."[208]

Childhood has A Lot to Answer For

Those in our sample who did engage in psychotherapy for help exiting and rehabilitating from white supremacy groups have had mixed results. Some reported therapists were ill-equipped and uninformed about white supremacism; some reported seeing therapists who feared them; one said she was refused treatment based on her previous participation in violent extremism. Others reported significant growth working through previous childhood traumas, particularly abuse, as well as dealing with anger management and traumatic experiences as an active extremist. In addition, some reported slowly expanding their ability to see minorities as fully human and all of humanity in more positive ways.

Many psychotherapists are not well versed in the subjects of trauma and dissociation and how obsession and compulsions can be engaged as dissociative defenses, i.e. keeping traumas hidden from conscious awareness. As Shaun Grimsley (West Midlands Infidels-

UK) tells me years after leaving his group, "I still get the urge to join anything and go mad at it. I'm fully aware this is a symptom. I have this empty feeling in my head." Shaun thinks this feeling is common in former members of the more extreme groups and asks, "I have seen people latch on to anything, but the hatred is the same?" Then Shaun seems to answer his own question with impressive acuity when I ask if he thinks an extremist can ever be fully rehabilitated given, we have seen recidivism even in those taking part in professional rehabilitation programs:

> There is always a chance they will revert to extremism. I recognize this in myself. Just like an ex-smoker can smoke again, extremists have the drive at the back of their heads. I know it's there and there are days when I'm under duress that it shows its ugly face. Hatred never leaves you, it just goes dormant sometimes. Stress and worry are triggers for it. The brain looks for ways to express this violence, it's a sort of default setting in your head. Yeah, you can cure the racism, but it just moves to something else, where something that a normie would maybe just get really annoyed over magnifies greatly in the extremist's head; if left unchecked it goes on loop and empathy and feelings disappear. The face completely relaxes and the eyes stare, you tend to answer people around in short words as your mind is elsewhere. The heart races and a sort of numbness takes hold. Luckily for me I can recognize it starting. It's like Jekyll and Hyde. I can be the kindest nicest person in the world and the nastiest evil person at the same time.

His response sounds dissociative, as if he loses a part of his conscious functioning temporarily, but he has learned to recognize and override it. Shaun agrees and further describes the process he goes through, "Sometimes it takes hold for a day or more. Then there's an emotional crash afterwards that is like what you feel you when you get drunk and do silly things and regret it next morning. I can fully understand why some extremists that appear rehabilitated flip out."

As is often the case, childhood trauma is among the root cause, "Yeah, having a mom who blamed you for having to stick with an abusive partner because you were born." Shaun was abused by both parents. "My mum used to wind my dad up into whipping me and stand and watch from about nine-years-old. So yeah, childhood has a lot to answer for."

When therapists understand how much trauma, abuse, and pain is hidden inside so many young men and women, and how that pain can manifest in a realm of symptoms which can be fueled by hate groups, we will see much better enduring rehabilitation outcomes and trustworthy reintegration of those who get into treatment programs.

Disengagement, Deradicalization and Reintegration

As we've seen, imprisonment can also mean disengagement, but plenty of radicalizers and extremist groups are inside prisons around the world.[209] Indeed, many militant jihadists who went to prison for petty crimes came out as lethal terrorists, as have many whites who've found supremacist ideologies inside prisons.[210] In the U.S., prison-based gangs and white extremist groups are the most violent, and in some cases follow a "blood in, blood out" recruitment strategy leaving death the only option to exit.

Most of our DVE interviewees who disengaged did so out of their own self-driven sense of disillusionment and most could be said to have, what we call, spontaneously deradicalized, although varying levels of lingering fear and hatred toward minorities continue in some, and disengagement without any real deradicalization was clear in at least two cases.

Because varied pressures on a disengaged member remain, it is ICSVE's view that those who disengage from a hate group, but don't deradicalize, remain highly vulnerable to reengaging and becoming dangerous once again. Shared hate ideology plays a powerful role in bonding white supremacists, as well as inspiring violent action. Individuals exiting and reverting to their groups or moving among various groups is common. So while we believe disengagement is clearly important, deradicalization needs to be the goal for sustainable rehabilitation and successful reintegration into society.[211]

Our 51 subjects offer insights into disillusionment, disengagement, and deradicalization, which need better understood, as does what support is needed to exit, rehabilitate, and reintegrate into society. The challenges are great, but as we've seen, failure to act can be deadly.

Disillusionment

Regardless of their status—from active or adhering to parts of their former ideology, to seeking a new identity, to feeling full remorse—our interviewees each noted particular experiences inside their hate group and out, that brought into question whether they wanted to continue to belong, and if the cause was noble or even correct after all.

Twenty-eight interviewees (of the first 50 included in our data analysis) reported processes which led to disillusionment with the ideology. For example, Jared Mickelberg (Aryan Brotherhood) recalls changing his views by participating in a court-ordered rehabilitation program that physically separated him from his group, got him off drugs, and infused a strong religious ideology. He says he went through a radical change and no longer believes everyone is out to get him and is only out for themself. "Jesus Christ came for the single race, not for the white race. I'm called to love my neighbor as myself and love my God. No room for hate in any of that. You can't operate in hate and love."

The second most commonly reported source of disillusionment by our sample was individual interactions with Black people (11). When interactions across races and ethnicities are positive, they can have a very strong effect and kick off disillusionment, then disengagement and the deradicalization process. For this reason, white supremacist groups try hard to create an echo chamber and isolate members from interactions with those they hate. Planned and positive interactions can be an active element of formal treatment, and even spontaneous and everyday interactions with people they were taught to hate can have as meaningful an effect. The resulting cognitive dissonance, for some, results in questioning what they were taught. It can even encourage spontaneous deradicalization.

For TM Garret (KKK), it was the generosity of a Turkish landlord at Christmas when he was desperate. Ryan LoRee (Rollingwood Skins) found compassion in prison when his fellow white supremacists didn't come to his aid but his Black cellmate did when he was attacked by a Black prisoner. Ivan Humble (English Defense League) recalls a conversation he had with a Muslim community leader: "He said, 'I'll give you a chance to say what you want, and I'll listen.' I ranted for an hour, tried to provoke him. After about an hour, he said, 'have you finished now?' We sniggered. One hundred barriers fell down…Mamar was prepared to listen to me and treat me as a human being."

Red (NSM) recounts this gripping experience working at a funeral home as an apprentice funeral director. He was in his mid-20s when a Black corpse his same age came in. "Here's this young man on my slab, could have easily been me…I am the one who had to contact the family." It was his first solo case. "As I was embalming this young man, you tap into the carotid and jugular veins and artery, it drains the blood out. Blood. He bled the same color I bled. Who the hell was I to be better than him?"

Brad Galloway (Canadian Volksfront) recalls the act of compassion he didn't feel he deserved after he got into a fight with a Vietnamese gang and ended up in the ER. "I was in all the gear. Orthodox Jewish doctor walks in. He didn't even bat an eye. Swastika on my shirt, jacket, and boots. He didn't mention anything. This guy shouldn't even help me." That encounter would come to haunt his memory and influence his decision to disengage.

Disengagement

Given the isolation and echo chambers that characterize white supremacist groups, disengaging is difficult. To really detach from white supremacism, some in our sample had to cut off all ties with group members who had become their friends and family; some had to abandon lucrative white power paraphernalia or music businesses they'd started; others had jobs embedded with white supremacists they had to leave; others saw their partners leave them.

We have also been told of some individuals, not included in our study, who find it hard to leave because their spouses refuse to exit. One woman phoned Jeff Schoep's *Beyond Barriers* exit organization asking for help because she knew her husband would not leave their hate group and she feared she could lose her children if she did. Many ISIS mothers didn't leave Syria for the same reasons. Their partners threatened to take their children if they tried to leave, or even worse, their home countries told them it was impossible to provide travel documents for children born in Syria, even if the mothers managed to make it across the border with their children to their consulates in Turkey.

Conversely, seven people in our sample reported interventions, pressures, and ultimatums from their families played a role in their decision to leave their group. Even from afar. Lauren Manning (Canadian Hammerskins) had joined after her father passed away. When the male group members told her that her role was not to fight but to have children, she felt her father's presence. "My dad was a pretty strong dude, raised me the same way. Near the end of my involvement, I thought, if my dad would come back from the dead, [he] would come back to beat my ass for putting up with this."

For Chris Knack (National Democratic Party of Germany) the

ultimatum came more formally, in a child custody case. "The judge said, due to my political opinions because I'm in the movement, the child can't come live with me. I had a new girlfriend; she made me think of everything. Then I started to think of getting out."

Søren (NSM) says he saw the hurt on people's faces during protests and it would bother him. "They are witnessing something horrible and awful; it was hard to deny that it was just a huge negative force in the world. In many ways I was a true believer and thought it would make the world a better place, but there are certain things you can't deny anymore." He was living with his girlfriend who tried to ignore and look past his actions "but she hated it. I was already disillusioned; she gave me an ultimatum."

Deradicalization

Three of the most important considerations when evaluating if someone is fully rehabilitated, are:

- What were their original reasons for joining, what needs did they hope to get fulfilled, and have they been redirected in a manner that those needs are now being met in a positive manner? If not, we can expect relapses and more trouble.
- What are they doing to get over all the traumas endured while in the group? Are they healing from that trauma or using and attempting to control other people to narcissistically heal their broken places? If the latter, we can also expect trouble.
- Upon exiting did they reevaluate what they'd been taught and undergo a change of heart or were they simply interested in saving their own skin? Are they sorry for what they've done and attempted to make amends?

We monitored these factors among ISIS cadres who we rated for their level of radicalization at the point they joined ISIS, the point when they were most highly radicalized, and how radicalized they were at the point of our interview. We found many joining out of the social need to belong, to have a sense of purpose, significance and dignity; for adventure, love, or the promise of a wife or sex slave; or more basic desires for a job and free housing. We saw the men often became most radicalized when they had undergone ISIS's intensive *shariah* training, indoctrination by learned sheiks who use Islamic scriptures to make their recruits believe ISIS was on the right path.

In the case of white supremacists, we also saw them become more radicalized the deeper they went into their groups through the process we call "Directed Hate." They join for a sense of belonging, significance, and purpose, and then come to believe they are part of an elite group due to their whiteness. In their eliteness, they believe they are privy to esoteric knowledge; that whites are subject to white genocide and white replacement with outsiders, particularly Jews, ultimately to blame; and violence must be endorsed to save their elite status as well as to ensure their continued belonging, purpose and significance in their group.

In ISIS, deradicalization occurred as disconfirming events, such as witnessing ISIS' un-Islamic nature through its brutality and corruption. This process greatly accelerated in prison when ISIS members were grouped together and began to share stories about how foul life was inside ISIS and how far off the mark of an Islamic utopian Caliphate the group had fallen. Thus, without any formal deradicalization process, we found 40 percent of our ICSVE sample had begun to spontaneously deradicalize.[212] Many came to despise and renounce ISIS on their own, but few made it the whole way to accepting full responsibility for their part in supporting a brutal terrorist organization or feeling remorse for their own actions or for the victims of ISIS.

Rehabilitation and Reintegration

These lessons apply to DVE and someone worth hearing from on that front is TM Garret. TM is dedicated to helping formers deradicalize and stay that way. He knows from personal experience the importance of early intervention and steady support which is why he started Be the Change, a nonprofit that includes an exit program from white supremacism. TM responds to texts and phone calls at all hours of the day and night with requests for help avoiding going back to prison, talking to a parole officer, avoiding former white supremacist gang members, and much more. He monitors social media posts of those he's supported and reins them in when they are backsliding into hate rhetoric.

His method of intervention is love, acceptance, and listening. Just like the recruiters, TM says he is seriously listening, "no matter how much I want to intervene." He finds out what they fear, why they think things are bad, what they see as the solution. "This is the first step. It begins with, 'I respect you. I want to listen. I want to know what's going in your life, what's wrong, and that I really care about you.'"

TM is not a licensed counselor, nor is he paid for his countless hours of intervention. In essence, he says, we compete with the recruiters. "Every kid has fear, a monster under the bed," and when they're small, "We hug them knowing there is no monster, but their fear is real." Then kids hit puberty and "we tell girls they have to be pretty, and boys have to be hard, and don't show unconditional love and compassion anymore." TM says, like the recruiters, we have to take their concerns, that "monster under the bed" seriously. Their fear is real. "With extremists, it's all fear-driven and if that fear is not acknowledged, then you get nowhere."

TM also believes exposure to those they once hated is valuable and will often take white supremacists he's working with to visit Jewish people and Black people who are willing to open their homes or places of worship to help with deradicalization efforts. When he invited Ken Parker, who joined the KKK and NSM after leaving the military, to a Jewish couple's home, Ken learned not all Jews are "libtards." This

Jewish couple voted for conservative Republicans and shared many of Ken's values.

As we've heard, tattoo removal may in fact be an integral part of rehabilitation and reentry into mainstream society. TM initially started to help white supremacists exit from hate groups in 2017 when he created *Erasing the Hate*. This program links current and former white supremacists, like Benji McDowell, to tattoo artists who help them cover or remove their white supremacist tattoos at no charge. It's a program that continues to grow, spanning multiple countries and continents.

In Europe, there are numerous government-supported exit programs that provide intensive counseling to greater success. Many are modeled after the pioneering efforts of Tore Bjørgo's Norwegian Project Exit program, which began in 1996, and has been replicated as EXIT programs in Sweden, Finland, Germany, Netherlands, and Sweden. These programs offer hotlines, relocation, housing, and re-employment support programs, connections to support services, and more, so white supremacists can fully remove themselves from their groups. They also offer parental and peer support groups and intensive individual counseling to help extremists fully deradicalize and reenter society. Unfortunately, the U.S. and Canada have fewer such groups, and these are usually poorly funded. Europeans also have a different view of the penal system as being rehabilitative versus punitive, something Americans might want to learn from given inmates are invited into hate groups and hateful ideologies are often learned in prison and without rehabilitation programs we may simply be delaying the next hate crime till incarceration is finished.

Those who successfully walk away from violent extremism and terrorism often regret the years lost in the movement, the neglect of partners and children, and hold guilt and trauma emanating from their own actions and experiences in the hate group. A lot of these feelings are centered on the self, however, and ignore their victims.

At ICSVE, we hold the view that total deradicalization, in order to be complete, should include a repentance process in which amends are made, if possible, to those harmed. It isn't always possible to make amends, or even apologize to victims who may revile or still fear them, but it is possible to be truly repentant and try to make up for the damage done. A repentance process involves taking responsibility for harmful actions to oneself and to others, feeling genuinely remorseful, fully rejecting anything that supports hate, and making amends. In our sample, some subjects had made efforts to make amends to their victims, in some cases with positive outcomes, in other cases they faced rejection which they needed to respect as well.

Countering Recruitment and Radicalization in the Military and Police

Military and police engagement in far-right extremism and white nationalism is a potentially lethal situation not easily remedied. Whether it's the problem of people inside the military being radicalized, or recruited to violent extremist groups once they've left, or members of DVE groups intentionally joining the military to receive weapons and tactical training, this troubling issue must be addressed holistically.

The Anti-Defamation League reports, "the military has tended to respond to major incidents with partial revisions or updates to the regulations or with investigations of specific units or groups." This piecemeal approach is part of the problem, permitting claims of a lack of clarity and specificity regarding military policies surrounding extremism, and contributing to the continued spread of violent extremism, particularly far-right ideologies, within the ranks.[213]

What can the military do when it finds an extremist in the ranks? Dishonorable discharge may appear to be the clearest course of action. This option allows the military to remove a violent extremist from their ranks who might radicalize other service members, recruit them to join their group, or even carry out an attack on civilians, military personnel, or military infrastructure. However, dishonorably discharging someone who has not yet been violent, without taking any other actions, can also be dangerous.

Keep in mind, every recruit receives firearms training during basic training, so it's not enough to just dismiss known white supremacists from military service. That simply unloads a dangerous and now weaponized individual with military know-how onto wider society. Dishonorable discharge without treatment sends a weapons-trained and militarized individual who is aggrieved and searching for an identity out into society, ripe for further radicalization and possible mobilization into violent acts. Intervention and treatment before or as an alternative to discharge is likely a more responsible option.[214]

Dishonorable discharge can also be seen as policing thoughts rather than actions, although in reality no one is discharged for thought crimes, and will likely engender a sense of grievance against the military and the U.S. government, which could be exploited by violent extremist recruiters following discharge. Finally, the need for a positive identity and belonging are key motivators for joining violent extremist groups and being dishonorably discharged essentially nullifies one's identity and sense of belonging as a member of the military, creating a void to be filled by a violent extremist group.[215]

After his discharge from the Army National Guard, Sean Gillespie (Aryan Nations) committed a series of hate crimes, including horrific acts of violence against Black men and attempting to firebomb a synagogue. Had there been an intervention rather than simple discharge, maybe he would have been pulled out of the Aryan Nations before, as he callously describes it, he "ran over some Black with my truck…beat up some Black guy with a baseball bat…etc."

In April 2021, U.S. Secretary of Defense Lloyd Austin rightly acknowledged the military has an extremism problem that needs routed out. He called for stand-down days during which time extremism in the ranks would be addressed within the military leadership. A video of Secretary Austin was played. Here is part of what he had to say:

> What is new is the speed and the pervasiveness with which extremist ideology can spread today, thanks to social media and the aggressive and organized and emboldened attitude that many of these hate groups and their sympathizers are now applying to their recruitment and to their operations…You know, it concerns me to think that anyone wearing the uniform of a soldier or a sailor, an airman, marine, or guardian, or Coast Guardsman would espouse these sorts of beliefs, let alone act on them. But they do. Some of them still do.
>
> Share with your leadership your own personal experiences with encountering extremism and extremist ideology in the military, should you have any. And I want your leadership to listen to those stories. And I want them to listen to any ideas that you might have to help us stamp out of the ranks the dangerous conduct that this ideology inspires.

However, sharing experiences was not the main focus of the stand down days. I know as I was a guest speaker, and I did share our ICSVE counter narrative video of Sean Gillespie's experiences inside and after discharge from the military. (See Chapter 4 for Sean's story.) However, the focus was defining terms and existing rules about impermissible behaviors, which moved from thoughts and beliefs (which are not regulated), to impermissible actions and behaviors (which are.) There was confusion about when it might be permissible to defend oneself against extremism, and if there was a list of banned groups (these were compiled after the event.) Absent were clear reporting guidelines and clearly defined intervention protocols (which the Secretary is now working toward creating.) Indeed, leadership provided only vague answers about what would be done if one did report extremism.

Unfortunately, Secretary Austin's sincere attempts over the past year to root out extremism in the military are now being overridden. The U.S. Senate has locked itself in a partisan divide over the scope of the problem. Some claim it is miniscule while others say it only takes a small few to create a disastrous problem. The result has been the Senate National Defense Authorization Act (NDAA) which called for immediately halting the U.S. Department of Defense's fight against extremism with the claim that extremism in the military is exceptionally rare and it's a waste of taxpayers' money to fund it.[216]

ICSVE's data focuses on the facts. Soldiers who do get recruited are indoctrinated into believing that inciting a racial war is necessary; these are men and women who are weapons trained; and they may have access to lethal weapons. In a recent report, ICSVE detailed open-source reporting on over 300 cases of military members involved in or investigated for violent extremism over the past five years. Some of the cases were extremely violent including former Marine Corps Matthew Belanger's Rapekrieg group discussed in Chapter 9.

As we also detailed in our peer-reviewed report[217] about extremism in the military, we believe violent extremism and radicalization in military members may be approached as a psychological issue, similar to PTSD and substance abuse. Such an approach would lead to promoting rehabilitation, rather than simply discharge which could lead to grievances and increase risks following discharge.

Violent extremism is not a mental illness, and those who commit acts of violent extremism should by all means be held accountable. However, violent extremism usually begins with alignment with violent actors and ideological indoctrination into virulently hateful beliefs and does arise as a result of a myriad of psychological and social factors. These factors can be addressed in a similar manner to other interventions where unhealthy choices are being made. Military-linked extremists can be rehabilitated with a combination of psychosocial treatment such as cognitive behavioral therapy, which addresses the underlying needs, vulnerabilities, and cognitive distortions that contribute to radicalization; and ideological challenge and redirection, which consists of serious conversations with credible messengers.[218]

There are detriments to this treatment pathway as well. Treating violent extremists similarly to service members struggling with PTSD and substance abuse risks reinforces that such ideologies and actions are somewhat tolerated in the military or could be interpreted as military leadership being somewhat sympathetic to it. Given the risks and benefits to dishonorable discharge and treatment, ICSVE proposes a middle ground. Once identified, violent extremists are required to undergo an intensive treatment program as long as they have not already committed a crime. If treatment is refused or if the individual is noncooperative in treatment, dishonorable discharge should be considered.[219] However, it remains incumbent upon the military to not simply discharge militarily trained and radicalized members out into the community without some sort of psychological intervention aimed at curbing their extremism.

The challenge for the military also lies not only in intervening when service members become radicalized or preventing them from radicalizing others. Focusing exclusively on active service members falls short. Veterans need to be considered for their vulnerabilities to recruitment into extremist groups, particularly those who are struggling with a loss of identity, depression, posttraumatic stress and difficulties with post-service employment. Effectively screening out potential recruits who hold violent extremist ideologies, so they do not receive military training and cannot radicalize and recruit fellow servicemembers, is of course crucial.

Similar challenges and caveats exist for police forces, and extremists are far more embedded in both the military and police than is publicly recognized. This problem is neither "miniscule" as elements of the post January 6 U.S. Senate claimed, nor is it something our government can afford to ignore given the potential lethality.

As of this writing, the U.S. Department of Defense, U.S. Department of Justice and the U.S. Department of Homeland Security have recently enlisted ICSVE to work with military and police respectively, to create a series of training courses to help each better identify and understand the radicalization in their ranks, intervene while keeping staff safe, and ensure they are not contributing to a wider problem and to also research the same.

All of us have a Role in the Battle against Hate

There are of course big picture structural issues that need tackled—like family dysfunction, abuse and neglect, drugs and alcohol abuse, economic stressors, etc. Then there is the need to increase programs to address crises among today's youth, from bullying and depression, self-harm and suicide, to street gangs and gun violence. We must include in this list the need to undercut the effectiveness of white supremacists' ability to successfully recruit those at risk.

Parents, teachers, coaches, religious leaders, and other influencers need to be cognizant that when the youth under their care have a sense of belonging, significance, and purpose, they are less likely to look for it elsewhere.

TM recalled for me a school scandal where a student who wrote a racial slur on a table was expelled. No one wanted a racist kid in school, so they "just put him in a box, labeled him a racist kid. This is exactly what happened to me." No one actually looked at that kid in the box. "We need to find out from the first signal, where does that kid stand? Is the family racist? Is it YouTube radicalization? Is he already in a group or just heard a racist slur on TV? We don't know, and the kid is kicked out and will carry the box to the next school where they will say, 'Oh my God, we are getting the racist kid, thank you!'" TM reiterates, "We need to open this box and see this human being inside. Not just put a label on a box."

When we see early signs of violent extremism in youth, we need to first take a caring approach rather than label and reject. The angry signs of violent extremism and hate are likely expressions of real pain. Youth need help to discover ways of belonging and they need healthy and nurturing people who can further their positive trajectory into adulthood.

We need a greater focus on our boys. While women do engage in DVE, DVE is primarily a white man's word; thus, a gendered approach is necessary. Boys and young men need to be provided with proactive and positive opportunities to gain their sense of dignity, purpose, significance and belonging in pro-social ways. Given religious and social institutions like church youth groups and Boy Scouts are in decline, we need to identify or create new ways to socialize boys as they come of age and move into manhood. Not to be forgotten are LGBTQ youth who suffer feelings of condemnation, self-hatred, and failure. Among our interviewees, some channeled their internalized prejudice and self-hatred by participating in overtly violent homophobic groups; some of these interviewees came out after leaving their hate groups.[220]

The physical and psychological assaults on young boys' sense of masculinity that draws them to toxic masculinity need addressed. Here we must include the pandemic of sexual abuse.

Just as the Me Too movement brought the experience of sexual violence into the open for women, we need to further acknowledge that boys are also molested and sexually assaulted at horrific rates in childhood, including here in the U.S. The data is deeply disturbing:

- Nearly a quarter of American men have experienced some form of physical sexual violence in their lifetime.[221]
- 2.6% of U.S. men (an estimated 2.8 million) experienced attempted or completed rape victimization in their lifetime. Approximately half of these (about 1.5 million) victims experienced such victimization prior to age 18; one quarter (718,000 victims) report their first victimization occurred

between the ages of 11 and 17, and another quarter (738,000 victims) at age 10 or younger.[222]

- Seven percent of boys in the juvenile justice system have experienced sexual abuse.[223] These are only the cases we know about.

Most of these minors will never tell anyone and as a result never receive treatment. We need to get much better at identifying all victims of childhood sexual abuse and intervene earlier and effectively. Both genders suffer. Male victims, in particular, may grow up with a festering sense of shame, humiliation and anger, and have problems controlling emotions, suffer from PTSD and depression, and turn to drugs and alcohol to cope. Extremists groups are only too ready to grab hold of these young men and turn them into a hateful, toxic version of masculinity.

School programs that teach tolerance for differences, build critical thinking, and help youth vet sources of information and correctly identify disinformation are part of the solution. One way we can protect our youth is to present what the extremists are presenting first, to help them be able to debunk false claims, think rationally, and not let their emotions get so engaged they skip over logical argumentation. Youth need our help to consider the consequences of involvement in any type of cult-like setting before they ever slip down that dark and dangerous path. ICSVE has long argued for providing inoculation programs for youth in 8th grade civics courses. Virulent and popular ideologies promulgated by extremists that spread over the internet can be presented in a controlled school setting in a way that allows students to analyze their claims rationally, not emotionally, with trained adult support. Students can work through the emotions recruiters attempt to engage and manipulate, to see their claims are not credible nor are their proposed violent solutions useful to society or to the student himself.[224]

This preemptive work builds upon an immunological metaphor proposed by social psychology researcher William McGuire. Just as the immune system can learn to mount a defense against a virus by being exposed to a weaker form of it, McGuire argues, exposing individuals to a persuasive message which contains weakened arguments and/ or messaging (e.g., showing both sides of a false argument; emotional manipulations; refutations of counterarguments), individuals can develop resistance against future persuasive attacks.[225]

We were pleased to see Dr. Kurt Braddock in the School of Communication at American University recently echo our call, arguing for inoculating youth by teaching them how to recognize disinformation and manipulation. He has demonstrated positive results, testing this theory in control group settings.[226]

ICSVE offers our *Breaking the ISIS Brand* and *Escape Hate* counter narrative videos and accompanying study guides as a way to bring such discussions into classrooms and youth groups and as an inoculation against terrorist and violent extremist claims and arguments.

The proliferation of assault weapons in the U.S. is also a dangerous burden on society when radicalized boys and men have such easy access to guns. When 20 first graders and six adults were gunned down at Sandy Hook Elementary School just before Christmas 2012, two grieving Sandy Hook parents created Sandy Hook Promise. More than a gun safety organization, it seeks to prevent bullying and a wide array of hate crimes by teaching students, teachers and administrators to "Know the Signs." Their "Say Something" initiative helps middle and high school students recognize the warning signs of someone at-risk of hurting themselves or others, and teaches students how to safely access help from a trusted adult. This data-proven program aligns with existing social-emotional learning (SEL) curriculum in schools and is available to schools and youth organizations at no cost. More at www. sandyhookpromise.org.)

We cannot discuss threats to our youth without centering the internet. Chances are, that is where the most virulent and popular ideologies, groups, and propaganda are going to reach our youth. Youth stumble into groups and ideologies and are lured into the violent extremist lifestyle from the presumed safety of their bedrooms. Parents are certainly aware that even a loving and protective family can't stop their home from being penetrated by forces entering online, but most don't conceive skinheads or Proud Boys or ISIS entering. I've spoken to parents whose children suddenly left home and traveled to Syria to join ISIS, totally blindsided by the internet recruitment going on right in their own home. If you have a phone or a computer and an internet connection, far-right extremists can reach our impressionable children at just the age when they are seeking to individuate and rebel from how they were raised. Parents need to keep communication channels open and discuss these topics with their teens always guiding them to nonviolent solutions to their feelings of grievance, and to addressing their fears and concerns. And when they see their child going down a rabbit hole of extremism, they need to engage knowledgeable professionals or formers to help them draw their child back out of hate movements.

Because dangerous disinformation is a serious problem when it comes to DVE, we need to hold those who promulgate their propaganda responsible. There are no easy fixes in this regard and it's difficult to police.

The main social media companies, Facebook, YouTube, Google, Twitter, etc. have strengthened takedown polices against extremist hate speech and incitement to violence and created machine learning programs that recognize and halt extremist propaganda in its tracks. However, many propagandists are smart and highly educated, and constantly innovate to keep ahead of counter terrorism moves. Terrorists and domestic violent extremists have found plenty of workarounds and encrypted platforms. ICSVE found militant jihadists avoiding takedown algorithms simply by spelling jihad with the numeral one (i.e., j1had), allowing them to continue to recruit for ISIS. Groups like ISIS also learned that all they had to do was blanket the internet with their virulent messaging—reaching billions—then sit back to see who responded with likes, shares, and comments. In a sense, social media platforms sorted out possible recruits, making recruitment an easier task. Recruiters could hone in on vulnerable and receptive individuals. Acacia Dietz, NSM's propagandist and social media lead, learned how to tone down and disguise hate speech just enough to avoid takedowns. Then those who responded to NSM's blander posts were migrated onto encrypted apps and platforms that allowed complete freedom of hate speech and further engagement.

Takedown efforts by the big social media companies are no doubt important, but perhaps the most important factor to understand is it's the people, not the posts, we really need to reach. The vast majority of violent extremist content is not eligible for taken down and even when content is removed, the human behind it still exists and continues to repost or move to another platform.

Allowing violent hate speech on social media platforms does a great disservice to society. Social media companies must continue to monitor and remove incitement to violence while abiding by important First Amendment considerations. Much as free speech is a foundational right for our country, social media platforms that allow for rampant dissemination of conspiracy theories and algorithms that magnify them, are bad for democracy. The point of our First Amendment rights was to stop the government from tyrannical control and allow citizens to criticize their governance without fear of repercussions, not to give a megaphone to those outside (and inside) government who might want to impose tyranny.

It is heartening to see most of the prominent companies have developed creative programs to address disinformation and hate speech: Facebook, for example, supports ICSVE's *Breaking the ISIS Brand* and *Escape Hate* campaigns by having donated over $600,000 in ad credits and hiring a consultant firm to help with ICSVE's counter narrative video campaigns, posted in 27 languages in more than 125 campaigns around the world.

Twitter instituted a stop and think initiative with a pop up that prompts the user to read an article before sharing it, to interrupt the quick retweeting of unread misinformation and propaganda. Likewise, recognizing that hate speech is often impulsively posted, they came up with a speed bump of sorts, a prompt that pops up for any post flagged as hate speech, asking the user to reconsider if they want to post or not. This gives the user a chance to stop and think before posting.

Google is also working on a system of pre-bunk (rather than to debunk) to get out ahead of extremist messaging. Users are warned what such extremist messages might look like and how to protect and equip themselves to avoid manipulation. For instance, by offerings warnings about fear mongering or cherry picking, this method was used quite well by many groups on multiple platforms during the Ukraine crisis to flag Russian fake content; content that can be extremely emotionally evocative; and the need to carefully vet sources before sharing potential disinformation. Google also has a redirect initiative that offers alternative and safer options to users who pose potentially dangerous search questions such as, "How do I join ISIS in Syria?" or "How do I become a skinhead?"

Many DVE supporters have exited Twitter and Facebook in the face of takedowns. However, internet platforms like Telegram, Gab, Parler, Truth Social, Discord, Twitch, and more continue to allow for hate speech and violent extremist activity. The problem is not the post, it's the poster. Perhaps some type of third-party intervention aimed at anyone about to be de-platformed may help. While it may sound naïve, given many violent extremists are looking for a sense of belonging and validation, a caring intervention may at least reach some.

Lethal free speech against our communities and our democracy has got to become unacceptable. While we will never return to the days of Walter Cronkite dishing out a presumed shared reality, we may need to think about how politically divisive and influential news punditry has become and require channels using our airwaves to rein it in and move toward less opinion and more responsible reporting. Other solutions are necessary for cable news outlets. Fox, in particular, is mainstreaming hate as are radio hosts like Rush Limbaugh. There is the media fringe of conspiracy promoters like Alex Jones and QAnon propagandists but perhaps more concerning are Fox's Tucker Carlson, Laura Ingram, Sean Hannity and a host of others who repeat conspiracies like the Great Replacement Theory or tell half-truths, fuel QAnon propaganda, repeat the lie of election fraud and push hate. Fox it appears is a master at propaganda which is different from leaning right or left and is dangerous to society because when a main news outlet makes a large segment of our citizens question the very institutions we rely upon for our democracy to function we could risk losing what we once cherished.

Likewise, politicians need to better police their own. The means cannot justify the ends and politicians promoting violence should never be tolerated. When Eric Greitens, a former Navy Seal and former Republican governor of Missouri, depicted himself hunting members of his own party with an actual rifle in a video ad for his race for the Senate, he went too far. Likewise, politicians who act and speak in ways that erode trust in our institutions and electoral processes do real damage to our country. When they encourage violence against our institutions and processes, they endanger our communities and our democracy. They must not be tolerated by any political party or party leadership.

From politics, police, and military to current members and kids online, an asset for prevention and deradicalization we would be wise to expand are former hate group members who can play a particularly effective role. Their engagement and various effective strategies and programs discussed throughout this book need increased support. With a caveat. Leaders in extremist and terrorist groups are used to attention and narcissistically crave it after they have left their movements. Able

to charismatically manipulate others, they may naturally gravitate
to continuing. That's why, while formers can be extremely powerful
helping others to exit, rehabilitate, and reintegrate, some will still need to
be carefully supervised and watched for lapses back into their old ways
of manipulating.

When someone has failed quite a bit in their life, it's important
to understand how seductive it is to be told the blame and responsibility
for one's failures lie elsewhere. One of the other really powerful ways
we've seen hearts and minds change is with simple interactions in
which hate group members were granted kindness and compassion by
members of minority groups they were convinced to hate. That's why,
like cults, white supremacist groups demand ideological and behavioral
loyalty from their members and try to isolate them from members of
the hated minority groups to prevent positive exposure. Interventions
and prevention measures designed to create positive interactions and
dialogue across racial, ethnic, and religious divides are valuable.

Which brings us to compassion.

It's not useful for parents, teachers, or clergy to lecture or engage
in condemnations and fear tactics when they see symbols of hate on
clothing and bodies, or in the case of law enforcement when engaging
with white supremacists. Instead, asking nonconfrontational questions
and listening to responses can open discussion and be far more effective.
Genuinely asking, "What is this doing for you? Why do you like this?"
could just open a door that points in more useful directions to meet a lost
person's needs.

When you see someone with marks of hate on his or her body
or clothes, you can rightly revile them or steer clear. But it may be
useful to think of former violent racist skinhead leader, Arno Michaelis,
who recalls the Black clerk who often served him with kindness and
compassion despite the hate marks tattooed on the hands in which she
placed his change. And former Volksfront, Brad Galloway, who could
never shake his amazement that an Orthodox Jewish emergency room

doctor treated him well and without any word of condemnation about the swastika on his shirt.

Søren (NSM) thinks there's really only one way to pull people out. "I know it sounds like someone obnoxious, but the only cure for that is love."

All of us can employ the power of compassion to rehumanize and remember that many of these people joined often after much personal pain and many failures in their lives. As TM reminds us, "If we don't pull these kids out of these boxes with those labels and put them back on track, the guys with the swastikas and white hoods, or QAnon, will do it. And then we may have lost another soul who may become the next synagogue shooter. This is the great power we have, to decide what happens to those individuals when they are in these boxes. The choice is ours."

Our EscapeHate.org webpage lists numerous exit programs that offer confidential help.

Chapter 19 - A Leader Leaves

He walked around like a presidential figure, dressed in a black suit with sunglasses and bodyguards flanking him, revered by his followers—with nothing more than a high school degree. After nearly two decades growing the NSM, Jeff Schoep was the glorified leader of a significant movement that intimidated others. He was constantly getting media attention. He fully identified with his grandfather and great uncles whom he saw as war heroes in Hitler's Germany.

"In the movement you have to be hard at all times or it is seen as weakness," Jeff tells me. "You don't show weakness, your humanity, or anything like that, or you can potentially become a victim yourself." Even when he was almost a victim of an assassination. The would-be assassin was someone who had moved from out of state to infiltrate his family and kill him. Jeff's kids became close to this new "uncle." Jeff survived an attack that split his head open. The NSM did not go to the police "We handled it ourselves. They were forced out of state." When his kids asked where their "uncle" was, Jeff offered no explanation, "'He's not your uncle and he's gone.'" Even his children saw him as emotionless.

Despite the hardships, members in hate movements get enough sense of pride and power, and opportunity to move up the ranks into leadership, that they will use up their vacations and volunteer countless unpaid hours, some working far more than they would in a full-time job.

When people would ask what they'd get out of joining, Jeff would tell them, "'You get blood, sweat, and tears. That you've done something good and noble for your people,'" falling back on the "noble cause" theme. But he has seen the downside of that noble cause narrative. He wistfully he adds, "I let go of my dreams from the beginning to do this. I saw it rip apart my family. I've seen people go to prison for 40 years. I've seen people die. There's nothing really positive; it's more a sacrifice."

"What did you get out of it?" I ask him.

"Blood, sweat and tears," he repeats, this time ruefully. "I gave up on everything I wanted to do in my life. I wanted to be a musician and a rock star. I cut my hair and gave it up for this."

The crack in Jeff's emotional armor, and the start of his exit, came from a most unexpected place—and it was caught on camera.

Daryl Davis and Deeyah Khan are two experts dedicated to effective efforts to deradicalize domestic violent white extremists. As you will see, they are two amazing people and those in our sample who engaged with either Deeyah or Daryl recall them having a powerful deradicalizing effect, which included painful personal work to fully disengage and deradicalize.

Daryl is an African American R&B and blues musician who has made it his life's mission to meet one-on-one with white supremacists. He was raised overseas in a Foreign Service family. When he returned home to find how awful racism is in the U.S., he hit upon a unique idea. He would arrange visits with members of racists groups, the KKK primarily, without telling them they were agreeing to meet a Black man. Then, seated with people who could just as easily kill him, he challenged them by asking, 'Why do you hate me?' Using this technique, Daryl has developed a whole system for challenging haters and has successfully pulled hundreds of men out of racist hate groups. He has collected the robes of over one hundred KKK members who decided to exit based on his interventions.[227]

Deeyah Khan is a documentary filmmaker and a Norwegian Muslim immigrant of Punjabi descent. Deeyah has filmed jihadists, men who abuse women, and white supremacists, challenging each as she films. Her website states, "After spending a number of months filming with members of the United States' largest neo-Nazi organization, including filming them on their notoriously violent march through Charlottesville in 2017, three high-ranking figures, including the leader, left the movement and rejected its white supremacist ideology. All of them credit their encounters with Deeyah as the catalyst for them to leave the extremist movement."[228]

Jeff tells me, "Deeyah Khan took down the entire executive leadership of the movement." He was one of them.

In her documentary, *White Right: Meeting the Enemy*, she went face-to-face with white supremacists to ask them why they hate her.[229] A pivotal moment for Jeff came during his interview. Jeff recounts his conversation with her during filming, when Deeyah told him, "'You know Jeff, when I was a little girl, it [racist groups] made me feel like less than a human being, ugly and hated.' I could see the sadness and feel her pain. That energy—I felt it. It was like getting kicked in the chest by a horse," Jeff recalls. "The cameraman picked up on it and zoomed in on my eyes." Deeyah later told him he would not like this part in the film. "It humanized me, it showed." When others saw the scene they told Jeff, "Deeyah made you look soft." Not a good look for a hate leader.

Søren, one of Jeff's deputies, recalls watching the documentary with his wife. He'd boasted to her about being friends with the big tough leader of the movement. "If you were going to make a movie, he'd be the perfect actor, the look, tough voice, but really smart." Then Søren watched the film with amazement. "I watched how she asked him questions. I saw mannerisms and body language. I know this guy; this is not how he normally was. I called it. I said, 'He's going to get out of this.'" Søren called Deeyah's soft technique brilliant. "It blew my mind to watch that unfold because it was really raw."

Jeff recalls Daryl also making an impact, telling him a similar story about being pelted with stones at a Boy Scout parade, and not understanding it was because he was Black. That a child would be attacked like this brought tears to Jeff's eyes. "It stuck with me to this day, this ideology, racism in general, could inspire someone to do something like that. For me, our enemies in the movement were adults. We didn't look at children in that way."

"I wanted to leave," Jeff confesses, "I didn't think I could leave. My whole life was promoting this stuff...I was not just ideologically committed. That was dissipating. My business was tied into the ideology." Jeff was making his living selling white supremacy and Nazi paraphernalia.

"People close to him who knew he was leaving didn't make it easy. They'd ask, "'What are you going to put on your job history? Nazi record label executive? Commander of the Nazi party?'" Jeff says they were trying to be helpful and also to reel him back in. "'I'm worried about you. What are you going to do with your life?'" A couple of them suggested he just run their hate music record label. Or retire and come back. They thought he was burnt out. "But I couldn't keep putting this sort of stuff out. It's hypocritical."

Many professional exit counselors in Europe advise cutting all ties with their former associates and going underground for their own protection, and to avoid being pulled back in. Jesse Morton, a former jihadist recruiter who advised all types of extremists, took an opposite view, and advised leaders in particular, to make public statements against their groups so they can never return. Jeff advises against this tactic. Though it will burn all bridges back into extremism, he advises those who exit to never speak against their former group as doing so can bring the group's violence down on them. But as for himself, "I already knew I was going to speak against them."

But at first, he just retired. "You are still beloved in the movement, whatever reason you left, burned out, or whatever. But if you speak out against it, you are a traitor. I knew I had to prepare for the threats."

"Were there threats?" I ask.

Jeff demurs. "If people think that I live in fear, it could cause them to second guess leaving," and adds he's very security minded because he's had assassination attempts in the past, and notes Antifa tried to assassinate him by hitting him with a tire iron that split the back of his skull. Always curious how white supremacists identify Antifa, a group they often blame for any violence that comes their way, I ask how he knew it was them.

"'Anti-Nazi league! We are here to kill you, motherfucker!'" and makes a striking movement with his arm. "They infiltrated the group at the time, in '97. They caught me from behind. I had layers of stitches."

When I asked Søren if Antifa's "Punch a Nazi in the Face" or doxxing strategies motivate members to exit hate groups, he thinks they have the opposite effect. "Yelling and shouting and hitting people and being violent towards those people, most who grew up in violent households, that's not what won me, or Jeff, over. It just fans the flames, both sides pushing back on each other." I agree. Reciprocal radicalization doesn't work, especially not with those already highly committed to the movement.[230] It simply confirms conspiracy claims and causes members to become more resolute. Indeed, many of our 51 respondents referenced violent interactions with alleged members of Antifa as radicalizing events for them and Antifa's doxxing was a mixed bag. Doxxing can prevent joining up or cause some people to leave a hate group, for fear of being publicly shamed, losing their job or being arrested. However, being doxxed was also a badge of honor for others, fusing them in deeper with their group. Doxxing also makes it more difficult for members to reintegrate into society if they do exit.[231]

"What do you regret?" I ask Jeff.

"All of it," he answers grimly. Less than a year after he left the NSM, he was speaking in California and a Jewish man told him this area was the base for his main California unit "and it stirred up a lot of crap. Everyone here knows who the NSM is. I'm scared talking to you even.'" Jeff realized he needed to apologize. "I took that on myself. I apologized to the public at that time. The ideology is incredibly damaging."

He says he can't change the past but would like to repair the damage he did. "Like when Deeyah told me how the movement made her feel like as a child, and Daryl Davis, too, he had a similar story…

This happened to thousands of people. Maybe I didn't choke the life out of them but the garbage I was spewing did an incredible amount of damage. I'll probably never understand it all, how it could have affected people so much."

Jeff is still making sense of the world he created out of hate, but inside, he knew it's impact. He has been married twice and has three children and he didn't allow them to participate. "They knew what I was doing and involved in. I didn't want it for them. I knew how hard it was and that it destroyed families. There were things where they'd ask to come to stuff. I'd say, 'When you're 18, you can make that decision.' Deep down I didn't want them to."

Jeff feels he's now found his noble cause. "Having a mission, having a sense of purpose, was really important to me and I have that now." *Beyond Barriers* is Jeff's mission. Even if one is cynical about motives, his engagement is significant. Jeff is still trusted and remains a role model. Many text him and ask him why he left the hate movement, which gives him something other practitioners might never gain—a brief cognitive opening for him to try to coax them out.

He shares a particular call about his exit with a young man that struck him because it was all too familiar. "I told him, 'It's a miracle that I'm alive, when I've seen so many others die and go to prison.' He was in his early 20s. I told him, 'You might not make it out.'"

The young man's response, "I might do like you did. I'll get out after 25 years."

"You missed my whole entire point," Jeff told him, and then shakes his head. "The kid answered back, 'If the cause that I stand for, if my ideology is correct, and what I'm fighting for is correct, my life means nothing. The cause means everything.' The second he said that it took my breath away. That's the exact thing I would have said when I was that age, at that juncture. It's true. That's how we thought."

"A lot of the formers are telling the people it's all about hate. That they hated people and that's why they were in the movement." Jeff disagrees. "I wouldn't have thrown away what I did all those years for hate. I believed it was good and noble." Jeff says this idea of the noble cause is the motivating and driving factor. Members really believe they are needed. They can't see issues, like the economy, are more than a white issue and affect everyone. They only see their own tribe and can't see the humanity of the other because they've been dehumanized. "It's okay to be proud of your heritage. Nobody is saying that's wrong. But holding someone else down, taking from them, it's not noble anymore. You've become the oppressor."

The feeling of victimhood is another powerful force. There's a mindset that "you are oppressed" and a constant victim. Even before January 6, they'd all been kicked off Facebook and Twitter, sending the message that "the white race is being victimized" and they would play on victimhood. They'd show videos out of South Africa showing farmers massacred "and say these may be isolated incidents, but this is what is coming to America, if we allow it."

The barriers to exiting are strong and they're also personal. Jeff shares more exit stories with me. A member's wife with four kids called *Beyond Barriers* saying she wants out, but her husband refuses to exit and she's afraid of him. Others fear they'll become friendless because they've built their whole life around white supremacism. Many have hate tattoos indelibly marked all over their bodies. Some fear repercussions—Antifa will doxx them, they can never get a job or rejoin normal society, or the group itself will punish them for leaving.

After our interview, Jeff arranged for his deputy at *Beyond Barriers,* former NSM leader, Acacia Dietz (whom I've also interviewed for *Escape Hate*), to grant our ICSVE team access to some of NSM's video archives for use in our counter narrative videos. The slick footage is professional and powerful, with NSM members in uniforms with banners, looking larger than life. We make productive use of it in our counter narrative videos with former NSM members.

Jeff also makes a counter narrative video for us. His advice, "There's more to life than throwing it away for a cause that is not even righteous," and tells his future internet audience: "It's going to send your life down a dark alleyway. When you take that road and get in extremist movements and when you are only worried about your own tribe and people, it's divisive."

Then as an aside, he says, "one could say the same thing about Black Lives Matter," illustrating, like many, he still doesn't really understand the difference between legitimate grievances that Black people are protesting as opposed to the threats posed by Domestic Violent Extremists. He explains both a common misperception about racism and Black Lives Matter, "it also is focused on one group of people, and it can cause racism, too," and a very real reaction to it: "Standing against Black Lives Matter is the reaction. Holding a fist up with Black power, you are going to get the white fist, too. I've heard people have said that it's the Black Klan."

Jeff continues his advice, "We'd say, 'One alone and together strong.' But you can band together with a party and not be involved in extremism. [Joining white supremacism] is going to send you down a bad path. Put it into something more palatable. The road you're on now is not a heroic or courageous road."

Then I hear another possible racist slip: "You don't have to become an oppressor. What is it about race that makes it so important? Not all Black people are going to rape and murder," then Jeff seems to try to correct himself. "White people invented lots of things around the world. China invented gunpowder. Jewish people invented penicillin. Different people have created wonderful things we all use." Exiting is hard and Jeff is in the process of having to unlearn his world of hate as he accepts responsibility for so much damage and tries to stop others from making his mistakes. He shakes his head, "I don't know why I stayed in there so long. In school I was standing up for kids that were being bullied."

For me it's clear. Jeff is a smart, charismatic, and natural leader. He was getting so many rewards from his role in the group, feelings of significance, dignity, living up to his childhood heroes and playing out their visions. He was walking tall with bodyguards and members put in long hours to serve his movement. People looked up to and feared him, women in the movement adored him, and he was making money. Why leave?

But he did leave. Part of his departure includes the lawsuit he is facing of the NSM's involvement in organizing the Charlottesville march that became deadly. In a great ironic twist, Jeff signed over the NSM's papers to a Black man, purportedly believing that would limit his legal liability. Later, he found having done so would not save him from prosecution, but now the NSM legally belongs to a Black man.

Despite these legal challenges, Jeff had also been ready to leave and Deeyah Khan and Daryl Davis broke through his noble cause and his shell of hate.

"Now I'm talking about my feelings," Jeff says. "In the movement it was never about feelings. It was ideology, cause, coming to power, what we were doing for the cause."

Fred Cook, Jeff's former chief of staff who left NSM before Jeff and his happy to have his friend back, says he sees a change in his former commander. "I had never saw Jeff smile and look so human." Indeed, so many white supremacists say exactly this—that once out they can finally feel their range of emotions, not just hateful ones.

Jeff resigned from the NSM in spring of 2019 and reemerged on August 12, 2019, to publicly issue this message on his new personal website: "I realized many of the principles I had once held so dearly and sacrificed so much for were wrong...It is now my mission to be a positive, peaceful influence of change and understanding for all humanity in these uncertain times." While I am convinced that Jeff's change of heart is real and he no longer supports white supremacism, he remains a skilled entrepreneur and leader at heart. Jeff is clearly putting

all his organizational and leadership skills, as well as his charisma
and past insights, into *Beyond Barriers,* working to build it into an
internationally recognized effort, which leaves some critics skeptical.
Despite the doubt, given his prominence among white supremacists,
and the fact that he is articulate in denouncing hate, we see his current
work as a powerful force for good. It remains to be seen how this former
leader will continue to remedy his past.

Conclusion - Making and Breaking Hate

The devastating Russian invasion of Ukraine may pose a new DVE threat we cannot afford to overlook. When Ukraine's president called foreigners to join the battle, most compelled to travel to Ukraine do so for legitimate reasons. However, this Ukrainian call has also excited white supremacists, particularly in Europe.

The Azov Battalion is a Ukrainian paramilitary militia. This far-right, ultra-nationalist, neo-Nazi group has become part of Ukraine's volunteer military. When hostilities with Russia began in 2014, we know some Americans and Europeans traveled to Ukraine to fight alongside the Azov Battalion. As of this writing, individuals are talking on messaging apps about the possibility of using the Russian-

Patriot Front Logo and Slogan

Ukraine war to obtain free weapons and battle training. Patriot Front members from the U.S. are already serving. The very real possibility exists that white supremacists could become battle-hardened in foreign conflicts, such as serving alongside the Azov volunteers, as they prepare for their own dream of RAHOWA. It could be all talk. But we need to watch this potential closely. We've seen it before.

More than 40,000 fighters from over 100 countries traveled to Syria in response to ISIS and other groups calling for men to take up arms; and in the case of ISIS, whole families were called to engage in state building. When ISIS fighters returned home to Belgium and France, it only took a few to wreak havoc by mounting terrorist attacks. What might battle-hardened white supremacists do when they return from Ukraine?

As scholars, practitioners, and law enforcement have made clear, DVE is a greater threat to American national security than international terrorism. This remains less true in other Western countries where the international terrorism threat from militant jihadists remains present as their domestic extremist threat also grows. America, however, has a uniquely homegrown and growing problem.

In 2020, law enforcement agencies submitted reports to the FBI involving 8,263 criminal incidents and 11,129 related offenses motivated by bias toward race, ethnicity, ancestry, religion, sexual orientation, disability, gender, and gender identity.[232] Since January 6, FBI data indicates a steady rise in hate crimes.[233]

We grow numb hearing of these incidents and tend to remember only those that were highly lethal. They soon blend into one another, and we forget if we are not a direct victim. However, it's important to remember since the January 6 insurrection we have seen numerous hate motivated threats and attacks carried out by domestic violent extremists aimed at election officials, members of Congress, a Supreme Court judge and the House Speaker herself. We witnessed a nauseating list of shootings, attacks on churches, synagogues, temples and mosques, attempted and actual murders of the LGBTQ community and have even seen children targeted for murder due to their race and national origin.[234] The specter of homegrown hate continues to cast a long shadow across our nation.

To be clear anyone who perpetrates violence in the name of hate must be held accountable. But we need to better understand the reasons for this particular kind of violence if we are going to prevent and not just punish. The 51 people I interviewed for ICSVE's *Escape Hate* study and this book made clear that a range of personal vulnerabilities creates a large pool of mostly boys and men, for recruiters to infiltrate. My work with extremists has led me to identify and categorize these vulnerabilities as the search for dignity, purpose, significance, and belonging. These needs can and must be redirected to better opportunities than those provided by violent extremist groups if we are going to make headway in prevention.

We also need to recognize that radicalization often has nothing to do with actual experiences with minority groups. Learning to hate is often the consequence of joining an extremist group, not the cause. ICSVE's conclusions do not support some theorists' views that grievances based on negative interactions with minority groups form the seeds of discontent that lead to white supremacist radicalization. In a minority of our cases that has been true, but most of the time, we've found belonging to a DVE group first fulfilled those clearly identifiable needs for dignity, purpose, significance and belonging; the growth of hate and violence was then nurtured.

The interviewees made clear hate could genuinely feel like pride and patriotism; and shared racial and ethnic hatred can bond group members and create identity fusion with hate and purpose when one believes their actions support their own people. Going along with hate, and even engaging in violence rather than losing their position as an elite insider in a hate group, is not worth risking by resisting the hate and violence.

We must take both systemic and casual racism more seriously as these make a violent racist belief system easier to adopt, spread, and even mainstream. Many in our sample who already had a racist background were more easily drawn into adopting hateful beliefs and actions once inside their group. Likewise, economic consequences of globalization and perceived social injustices leave people feeling left behind and increase their vulnerability to recruitment. When white men in particular are failing in life, they are suspectable to shifting blame onto others as white supremacists do—blaming minority groups and ultimately Jews as the primary enemy.

As I always say, no one joins a terrorist or violent extremist group unless they believe the group will at least initially meet their needs. Designing programs based on this knowledge will make efforts at prevention, disengagement, and deradicalization more effective.

For our part, ISCVE continues our research into the causes and solutions of international and domestic terrorism through the lived experiences of those at the center of hate. We will continue to publish peer-reviewed studies, work with the media and government agencies including the U.S. Departments of Defense, Justice and Homeland Security, and create trainings for the military and police. Like domestic violent extremists, we are also learning from ISIS, the master at manipulating emotions. We continue to design our *Breaking the ISIS Brand* and *Escape Hate* counter narrative videos to be highly emotional, with graphic video imagery, and evocative music. We took a page out of ISIS's playbook and are turning their tactics back on them. We are grateful to the dozens of former domestic violent extremists who have permitted us to publicly share their very personal and often traumatic experiences in these counter narratives, in an effort to prevent others from taking the bleak and hostile journey they've taken.

Accountability is called for, as is empathy and support. Exiting is not easy. Exiting involves personal losses including family, friends, business revenues and more; it means reckoning with complex emotions and the reality of the harm done to others. For those who leave white supremacism and deradicalize, spontaneously or with the help of a program or professional, the risk of re-engagement remains.

We remind you that ICSVE's EscapeHate.org lists numerous exit programs that offer confidential help.

Should you wish to make a tax-deductible contribution to ICSVE's work, you can learn more at www.icsve.org.

Epilogue - Where are they now?

Josh Pruitt, Proud Boys (Chapter 1): I interviewed Josh just days after the January 6, 2021 insurrection when he invaded the Capitol Building with the Proud Boys. He pleaded guilty in June 2022 to obstructing the congressional vote count certifying President Biden's victory. At age 39 he faced a statutory maximum of 20 years in prison and a fine of up to $250,000. Due to his plea deal in which he agreed to meet the FBI once to confer on their efforts to round up perpetrators, in August 2022 he received a reduced sentence of 55 months (4 years and 7 months) which he is currently serving.[235]

 Handing down his sentence, the judge said Josh was "at the forefront of that mob" and "snapped our previously unbroken tradition of the peaceful transition of power."[236] His defense attorney said Josh accepts responsibility and though his original intent was to simply exercise his constitutional rights, "he realizes that his actions went beyond a peaceful demonstration."[237] Though Josh insisted during our interview he was helping police on January 6, prosecutors disagreed. "They anticipated going to the Capitol to stop the certification of the election and confronting police who might try to stand in their way."[238] Wherever the truth lies, Josh is paying the price.

Sean Gillespie, Aryan Nations (Chapter 4): Sean, who was turned in to the FBI by an informant after a hate crime spree that included bombing a synagogue and beating a Black man with a baseball bat, now publicly speaks against white supremacism. He is particularly focused on reaching youth who are lost like he was as a kid; and he remains frustrated that his childhood sexual abuser remains free and he has not found a way to have him brought to justice. Sean also spends a lot of his free time in a gym shared by many races and ethnicities, sparing and training as a mixed martial arts fighter, and is now competing for glory in that realm.

Ryan Lo'Ree, Aryan Brotherhood (Chapter 5): When Ryan
returned to an economically struggling Flint, Michigan, after a grueling
deployment in Iraq, he was introduced to the Aryan Brotherhood by the
uncle who had sexually abused him when he was a boy. Ryan rose up
the ranks but wound up in prison, where a Black cell mate helped him
deradicalize. Ryan became politically active upon release and in the year
following our interview, he has spoken at ICSVE trainings where he was
extremely well received.

He continues his social justice activism in Michigan with *Parallel
Networks* and works in collaboration with *Cure Violence* on a project in
Portland, Oregon, where battles between far right anti-government and
white supremacists, and Antifa, have been rife. Ryan's work to combat
polarization, structural injustice, racism, hate, and violent extremism
often occurs through direct dialogue with DVE members.

The Wolverine Watchmen (Chapter 5): In October of 2022 jurors in
Michigan convicted Paul Bellar, Joseph Morrison and Pete Musico of
aiding in a plot to kidnap Michigan's Governor Gretchen Whitmer, a
crime for which Adam Fox was already convicted in federal court.[239]
Though all three men had been named regularly in testimony at the other
trials, none of them faced federal charges in the conspiracy to kidnap
Ms. Whitmer at her vacation home and possibly kill her. Instead, they
were charged in state court with providing support for terrorist acts,
including training with one of the federal defendants. They were also
accused of illegal gang membership because of their affiliation with
the Wolverine Watchman, a militia whose members spoke of hanging
politicians and harming police officers. While the defense argued that the
men were not plotting but simply exercising their first amendment rights
the prosecution stated, "These are not merely acts of 'harmless chatter'
and 'wishful thinking. These are criminal conspiracies to conduct
dangerous acts, and it is incumbent upon law enforcement to treat this
activity as such."

Jurors convicted the three men on all charges, the most serious of which carry prison terms of up to 20 years. Sentencing is scheduled for Dec. 15, 2022. After the verdict Ms. Whitmer gave her opinion of the growing acts of political violence against public officials: "They are the logical, disturbing extension of radicalization, hatred and conspiratorial thinking that festers in America, threatening the foundation of our republic."[240]

In December 2022 five additional men involved in the foiled kidnapping plot were turned over for trial in Michigan on charges of providing material support for terrorist acts and gun crime. The legal brief entered in their case stated that the conspiracy evolved from targeting law enforcement to "politicians in general, and lastly a plot to kidnap Governor Whitmer" and each defendant made statements recorded in audio, video or online chat that had "the singular purpose of advocating the Boogaloo ideology with the goal of seeing civil war erupt in the United States and the overthrow of existing governments."[241]

Jason Van Tatenhove, Oath Keepers (Chapter 6): In July 2022, this former propagandist for the Oath Keepers made a memorable tattooed presence as his testimony before the House Select Committee to Investigate the January 6th Attack was televised nationally. He reiterated what he had shared with me a month before, "I think we need to quit mincing words and just talk about truths, and what it was going to be was an armed revolution," he told the nation. "I mean, people died that day. Law enforcement officers died this day. There was a gallows set up in front of the Capitol. This could have been the spark that started a new civil war."[242] Jason also told the committee he believes the Oath Keepers› involvement in January 6th gave their founder, Stewart Rhodes, a sense of legitimacy as a paramilitary leader. "The fact that [President Donald Trump] was communicating, whether directly or indirectly messaging—that gave him the nod. All I can do is thank the gods that things did not go any worse."

In his prepared written statement, Jason expanded on the Oath Keepers true motivations, and it is not the propaganda they push. The goals are to raise money and gain influence by catering to the conspiracy theories of the day and connect with ever-radicalizing communities within the alt-right, white nationalists, and racists. Citing January 6th, he says their ability to whip people into violent action continues to be "a dangerous proposition for our country. We cannot allow these groups to continue threatening our democracy."

He informed the House committee that the Oath Keepers are still able to widely disseminate violent messaging and radicalize followers, and he laid blame on former President Trump from whom it only took a nod to activate them.[243] Underestimating them is a mistake he says he made. "Because in the end, they were able to muster a group of heavily armed and outfitted members who had been trained in modern warfare techniques, including those we now know had explosives, to storm the Capitol to stop the process of inaugurating the duly elected president. It is time to speak the truth about these groups and the violent influence they wield. It is time to show an exit ramp to others like me who may have been caught up in the rhetoric of these groups and used as pawns in a dishonest campaign to capture more money, influence, and power."

Jason is writing a book about his time in the Oath Keepers.

Stewart Rhodes (Chapter 6): Stewart Rhodes, the leader of the far-right Oath Keepers militia and employer of Jason Van Tatenhove, was convicted on November of 2022 along with one of his subordinates of seditious conspiracy. The jury found them guilty of seeking to keep former President Donald J. Trump in power through an extensive plot that started after the 2020 election and culminated in the mob attack on the Capitol.[244]

TM Garret, KKK (Chapter 10): This former hard rocker of hate continues to work with ICSVE as well as run Erasing the Hate tattoo removal project and Be the Change. He routinely checks on formers who call upon him for support in exiting hate groups, including Benji McDowell, who has taken a turn for the worse. TM is also a speaker for the Simon Wiesenthal Center, often visiting synagogues to bring understanding of violent extremism. TM remains a well-loved member of his local Jewish synagogue.

Shane Johnson, KKK (Chapter 16): Once raised by the Klan, Shane continues his work as a pastor and helps violent extremists facing criminal charges deal with drug and alcohol problems in treatment centers rather than in prison.

Benji McDowell, KKK (Chapter 17): At the time of this writing, Benji is back in custody in South Carolina with the order that "detention is warranted."[245] Recall, Benji was set up in an FBI sting by his Grand Wizard when he threatened to shoot up a synagogue in South Carolina, for which he served prison time. Since his release, Benji was basically living peacefully and we learned he was even using our counter narrative video of him to speak to Black audiences about how he fell into hate, and how he now regrets and renounces that lifestyle.

However, an arrest warrant was obtained July 2022 and Benji was arrested the following month. While charges have yet to be filed, Benji is accused of violating the terms of his supervised release which required him to spend the first year on home confinement with electronic monitoring, participate in a drug treatment program, undergo mental health treatment, and receive vocational training. In June 2020, the court learned he was using illegally obtained suboxone, a prescription medication used to treat opioid addictions, and six months later, he admitted to using marijuana on three separate occasions. He was given a violation of abeyance. Later the court was told Benji was not taking his mental health medications.[246]

Documents related to this arrest, initial court appearance, and preliminary hearing are sealed. When we contacted the head of the detention center, we were unable to reach Benji to learn more. We did learn the Council on American-Islamic Relations, CAIR, reached out to local news calling for Benji to stay imprisoned, "Mr. McDowell's criminal record and his recent behavior make it abundantly clear that he remains a threat to the security of minority communities and our society as a whole…Authorities must do everything in their power to ensure he is not given a chance to act on his bigoted views through acts of violence. He should serve his full sentence."[247]

Jeff Schoep, NSM, (Chapters 11-12, 19): The man who grew the single largest neo-Nazi group in the U.S. continues to run *Beyond Barriers* with his former NSM propagandist, Acacia Dietz, working to disengage and deradicalize extremists. Jeff, like TM, is also a consultant and speaker for the Simon Wiesenthal Center, and a speaker for Conscious Campus which consults for the U.S. Office of Juvenile Justice and Delinquency Prevention to conduct law enforcement trainings on extremism. Jeff often speaks at events with Daryl Davis and Deeyah Khan, two of the influencers who helped him rethink white supremacism, and with Ken Nwadike, one of the men who filmed the car attack at the 2017 "Unite the Right" rally in Charlottesville (and was nearly run over in the process.)

Jeff was one of the two dozen defendants among prominent white supremacist and neo-Nazi leaders and hate groups tried in the civil lawsuit, Sines v. Kessler, for the violence that took place at the "Unite the Right" rally. Verdicts handed out in November 2021 held the various defendants liable on claims of civil conspiracy and race-based harassment or violence. The jury awarded plaintiffs more than 25 million dollars in damages.[248] Jeff was individually ordered to pay a half million dollars for his part in the rally. He has appealed, citing the award an insurmountable amount for him to pay.

About The Author

Anne Speckhard, Ph.D., is Director of the International Center for the Study of Violent Extremism (ICSVE). She serves as Adjunct Associate Professor of Psychiatry at Georgetown University School of Medicine and an Affiliate in the Center for Security Studies, Georgetown University.

She has interviewed over 800 terrorists, violent extremists, their family members and supporters around the world, including in Western Europe, the Balkans, Central Asia, the Former Soviet Union and the Middle East. Over the past five years, she has conducted in-depth psychological interviews with 273 ISIS defectors, returnees and prisoners, as well as 16 al Shabaab cadres (as well as family members and ideologues,) studying their trajectories into and out of terrorism, and their experiences inside ISIS and al Shabaab.

Speckhard developed the ICSVE *Breaking the ISIS Brand Counter Narrative Project* from these interviews, which includes over 250 short counter narrative videos that mimic ISIS recruitment videos but contain actual terrorists strongly denouncing ISIS as un-Islamic, corrupt and brutal. These videos have been utilized in over 200 Facebook and Instagram campaigns globally. Beginning in 2020, she launched the ICSVE *Escape Hate Counter Narrative Project,* interviewing dozens of white supremacists and members of hate groups, developing counternarratives from their interviews, and creating anti-recruitment videos. She has also conducted rare interviews with five Antifa activists (Antifa protestors rarely grant interviews.)

Dr. Speckhard is also an expert in rehabilitation and repatriation of terrorists and their families. In 2007, she designed the psychological and Islamic aspects of the Detainee Rehabilitation Program in Iraq to be applied to 20,000+ detainees and 800 juveniles. This work led to consulting with foreign governments on issues of terrorist prevention, interventions and repatriation; and the rehabilitation and reintegration of ISIS foreign fighters, wives and children. She has worked with NATO, the Organization for Security and Cooperation in Europe (OSCE), UN Women, United Nations Countering Terrorism Committee Executive Directorate (UNCTED), United Nations Office of Drug and Crime (UNODC), the EU Commission and EU Parliament, and consulted to the U.S. Senate & House, Departments of State, Defense, Justice, Homeland Security, Health & Human Services, and the FBI.

Today Dr. Speckhard actively trains key stakeholders in law enforcement, intelligence, elite hostage negotiation teams, educators, and other professionals in countering violent extremism, locally and internationally. Her focus is on the psychology of terrorism, the effective use of counter-narrative messaging materials produced by ICSVE, as well as studying the use of children as violent actors by groups such as ISIS. Her consultations and trainings include U.S., Canadian, German, British, Dutch, Austrian, Swiss, Belgian, Danish, Iraqi, Syrian, Jordanian and Thai national police and security officials, among others.

Dr. Speckhard is the author of five books: *Homegrown Hate, Talking to Terrorists, Bride of ISIS, Undercover Jihadi,* and *ISIS Defectors: Inside Stories of the Terrorist Caliphate.* She has appeared on CNN, BBC, NPR, Fox News, MSNBC, CTV, CBC, and in the *New York Times, Washington Post, London Times,* TIME Magazine, *Newsweek, Daily Beast* and more. She regularly writes a column for *Homeland Security.* Her research has been published in *Global Security: Health, Science and Policy, Behavioral Sciences of Terrorism and Political Aggression, Journal of African Security, Journal of Strategic Security,* the *Journal of Human Security, Bidhaan: An International Journal of Somali Studies, Journal for Deradicalization, Perspectives on Terrorism* and the *International Studies Journal.* Her academic publications are found at https://georgetown.academia.edu/AnneSpeckhard and www. icsve.org.

ICSVE's research has been funded by the EU Commission; U.S. Departments of State, Homeland Security, Defense and Justice; UN Women; and the Embassy of Qatar.

Follow @AnneSpeckhard

Acknowledgements

*E*scape Hate represents a year and a half of intensive research, involving tracking down and convincing former and active white supremacists in five countries and across three continents to engage in a two-hour research interview. Once willing to participate and with their permission, our team also created a short video counter narrative of their story to disrupt online and face-to-face white supremacist recruitment which we are now partnering with Facebook to distribute around the world.

TM Garret and Jeff Schoep helped me find subjects for this research and some of the subjects, Ed Schofield for example, also referred others into the project. I was able to find some myself on Twitter and elsewhere. Sophia Abi Najm worked as an intern joining us right after the January 6th insurrection and took on the arduous task of contacting those who posted videos of themselves in the Capitol, often finding their social media posts and entire profiles disappearing as fast as she could contact them. She reached Joshua Pruitt only days after the events who agreed to an interview, while others became hostile to being contacted after advertising their follies on social media. Tiffany Dove helped us with our military and police research and helped track down Jason Van Tatenove for an interview.

Molly Ellenberg is the brains behind all our statistical analysis. Together we decided on a coding scheme of 443 variables for my ISIS interviews and when we started the white supremacist encounters, we went over those variables and decided which applied and what needed to be added and deleted to come up with 375 variables for these interviews. Molly did all the coding, statistical analysis, wrote up of the first round of results from the fifty interviews, compared our work to the existing academic literature, and did much of the reference work for this book. She is also the engine behind many of our academic reports which go into deeper statistical and analytical details on both ISIS and DVE. She is a much appreciated and highly valued research partner.

TM Garret advised throughout the project, often pointing out esoteric details that would otherwise have been missed, such as differentiating between local KKK klaverns that take on prison gang names, such as Aryan Brotherhood and Aryan Nations, and the actual white supremacist prison gangs. He added to the analysis in areas he is expert in due to his unique history inside these groups, and his informal and compassionate intervention work over the past decades. Zack Baddorf, our former Director of Video Productions, produced the early counter narrative videos, and TM produced the rest. I helped to script and provided production input for all the videos. TM also translated for the Germans who could not speak English well and helped me understand cultural references. Jeff Schoep graciously explained concepts and experiences in the NSM as questions arose. Daryl Davis helped to explain his interventions and methodologies with white supremacists, and he graciously wrote the foreword for this book.

Jesse Morton, who briefly worked with ICSVE in the Fall of 2020 made our first interview introductions for studying white supremacists. Jesse and I along with a group brought together by Cure Violence was following online DVE chat during the Fall leading up to the Capitol Hill riots underlining how serious the DVE problem was becoming. Without Jesse's initial push, I'm not sure I would have made the leap for ICSVE to study white supremacists and domestic violent extremists.

Molly, TM, and Kate Strezishar read the book in its entirety while still a draft and made many suggestions and edits for which I'm very grateful. Kate wrote the first version of the glossary.

Susan K. Barnett, a former award-winning journalist, is the editor of this book and I always say Susan brings anything I write to an entirely new and improved level, often asking hard questions, researching topics and rephrasing things to be much more palatable for the nonacademic reader. This is the second book we've done together. She was also the editor for *ISIS Defectors* and I found she remembered everything from that study to apply here as well. Susan is sharp, funny, an excellent writer herself and catches everything, and she is a real joy to work with. She also always keeps me motivated to keep plugging ahead.

Lastly, the Embassy of Qatar deserves thanks for generously funding our think tank, ICSVE, for five years now and as the founding funder of our highly successful *Breaking the ISIS Brand Counter Narrative Project*, after which we emulated the *Escape Hate Counter Narrative Project*.

While COVID made staying home and taking the time to interview so many people week-by- week possible, I hated the isolation and having my travel wings clipped. However, I am now grateful for the lonely times which made it even more precious to sit down and listen carefully to stories of heartbreak, misguided steps, painful experiences, and journeys into and back out of white supremacism. While I can never endorse hate, I'm ever so grateful to every single person who took the time to talk to me and who trusted me enough to really open up about very personal and often painful issues, including harms done to and by them.

I learned a lot and I trust you, the reader, have as well. I hope if nothing else, I've accomplished two goals: I've convinced you we have a serious domestic violence issue in this country that needs addressed both in terms of prevention and remediation; and we are all reminded that behind every single story is a real human being who didn't start out life as a hater, a fact that tells us there is plenty of hope for prevention efforts.

Glossary

Accelerationism: A politically based range of ideas within critical and social theory advocating for specific forces, usually economic, to be accelerated to promote social change. Violent extremist groups have adopted a version of accelerationism to promote violence and radicalism with the intent to discredit existing governmental institutions, and in the case of white supremacists, to quicken the fall of liberal democracy in favor of the white authoritarian rule they envision for society.

Alt-Right: An ideological movement mainstreamed into right-wing politics based in the United States, in which the members reject mainstream conservative beliefs, and instead promote extremist and potentially violent rhetoric focused on white nationalism, and oppose concepts such as racial, religious, and gender equality.

Anti-Defamation League (ADL): The ADL is a leading anti-hate organization in the world. Founded in 1913, the ADL is a global leader in combating antisemitism, countering extremism, and battling bigotry; the ADL works to protect democracy and ensure a just and inclusive society for all.

Antifa: Short for anti-fascism. Loosely affiliated autonomous leftist groups and individuals who utilize political protests, property destruction, doxxing and in some cases violence, to contest what they define as fascism and other right-wing ideologies. Antifa members vary in their political affiliations from communists, anarchists, socialists, democrats, etc. as well as range in their endorsement for the legitimate use of violence to stop white supremacism and fascist movements.

Anti-Racist Action Network (ARA): A decentralized network originating in the 1980's among punk skinheads in the U.S., and spreading to Canada, made up of far-leftist activists engaged in direct action, including in some cases, violence and doxxing against far-right actors whom they deem as racist or fascist.

Arastrú/Odinism/Wotanism: A sect that revives pre-Christian beliefs and practices dedicated to Norse and Germanic gods, specifically the chief god, Odin. Odinism, or Wotanism, is the form of Arastrú that white supremacists often adapt as it promotes northern European white tribalism and is interpreted as a warrior religion that values of honor and valor within its followers.

Aryan Brotherhood: A neo-Nazi prison gang and organized crime syndicate within the United States. Created in the 1960's at San Quentin State prison, the gang evolved from a lone prison gang to a white supremacy group spanning the U.S., promoting racial violence, and using intimidation to control its own members.

Aryan Nations: A white supremacist organization created in the late 1970's based in the Christian Identity beliefs promoted by Wesley Swift, founder of the highly antisemitic and white supremacist Church of Jesus Christ–Christian. The Aryan Nations is known for violence against other religions and races and terrorist acts. Richard Butler, who led the Aryan Nations for two decades, was an ardent admirer of Adolph Hitler and dreamed of a white homeland. He bought land in Idaho to create a refuge for those who believed in white supremacy and antisemitism. This compound was later lost in a civil lawsuit brought by the Southern Poverty Law Center.

Blood and Honor: An international coalition of racist skinhead gangs based out of the U.K. It grew out of the skinhead music scene in the 1980s. It was founded by Ian Stuart, the lead singer of the influential hate rock band, Skrewdriver.

Christian Identity: An interpretation of Christianity that states the white race is descended from Adam and Eve and all others are descended from Satan or are beasts created apart from humankind. Depending on the theory, Jews and non-whites fall into the one-seed theory, where they are beasts to be dominated by whites; or the two-seed theory, where non-whites are beasts and Jews are the cursed offspring of Eve's literal sexual liaison with the devil in the form of a serpent. Christian Identity promotes non-whites as inferior to whites, and Jews craftily trying to replace whites with minorities to achieve global domination.

Creativity Movement: A white supremacist religion that promotes the white race as the only true humans and endorses pseudo-scientific racism and religious naturalism.

Day of the Rope: A concept introduced in the fictional book, *The Turner Diaries,* in which non-whites, Jews, liberals, and race traitors are rounded up and executed by hanging on "the day of the rope." QAnon currently echoes this concept, referring to it as the "Great Reckoning" in which liberals and alleged sexual predatory elites will be rounded up and hung.

Doc Martens: Brand of boots popular with skinheads. Racist skinheads often lace their boots differently and wear either white or red laces to distinguish themselves from other wearers of the trendy footwear. Red bootlaces indicate the wearer has shed blood for the racist skinhead movement. Racist skinheads will often randomly attack non-whites to "earn" their red laces. White bootlaces indicate a skinhead is identified with "white power," opposed to non-racist or anti-racist skinheads.

Domestic Violent Extremism (DVE): Defined by the FBI as "violent, criminal acts committed by individuals and/or groups to further ideological goals stemming from domestic influences, such as those of a political, religious, social, racial, or environmental nature," DVE is recognized as the leading terrorism-related threat to the United States.

Doxxing: The abbreviation for "dropping docs" (documents) refers to publicly releasing private information about someone with malicious intent, usually over the internet. Antifa has adopted this practice to publicly identify and shame individuals participating in white supremacy movements to prevent them from holding jobs, forming relationships, and at times making them unable to do errands without being hassled. However, Antifa activists, particularly women, have also been ruthlessly doxxed by white supremacists and far right actors for the purpose of harassment and intimidation.

Fascism: A far-right authoritarian government structure based in ultra-nationalism and dictatorial power, with forcible suppression of opposition and a regimented society. Neo-fascism is a post-World War II ideology that includes significant elements of fascism.

Fourteen Words: "We must secure the existence of our people and a future for white children." This well-known and often-quoted white nationalist slogan originated with David Lane, idealogue and member of the American terrorist group, The Order, which engaged in armed robberies, terrorist bombings, and assassinations. The 14 Words often serves as a call-to-action for white nationalists around the world and the number 14 is the common white supremacist code for the "14 words".

Great Replacement: The Great Replacement theory was conceived by Renaud Camus in France, who wrote the 2011 book *Le Grand Remplacement*. This white supremacist, xenophobic, and anti-immigrant conspiracy theory posits that white people living in their so-called "home" countries are being replaced by immigrants, Muslims, and other people of color, and often blames the "elite" and Jews for orchestrating these changing demographics. The theory, which is also referred to as white genocide, has spread through Europe, the Balkans, United States, Canada, New Zealand and Australia, and is now often cited as a call-to-arms by white supremacist mass shooters who want to kick off a race war.

Hammerskins: A white supremacist group formed in 1988 in Dallas, Texas, focused on disseminating white power rock music. Also known as Hammerskin Nation, they once dominated the racist skinhead movement in the U.S. with regional factions and chapters.

Hitler, Adolph: The leader of Nazi Germany and perpetrator of the Holocaust remains an important inspiration among domestic violent extremists. The number 88 is the common white supremacist code for "Heil Hitler", as H is the eighth letter of the alphabet.

Holocaust Denial: An antisemitic conspiracy theory falsely claiming the World War II genocide of six million Jews under the orders of Adolf Hitler is a fabrication. Believers claim Jews were only deported; the use of death camps and gas chambers is a lie; and the Allies inflated the number of Jewish people who were murdered.

Ku Klux Klan: Known as the KKK, this secret organization was founded on white supremacy, violence, and right-wing extremism in the United States after the Civil War. Famous for the image of men cloaked in white hoods, robes holding cross burnings, the KKK targeted non-whites, specifically lynching African Americans, as well as directing hate toward Jews, Catholics, immigrants, members of the LGBTQ community, Muslims, and liberals. Broken up decades ago, the KKK today consists of many isolated and competing regional groups functioning independently of one another.

Lane, David: Lane, who wrote the 14 Words, was a white separatist, neo-Nazi, and member of The Order. He was convicted in 1984 for multiple crimes including the violation of civil rights of Alan Berg, a Jewish radio host who was murdered by a member of The Order. Lane drove the getaway car. He died in prison.

Mein Kampf: Book written by Nazi leader Adolf Hitler in 1924, translates to "My Struggle." Part autobiography and part political treatise, it promoted Nazism through intense antisemitism, racism, and aggressive foreign policy.

Militia: Civilian forces who come together to create a paramilitary force, usually to supplement or act independently of a regular army. Many armed militias across the U.S. have adopted anti-government and white supremacist philosophies.

National Socialist Movement (NSM): Founded in 1994 in Detroit, Michigan, NSM is a far-right organization based on neo-Nazism and white supremacy. Known for its antisemitic and racist rhetoric, NSM was the largest organized neo-Nazi group in the United States throughout the 2000s.

Neo-Nazism: A global political, social, and militant movement to revitalize and implement Nazi ideology. Followers often use this ideology to further hatred and white supremacy, with attacks against racial and ethnic minorities. Some members hope to initiate a fascist state.

The Protocols of the Elders of Zion: A fictitious antisemitic publication falsely claiming Jews are involved in a global conspiracy for worldwide dominance. Though its exact origins are unknown, it was first published in Russia in 1905 then republished and widely disseminated throughout the 20th century. Many white supremacists and far-right extremists today believe the *Protocols* is true and use it to validate their hatred and violence toward Jews.

Order, The: A white supremacist terrorist organization, also known as the Brüder Schweigen (German for *Brothers Keep Silent* or *Brothers' Silence)*, was a white supremacist terrorist organization active in the United States between September 1983 and December 1984. Founded by Robert Jay Mathews, the group was named after and emulated a group appearing in the fictional *The Turner Diaries* with the intent of overthrowing the U.S. government in favor of installing a whites-only homeland. The group raised funds via armed robberies and participated in terrorist bombings and political assassinations. The group was short-lived as ten members were tried and convicted for racketeering and two were convicted for their role in the 1984 murder of Jewish radio talk show host Alan Berg. David Lane, who coined the 14 words, was a member of The Order.

Pierce, William: Far-right political activist, white supremacist, and neo-Nazi, Pierce was one of the most influential members of the white nationalist movement for over 30 years as author of the fictional *The Turner Diaries*, which was and remains the inspiration for many white supremacists' hate crimes.

Proud Boys: A violent right-wing extremist group mainly within the United States, with some international chapters. The group primarily promotes misogyny, Islamophobia, transphobia, and anti-immigration policies. Many members also engage with white supremacy and antisemitism. Members have been known to be violent at public rallies and protests. Many have been convicted of violent crimes, and many were involved in the January 6th, 2021, storming of the Capitol Building and face criminal charges.

Oath Keepers: A U.S.-based, far-right and anti-government militia founded in 2009 on the belief they are the defenders of the U.S. Constitution as they interpret it. Many members are former or active-duty military and law enforcement who often appear heavily armed at public protests and far-right events. Oath Keepers promote conspiracy theories and were also well represented in the January 6th, 2021, storming of the Capitol Building. Their leader, Stewart Rhodes, has been indicted for seditious conspiracy in the January 6th attack.

QAnon: An umbrella for a set of conspiracy theories alleging the world is run by a liberal cabal of Satan-worshiping elites, pedophiles trafficking in children, who kill and eat their young victims to extract a life-extending chemical called adrenochrome. QAnon adherents believe this cabal includes top Democrats like President Joseph R. Biden Jr., Hillary Clinton, Barack Obama, and George Soros, as well as religious figures including Pope Francis and the Dalai Lama. QAnon followers are often also anti-vaxxers and conservative Christians who believe President Donald J. Trump is the "savior" who will break up this criminal conspiracy and bring its members to justice in a day called the "Great Reckoning".

Race Traitor: A derogatory term referring to a person seen to be acting against their own race. Often refers to a white person in a relationship with a non-white or a person working to promote the interests and successes of other races.

RAHOWA - Acronym for "Racial Holy War". Coined by the Creativity Movement, RAHOWA is a rallying call for predicted violent revolution on behalf of white supremacy.

SHARPS: Acronym for Skinheads Against Racial Prejudice. SHARPS are anti-racist skinheads who oppose white power skinheads, neo-fascists, and other white supremacists. Members are multiethnic and multiracial and include blacks, Latinos, and Asians.

Skinhead: A global youth subculture originating among the British working class in the 1960s. Identifiable by their shaved heads and working-class attire, they were originally motivated by social alienation and pride in the working class. As the movement progressed, the culture gained a political component, with individuals splintering off between far-right neo-Nazi skinheads and left-leaning skinheads against racial prejudice.

Southern Poverty Law Center (SPLC): The SPLC is a leading U.S. non-profit organization monitoring activities of domestic hate groups and other extremists. It currently tracks more than 1,600 extremist groups operating across the country and publishes investigative reports, trains law enforcement, shares key intelligence, and offers expert analysis.

Three Percenters (also written as 3 Percenters, 3%ers and III%ers): Established in 2008, this far-right libertarian anti-government militia in the United States and Canada is based on a false historical ideology that only three percent of Americans fought against the British in the American Revolutionary War. They promote defense of the Second Amendment and gun ownership rights, as well as extreme opposition to the U.S government.

The Turner Diaries: An explicitly antisemitic and racist novel written by William Pierce in 1978. The premise of the book revolves around a violent revolution in the U.S. where the federal government is overthrown, countries engage in nuclear war, and it ends with a race war that commits genocide against non-whites and race traitors. The book promotes the idea of the "Day of the Rope" in which non-whites and race traitors are rounded up and hung. The book is influential in recruiting individuals to the far right and is a key perpetrator of the conspiracy theory of white genocide. Timothy McVeigh's 1995 attack on the Alfred P. Murrah Federal Building in Oklahoma City, among other terrorist acts, are believed to have been inspired by this book.

White Aryan Resistance (WAR): Founded in the 1980s by white supremacist Tom Metzger, a former Grand Dragon in the KKK, to build a network of racist skinheads. Several racist groups use the name including a large prison gang in Arkansas and skinheads in prisons in the western U.S. who go by White Aryan Resistance or Warskins.

White Genocide: A conspiracy theory promoted by white supremacists that individuals, usually Jews, are plotting against the white race by diminishing the white race through interracial marriage, miscegenation, non-white immigration, low white fertility rates, and abortion. The conspiracy also indicates land belonging to whites is being stolen, and whites are the victims of organized violence. Other racial and ethnic minorities are seen as part of the problem, but not the masterminds. This political myth is used to promote white nationalism and validate violence against minorities. White genocide is often associated with the white replacement conspiracy theory.

White Nationalism: A form of racial nationalism promoting the belief that white people are a superior race, it pushes for the creation of a white ethnostate. Often overlapping with white supremacism and white separatism, white Nationalists seek to ensure the survival of the white race and believe whites should maintain their economic and political dominance in majority-white countries.

White Replacement Theory: A conspiracy theory, much like white genocide, that says nonwhite people or foreigners will overtake the nation via immigration, reproduction, and seizure of political power, orchestrated by an elite Jewish cabal. (See also Great Replacement Theory.)

White Separatism: A movement with political and social roots seeking to segregate white people from other races and ethnicities, potentially installing a white ethnostate by removing non-whites from communities or creating white-only communities elsewhere. Viewed as a form of white supremacy.

White Supremacism: Belief that white people are superior to other races and ethnicities, and whites should be in positions of power and privilege. This belief is at times bolstered by claims white Europeans were great colonial powers and therefore proven as the superior race or is based on religious interpretations such as those made by the Christian Identity or Creativity movements.

Zionist Occupied Government (ZOG): A white supremacist belief that the U.S. government is controlled by Jews.

Endnotes

1   Tucker, E., & Jalonick, M. (2021, March 2). FBI chief warns violent 'domestic terrorism' growing in US. *Associated Press*. Retrieved from https://apnews.com/article/fbi-chris-wray-testify-capitol-riot-9a5539af34b15338bb5c4923907eeb67

2   Speckhard, A (2011) Talking to Terrorists. Advances Press. Speckhard, A. (2011). Prison and community-based disengagement and de-radicalization programs for extremist involved in militant jihadi terrorism ideologies and activities. *Psychosocial, organizational   and cultural aspects of terrorism*, 1-14. *NATO*. Retrieved from https://apps.dtic.mil/sti/pdfs/ADA555076.pdf

3   About Breaking the ISIS Brand. *International Center for the Study of Violent Extremism*. Retrieved from https://www.icsve.org/about-breaking-the-isis-brand/

4   About Breaking the ISIS Brand. *International Center for the Study of Violent Extremism*. Retrieved from https://www.icsve.org/about-breaking-the-isis-brand/

5   Farivar, M. (2021, January 16). Researchers: More than a dozen extremist groups took part in Capitol riots. *VOA*. Retrieved from https://www.voanews.com/a/2020-usa-votes_researchers-more-dozen-extremist-groups-took-part-capitol-riots/6200832.html Gais, H. (2020, April 17). Hate groups and racist pundits spew COVID-19 misinformation on social media despite companies' pledges to combat it. *Southern Poverty Law Center*. Retrieved from https://www.splcenter.org/hatewatch/2020/04/17/hate-groups-and-racist-pundits-spew-covid-19-misinformation-social-media-despite-companies.

6   Renshaw, J., & Wolfe, J. (2021, June 15). U.S. lays out plan to confront white supremacist violence. *Reuters*. Retrieved from https://www.reuters.com/world/us/biden-administration-unveils-plan-tackle-domestic-terrorism-2021-06-15/

7   Tucker, E., & Jalonick, M. C. (2021, March 2). FBI chief warns violent 'domestic terrorism' growing in US. *AP*. Retrieved from https://apnews.com/article/fbi-chris-wray-testify-capitol-riot-9a5539af34b15338bb5c4923907eeb67

8   Wild, W. (2022, March 7). Dozens more US Capitol Police officers were injured on January 6 than previously known, report says. *CNN*. Retrieved from https://www.cnn.com/2022/03/07/politics/capitol-police-injuries/index.html

9   Browning, K.; Thrush, G. & Arango, T. (2022, October 31). Intruder wanted to break Speaker Pelosi's kneecaps federal complaint says. The New York Times. Retrieved from https://www.nytimes.com/2022/10/31/us/pelosi-home-attack-suspect-charged.html?action=click&pgtype=Article&state=default&module=styln-pelosi-attack&variant=show&region=MAIN_CONTENT_1&block=storyline_top_links_recirc

10 Farley, R. (2022, March 21). How many died as a result of Capitol Riot? *FactCheck.org*. Retrieved from https://www.factcheck.org/2021/11/how-many-died-as-a-result-of-capitol-riot/

11 Farley, R. (2022, March 21). How many died as a result of Capitol Riot? *FactCheck.org*. Retrieved from https://www.factcheck.org/2021/11/how-many-died-as-a-result-of-capitol-riot/

12   Connolly, G. (2020, July 5). Former Trump aide Flynn appears to make pledge to QAnon in July 4 video. *Independent*. Retrieved from https://www.independent. co.uk/news/world/americas/us-politics/trump-flynn-qanon-conspiracy-theory-independence-day-speech-slogan-a9602596.html and Mogenson, J. (July 5, 2020). To celebrate the fourth, Michael Flynn posts a pledge to conspiracy groups QAnon. *Mother Jones*. Retrieved from https://www.independent.co.uk/news/world/americas/us-politics/michael-flynn-cnn-qanon-oath-b1879970.html https://www.motherjones.com/politics/2020/07/to-celebrate-the-fourth-michael-flynn-posts-a-pledge-to-conspiracy-group-qanon/

13   Speckhard & Ellenberg (2022, July 12). How interactions with Antifa can fuel white supremacist groups. *Homeland Security Today*. Retrieved from https://www.hstoday.us/subject-matter-areas/counterterrorism/how-interactions-with-antifa-can-fuel-white-supremacist-groups/; Speckhard & Ellenberg (in press). Fuel for the fire or pressure to leave? The effects of Antifa encounters on white supremacist radicalization.

14   Proud Boys. *Southern Poverty Law Center*. Retrieved from https://www.splcenter.org/fighting-hate/extremist-files/group/proud-boys

15   Jacobs, E. (March 2, 2021). Proud Boys named terrorist entity in Canada. *NPR*. Retrieved from https://www.npr.org/2021/05/02/992846086/proud-boys-named-terrorist-entity-in-canada

16   Kuznia, Rob & Devine, Curt. (2022, January 5). The Proud Boy. *CNN* Retrieved from https://www.cnn.com/interactive/2021/06/us/capitol-riot-paths-to-insurrection/josh-pruitt.html

17   Kuznia, Rob & Devine, Curt. (2022, January 5). The Proud Boy. *CNN* Retrieved from https://www.cnn.com/interactive/2021/06/us/capitol-riot-paths-to-insurrection/josh-pruitt.html

18   Kuznia, Rob & Devine, Curt. (2022, January 5). The Proud Boy. *CNN* Retrieved from https://www.cnn.com/interactive/2021/06/us/capitol-riot-paths-to-insurrection/josh-pruitt.html

19   Kuznia, Rob & Devine, Curt. (2022, January 5). The Proud Boy. *CNN* Retrieved from https://www.cnn.com/interactive/2021/06/us/capitol-riot-paths-to-insurrection/josh-pruitt.html

20   Kuznia, Rob & Devine, Curt. (2022, January 5). The Proud Boy. *CNN* Retrieved from https://www.cnn.com/interactive/2021/06/us/capitol-riot-paths-to-insurrection/josh-pruitt.html

21   Sarnoff, Marisa. (2022, June 3). Proud Boy Who Nearly Came Face to Face with Chuck Schumer Inside the Capitol on Jan. 6 Pleads Guilty to a Felony. *Law and Crime*. Retrieved from https://lawandcrime.com/u-s-capitol-breach/proud-boy-who-nearly-came-face-to-face-with-chuck-schumer-inside-the-capitol-on-jan-6-pleads-guilty-to-a-felony/

22   Breuninger, K., Franck, T., Mangan, D. & Macias, A. (July 7, 2022). Trump instigated his supporters' attack on Congress and threats against Pence, Jan. 6 committee says. *CNBC News*. Retrieved from https://www.cnbc.com/2022/07/21/jan-6-committee-hearing-live-coverage-and-latest-updates-day-8.html

23 Weiner, Rachel (2022, June 3). D.C. Proud Boy and bartender pleads guilty
to felony in Capitol riot. *Washington Post.* Retrieved from https://www.
washingtonpost.com/dc-md-va/2022/06/03/proud-boy-pruitt-pleads-guilty-jan6/
24 Sarnoff, Marisa. (2022, June 3). Proud Boy Who Nearly Came Face to Face with
Chuck Schumer Inside the Capitol on Jan. 6 Pleads Guilty to a Felony. *Law and
Order.* Retrieved from https://lawandcrime.com/u-s-capitol-breach/proud-boy-
who-nearly-came-face-to-face-with-chuck-schumer-inside-the-capitol-on-jan-6-
pleads-guilty-to-a-felony/
25 Renshaw, J., & Wolfe, J. (2021, June 15). U.S. lays out plan to confront white
supremacist violence. *Reuters.* Retrieved from https://www.reuters.com/world/
us/biden-administration-unveils-plan-tackle-domestic-terrorism-2021-06-15/
26 Ali, Wajahat (August 27, 2022). Law enforcement has an extremist problem in
its own backyard. *Yahoo News.* Retrieved from https://news.yahoo.com/law-
enforcement-extremist-problem-own-032845486.html?guccounter=1&guce_
referrer=aHR0cHM6Ly93d3cuZ29vZ2xlLmNvbS88&guce_referrer_
sig=AQAAANuh3-Lo8kj2OBOxJMHc9WaWA4r2LIEBO-
i0jRJBFiMMEZI0bUW_Mul1W3DW2U-2KC0uF8SaLIj5LKInWUXx6uZ9h3B
Yb8SQfrkUohsOZn86G16gkXZ_be_8L6uxhDE3Y1-g1mpU3iDeNpkCKtz6Ol4
RIyou6DMulFhAhwduiVQO
27 Milton, D., & Mines, A. (2021). "This Is War": Examining Military Experience
Among the Capitol Hill Siege Participants. *CTC Sentinel.* Retrieved from https://
ctc.westpoint.edu/this-is-war-examining-military-experience-among-the-capitol-
hill-siege-participants/
28 Tucker, E., & Jalonick, M. (2021). FBI chief warns violent 'domestic terrorism'
growing in US. *Associated Press.* Retrieved from https://apnews.com/article/fbi-
chris-wray-testify-capitol-riot-9a5539af34b15338bb5c4923907eeb67
29 Anti-Defamation League. (2019). Murder and Extremism in the United States in
2018. *ADL Center on Extremism.* Retrieved from https://www.adl.org/resources/
report/murder-and-extremism-united-states-2018
30 Macklin, G. (2019). The Christchurch attack livestream terror in the viral
video age. *CTC Sentinel.* Vol 12 (6). retrieved from https://ctc.westpoint.edu/
christchurch-attacks-livestream-terror-viral-video-age/; Smith-Spark, L. (2021)
A far-right extremist killed 77 people in Norway. A decade on, 'the hatred is still
out there' but attacker's influence is seen as low. *CNN.* Retrieved from https://
www.cnn.com/2021/07/22/europe/anders-breivik-july-22-attacks-norway-
anniversary-cmd-intl/index.html
31 Meier, A. (2022). Germany's white supremacism problem and what it means for
the United States. *Lawfare Blog.* Retrieved from https://www.lawfareblog.com/
germanys-white-supremacist-problem%E2%80%94and-what-it-means-united-
states
32 Milekic, S. (2017). US condemns Croatian Neo-Nazi march for Trump. *Balkan
Transitional Justice.* Retrieved from https://balkaninsight.com/2017/02/27/us-
condemns-zagreb-neo-nazi-march-for-trump-02-27-2017/
33 *Applebome, Peter (April 26, 1995). "Terror in Oklahoma: The Background. The
New York Times. Retrieved from https://www.nytimes.com/1995/04/26/us/terror-*

in-oklahoma-the-background-a-bombing-foretold-in-extreme-right-bible.html

34   "Extremism in America: The Turner Diaries". ADL.org. Anti-Defamation
      League. 2007. Retrieved December 26, 2018. Retrieved from https://www.adl.
      org/resources/backgrounders/turner-diaries

35   *Jackson, Camille (October 14, 2004). "Turner Diaries, Other Racist Novels
      Inspire Extremist Violence". Southern Poverty Law Center.* Retrieved December
      26, 2018 *from https://www.splcenter.org/fighting-hate/intelligence-report/2004/
      turner-diaries-other-racist-novels-inspire-extremist-violence*

36   McAlear, R. (2009). Hate, narrative, and propaganda in the Turner diaries. *The
      Journal of American Culture, 32*(3), 192.

37   Wilkerson, Isabel. (2020). *Caste: The origins of our discontent.* Random House.

38   Schuetze, C. (2020, March 19). Germany shuts down far-right clubs that deny
      the modern state. *The New York Times.* Retrieved from https://www.nytimes.
      com/2020/03/19/world/europe/germany-reich-citizens-ban.html

39   Bennhold, K. & Solomon, E. (2022, December 7). Germany arrests 25 suspected
      of planning to overthrow the government. *The New York Times.* Retrieved from
      https://www.nytimes.com/2022/12/07/world/europe/germany-coup-arrests.
      html?smid=nytcore-ios-share&referringSource=articleShare

40   Hoffman, B (January 5, 2022) A year after January 6, is accelerationism the new
      terrorist threat? *Council on Foreign Relations.* Retrieved from https://www.cfr.
      org/in-brief/year-after-january-6-accelerationism-new-terrorist-threat

41   Sarnoff, Marisa. (2022, June 3). Proud Boy Who Nearly Came Face to Face with
      Chuck Schumer Inside the Capitol on Jan. 6 Pleads Guilty to a Felony. *Law and
      Order.* Retrieved from https://lawandcrime.com/u-s-capitol-breach/proud-boy-
      who-nearly-came-face-to-face-with-chuck-schumer-inside-the-capitol-on-jan-6-
      pleads-guilty-to-a-felony/

42   Weiner, Rachel (2022, June 3). D.C. Proud Boy and bartender pleads guilty
      to felony in Capitol riot. *Washington Post.* Retrieved from https://www.
      washingtonpost.com/dc-md-va/2022/06/03/proud-boy-pruitt-pleads-guilty-jan6/

43   Kuznia, Rob & Devine, Curt. (2021). The Proud Boy. *CNN* Retrieved from
      https://www.cnn.com/interactive/2021/06/us/capitol-riot-paths-to-insurrection/
      josh-pruitt.html

44   Marisa Sarnoff. (2022, January 13). Judge orders jail for Proud Boy seen
      throwing 'Quiet Please' sign across Capitol atrium on Jan. 6 after multiple
      curfew violations. *Law and Crime.* Retrieved from https://lawandcrime.com/u-s-
      capitol-breach/judge-orders-jail-for-proud-boy-seen-throwing-quiet-please-sign-
      across-capitol-atrium-on-jan-6-after-multiple-curfew-violations/

45   BBC. (2019). Christchurch shootings: How the attacks unfolded. Retrieved from
      https://www.bbc.com/news/world-asia-47582183

46   Charlton, L (August 6, 2019) What is the great replacement? *The New York
      Times.* Retrieved from https://www.nytimes.com/2019/08/06/us/politics/grand-
      replacement-explainer.html

47   Smith, A., Radnofsky, C., Givetash, L & Banic, V. (2019). New Zealand mosque
      shooting attackers apparent manifesto probed. *NBC* Retrieved from https://www.
      nbcnews.com/news/world/new-zealand-mosque-terrorist-may-have-targeted-

country-because-it-n983601; BBC. (2020). Christchurch shooting: Gunman Tarrant wanted to kill 'as many as possible'. Retrieved from https://www.bbc.com/news/world-asia-53861456

48   ADL. (2022). Creativity Movement. Retrieved July 13, 2022 from https://www.adl.org/education/references/hate-symbols/creativity-movement

49   Fearnow, B. (2019). Don't 'blame Trump': Manifesto tied To El Paso shooting rants about Democrats, Hispanics invading country. *Newsweek.* Retrieved from
https://www.newsweek.com/el-paso-shooter-manifesto-defends-donald-trump-fake-news-blame-immigration-1452484#:~:text=Don%27t%20%27Blame%20Trump%27%3A%20Manifesto%20Tied%20To%20El%20Paso%20Shooting%20Rants%20About%20Democrats%2C%20Hispanics%20Invading%20Country; Franklin, J. (2022). Parts of the Buffalo shooters alleged screed were copied from other sources. *NPR.* Retrieved from https://www.npr.org/2022/05/18/1099372659/parts-of-the-buffalo-shooters-alleged-screed-were-copied-from-other-sources

50   Southern Poverty Law Center. (2022). Church of the Creator founder Ben Klassen's writings reveal militarism, racism and Nazism. Retrieved from https://www.splcenter.org/fighting-hate/intelligence-report/1999/church-creator-founder-ben-klassen%E2%80%99s-writings-reveal-militarism-racism-and-nazism

51   Southern Poverty Law Center. (2022). Creativity Movement. Retrieved from https://www.splcenter.org/fighting-hate/extremist-files/group/creativity-movement-0

52   ADL. (2022). RAHOWA. Retrieved from https://www.adl.org/education/references/hate-symbols/RAHOWA

53   *Southern Poverty Law Center*. (2022). Proud Boys. Retrieved from https://www.splcenter.org/fighting-hate/extremist-files/group/proud-boys

54   Staples, B. (2019, October 12). Opinion: How Italians became 'white.' *New York Times*. Retrieved from https://www.nytimes.com/interactive/2019/10/12/opinion/columbus-day-italian-american-racism.html

55   Southern Poverty Law Center. (2022). Creativity Movement. Retrieved from https://www.splcenter.org/fighting-hate/extremist-files/group/creativity-movement-0

56   Southern Poverty Law Center. (2022). Creativity Movement. Retrieved from https://www.splcenter.org/fighting-hate/extremist-files/group/creativity-movement-0

57   Keller, L. (2011, February 27). et Creativity Movement is back. *Southern Poverty Law Center*. Retrieved from https://www.splcenter.org/fighting-hate/intelligence-report/2015/neo-nazi-creativity-movement-back

58   Southern Poverty Law Center. (2015). Active hate groups in the United States in 2015. Retrieved from https://www.splcenter.org/fighting-hate/intelligence-report/2016/active-hate-groups-united-states-2015

59   ADL.(2017). Ricin found in car of Georgia white supremacist. Retrieved from https://www.adl.org/blog/ricin-found-in-car-of-georgia-white-supremacist

60   Joyner, C. (2017, February 23). AJC Watchdog: North Ga. man arrested for ricin radicalized online. *The Atlanta Journal-Constitution*. Retrieved from https://

www.ajc.com/news/state--regional/ajc-watchdog-north-man-arrested-for-ricin-radicalized-online/wdxws9G7zMmaUDmm22njYK/

61   Nazi collaborator monuments (2022). *The Forward.* https://forward.com/series/nazi-collaborator-monuments-around-the-world/

62   Join Our Church. (2022). *The Creativity Alliance.* Retrieved from https://creativityalliance.com/about-our-church/join-our-church/

63   Lee, M. (2017) How right-wing extremists stalk, dox and harass their enemies. The Intercept. Retrieved from https://theintercept.com/2017/09/06/how-right-wing-extremists-stalk-dox-and-harass-their-enemies/

64   Speckhard, A. (2016). The lethal cocktail of terrorism: the four necessary ingredients that go into making a terrorist & fifty individual vulnerabilities/motivations that may also play a role. *International Center for the Study of Violent Extremism: Brief Report.*

65   Southern Poverty Law Center. (2022). Kingdom Identity Ministries. Retrieved from https://www.splcenter.org/fighting-hate/extremist-files/group/kingdom-identity-ministries

66   Federal Bureau of Investigation (FBI). (2021, March 21). The Covenant, the Sword, the Arm of the Lord, File: 100-HQ-487200". FBI Vault. Retrieved from https://vault.fbi.gov/The Covenant The Sword The Arm of the Lord

67   Noble, K. (1998). Tabernacle of Hate: Why they Bombed Oklahoma City. Voyageur Publishers.

68   Geranios, N. K. (2006, January 7). Aryan Nations founder moves. *ABC News.* Retrieved from https://abcnews.go.com/US/story?id=95272&page=1

69   Speckhard, A., Ellenberg, M. & Strezishar, K. (2022). ICSVE Research Reports.

70   ADL. (September 6, 2022). Leaked Oath Keepers' Membership List Reveals Hundreds of Current & Former Law Enforcement Officers, Members of Military, and Elected Officials. Retrieved from https://www.adl.org/resources/press-release/new-adl-leaked-oath-keepers-membership-list-reveals-hundreds-current-former

71   Donnelly, F. X., & duMond, C. (2020, October 12). Inside alleged Whitmer plotters' training site: Shotgun shells, human silhouettes. *The Detroit News*. Retrieved from https://www.detroitnews.com/story/news/local/michigan/2020/10/12/alleged-whitmer-plotters-training-site-had-shotgun-shells-human-silhouettes/5970961002/

72   Donnelly, F. X., & duMond, C. (2020, October 12). Inside alleged Whitmer plotters' training site: Shotgun shells, human silhouettes. *The Detroit News*. Retrieved from https://www.detroitnews.com/story/news/local/michigan/2020/10/12/alleged-whitmer-plotters-training-site-had-shotgun-shells-human-silhouettes/5970961002/

73   Cranney, J. (2020, October 9). Former soldier accused in Michigan governor kidnap plot arrested in Columbia. *The Post and Courier*. Retrieved from https://www.postandcourier.com/columbia/former-soldier-accused-in-michigan-governor-kidnap-plot-arrested-in-columbia/article_3faf26b8-0a4a-11eb-b2d9-bfcdf496a059.html

74   Watson, E., & Legare, R. (2021, December 15). Over 80 of those charged in

the January 6 investigation have ties to the military. *CBS News* Retrieved from https://www.cbsnews.com/news/capitol-riot-january-6-military-ties/

75 Westervelt, Eric. (2021, January 15). Off-duty police officers investigated, charged With participating in capitol riot. *NPR*. Retrieved from https://www.npr.org/2021/01/15/956896923/police-officers-across-nation-face-federal-charges-for-involvement-in-capitol-ri

76 Morton, J. (2019). Combatting violent extremism and terrorism. *C-Span*. Retrieved from https://www.c-span.org/video/?466011-1/combating-violent-extremism-terrorism

77 Southern Poverty Law Center. (2022). National Socialist Movement. Retrieved from https://www.splcenter.org/fighting-hate/extremist-files/group/national-socialist-movement

78 Speckhard, A., Ellenberg, M. & Garret, T.M. (2022). Directed hate: The three stages in adopting white supremacist ideologies. *Homeland Security Today.* Retrieved from https://www.hstoday.us/subject-matter-areas/counterterrorism/directed-hate-the-three-stages-in-adopting-white-supremacist-ideologies/

79 Ribuffo, L. P. (1980). Henry Ford and "The International Jew." *American Jewish History*, *69*(4), 437–477. http://www.jstor.org/stable/23881872

80 Mickle, B. (2007). "Skins" white supremacist group making itself known in Flint. *Flint Journal*. Retrieved from https://www.mlive.com/flintjournal/newsnow/2007/09/skins_white_supremacist_group.html

81 Lister, C. (2022). We cannot ignore Syria's emergence as a narco-state. *Middle East Institute*. Retrieved from https://www.mei.edu/publications/we-cannot-ignore-syrias-emergence-narco-state

82 Miller-Idriss, C. (2022). *Hate in the Homeland*. Princeton University Press.

83 Kennedy, M. (2016) Lead-laced water in Flint: A step-by-step look at the makings of a crisis. *NPR*. Retrieved from https://www.npr.org/sections/thetwo-way/2016/04/20/465545378/lead-laced-water-in-flint-a-step-by-step-look-at-the-makings-of-a-crisis

84 Flint police ID homicide victim. *MLive*. Retrieved from https://www.mlive.com/news/flint/2018/06/police_id_homicide_victim_in_f.html

85 Cappelleti, J and White, E (August 23, 2022). 2 men convicted in plot to kidnap Michigan Gov. Whitmer. ABC News. Retrieved from https://abcnews.go.com/Politics/wireStory/deliberations-start-men-charged-gov-whitmer-plot-88733412?cid=social_twitter_abcn

86 Cappelleti, J and White, E (August 23, 2022). 2 men convicted in plot to kidnap Michigan Gov. Whitmer. ABC News. Retrieved from https://abcnews.go.com/Politics/wireStory/deliberations-start-men-charged-gov-whitmer-plot-88733412?cid=social_twitter_abcn

87 Cappelleti, J and White, E (August 23, 2022). 2 men convicted in plot to kidnap Michigan Gov. Whitmer. ABC News. Retrieved from https://abcnews.go.com/Politics/wireStory/deliberations-start-men-charged-gov-whitmer-plot-88733412?cid=social_twitter_abcn

88 The United States Attorney's Office District of Columbia. (2022, January 13). Leader of Oath Keepers and 10 other individuals indicted in federal court for

seditious conspiracy and other offenses related to U.S. Capitol breach. Retrieved from https://www.justice.gov/usao-dc/pr/leader-oath-keepers-and-10-other-individuals-indicted-federal-court-seditious-conspiracy

89   The United States Attorney's Office District of Columbia. (2022, January 13). Leader of Oath Keepers and 10 other individuals indicted in federal court for seditious conspiracy and other offenses related to U.S. Capitol breach. Retrieved from https://www.justice.gov/usao-dc/pr/leader-oath-keepers-and-10-other-individuals-indicted-federal-court-seditious-conspiracy

90   U.S. Department of Justice. (2022, May 4). Leader of North Carolina Chapter of Oath Keepers pleads guilty to seditious conspiracy and obstruction of Congress for efforts to stop transfer of power following 2020 presidential election. *Justice News.* Retrieved from https://www.justice.gov/opa/pr/leader-north-carolina-chapter-oath-keepers-pleads-guilty-seditious-conspiracy-and-obstruction

91   U.S. Department of Justice. (2022, May 4). Leader of North Carolina Chapter of Oath Keepers pleads guilty to seditious conspiracy and obstruction of Congress for efforts to stop transfer of power following 2020 presidential election. *Justice News.* Retrieved from https://www.justice.gov/opa/pr/leader-north-carolina-chapter-oath-keepers-pleads-guilty-seditious-conspiracy-and-obstruction

92   Southern Poverty Law Center. (2022, August 10). Oath Keepers. Retrieved from https://www.splcenter.org/fighting-hate/extremist-files/group/oath-keepers

93   Southern Poverty Law Center. (2022, August 10). Oath Keepers. Retrieved from https://www.splcenter.org/fighting-hate/extremist-files/group/oath-keepers

94   Southern Poverty Law Center. (2022, August 10). Oath Keepers. Retrieved from https://www.splcenter.org/fighting-hate/extremist-files/group/oath-keepers

95   Oathkeepers. (September, 29 2022). Retrieved from http://oath-keepers.blogspot.com/ These ten orders include the following:

1.   We will NOT obey orders to disarm the American people.
2.   We will NOT obey orders to conduct warrantless searches of the American people
3.   We will NOT obey orders to detain American citizens as "unlawful enemy combatants" or to subject them to military tribunal.
4.   We will NOT obey orders to impose martial law or a "state of emergency" on a state.
5.   We will NOT obey orders to invade and subjugate any state that asserts its sovereignty.
6.   We will NOT obey any order to blockade American cities, thus turning them into giant concentration camps.
7.   We will NOT obey any order to force American citizens into any form of detention camps under any pretext.
8.   We will NOT obey orders to assist or support the use of any foreign troops on U.S. soil against the American people to "keep the peace" or to "maintain control."
9.   We will NOT obey any orders to confiscate the property of the American people, including food and other essential supplies.
10.   We will NOT obey any orders which infringe on the right of the people to

free speech, to peaceably assemble, and to petition their government for a redress of grievances.

96   Montgomery, Peter. (2020, December 17). Oath Keepers' Stewart Rhodes repeats demand that Trump declare martial law to avoid militia-led civil war. *Right Wing Watch.* Retrieved from https://www.rightwingwatch.org/post/oath-keepers-stewart-rhodes-repeats-demand-that-trump-declare-martial-law-to-avoid-militia-led-civil-war/

97   Montgomery, Peter. (2020, December 17). Oath Keepers' Stewart Rhodes repeats demand that Trump declare martial law to avoid militia-led civil war. *Right Wing Watch.* Retrieved from https://www.rightwingwatch.org/post/oath-keepers-stewart-rhodes-repeats-demand-that-trump-declare-martial-law-to-avoid-militia-led-civil-war/

98   Lawrence, Drew. (2022, May 6). What the military records of the Oath Keepers leader actually say about his service. *Military.com* Retrieved from https://www.military.com/daily-news/2022/05/06/he-hinted-hardened-service-oath-keepers-leaders-military-records-dont-back.html

99   Montgomery, Peter. (2020, December 17). Oath Keepers' Stewart Rhodes repeats demand that Trump declare martial law to avoid militia-led civil war. *Right Wing Watch.* Retrieved from https://www.rightwingwatch.org/post/oath-keepers-stewart-rhodes-repeats-demand-that-trump-declare-martial-law-to-avoid-militia-led-civil-war/

100 Reavis, Dick. (1995). *The Ashes of Waco: An Investigation.* New York: Simon and Schuster, p, 13.

101 Reilly, Ryan. (2022, May 28). New evidence reveals coordination between Oath Keepers, Three Percenters on Jan. 6. *NBC News.* Retrieved from https://www.nbcnews.com/politics/justice-department/new-evidence-reveals-coordination-oath-keepers-three-percenters-jan-6-rcna30355

102 Yglesias, Matthew. (2015) The amazing Jade Helm conspiracy theory, explained. *Vox.* Retrieved from https://www.vox.com/2015/5/6/8559577/jade-helm-conspiracy

103 Southern Poverty Law. (August 31, 2020). What we know about Patriot Prayer. https://www.splcenter.org/hatewatch/2020/08/31/what-we-know-about-patriot-prayer

104 Nickerson, Charlotte. (2021, November 10). Looking-glass self: Theory, definition & examples. *Simply Psychology.* Retrieved from https://www.simplypsychology.org/charles-cooleys-looking-glass-self.html

105 Speckhard, A., Ellenberg, M. & Garret, T.M. (2022) White supremacists speak: Recruitment, radicalization and experience of engaging and disengaging from hate groups. *ICSVE Research Reports.* Retrieved from https://www.icsve.org/white-supremacists-speak-recruitment-radicalization-experiences-of-engaging-and-disengaging-from-hate-groups-2/

106 Felitti, V. J., Anda, R. F., Nordenberg, D., Williamson, D. F., Spitz, A. M., Edwards, V., & Marks, J. S. (1998). Relationship of childhood abuse and household dysfunction to many of the leading causes of death in adults: The Adverse Childhood Experiences (ACE) Study. *American Journal of Preventive*

Medicine, 14(4), 245-258.

107   Speckhard, A. and Ellenberg, M. (2020). ISIS in Their Own Words:
       Recruitment History, Motivations for Joining, Travel, Experiences in ISIS,
       and Disillusionment over Time – Analysis of 220 In-depth Interviews of ISIS
       Returnees, Defectors and Prisoners. *Journal of Strategic Security* 13 (1) pp. 82-
       127. Retrieved from https://digitalcommons.usf.edu/jss/vol13/iss1/5; Speckhard,
       A. and Ellenberg, M. (2020). Is internet recruitment enough to seduce a
       vulnerable individual into terrorism? *Homeland Security Today*. Retrieved from
       https://www.icsve.org/is-internet-recruitment-enough-to-seduce-a-vulnerable-
       individual-into-terrorism/

108   Lautaru, A. (2017, August 28). Prisoners describe what it's like to get a tattoo
       behind bars. *VICE*. https://www.vice.com/en/article/kzzgxm/prisoners-describe-
       what-its-like-to-get-a-tattoo-behind-bars

109   Southern Poverty Law Center. (2022). New brand of racist Odinist religion on
       the march. Retrieved from https://www.splcenter.org/fighting-hate/intelligence-
       report/1998/new-brand-racist-odinist-religion-march

110   Southern Poverty Law Center. (2022). New brand of racist Odinist religion on
       the march. Retrieved from https://www.splcenter.org/fighting-hate/intelligence-
       report/1998/new-brand-racist-odinist-religion-march

111   Southern Poverty Law Center. (2022). New brand of racist Odinist religion on
       the march. Retrieved from https://www.splcenter.org/fighting-hate/intelligence-
       report/1998/new-brand-racist-odinist-religion-march

112   BBC. (2019). Christchurch shootings: How the attacks unfolded. Retrieved from
       https://www.bbc.com/news/world-asia-47582183

113   Speckhard, A., Ellenberg, M. & Garret, T.M. (2022, May 17). White
       supremacists speak: Recruitment, radicalization and experience of engaging
       and disengaging from hate groups. *ICSVE Research Reports*. Retrieved from
       https://www.icsve.org/white-supremacists-speak-recruitment-radicalization-
       experiences-of-engaging-and-disengaging-from-hate-groups-2/

114   Speckhard, Anne, and Ellenberg, Molly, and Garret, TM. (2021, November 11).
       The Challenge of Extremism in the Military Is Not Going Away Without a New
       Perspective. *ICSVE Research Reports*. Retrieved from https://www.icsve.org/
       the-challenge-of-extremism-in-the-military-is-not-going-away-without-a-new-
       perspective/; Speckhard, Anne, and Ellenberg, Molly (2021, May 17). White
       Supremacists Speak: Recruitment, Radicalization & Experiences of Engaging
       and Disengaging from Hate Groups. *ICSVE Research Reports*. Retrieved from
       https://www.icsve.org/white-supremacists-speak-recruitment-radicalization-
       experiences-of-engaging-and-disengaging-from-hate-groups-2/

115   Berlet, C., & Vysotsky, S. (2006). Overview of US white supremacist
       groups. *Journal of Political & Military Sociology*, 11-48.

116   Franklin, J. (2022). Parts of the Buffalo shooters alleged screed were
       copied from other sources. *NPR*. Retrieved from https://www.npr.
       org/2022/05/18/1099372659/parts-of-the-buffalo-shooters-alleged-screed-were-
       copied-from-other-sources

117   Fearnow, B. (2019). Don't 'blame Trump': Manifesto tied To El Paso shooting

rants about Democrats, Hispanics invading country. *Newsweek.* Retrieved from
https://www.newsweek.com/el-paso-shooter-manifesto-defends-donald-trump-fake-
news-blame-immigration-1452484#:~:text=Don%27t%20%27Blame%20
Trump%27%3A%20Manifesto%20Tied%20To%20El%20Paso%20
Shooting%20Rants%20About%20Democrats%2C%20Hispanics%20
Invading%20Country

118   Smith, A., Radnofsky, C., Givetash, L & Banic, V. (2019). New Zealand mosque
shooting attackers apparent manifesto probed. *NBC* Retrieved from https://www.
nbcnews.com/news/world/new-zealand-mosque-terrorist-may-have-targeted-
country-because-it-n983601; BBC. (2020). Christchurch shooting: Gunman
Tarrant wanted to kill 'as many as possible'. Retrieved from https://www.bbc.
com/news/world-asia-53861456

119   Speckhard, A. & Ellenberg, M. (2022, August 1) Projected hate: Gender identity,
sexual orientation, and white supremacism. *Homeland Security Today.* Retrieved
from https://www.hstoday.us/featured/perspective-projected-hate-gender-
identity-sexual-orientation-and-white-supremacism/

120   Shah, S. (2016). Constructing an alternative pedagogy of Islam: the experiences
of lesbian, gay, bisexual and transgender Muslims. *Journal of Beliefs &
Values*, *37*(3), 308-319.

121   Schafer, J. A., Mullins, C. W., & Box, S. (2014). Awakenings: The emergence of
white supremacist ideologies. *Deviant Behavior*, *35*(3), 173-196.

122   Schafer, J. A., Mullins, C. W., & Box, S. (2014). Awakenings: The emergence of
white supremacist   ideologies. *Deviant Behavior*, *35*(3), 173-196.

123   Speckhard, A., Ellenberg, M. & Garret, T.M. (2022). Directed hate: The three
stages in adopting white supremacist ideologies. *Homeland Security Today.*
Retrieved from https://www.hstoday.us/subject-matter-areas/counterterrorism/
directed-hate-the-three-stages-in-adopting-white-supremacist-ideologies/

124   Speckhard, A., Ellenberg, M. & Garret, T.M. (2022). Directed hate: The three
stages in adopting white supremacist ideologies. *Homeland Security Today.*
Retrieved from https://www.hstoday.us/subject-matter-areas/counterterrorism/
directed-hate-the-three-stages-in-adopting-white-supremacist-ideologies/

125   Speckhard, A. & Ellenberg, M. (2022). Are Antifa activists achieving their goals?
ICSVE Brief Reports. Retrieved from https://www.icsve.org/are-antifa-activists-
achieving-their-goals/?utm_source=rss&utm_medium=rss&utm_campaign=are-
antifa-activists-achieving-their-goals

126   Atran, S. (2016). The devoted actor: unconditional commitment and intractable
conflict across cultures. *Current Anthropology*, *57*(S13), S192-S203.

127   Windisch, S., Simi, P., Blee, K., & DeMichele, M. (2018). Understanding
the micro-situational dynamics of white supremacist violence in the United
States. *Perspectives on Terrorism*, *12*(6), 23-37.

128   Atran, S. (2016). The devoted actor: unconditional commitment and intractable
conflict across cultures. *Current Anthropology*, *57*(S13), S192-S203.

129   Bray, M. (2017). *Antifa: The anti-fascist handbook*. Melville House.

130   Huang, M. (2021, April 22). Oklahoma City Bombing: 26 years later, the same
extremist threats prevail. *Southern Poverty Law Center.* Retrieved from https://

www.splcenter.org/news/2021/04/22/oklahoma-city-bombing-26-years-later-same-extremist-threats-prevail

131   BBC. (2022, February 1). Norway mass killer Anders Breivik ordered to stay in jail. *BBC News*. Retrieved from https://www.bbc.com/news/world-europe-60219876

132   Yaccino, S., Schwirtz, M., & Santora, M. (2012, August 5). Gunman kills 6 at a Sikh temple near Milwaukee. *The New York Times*. Retrieved from https://www.nytimes.com/2012/08/06/us/shooting-reported-at-temple-in-wisconsin.html

133   Kinnard, M. (2022, March 2). Dylann Roof takes church shooting appeal to U.S. Supreme Court. *ABC News*. Retrieved from https://abcnews.go.com/US/wireStory/dylann-roof-takes-church-shooting-appeal-us-supreme-83207302

134   Robertson, C., Mele, C., & Tavernise, S. (2018, October 27). 11 killed in synagogue massacre; suspect charged with 29 counts. *The New York Times*. Retrieved from https://www.nytimes.com/2018/10/27/us/active-shooter-pittsburgh-synagogue-shooting.html

135   Radio New Zealand. (2019). Police with the latest information on the mosque shootings. Retrieved from https://www.radionz.co.nz/news/national/384896/police-with-the-latest-information-on-the-mosque-shootings

136   Tress, L (2022, May 15) Manifesto attributed to Buffalo shooting suspect pushes anti-Semitic conspiracies. *Times of Israel*. Retrieved from https://www.timesofisrael.com/manifesto-attributed-to-buffalo-shooting-suspect-pushes-antisemitic-conspiracies/

137   Speckhard, A., Warren, W., Strezishar, K. & Ellenberg, M. (2022, April 5). A summer inside QAnon and white supremacist forums. *Homeland Security Today*. Retrieved from https://www.hstoday.us/subject-matter-areas/counterterrorism/perspective-a-summer-inside-qanon-and-white-supremacist-online-forums/

138   Montgomery, P. (February 8, 2021). The religious right's rhetoric fueled the insurrection. *The American Prospect*. https://prospect.org/politics/religious-right-rhetoric-fueled-the-capitol-insurrection/

139   Milton, D., & Mines, A. (2021, April 12). "This Is War": Examining Military Experience Among the Capitol Hill Siege Participants. *West Point Sentinel*. Retrieved from https://ctc.usma.edu/this-is-war-examining-military-experience-among-the-capitol-hill-siege-participants/

140   Milton, D., & Mines, A. (2021). "This Is War": Examining Military Experience Among the Capitol Hill Siege Participants. *CTC Sentinel*. Retrieved from https://ctc.westpoint.edu/this-is-war-examining-military-experience-among-the-capitol-hill-siege-participants/

141   Speckhard, A. & Ellenberg, M. (2022, June 27) The Oath Keepers wanted a coup. *Homeland Security Today*. Retrieved from https://www.hstoday.us/subject-matter-areas/counterterrorism/perspective-the-oath-keepers-wanted-a-coup/

142   Shane, L. (February 6, 2020). Signs of white supremacy extremism up again in poll of active-duty troops. *Military Times*. Retrieved from https://www.militarytimes.com/news/pentagon-congress/2020/02/06/signs-of-white-supremacy-extremism-up-again-in-poll-of-active-duty-troops/

143   National Coordinator for Counterterrorism and Security. (2022, May 17). NCTV

Terrorist Threat Assessment: threat of terrorist attack remains conceivable, but there are no specific indications of one. Retrieved from https://english.nctv.nl/topics/terrorist-threat-assessment-netherlands/news/2022/05/17/nctv-terrorist-threat-assessment-threat-of-terrorist-attack-remains-conceivable-but-there-are-no-specific-indications-of-one

144 Speckhard, A., Ellenberg, M., & Garret, TM. (2021, Nov 16). The Challenge of Extremism in the Military Is Not Going Away Without a New Perspective. *Military Times.* Retrieved from https://www.militarytimes.com/opinion/commentary/2021/11/16/the-challenge-of-extremism-in-the-military-is-not-going-away-without-a-new-perspective/

145 Kifner, J. (2006, July 7). Hate groups are infiltrating the military, group asserts. *The New York Times.* Retrieved from https://www.nytimes.com/2006/07/07/washington/hate-groups-are-infiltrating-the-military-group-asserts.html

146 Blevins, C. A., Weathers, F. W., Davis, M. T., Witte, T. K., & Domino, J. L. (2015). The posttraumatic stress disorder checklist for DSM-5 (PCL-5): Development and initial psychometric evaluation. *Journal of traumatic stress*, *28*(6), 489-498.

147 Speckhard, Anne, and Ellenberg, Molly, and Garret, TM. (2021, November 11). The Challenge of Extremism in the Military Is Not Going Away Without a New Perspective. *ICSVE Research Reports.* Retrieved from https://www.icsve.org/the-challenge-of-extremism-in-the-military-is-not-going-away-without-a-new-perspective/; Speckhard, Anne, and Ellenberg, Molly (2021, May 17).

148 Schogol, J. (July 27, 2022). Ex-Marine booted for extremist activities accused of calling for Nazi- inspired mass rape and murder. Task and Purpose. Retrieved from https://taskandpurpose.com/news/marine-accused-neo-nazi-group/

149 Bray, M. (2017). *Antifa: The anti-fascist handbook.* Melville House.

150 Roston, Aram. (2021, August 25). Antifa: A woman's journey from Girl Scout to anarchist street warrior. *Reuters.* Retrieved from https://www.reuters.com/investigates/special-report/usa-antifa-profile/

151 DW. Neo-Nazi Sturmbrigade 44: How serious of a threat is it? Retrieved from https://www.dw.com/en/neo-nazi-sturmbrigade-44-how-serious-of-a-threat-is-it/a-55788441; BBC. (2021, May 20). German officer who posed as Syrian refugee in terror trial. Retrieved from https://www.bbc.com/news/world-europe-57184527; Meier, A. (2022, January 30). Germany's white supremacist problem – and what it means for the United States. *Lawfare.* Retrieved from https://www.lawfareblog.com/germanys-white-supremacist-problem%E2%80%94and-what-it-means-united-states

152 ADL (2018, December 26). Extremism in America: The Turner Diaries. Retrieved from https://www.adl.org/resources/backgrounders/turner-diaries

153 Yaccino, S., Schwirtz, M., & Santora, M. (2012, August 5). Gunman kills 6 at a Sikh temple near Milwaukee. *The New York Times.* Retrieved from https://www.nytimes.com/2012/08/06/us/shooting-reported-at-temple-in-wisconsin.html

154 Milton, D., & Mines, A. (2021, April 12). "This Is War": Examining Military Experience Among the Capitol Hill Siege Participants. *West Point Sentinel.* Retrieved from https://ctc.usma.edu/this-is-war-examining-military-experience-

among-the-capitol-hill-siege-participants/

155   Southern Poverty Law Center. (2022). In 2021, we tracked 733 hate groups across the U.S. Retrieved from https://www.splcenter.org/hate-map

156   Southern Poverty Law Center. (2022). Jeff Schoep. Retrieved from https://www. splcenter.org/fighting-hate/extremist-files/individual/jeff-schoep

157   Holthouse, D. (2006, April 19). Racial tensions high in Toledo-area neighborhood after National Socialist Movement march. *Southern Poverty Law Center*. Retrieved from https://www.splcenter.org/fighting-hate/intelligence-report/2006/racial-tensions-high-toledo-area-neighborhood-after-national-socialist-movement-march

158   Southern Poverty Law Center. National Socialist Movement. (2022). Retrieved from https://www.splcenter.org/fighting-hate/extremist-files/group/national-socialist-movement

159   Southern Poverty Law Center. National Socialist Movement. (2022). Retrieved from https://www.splcenter.org/fighting-hate/extremist-files/group/national-socialist-movement

160   Holthouse, D. (2006, April 19). Racial tensions high in Toledo-area neighborhood after National Socialist Movement march. *Southern Poverty Law Center*. Retrieved from https://www.splcenter.org/fighting-hate/intelligence-report/2006/racial-tensions-high-toledo-area-neighborhood-after-national-socialist-movement-march

161   Southern Poverty Law Center. (2022). William Pierce. Retrieved from https:// www.splcenter.org/fighting-hate/extremist-files/individual/william-pierce; Southern Poverty Law Center. (2022). Richard Butler. Retrieved from https:// www.splcenter.org/fighting-hate/extremist-files/individual/richard-butler; Southern Poverty Law Center. (2022). Matt Hale. Retrieved from https://www. splcenter.org/fighting-hate/extremist-files/individual/matt-hale

162   Kim, T. K. (2006, April 19). A look at White Power music today. *Southern Poverty Law Center*. Retrieved from https://www.splcenter.org/fighting-hate/ intelligence-report/2006/look-white-power-music-today

163   Southern Poverty Law Center. (2022). National Socialist Movement. Retrieved from https://www.splcenter.org/fighting-hate/extremist-files/group/national-socialist-movement

164   ADL. (2022). Othala Rune. Retrieved from https://www.adl.org/education/ references/hate-symbols/othala-rune

165   Jackson, C., & Potok, M. (2004, July 20). National Socialist Movement Recruits Young Children. *Southern Poverty Law Center*. Retrieved from https://www. splcenter.org/fighting-hate/intelligence-report/2004/national-socialist-movement-recruits-young-children

166   Silverman, E. (2021, November 4). Neo-Nazi told leader of group at deadly 2017 Charlottesville rally: 'We're all doing it together.' *The Washington Post*. Retrieved from https://www.washingtonpost.com/dc-md-va/2021/11/04/ charlottesville-lawsuit-nazis-heimbach-trial/

167   Helmore, E. (2021, November 7). Far-right figures in Charlottesville court over deadly violence of 2017. *The Guardian*. Retrieved from https://www.

theguardian.com/us-news/2021/nov/07/charlottesville-virginia-court-trial-violence

168 Miller, M. E. (2017, August 21). The shadow of an assassinated American Nazi commander hangs over Charlottesville. *The Washington Post*. Retrieved from https://www.washingtonpost.com/news/retropolis/wp/2017/08/21/the-shadow-of-an-assassinated-american-nazi-commander-hangs-over-charlottesville/

169 Southern Poverty Law Center. (2022). National Socialist Movement. Retrieved from https://www.splcenter.org/fighting-hate/extremist-files/group/national-socialist-movement

170 Southern Poverty Law Center. (2022). National Socialist Movement. Retrieved from https://www.splcenter.org/fighting-hate/extremist-files/group/national-socialist-movement

171 Holthouse, D. (2006, April 19). Racial tensions high in Toledo-area neighborhood after National Socialist Movement march. *Southern Poverty Law Center*. Retrieved from https://www.splcenter.org/fighting-hate/intelligence-report/2006/racial-tensions-high-toledo-area-neighborhood-after-national-socialist-movement-march

172 Southern Poverty Law Center. (2022). Richard Butler. Retrieved from https://www.splcenter.org/fighting-hate/extremist-files/individual/richard-butler

173 Barrett, H. M. (2001). *Pioneer Little Europe: PLE Prospectus: Aka" stormfronts of the Street"*. Retrieved from https://archive.org/details/pleprospectus

174 Christian Science Monitor. (2013, November 19). White supremacists arrested in North Dakota for terrorizing citizens. Retrieved from https://www.csmonitor.com/USA/Latest-News-Wires/2013/1119/White-supremacists-arrested-in-North-Dakota-for-terrorizing-citizens

175 Southern Poverty Law Center. (2022). Craig Cobb. Retrieved from https://www.splcenter.org/fighting-hate/extremist-files/individual/craig-cobb; Southern Poverty Law Center. (2014, May). Would-be führer of Leith, N.D. pleads to felony terrorizing. Retrieved from https://www.splcenter.org/fighting-hate/intelligence-report/2014/would-be-f%C3%BChrer-leith-nd-pleads-felony-terrorizing

176 Southern Poverty Law Center (2013, November 20). Closed circuit. https://www.splcenter.org/fighting-hate/intelligence-report/2013/closed-circuit

177 Southern Poverty Law Center. (2022). JT Ready. Retrieved from https://www.splcenter.org/fighting-hate/extremist-files/individual/jt-ready

178 Mandel, D. (2021, November) The role of instigators in radicalization. In Anne Speckhard, (Ed.), *Psychosocial, Organizational and Cultural Aspects of Terrorism NATO HFM 140 Final Report* (pp. 29-38). NATO.

179 Hassan, S. A. (2020). *The BITE Model of Authoritarian Control: Undue Influence, Thought Reform, Brainwashing, Mind Control, Trafficking and the Law* (Doctoral dissertation, Fielding Graduate University).

180 Southern Poverty Law Center. (2022). Racist Skinhead. *Southern Poverty Law Center*. Retrieved from https://www.splcenter.org/fighting-hate/extremist-files/ideology/racist-skinhead; Two films offer realistic depictions of skinhead life: "Romper Stomper" with Russell Crowe (1992), is set in Melbourne, Australia,

and "American History X" with Ed Norton (1998) is set in California.

181   Southern Poverty Law Center. (2022). Stefan Molyneux. Retrieved from https://www.splcenter.org/fighting-hate/extremist-files/individual/stefan-molyneux

182   Wilding, Mark (March 12, 2018). The rise and demise of the EDL. *Vice News.* Retrieved from https://www.vice.com/en/article/qve8wm/the-rise-and-demise-of-the-edl

183   Southern Poverty Law Center. (2022). Alex Jones. Retrieved from https://www.splcenter.org/fighting-hate/extremist-files/individual/alex-jones

184   ADL. (2017, May 23). Despite internal turmoil Klan groups persist. Retrieved from https://www.adl.org/resources/report/despite-internal-turmoil-klan-groups-persist

185   ADL. (2022). Stormfront. Retrieved from https://www.adl.org/education/references/hate-symbols/stormfront

186   Speckhard, A., & Ellenberg, M. (2020, August 3). Spontaneous deradicalization and the path to repatriate some ISIS   members. *Homeland Security Today.* Retrieved from https://www.hstoday.us/subject-matter-areas/counterterrorism/perspective-spontaneous-deradicalization-and-the-path-to-repatriate-some-isis-members/

187   Enzinna, W. (2018, July/August). Inside the Radical, Uncomfortable Movement to Reform White Supremacists. *Mother Jones.* Retrieved from https://www.motherjones.com/politics/2018/07/reform-white-supremacists-shane-johnson-life-after-hate/

188   Where God Leads Correctional Ministries. (2020). Retrieved from https://www.facebook.com/wglcm

189   O'Hara, M. E. (2017, February 16). FBI arrests man who allegedly planned Dylann Roof-style attack. *NBC News.* Retrieved from https://www.nbcnews.com/news/us-news/fbi-arrests-man-after-planning-dylann-roof-style-attack-n721881

190   Kinnard, M. (2018, July 12). Man who said he planned attack at Myrtle Beach synagogue gets nearly 3 years. *ABC News 4.* Retrieved from https://abcnews4.com/news/crime-news/man-who-said-he-planned-attack-at-myrtle-beach-synagogue-gets-nearly-3-years

191   Speckhard, A. (2012). *Talking to Terrorists: Understanding the Psycho-social Motivations of Militant Jihadi Terrorists, Mass Hostage Takers, Suicide Bombers &" martyrs".* McLean, VA: Advances Press.

192   Speckhard, A. (2012). *Talking to Terrorists: Understanding the Psycho-social Motivations of Militant Jihadi Terrorists, Mass Hostage Takers, Suicide Bombers &" martyrs".* McLean, VA: Advances Press.

193   Speckhard, A. (2012). *Talking to Terrorists: Understanding the Psycho-social Motivations of Militant Jihadi Terrorists, Mass Hostage Takers, Suicide Bombers &" martyrs".* McLean, VA: Advances Press.

194   Speckhard, A. (2012). *Talking to Terrorists: Understanding the Psycho-social Motivations of Militant Jihadi Terrorists, Mass Hostage Takers, Suicide Bombers &" martyrs".* McLean, VA: Advances Press.

195   Speckhard, A., Jacuch, B., & Vanrompay, V. (2012). Taking on the persona of a suicide bomber: A thought experiment. *Perspectives on Terrorism, 6*(2), 51-73.

Retrieved from https://www.researchgate.net/publication/271195742_Taking_
on_the_Persona_of_a_Suicide_Bomber_a_Thought_Experiment

196 O'Hara, M. E. (2017, February 16). FBI arrests man who allegedly planned
Dylann Roof-style attack. *NBC News*. Retrieved from https://www.nbcnews.com/
news/us-news/fbi-arrests-man-after-planning-dylann-roof-style-attack-n721881

197 Mandel, D. (2021, November) The role of instigators in radicalization. In
Anne Speckhard, (Ed.), *Psychosocial, Organizational and Cultural Aspects of
Terrorism NATO HFM 140 Final Report* (pp. 29-38). NATO.

198 Speckhard, A. (2016, Feb 25). The lethal cocktail of terrorism: the four necessary
ingredients that go into making a terrorist & fifty individual vulnerabilities/
motivations that may also play a role. *International Center for the Study of
Violent Extremism: Brief Report*. Retrieved from https://www.icsve.org/the-
lethal-cocktail-of-terrorism/

199 Kinnard, M. (2018, July 12). Man who said he planned attack at Myrtle Beach
synagogue gets nearly 3 years. *ABC News 4*. Retrieved from https://abcnews4.
com/news/crime-news/man-who-said-he-planned-attack-at-myrtle-beach-
synagogue-gets-nearly-3-years

200 BBC. (2019, December 3). London Bridge: What we know about the attack.
BBC News. Retrieved from https://www.bbc.com/news/uk-50594810.

201 Speckhard, A. & Ellenberg, M. (2022). A data-driven approach to the
deradicalization disengagement debate. *Journal of Deradicalization.*; Speckhard,
Anne (2011) "Deradicalization/Disengagement Strategies: Challenging Terrorist
Ideologies and Militant Jihadis" in Laurie Fenstermacher, Special Rapporteur
and Anne Speckhard, editors Social Sciences Support to Military Personnel
Engaged in Counter-Insurgency and Counter-Terrorism Operations: Report of
the NATO Research and Technology Group 172 on Social Sciences Support
to Military Personnel Engaged in Counter-Insurgency and Counter-Terrorism
Operations Symposium held in St. Petersburg, Russia June 18-20, 2009.
Retrieved from https://www.researchgate.net/publication/271195266_Prison_
and_Community_Based_Disengagement_and_De-Radicalization_Programs_for_
Extremists_Involved_in_Militant_Jihadi_Terrorism_Ideologies_and_Activities

202 Speckhard, A. & Ellenberg, M. (2022). A data-driven approach to the
deradicalization disengagement debate. *Journal of Deradicalization.*; Speckhard,
Anne (2011) "Deradicalization/Disengagement Strategies: Challenging Terrorist
Ideologies and Militant Jihadis" in Laurie Fenstermacher, Special Rapporteur
and Anne Speckhard, editors Social Sciences Support to Military Personnel
Engaged in Counter-Insurgency and Counter-Terrorism Operations: Report of
the NATO Research and Technology Group 172 on Social Sciences Support
to Military Personnel Engaged in Counter-Insurgency and Counter-Terrorism
Operations Symposium held in St. Petersburg, Russia June 18-20, 2009.
Retrieved from https://www.researchgate.net/publication/271195266_Prison_
and_Community_Based_Disengagement_and_De-Radicalization_Programs_for_
Extremists_Involved_in_Militant_Jihadi_Terrorism_Ideologies_and_Activities

203 Speckhard, A. (2011). Prison and community-based disengagement and deradicalization programs for extremist involved in militant jihadi terrorism

ideologies and activities. In A. Speckhard. (Ed.) *Psychosocial, organizational and cultural aspects of terrorism* (pp. 109-122). Brussels. NATO. Retrieved from https://apps.dtic.mil/sti/pdfs/ADA555076.pdf

204   Speckhard, A. (2020, February 12). Psycho-social and Islamic challenge approaches to in-prison treatment of militant jihadis. *ICSVE Research Reports.* Retrieved from https://www.icsve.org/psycho-social-and-islamic-challenge-approaches-to-in-prison-treatment-of-militant-jihadis/

205   Speckhard, A. & Ellenberg, M. (2020, August 3). Spontaneous deradicalization and the path to repatriate some ISIS members. *Homeland Security Today.* Retrieved from https://www.hstoday.us/subject-matter-areas/counterterrorism/perspective-spontaneous-deradicalization-and-the-path-to-repatriate-some-isis-members/

206   Hofmann, S. G., Asnaani, A., Vonk, I. J., Sawyer, A. T., & Fang, A. (2012). The efficacy of cognitive behavioral therapy: A review of meta-analyses. *Cognitive therapy and research*, *36*(5), 427-440.

207   Brown, R. A., Helmus, T. C., Ramchand, R., Palimaru, A. I., Weilant, S., Rhoades, A. L., & Hiatt, L. (2021). What do former extremists and their families say about radicalization and deradicalization in America? *RAND Corporation.* Retrieved from https://www.rand.org/pubs/research_briefs/RBA1071-1.html

208   Morton, J. (2019). Combatting violent extremism and terrorism. *C-Span.* Retrieved from https://www.c-span.org/video/?466011-1/combating-violent-extremism-terrorism

209   LaFree, G., Jiang, B., & Porter, L. C. (2020). Prison and violent political extremism in the United States. *Journal of quantitative criminology*, *36*(3), 473-498.

210   Basra, R., Neumann, P. R. & Brunner, C. (2016). Criminal pasts, terrorist futures: European jihadists and the new crime-terror nexus. *Perspectives on Terrorism*, *10*(6), 25-40. Retrieved from https://icsr.info/wp-content/uploads/2016/10/ICSR-Report-Criminal-Pasts-Terrorist-Futures-European-Jihadists-and-the-New-Crime-Terror-Nexus.pdf

211   Speckhard, A. & Ellenberg, M. (2022, July 18). The disengagement and deradicalization debate: Both are needed for true rehabilitation. *Homeland Security Today.* Retrieved from https://www.hstoday.us/subject-matter-areas/counterterrorism/the-disengagement-and-deradicalization-debate-both-are-needed-for-true-rehabilitation/

212   Speckhard, A. & Ellenberg, M. (2020, August 3). Spontaneous deradicalization and the path to repatriate some ISIS members. *Homeland Security Today.* Retrieved from https://www.hstoday.us/subject-matter-areas/counterterrorism/perspective-spontaneous-deradicalization-and-the-path-to-repatriate-some-isis-members/

213   Anti-Defamation League. (2021, March 9). Extremism in the U.S. military: Problems and solutions. *ADL.* Retrieved from https://www.adl.org/blog/extremism-in-the-us-military-problems-and-solutions; Buck, K. R., Rose, A. E., Wiskoff, M. F., & Liverpool, K. M. (2005). *Screening for potential terrorists in the enlisted military accessions process.* Defense Personnel Security Research

Center. Monterrey, CA.; Dawson, J. (2021). Cyber Extremism: Extremist Ideologies Targeting the US Military Online. *SOCarXiv*. Retrieved from https://osf.io/preprints/socarxiv/7km4e/

214 Speckhard, Anne, and Ellenberg, Molly, and Garret, TM. (2021, November 11). The Challenge of Extremism in the Military Is Not Going Away Without a New Perspective. *ICSVE Research Reports*. Retrieved from https://www.icsve.org/the-challenge-of-extremism-in-the-military-is-not-going-away-without-a-new-perspective/; Speckhard, Anne, and Ellenberg, Molly (2021, May 17).

215 Simi, P., Bubolz, B. F., & Hardman, A. (2013). Military experience, identity discrepancies, and far right terrorism: An exploratory analysis. *Studies in Conflict & Terrorism*, *36*(8), 654-671.

216 Donnelly, J. (2022, July 20). Senate NDAA to the Pentagon: 'Immediately' halt fight against extremism. *Roll Call* Retrieved from https://rollcall.com/2022/07/20/senate-ndaa-to-pentagon-immediately-halt-fight-against-extremism/

217 Speckhard, Anne, and Ellenberg, Molly, and Garret, TM. (2021, November 11). The Challenge of Extremism in the Military Is Not Going Away Without a New Perspective. *ICSVE Research Reports*. Retrieved from https://www.icsve.org/the-challenge-of-extremism-in-the-military-is-not-going-away-without-a-new-perspective/

218 Speckhard, A. (2011). Prison and community-based disengagement and de-radicalization programs for extremist involved in militant jihadi terrorism ideologies and activities. In A. Speckhard. (Ed.) *Psychosocial, organizational and cultural aspects of terrorism* (pp. 109-122). Brussels. NATO. Retrieved from https://apps.dtic.mil/sti/pdfs/ADA555076.pdf

219 Speckhard, Anne, and Ellenberg, Molly, and Garret, TM. (2021, November 11). The Challenge of Extremism in the Military Is Not Going Away Without a New Perspective. *ICSVE Research Reports*. Retrieved from https://www.icsve.org/the-challenge-of-extremism-in-the-military-is-not-going-away-without-a-new-perspective/

220 Speckhard, Anne & Ellenberg, Molly (2022, August 1). Projected hate, gender identity, sexual orientation and white supremacism. *Homeland Security Today*. Retrieved from https://www.hstoday.us/featured/perspective-projected-hate-gender-identity-sexual-orientation-and-white-supremacism/

221 Smith, S. G., Zhang, X., Basile, K. C., Merrick, M. T., Wang, J., Kresnow, M. J., & Chen, J. (2018). The national intimate partner and sexual violence survey: 2015 data brief–updated release.

222 Smith, S. G., Zhang, X., Basile, K. C., Merrick, M. T., Wang, J., Kresnow, M. J., & Chen, J. (2018). The national intimate partner and sexual violence survey: 2015 data brief–updated release.

223 Baglivio, Michel, Epps, Nathan et al. (2014, Spring). The prevalence of adverse childhood experiences (ACE) in the lives of juvenile offenders. *Journal of Juvenile Justice* 3(2). Retrieved from https://www.prisonpolicy.org/scans/Prevalence_of_ACE.pdf

224 Speckhard, Anne (2007). De-legitimizing terrorism: Creative engagement

and understanding of the psycho-social and political processes involved in ideological support for terrorism. *Democracy & Security. 3:251-277.* Retrieved from https://www.jstor.org/stable/48602590

225   McGuire W. J. (1964). Inducing resistance to persuasion: some contemporary approaches, in *Advances in Experimental Social Psychology, Vol. 1*, ed Berkowitz L. (New York, NY: Academic Press;), 191–229.

226   Braddock, Kurt. (2019). Vaccinating against hate: Using attitudinal inoculation to confer resistance to persuasion by extremist propaganda." *Terrorism and Political Violence* (November). Retrieved from https://www.tandfonline.com/doi/full/10.1080/09546553.2019.1693370

227   Davis, D. (1997). *Klan-Destine Relationships*. New Horizon Press; 1st edition.

228   About Deeyah. *Deeyah.* Retrieved from https://deeyah.com/about-deeyah/

229   Khan, D. (Director). (2017). *White right: Meeting the Enemy.* Fuuse.

230   Speckhard, A. & Ellenberg, M. (2022). Are Antifa activists achieving their goals? *ICSVE Brief Reports.* Retrieved from https://www.icsve.org/are-antifa-activists-achieving-their-goals/?utm_source=rss&utm_medium=rss&utm_campaign=are-antifa-activists-achieving-their-goals

231   Speckhard, Anne & Ellenberg, Molly (2022, July 11). How interactions with Antifa can fuel white supremacist groups. *Homeland Security Today.* Retrieved from https://www.hstoday.us/featured/how-interactions-with-antifa-can-fuel-white-supremacist-groups/

232   Department of Justice. (2021, October 21). FBI releases updated hate crime statistics. Retrieved from https://www.fbi.gov/news/press-releases/press-releases/fbi-releases-updated-2020-hate-crime-statistics

233   Department of Justice. (2021, August) FBI Hate Crime Statistics 2020. Retrieved from https://www.justice.gov/crs/highlights/2020-hate-crimes-statistics

234   U.S. Department of Justice (2022). Hate crimes case examples. Retrieved from https://www.justice.gov/hatecrimes/hate-crimes-case-examples

235   Lybrand, Holmes. (2022, August 29). Proud Boy who came within seconds of Sen. Schumer on January 6 sentenced to 55 months in prison. *CNN.* Retrieved from https://edition.cnn.com/2022/08/29/politics/joshua-pruitt-rioter-proud-boys-sentenced/index.html

236   Lybrand, Holmes. (2022, August 29). Proud Boy who came within seconds of Sen. Schumer on January 6 sentenced to 55 months in prison. *CNN.* Retrieved from https://edition.cnn.com/2022/08/29/politics/joshua-pruitt-rioter-proud-boys-sentenced/index.html

237   Weiner, Rachel. (2022, June 3). D.C. Proud Boy and bartender pleads guilty to felony in Capitol riot. *Washington Post.* Retrieved from https://www.washingtonpost.com/dc-md-va/2022/06/03/proud-boy-pruitt-pleads-guilty-jan6/

238   Lybrand, Holmes. (2022, August 29). Proud Boy who came within seconds of Sen. Schumer on January 6 sentenced to 55 months in prison. *CNN.* Retrieved from https://edition.cnn.com/2022/08/29/politics/joshua-pruitt-rioter-proud-boys-sentenced/index.html

239   Smith, Mitch (2022, August 23). Two men convicted in plot to kidnap Michigan's governor. *The New York Times.* Retrieved from https://www.nytimes.

com/2022/08/23/us/verdict-trial-gretchen-whitmer-kidnap.html

240   Smith, Mitch. (2022, October 22). Jury convicts men accused of supporting plot to kidnap Michigan governor. The New York Times. Retrieved from https://www.nytimes.com/2022/10/26/us/michigan-wolverine-watchmen-trial. html?smid=nytcore-ios-share&referringSource=articleShare

241   Flesher, J. (2022, December 7). Wolverine Watchmen: Trial ordered for 5 men in plot to kidnap Michigan Gov. Gretchen Whitmer. Fox2 Detroit. Retrieved from https://www.fox2detroit.com/news/wolverine-watchmen-trial-ordered-for-5-men-in-plot-to-kidnap-michigan-gov-gretchen-whitmer

242   Powell, E. (2022, July 13). Coloradan and former Oath Keeper spokesman testifies Jan. 6 violence could have been much worse. *9 News.* Retrieved from https://www.9news.com/article/news/local/next/jan-6-oath-keeper-testimony-colorado-jason-van-tatenhove/73-5e0b4bf7-fbaa-4164-84ef-679909948064

243   Allam, H. (2022, July 12). Ex-Oath Keeper outlines dark worldview behind U.S. Capitol attack. *The Washington Post.* Retrieved from https://www.washingtonpost.com/national-security/2022/07/12/jason-van-tatenhove-oath-keepers-jan-6/

244   Feuer, A. & Montague, Z. (2022, November 29). Oath keepers leader convicted of sedition in landmark Jan 6 case. The New York Times. Retrieved from https://www.nytimes.com/2022/11/29/us/politics/oath-keepers-trial-verdict-jan-6.html

245   Rowles, Courtney (2022, August 15). Authorities want Conway man with "white supremacist" views to stay in jail: Court records. *ABC 15 News.* Retrieved from https://wpde.com/news/local/conway-man-benjamin-thomas-samuel-mcdowell-white-supremacist-views-dylan-roof-style-attack-to-stay-in-jail-court-records-july-15-2022

246   Dodson, Braley (2022, August 15). Federal authorities want Conway white supremacist to stay in jail. *WBTW News 13.* Retrieved from https://www.wbtw.com/news/grand-strand/conway/federal-authorities-want-conway-white-supremacist-to-stay-in-jail/

247   Dodson, Braley (2022, August 15). Federal authorities want Conway white supremacist to stay in jail. *WBTW News 13.* Retrieved from https://www.wbtw.com/news/grand-strand/conway/federal-authorities-want-conway-white-supremacist-to-stay-in-jail/

248   Sganga, Nicole (2021, November 24). Jury awards $26 million in "Unite the Right" rally civil case. *CBS News.* Retrieved from https://www.cbsnews.com/news/charlottesville-unite-the-right-rally-trial-verdict-26-million/